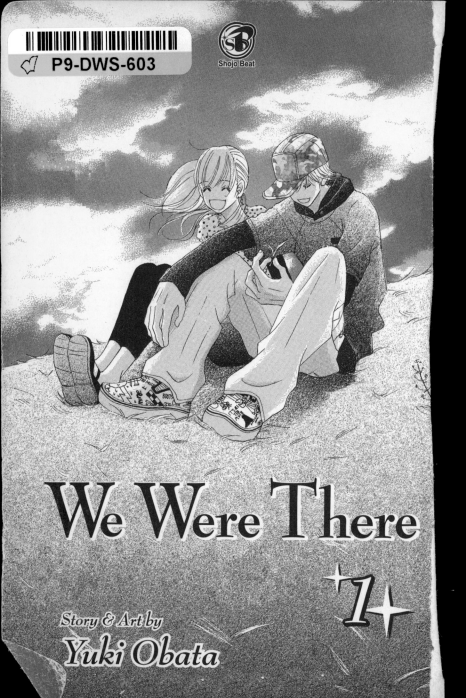

Shojo Beat

We Were There

+1+

Story & Art by
Yuki Obata

Contents

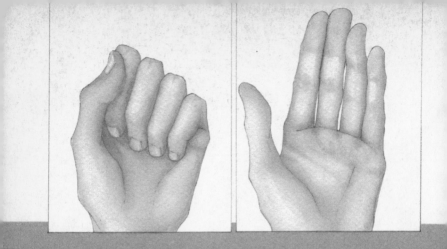

AT THE TIME, HE WAS 15 YEARS OLD.

AND NOW, HE'S ONLY 16.

BUT THE REALITY HE MUST FACE...

...IS FAR GREATER THAN YOUTH WILL ALLOW.

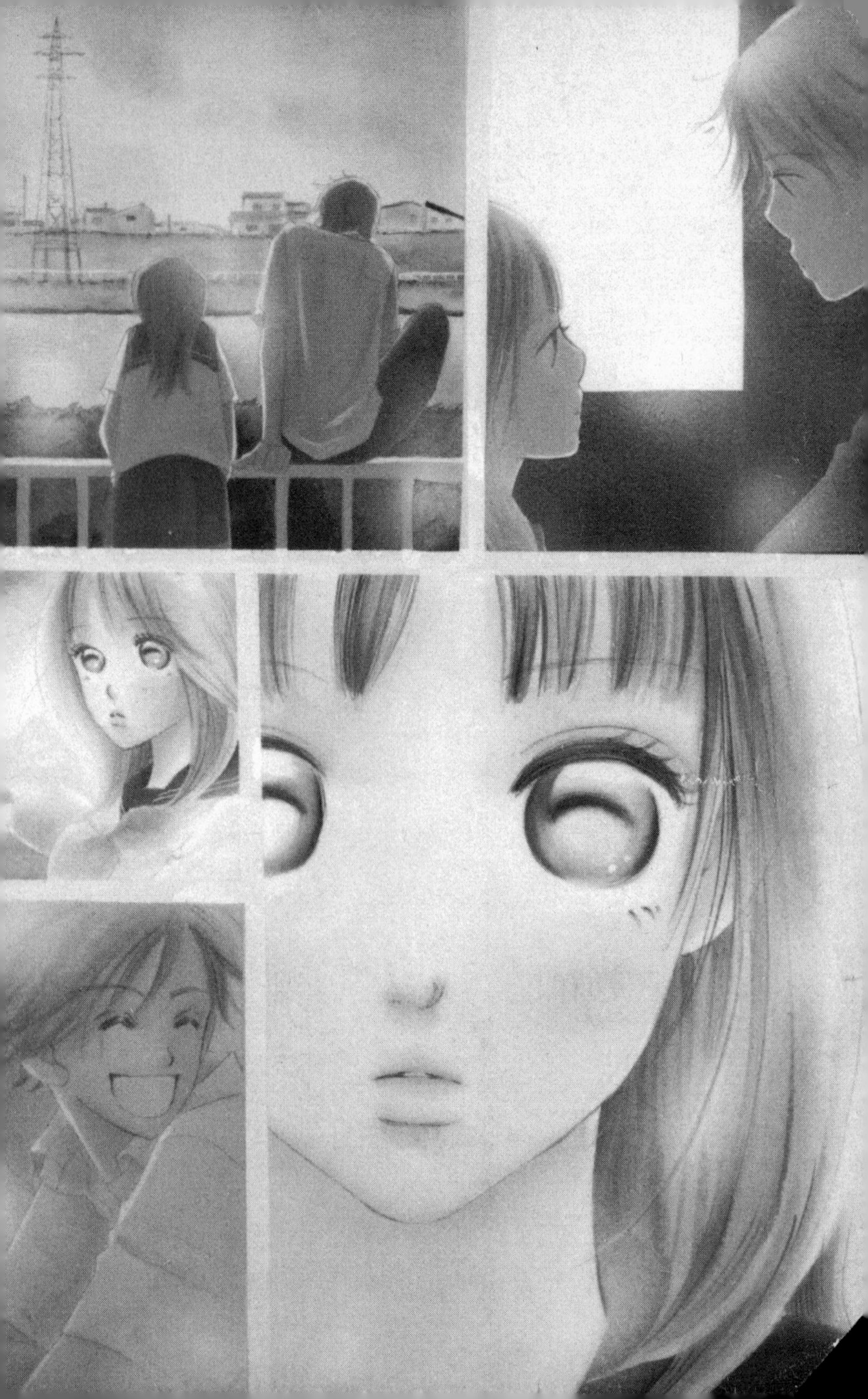

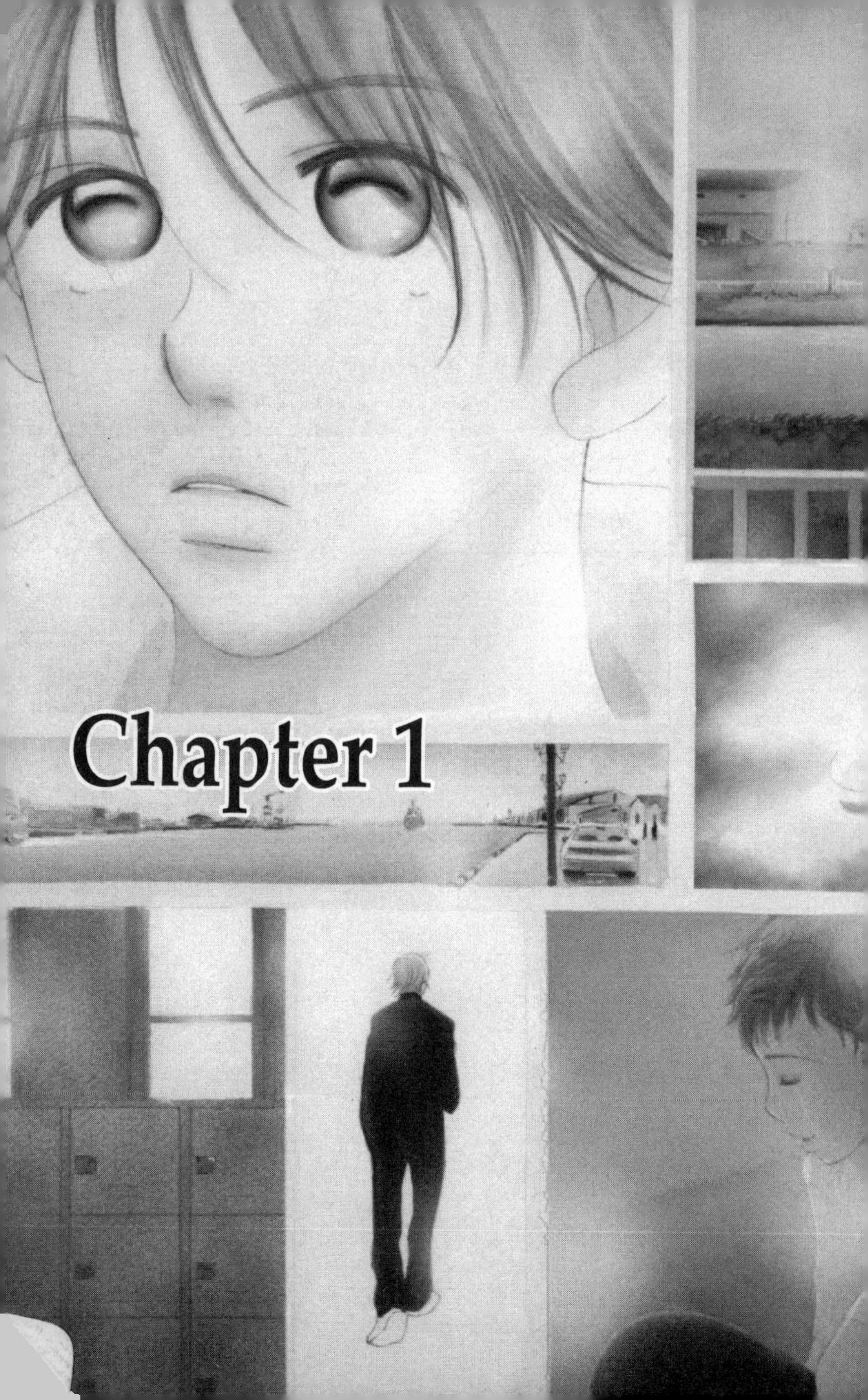
Chapter 1

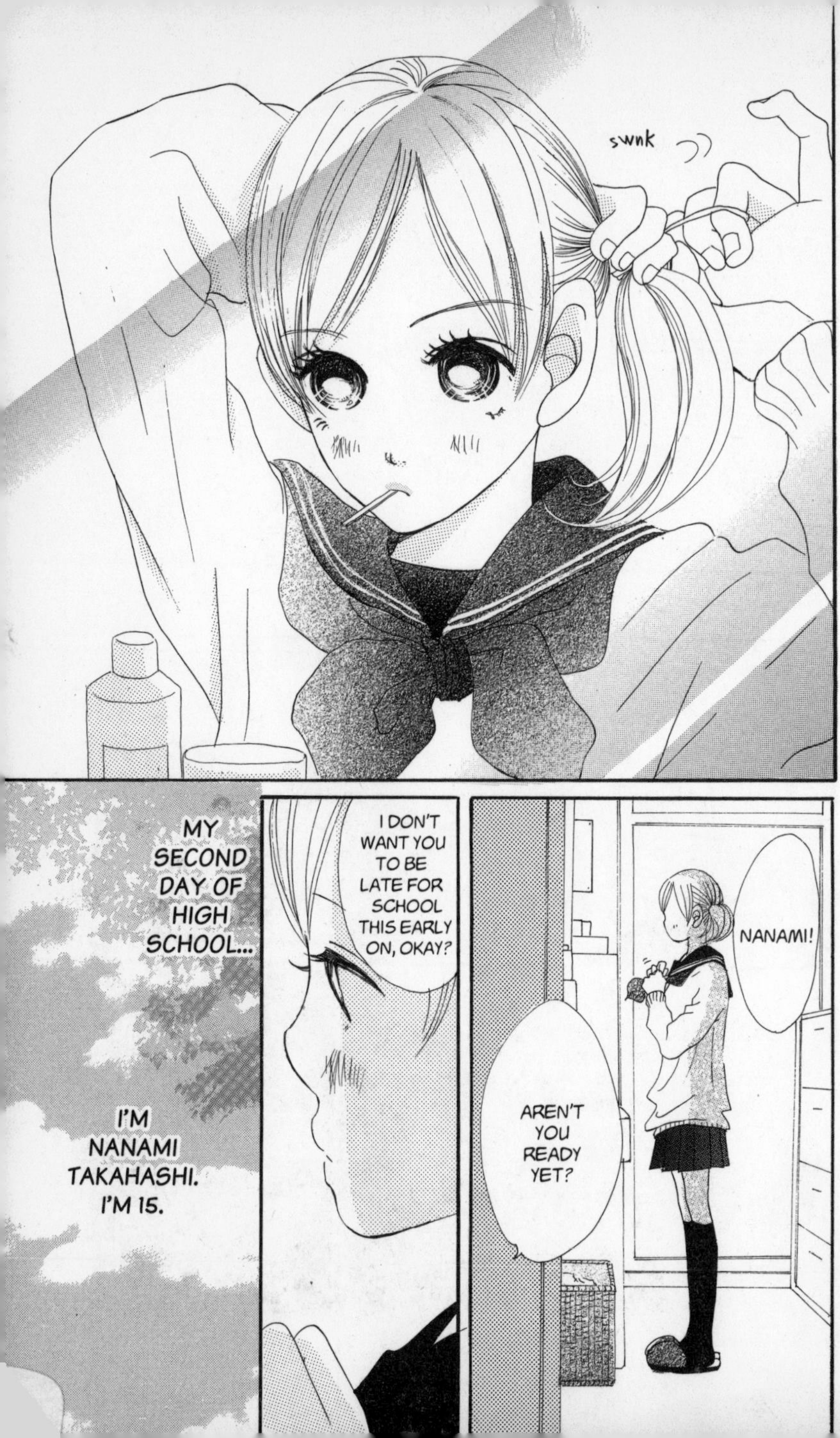
swnk
NANAMI!
AREN'T YOU READY YET?
I DON'T WANT YOU TO BE LATE FOR SCHOOL THIS EARLY ON, OKAY?
MY SECOND DAY OF HIGH SCHOOL...
I'M NANAMI TAKAHASHI. I'M 15.

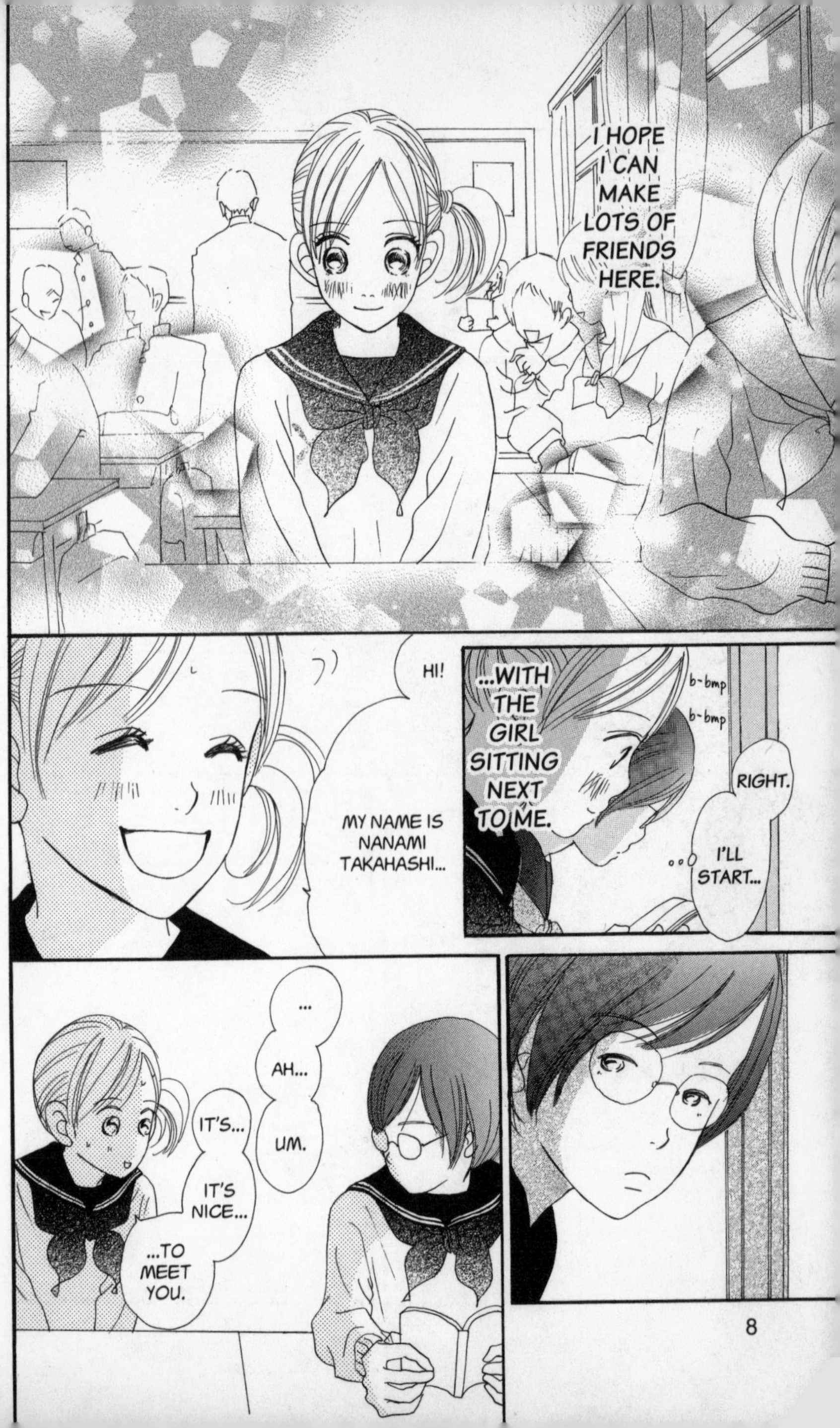
I HOPE I CAN MAKE LOTS OF FRIENDS HERE.
...WITH THE GIRL SITTING NEXT TO ME.
b-bmp
b-bmp
RIGHT.
I'LL START...
HI!
MY NAME IS NANAMI TAKAHASHI...
...
AH...
UM.
IT'S...
IT'S NICE...
...TO MEET YOU.

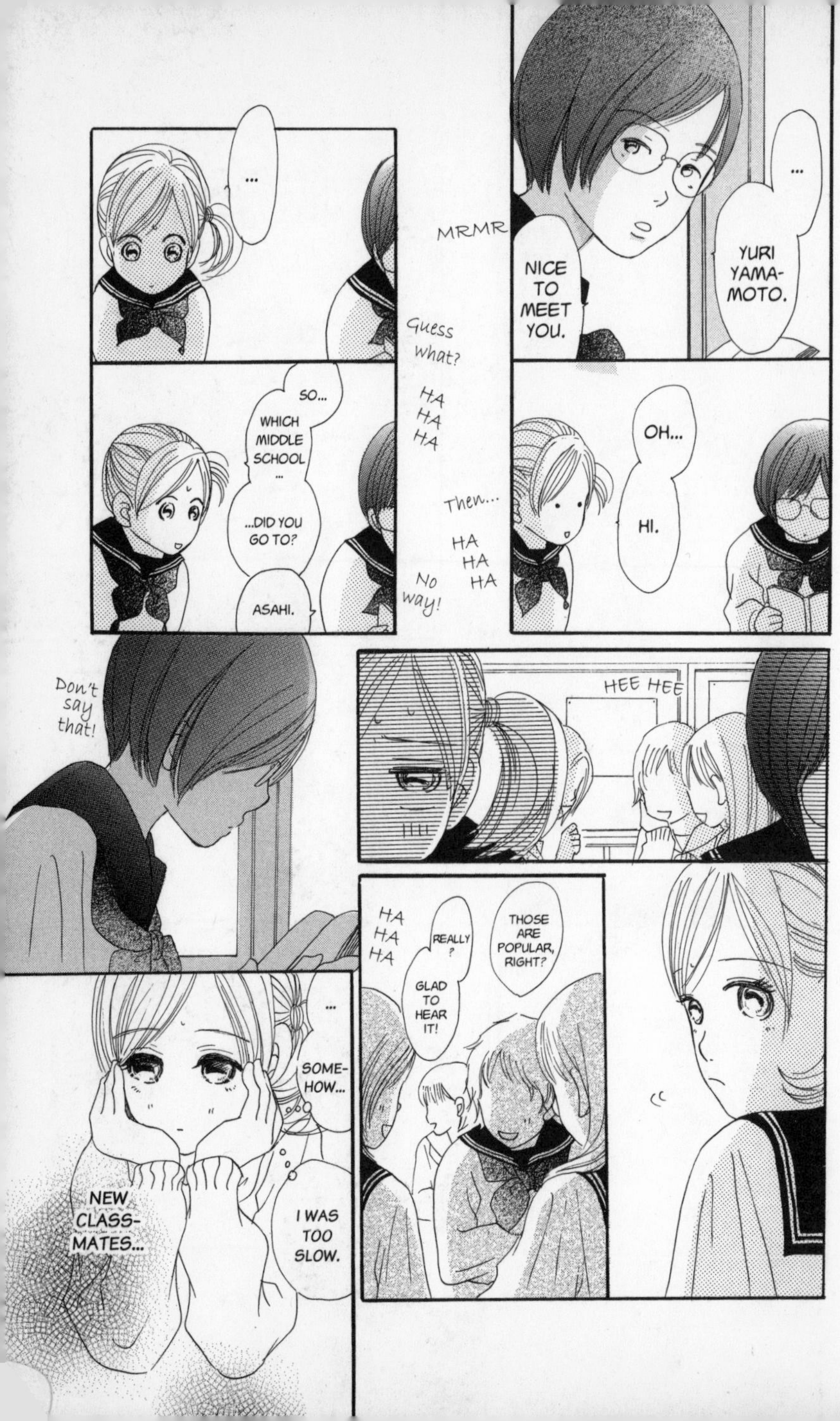
...
YURI YAMAMOTO.
MRMR
NICE TO MEET YOU.
...
OH... HI.
SO... WHICH MIDDLE SCHOOL ... ...DID YOU GO TO?
ASAHI.
Guess what?
HA HA HA
Then...
HA HA HA
No way!
HEE HEE
Don't say that!
THOSE ARE POPULAR, RIGHT?
REALLY? GLAD TO HEAR IT!
HA HA HA
...
SOMEHOW...
I WAS TOO SLOW.
NEW CLASSMATES...

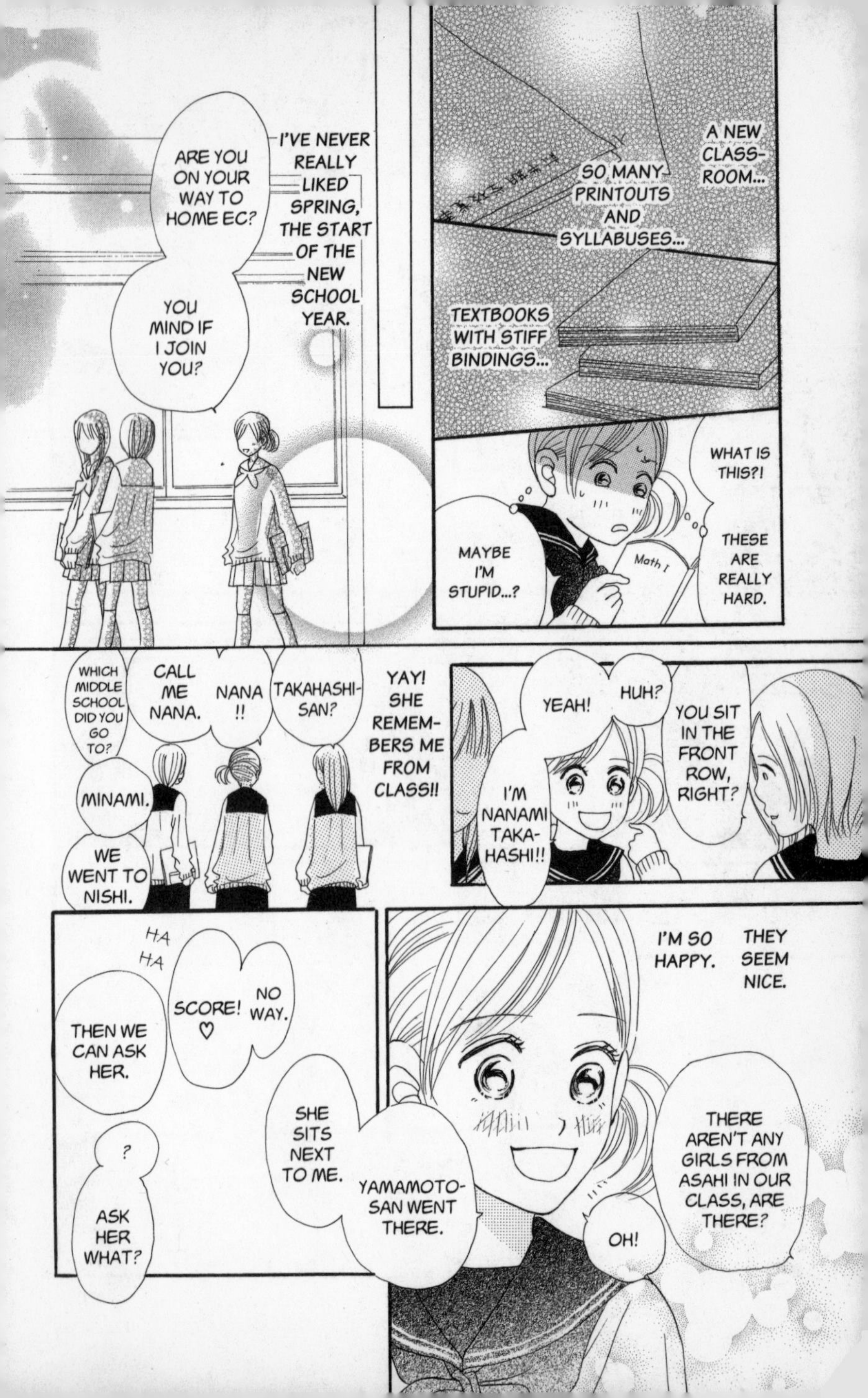
A NEW CLASS-ROOM...
SO MANY PRINTOUTS AND SYLLABUSES...
TEXTBOOKS WITH STIFF BINDINGS...
WHAT IS THIS?!
THESE ARE REALLY HARD.
Math I
MAYBE I'M STUPID...?
I'VE NEVER REALLY LIKED SPRING, THE START OF THE NEW SCHOOL YEAR.
ARE YOU ON YOUR WAY TO HOME EC?
YOU MIND IF I JOIN YOU?
YOU SIT IN THE FRONT ROW, RIGHT?
HUH?
YEAH!
I'M NANAMI TAKAHASHI!!
YAY! SHE REMEMBERS ME FROM CLASS!!
TAKAHASHI-SAN?
NANA!!
CALL ME NANA.
WHICH MIDDLE SCHOOL DID YOU GO TO?
MINAMI.
WE WENT TO NISHI.
THEY SEEM NICE.
I'M SO HAPPY.
THERE AREN'T ANY GIRLS FROM ASAHI IN OUR CLASS, ARE THERE?
OH!
YAMAMOTO-SAN WENT THERE.
SHE SITS NEXT TO ME.
NO WAY.
SCORE! ♡
HA HA
THEN WE CAN ASK HER.
?
ASK HER WHAT?

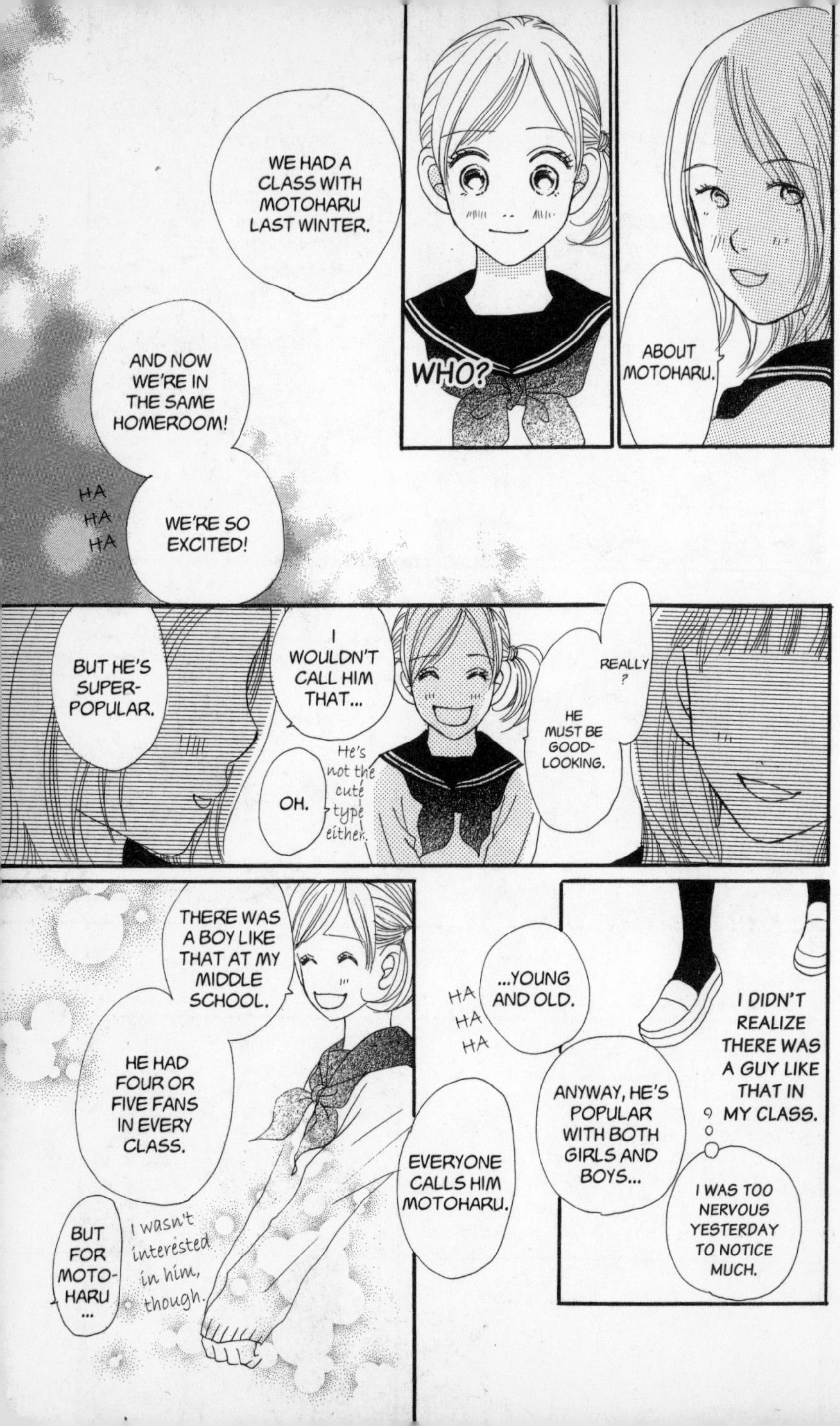
ABOUT MOTOHARU.
WHO?
WE HAD A CLASS WITH MOTOHARU LAST WINTER.
AND NOW WE'RE IN THE SAME HOMEROOM!
HA HA HA
WE'RE SO EXCITED!
REALLY?
HE MUST BE GOOD-LOOKING.
I WOULDN'T CALL HIM THAT...
He's not the cute type either.
BUT HE'S SUPER-POPULAR.
OH.
EVERYONE CALLS HIM MOTOHARU.
ANYWAY, HE'S POPULAR WITH BOTH GIRLS AND BOYS...
...YOUNG AND OLD.
HA HA HA
I DIDN'T REALIZE THERE WAS A GUY LIKE THAT IN MY CLASS.
I WAS TOO NERVOUS YESTERDAY TO NOTICE MUCH.
THERE WAS A BOY LIKE THAT AT MY MIDDLE SCHOOL.
HE HAD FOUR OR FIVE FANS IN EVERY CLASS.
BUT FOR MOTO-HARU...
I wasn't interested in him, though.

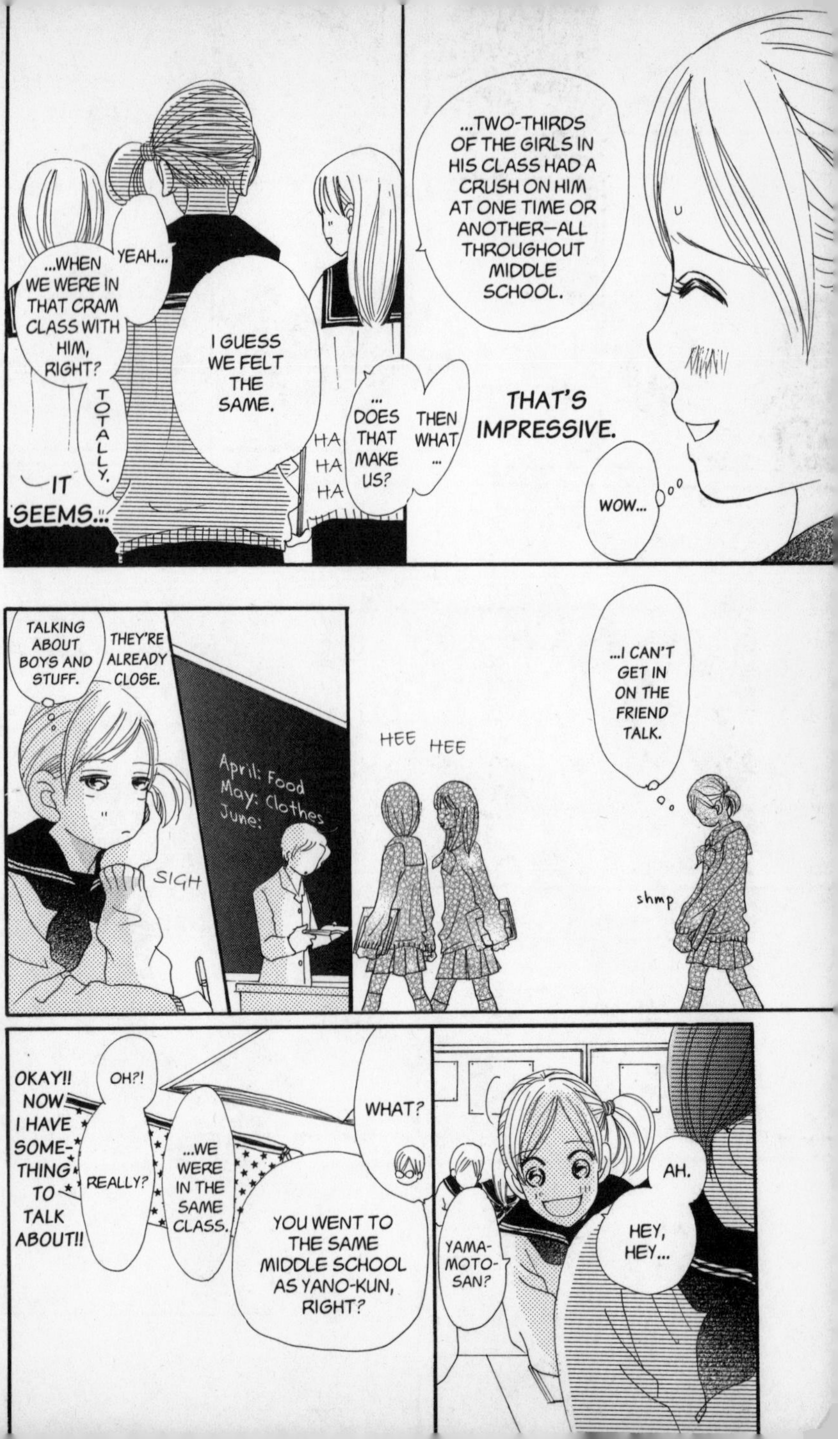
...TWO-THIRDS OF THE GIRLS IN HIS CLASS HAD A CRUSH ON HIM AT ONE TIME OR ANOTHER—ALL THROUGHOUT MIDDLE SCHOOL.
THAT'S IMPRESSIVE.
WOW...
THEN WHAT ...
... DOES THAT MAKE US?
HA HA HA
I GUESS WE FELT THE SAME.
YEAH...
...WHEN WE WERE IN THAT CRAM CLASS WITH HIM, RIGHT?
TOTALLY.
IT SEEMS...
...I CAN'T GET IN ON THE FRIEND TALK.
HEE HEE
shmp
THEY'RE ALREADY CLOSE.
TALKING ABOUT BOYS AND STUFF.
April: Food
May: Clothes
June:
SIGH
AH.
HEY, HEY...
YAMA-MOTO-SAN?
WHAT?
YOU WENT TO THE SAME MIDDLE SCHOOL AS YANO-KUN, RIGHT?
...WE WERE IN THE SAME CLASS.
OH?!
REALLY?
OKAY!! NOW I HAVE SOME-THING TO TALK ABOUT!!

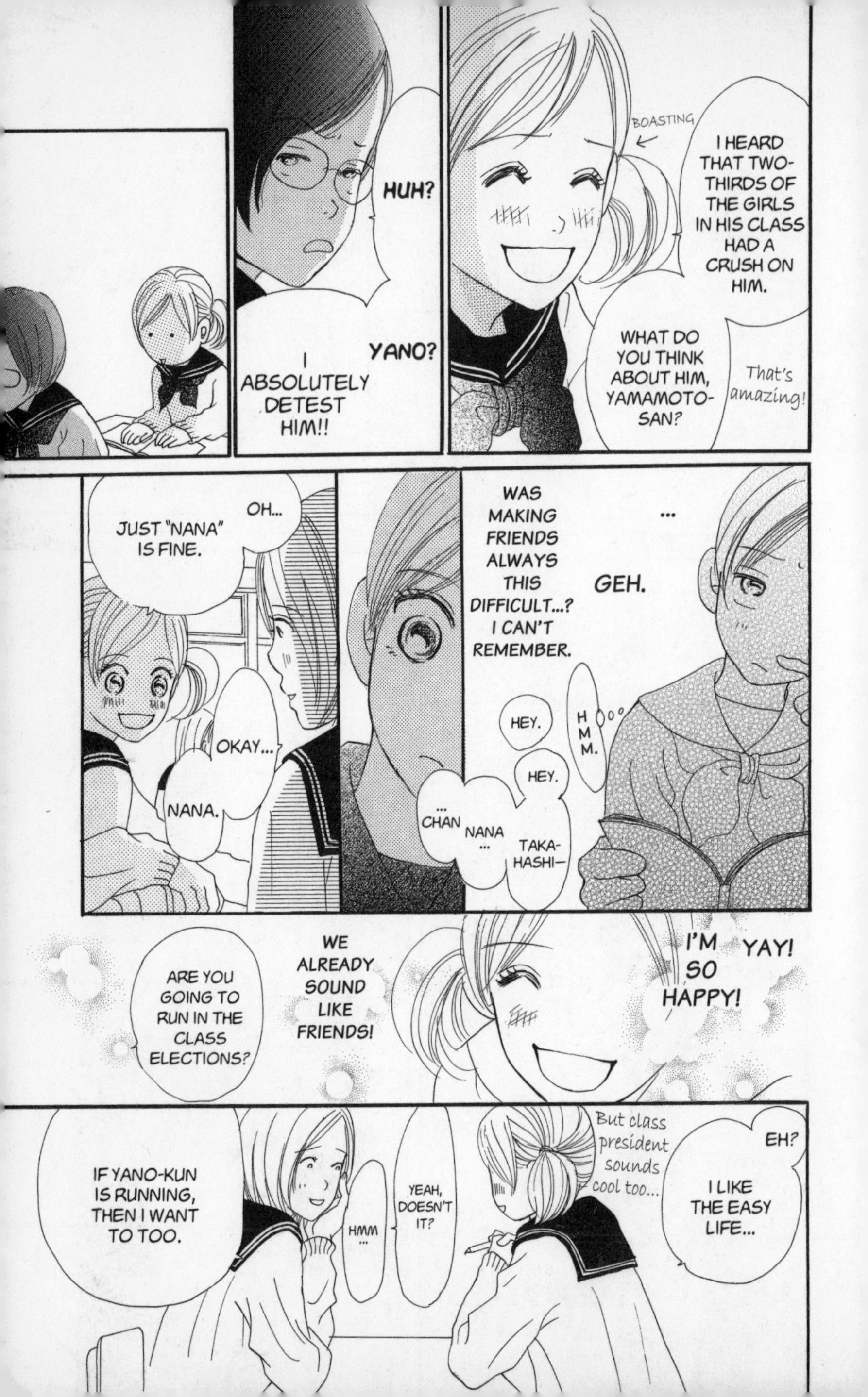
BOASTING
I HEARD THAT TWO-THIRDS OF THE GIRLS IN HIS CLASS HAD A CRUSH ON HIM.
That's amazing!
WHAT DO YOU THINK ABOUT HIM, YAMAMOTO-SAN?
HUH?
YANO?
I ABSOLUTELY DETEST HIM!!
...
WAS MAKING FRIENDS ALWAYS THIS DIFFICULT...? I CAN'T REMEMBER.
GEH.
HMM.
HEY.
HEY.
TAKAHASHI-
NANA...
...CHAN
OH...
JUST "NANA" IS FINE.
OKAY...
NANA.
YAY!
I'M SO HAPPY!
WE ALREADY SOUND LIKE FRIENDS!
ARE YOU GOING TO RUN IN THE CLASS ELECTIONS?
EH?
I LIKE THE EASY LIFE...
But class president sounds cool too...
YEAH, DOESN'T IT?
HMM...
IF YANO-KUN IS RUNNING, THEN I WANT TO TOO.

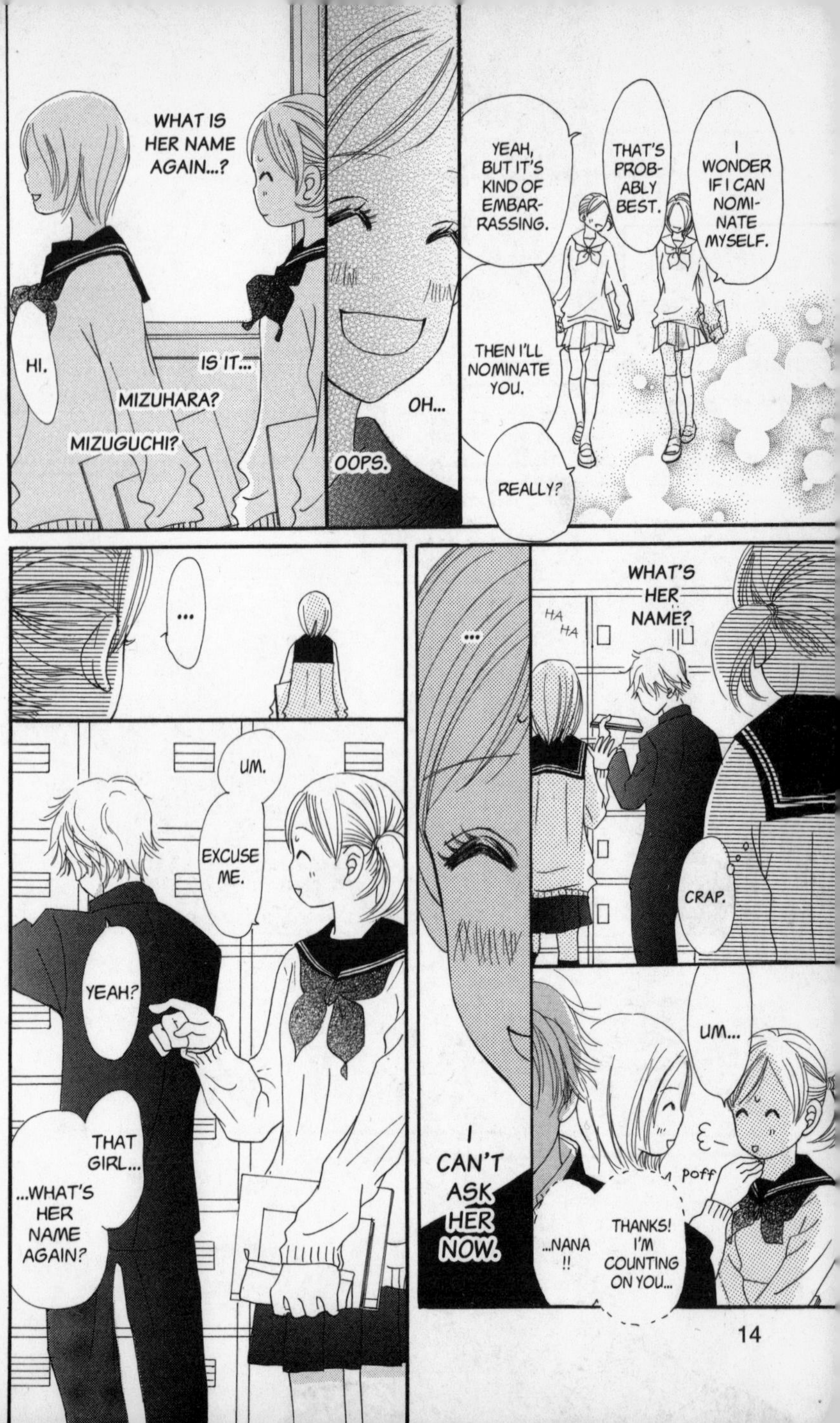
I WONDER IF I CAN NOMINATE MYSELF.
THAT'S PROBABLY BEST.
YEAH, BUT IT'S KIND OF EMBARRASSING.
THEN I'LL NOMINATE YOU.
REALLY?
OH...
OOPS.
WHAT IS HER NAME AGAIN...?
IS IT...
HI.
MIZUHARA?
MIZUGUCHI?
WHAT'S HER NAME?
HA HA
CRAP.
UM...
poff
THANKS! I'M COUNTING ON YOU...
...NANA !!
...
I CAN'T ASK HER NOW.
...
UM.
EXCUSE ME.
YEAH?
THAT GIRL...
...WHAT'S HER NAME AGAIN?

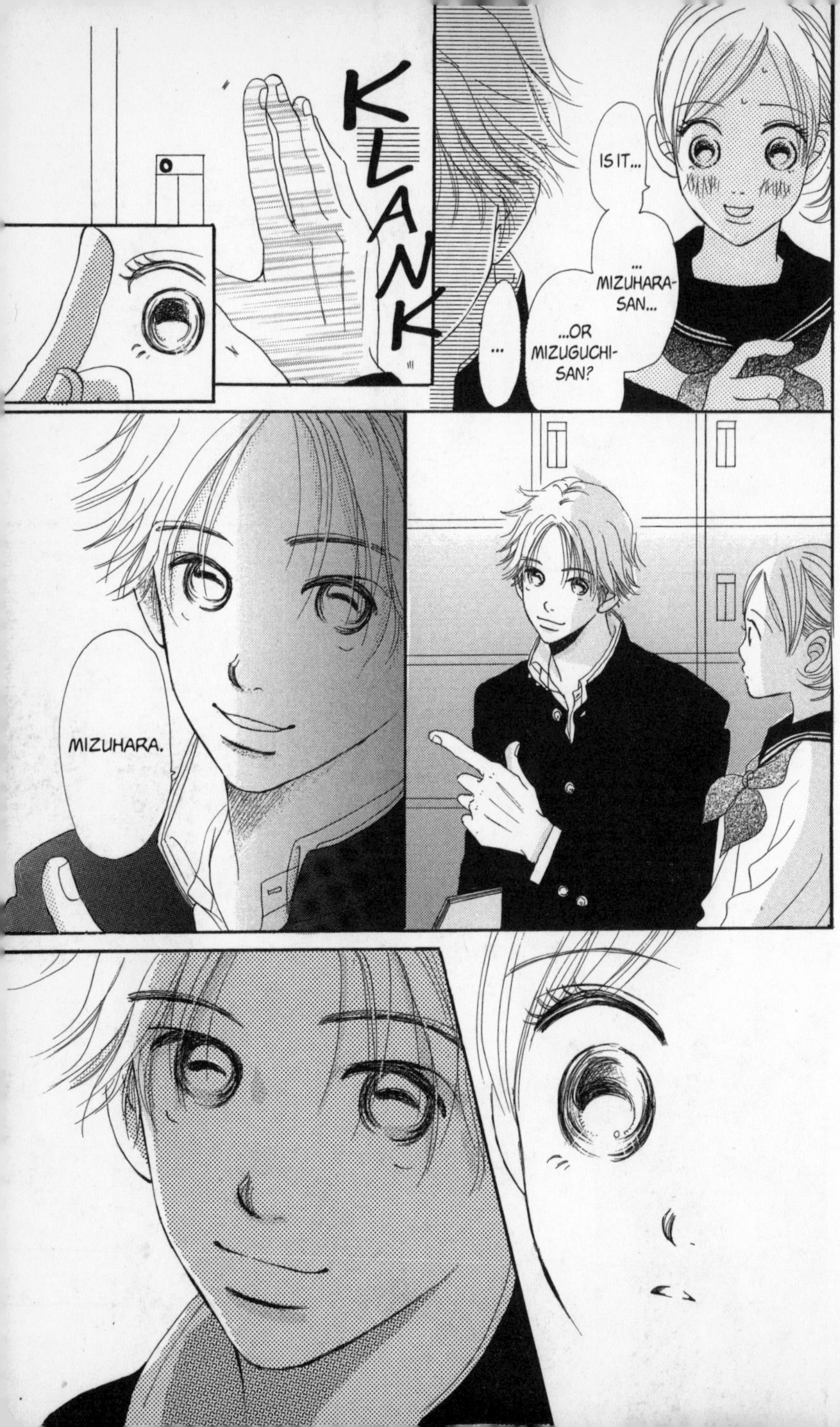
IS IT...
... MIZUHARA-SAN...
...OR MIZUGUCHI-SAN?
...
KLANK
MIZUHARA.

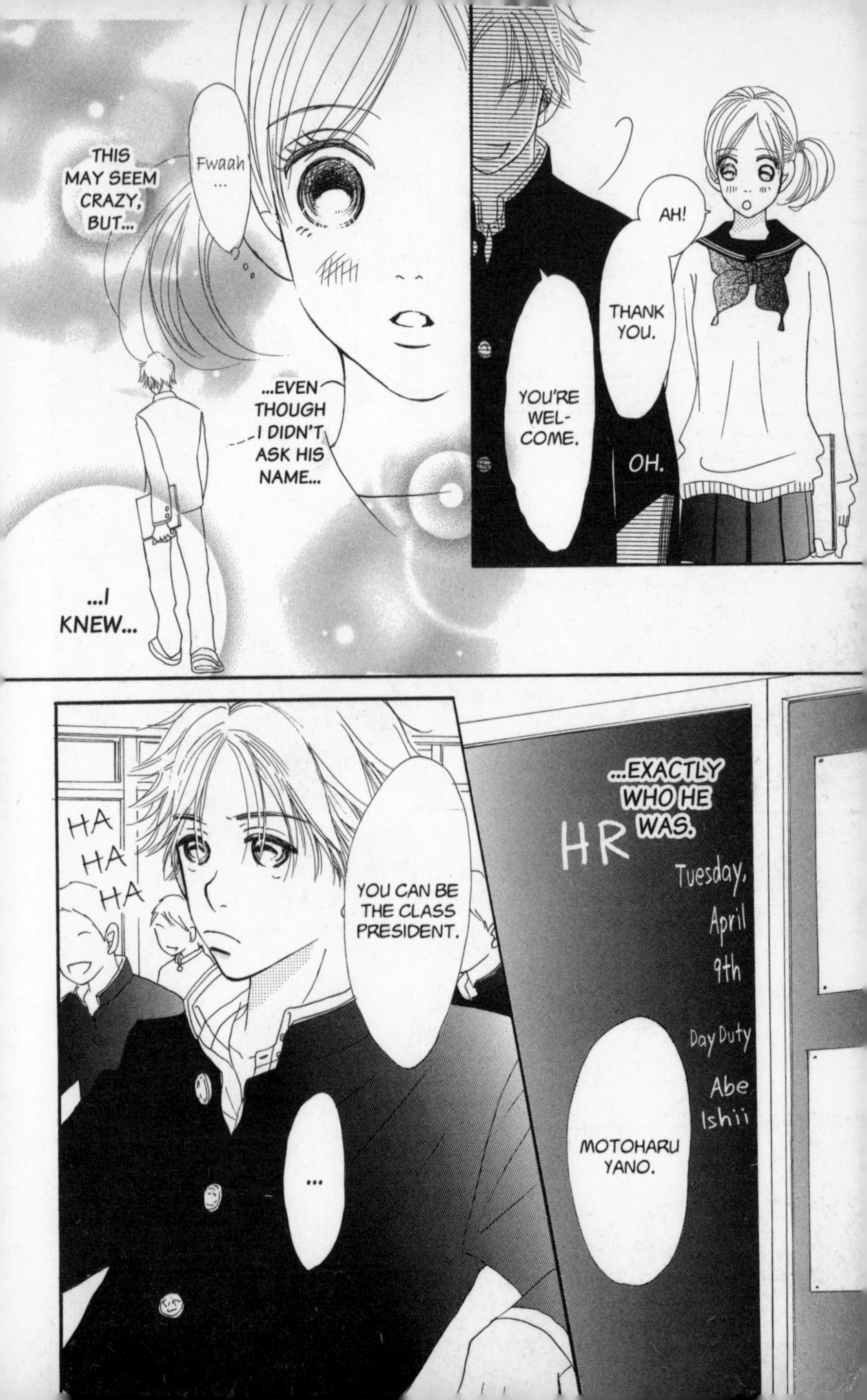
AH!
THANK YOU.
YOU'RE WEL-COME.
OH.
Fwaah ...
THIS MAY SEEM CRAZY, BUT...
...EVEN THOUGH I DIDN'T ASK HIS NAME...
...I KNEW...
...EXACTLY WHO HE WAS.
HR
Tuesday, April 9th
Day Duty
Abe
Ishii
MOTOHARU YANO.
YOU CAN BE THE CLASS PRESIDENT.
...
HA HA HA

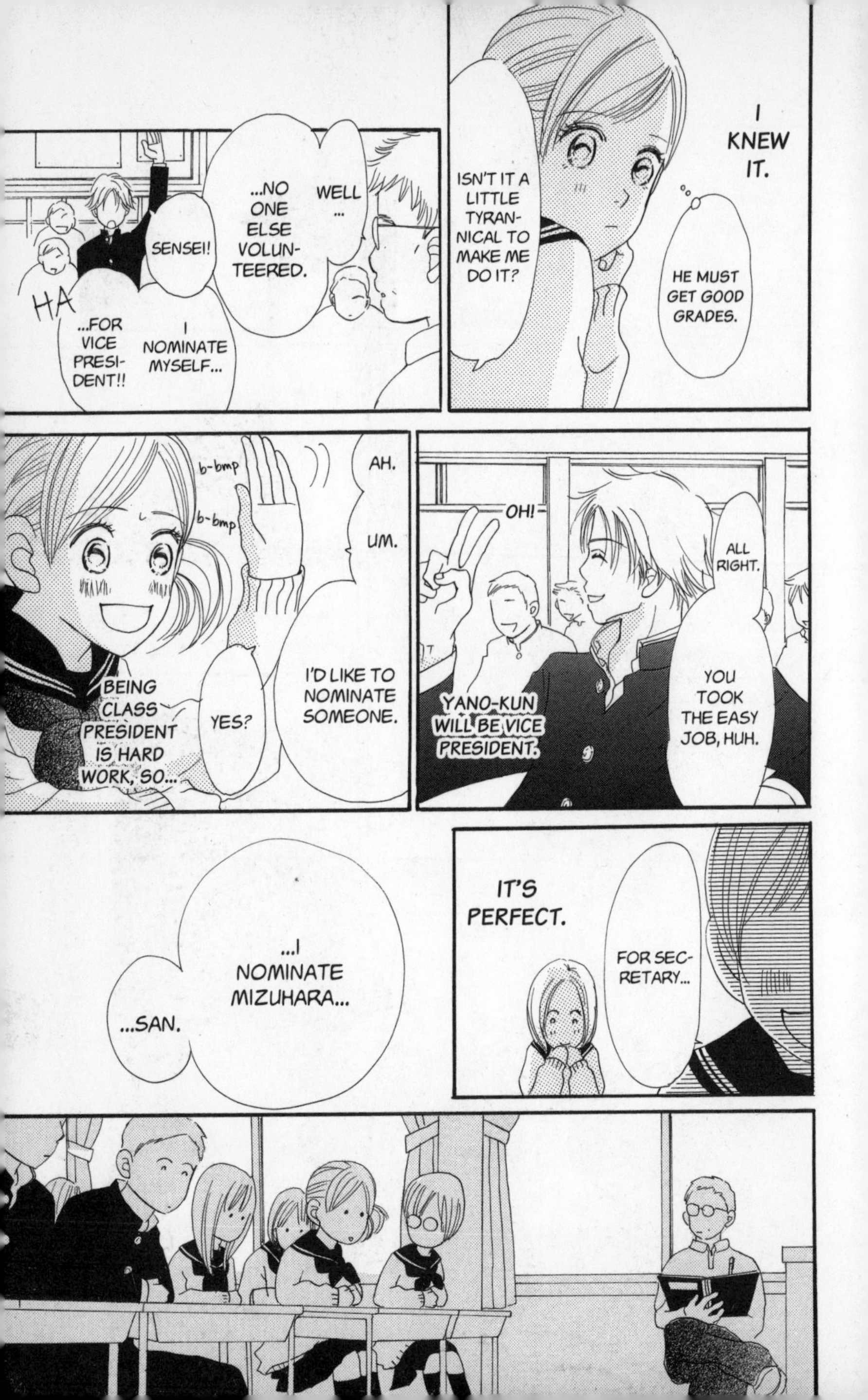
I KNEW IT.
HE MUST GET GOOD GRADES.
ISN'T IT A LITTLE TYRANNICAL TO MAKE ME DO IT?
WELL ...
...NO ONE ELSE VOLUNTEERED.
SENSEI!
I NOMINATE MYSELF...
...FOR VICE PRESIDENT!!
HA
ALL RIGHT.
OH!
YOU TOOK THE EASY JOB, HUH.
YANO-KUN WILL BE VICE PRESIDENT.
AH.
UM.
b-bmp
b-bmp
I'D LIKE TO NOMINATE SOMEONE.
YES?
BEING CLASS PRESIDENT IS HARD WORK, SO...
FOR SECRETARY...
IT'S PERFECT.
...I NOMINATE MIZUHARA...
...SAN.

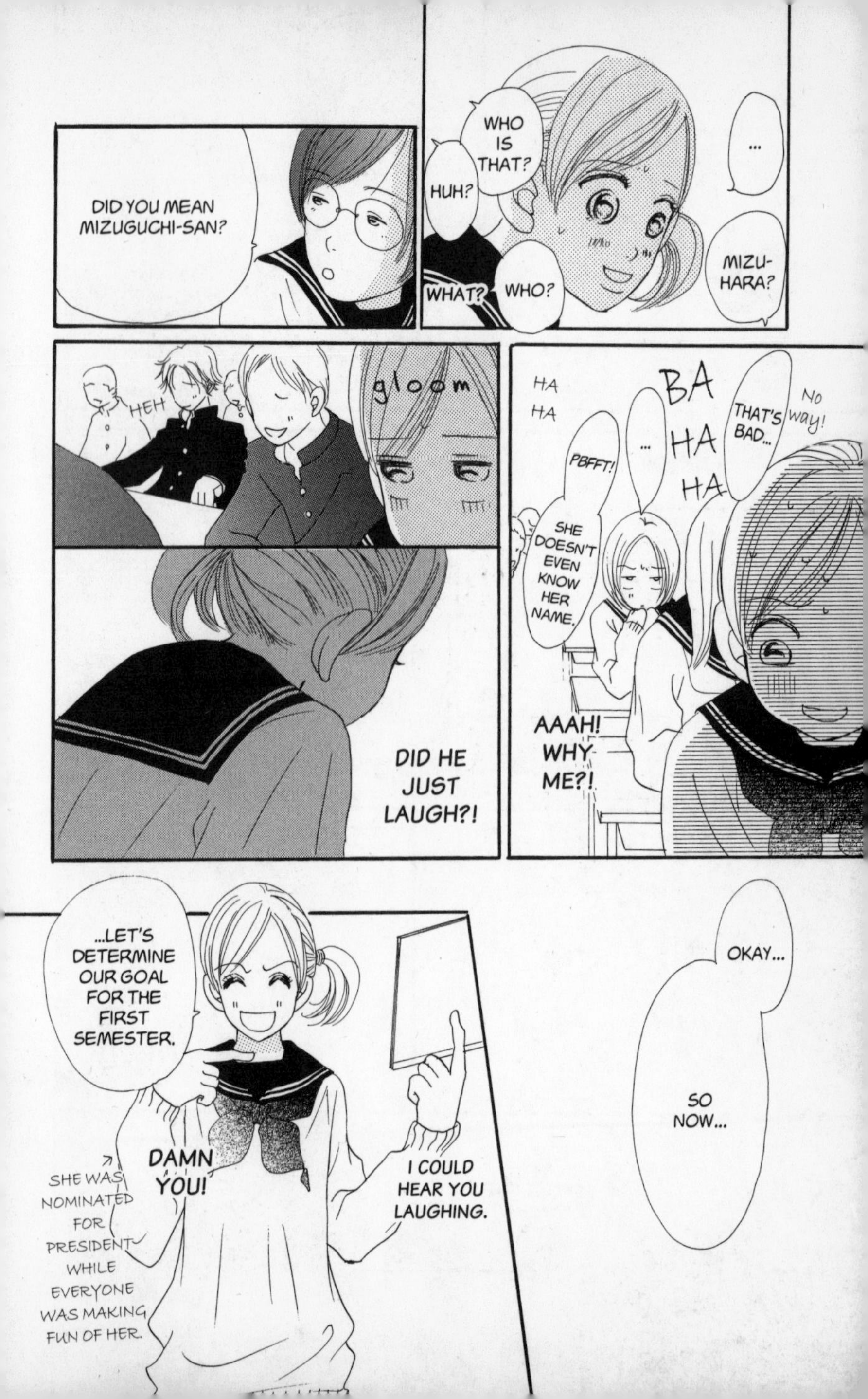
...
MIZU-HARA?
WHO IS THAT?
HUH?
WHO?
WHAT?
DID YOU MEAN MIZUGUCHI-SAN?
No way!
THAT'S BAD...
BA HA HA
...
HA HA
PBFFT!
SHE DOESN'T EVEN KNOW HER NAME.
AAAH! WHY ME?!
gloom
HEH
DID HE JUST LAUGH?!
OKAY...
SO NOW...
...LET'S DETERMINE OUR GOAL FOR THE FIRST SEMESTER.
I COULD HEAR YOU LAUGHING.
DAMN YOU!
SHE WAS NOMINATED FOR PRESIDENT WHILE EVERYONE WAS MAKING FUN OF HER.

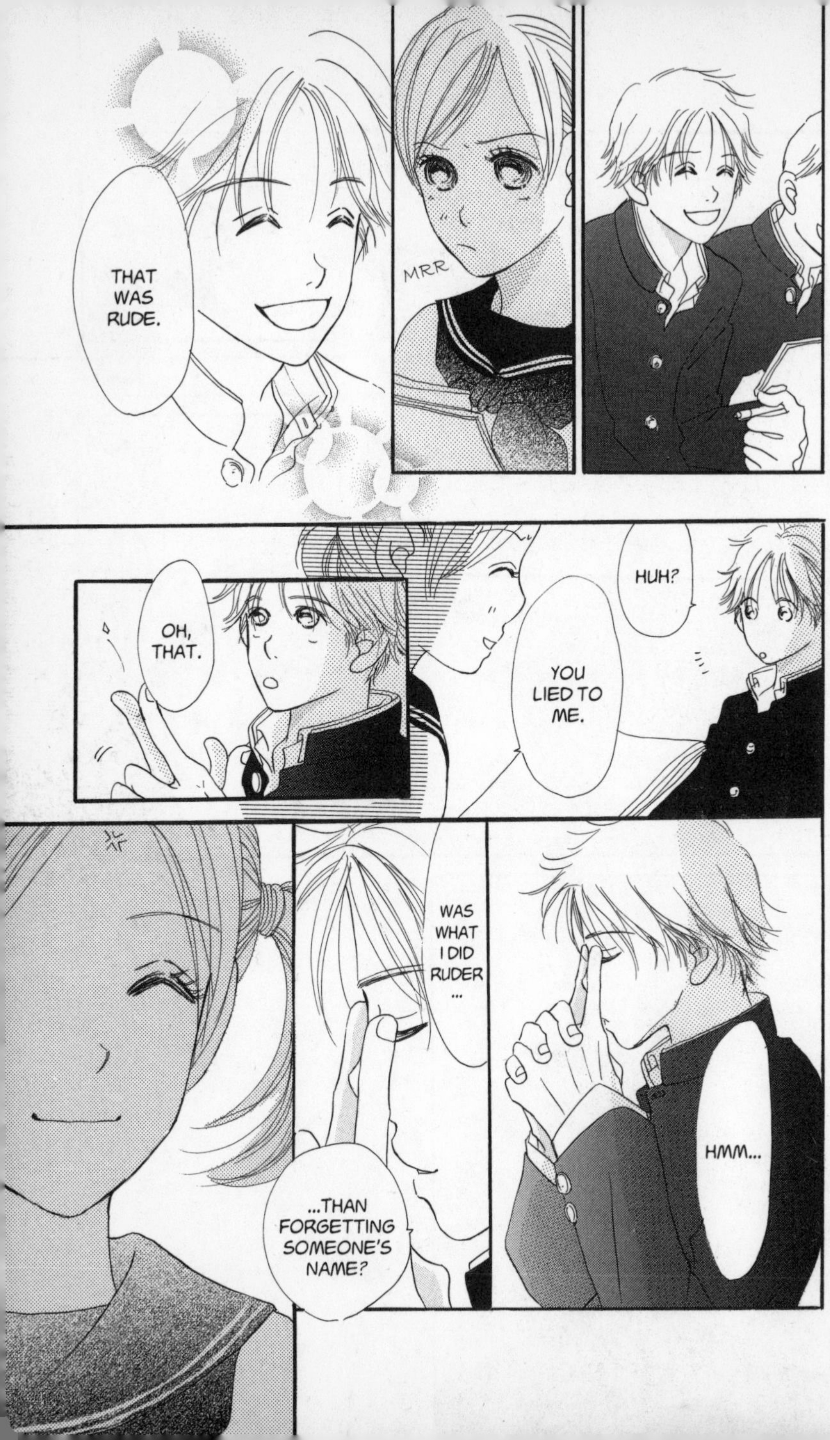
MRR
THAT WAS RUDE.
HUH?
YOU LIED TO ME.
OH, THAT.
HMM...
WAS WHAT I DID RUDER ...
...THAN FORGETTING SOMEONE'S NAME?

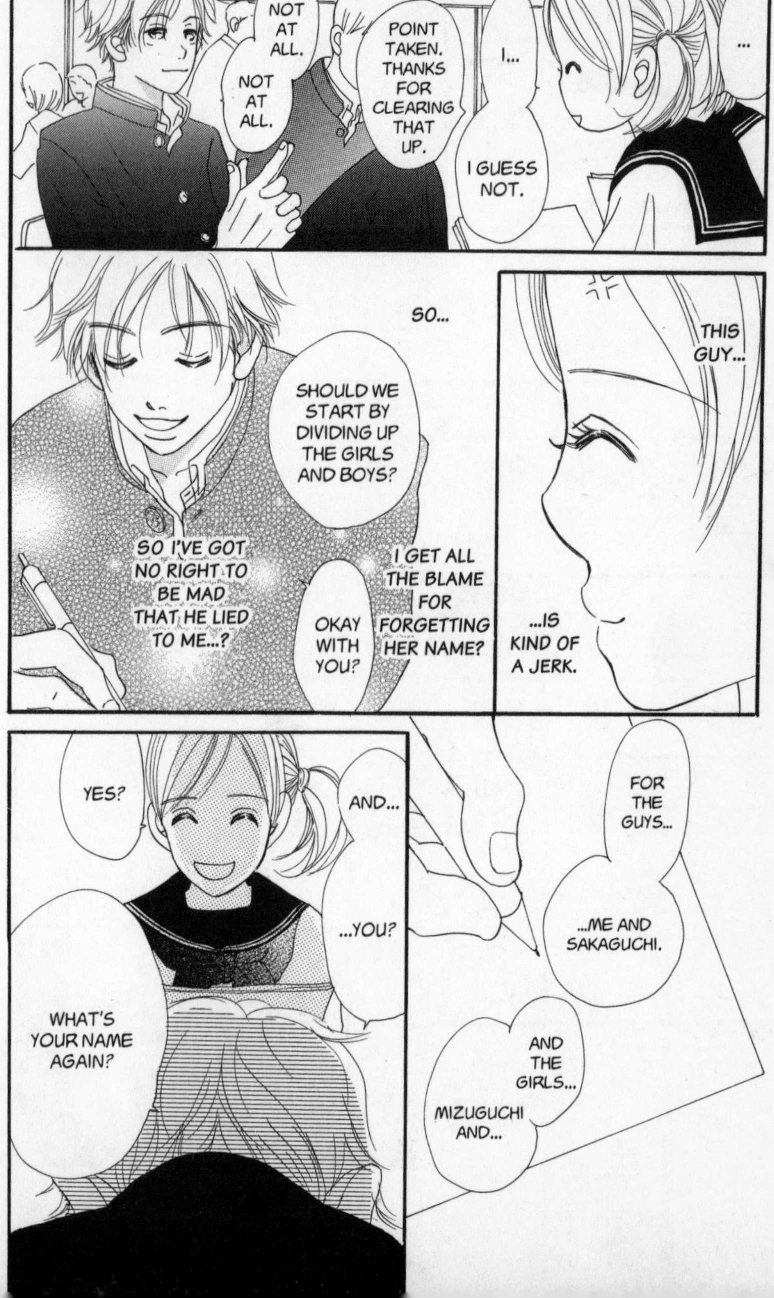
...
I...
I GUESS NOT.
POINT TAKEN. THANKS FOR CLEARING THAT UP.
NOT AT ALL.
NOT AT ALL.
THIS GUY...
...IS KIND OF A JERK.
SO...
SHOULD WE START BY DIVIDING UP THE GIRLS AND BOYS?
I GET ALL THE BLAME FOR FORGETTING HER NAME?
OKAY WITH YOU?
SO I'VE GOT NO RIGHT TO BE MAD THAT HE LIED TO ME...?
FOR THE GUYS...
...ME AND SAKAGUCHI.
AND THE GIRLS...
MIZUGUCHI AND...
AND...
...YOU?
YES?
WHAT'S YOUR NAME AGAIN?

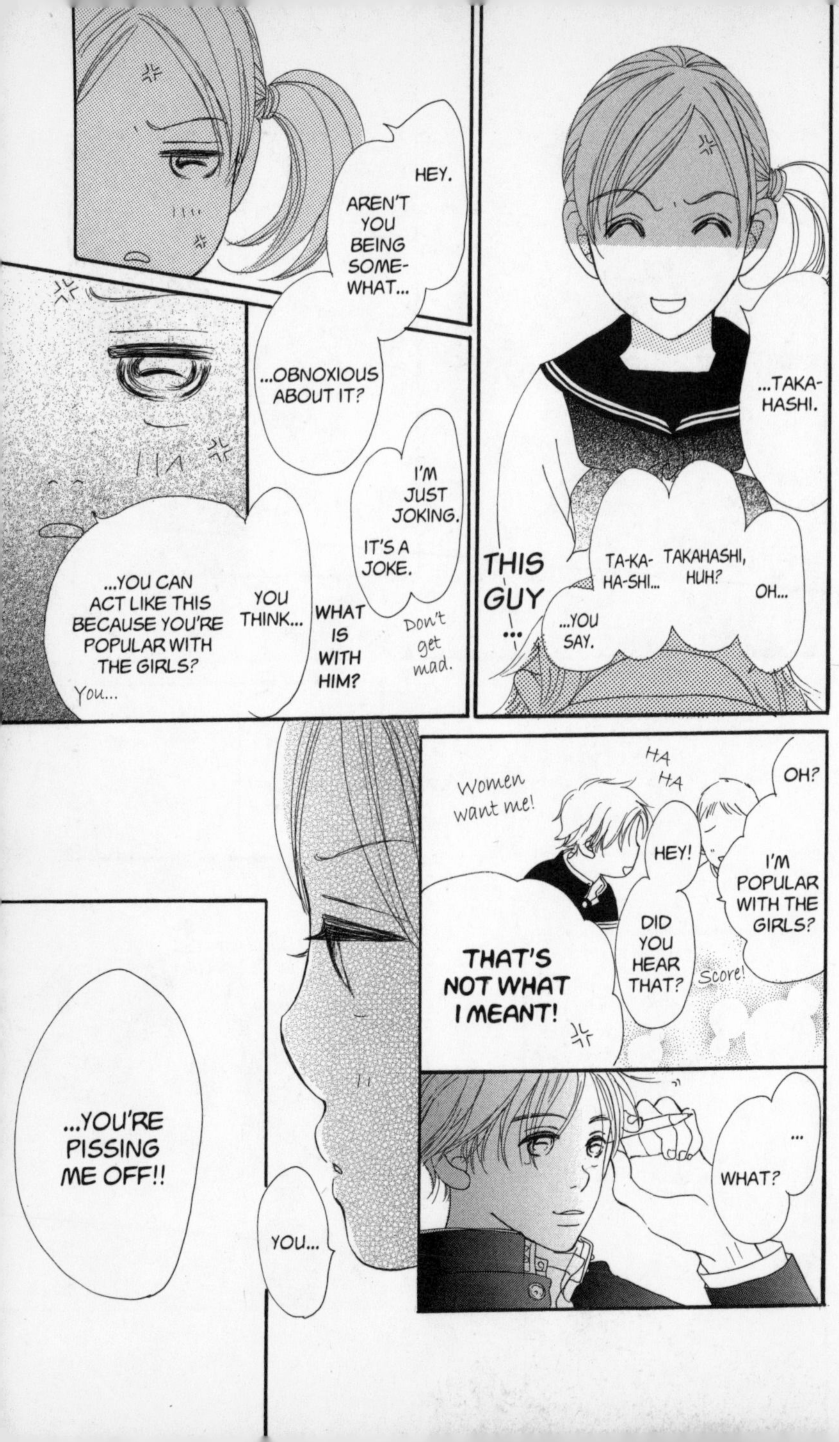
...TAKA-HASHI.
OH...
TAKAHASHI, HUH?
TA-KA-HA-SHI...
...YOU SAY.
THIS GUY...
HEY.
AREN'T YOU BEING SOME-WHAT...
...OBNOXIOUS ABOUT IT?
I'M JUST JOKING.
IT'S A JOKE.
Don't get mad.
WHAT IS WITH HIM?
YOU THINK...
...YOU CAN ACT LIKE THIS BECAUSE YOU'RE POPULAR WITH THE GIRLS?
You...
OH?
I'M POPULAR WITH THE GIRLS?
HA HA
HEY!
DID YOU HEAR THAT?
Score!
Women want me!
THAT'S NOT WHAT I MEANT!
...
WHAT?
YOU...
...YOU'RE PISSING ME OFF!!

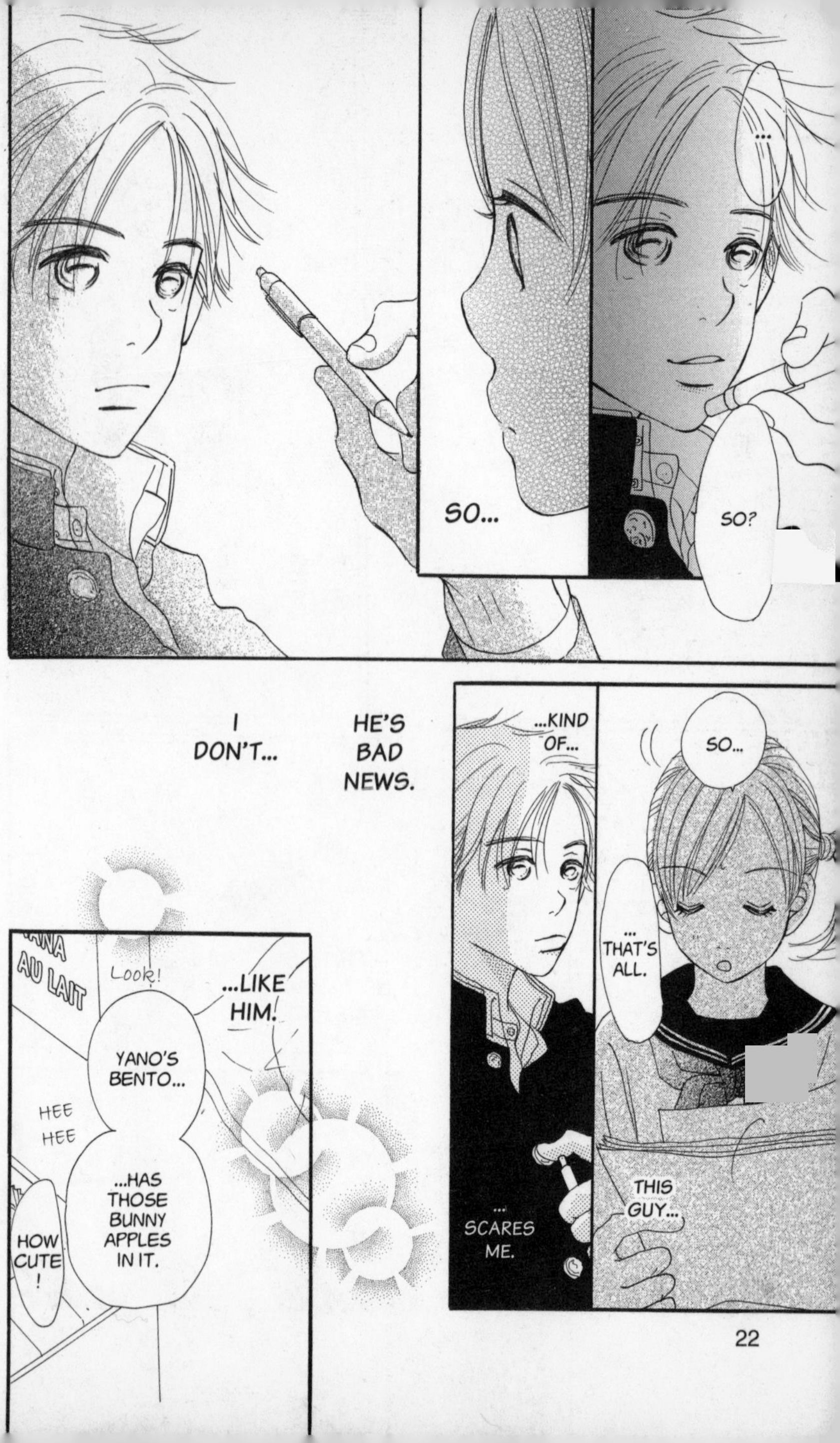
...
SO?
SO...
SO...
...THAT'S ALL.
THIS GUY...
...KIND OF...
...SCARES ME.
HE'S BAD NEWS.
I DON'T...
...LIKE HIM!
ANA AU LAIT
Look!
YANO'S BENTO...
...HAS THOSE BUNNY APPLES IN IT.
HEE HEE
HOW CUTE!

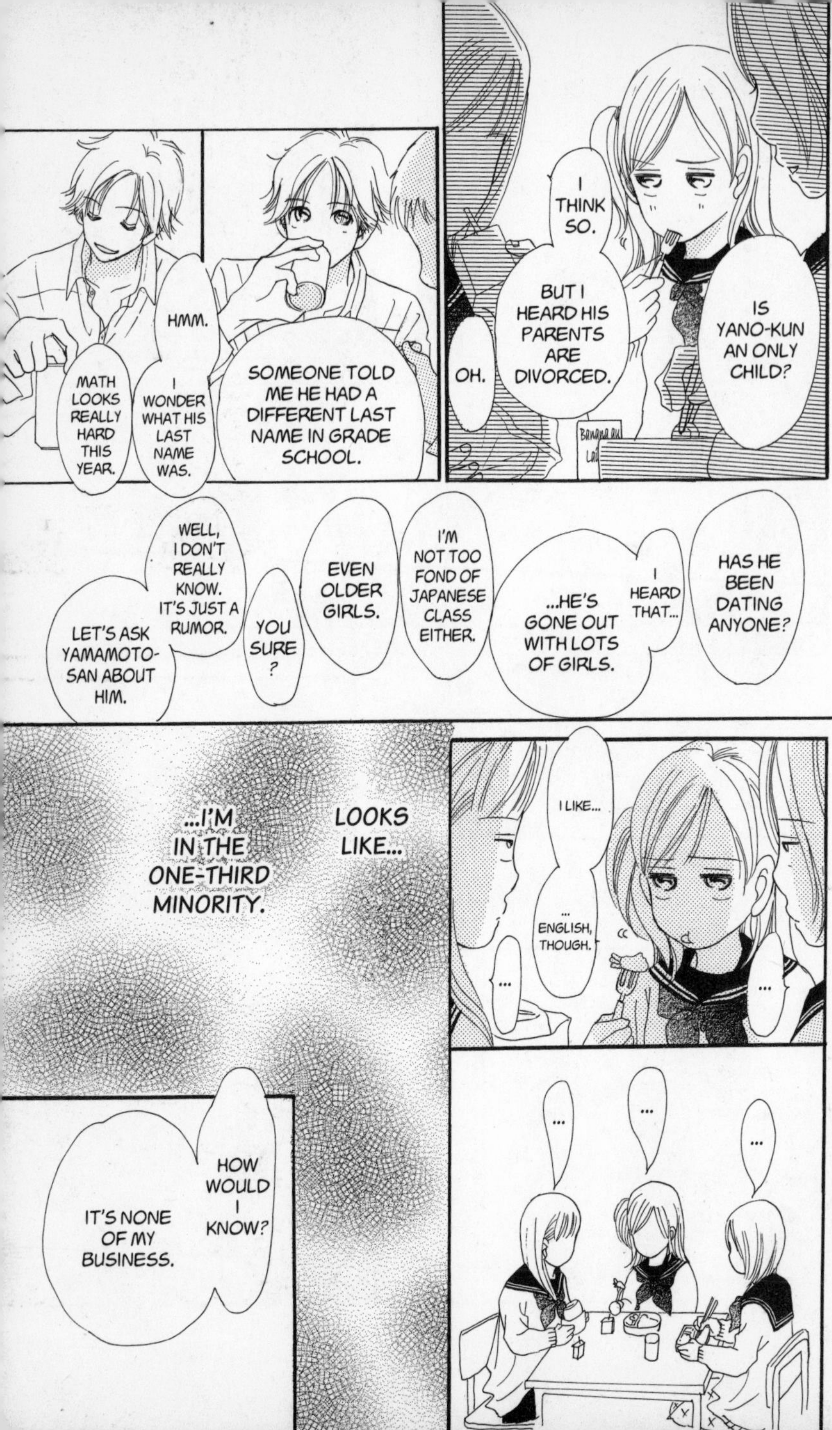
IS YANO-KUN AN ONLY CHILD?
I THINK SO.
BUT I HEARD HIS PARENTS ARE DIVORCED.
OH.
SOMEONE TOLD ME HE HAD A DIFFERENT LAST NAME IN GRADE SCHOOL.
HMM.
I WONDER WHAT HIS LAST NAME WAS.
MATH LOOKS REALLY HARD THIS YEAR.
HAS HE BEEN DATING ANYONE?
I HEARD THAT...
...HE'S GONE OUT WITH LOTS OF GIRLS.
I'M NOT TOO FOND OF JAPANESE CLASS EITHER.
EVEN OLDER GIRLS.
YOU SURE?
WELL, I DON'T REALLY KNOW. IT'S JUST A RUMOR.
LET'S ASK YAMAMOTO-SAN ABOUT HIM.
I LIKE...
... ENGLISH, THOUGH.
...
...
...
...
...
LOOKS LIKE...
...I'M IN THE ONE-THIRD MINORITY.
HOW WOULD I KNOW?
IT'S NONE OF MY BUSINESS.

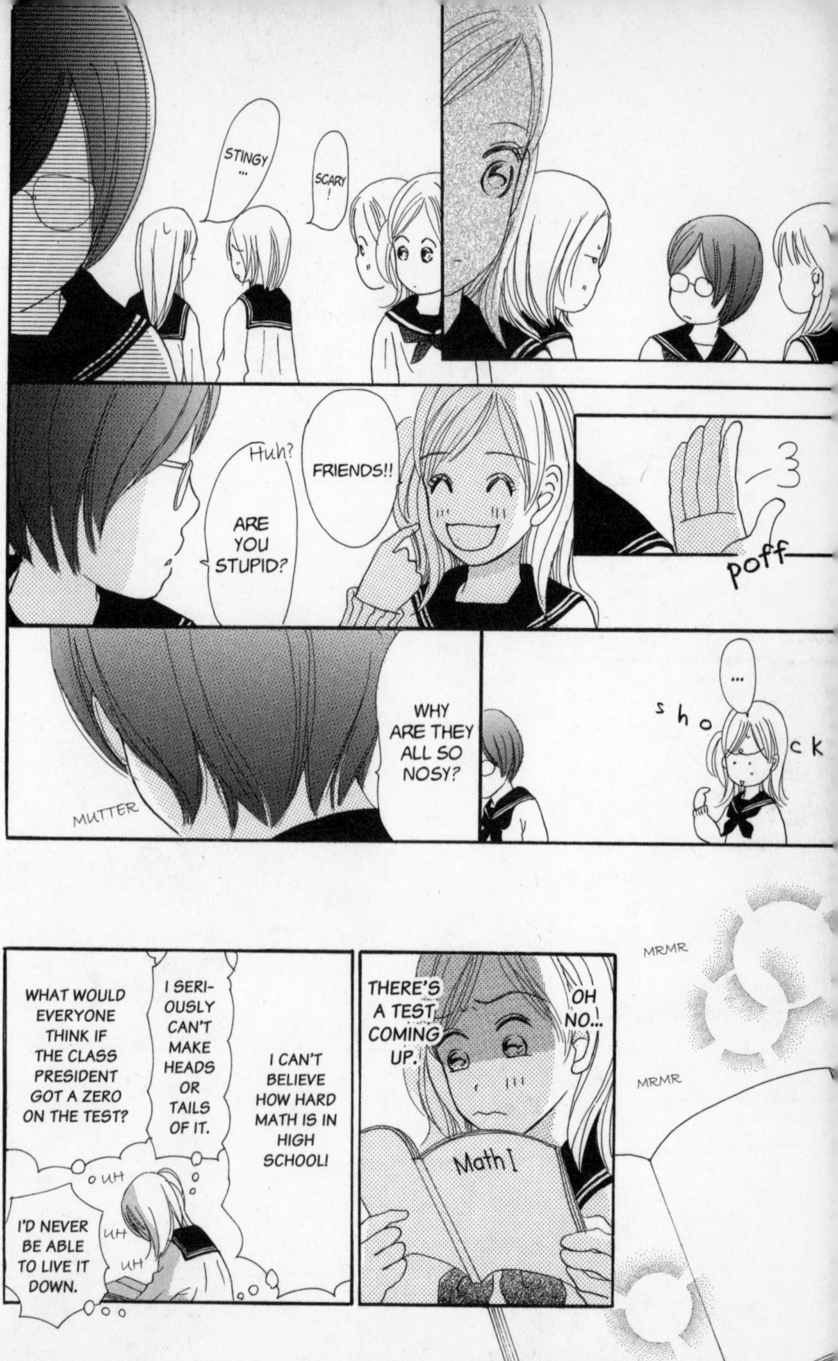

SCARY!
STINGY...
3
poff
FRIENDS!!
Huh?
ARE YOU STUPID?
...
shock
WHY ARE THEY ALL SO NOSY?
MUTTER
MRMR
MRMR
OH NO...
THERE'S A TEST COMING UP.
Math I
I CAN'T BELIEVE HOW HARD MATH IS IN HIGH SCHOOL!
I SERIOUSLY CAN'T MAKE HEADS OR TAILS OF IT.
WHAT WOULD EVERYONE THINK IF THE CLASS PRESIDENT GOT A ZERO ON THE TEST?
OUH
UH
UH
I'D NEVER BE ABLE TO LIVE IT DOWN.

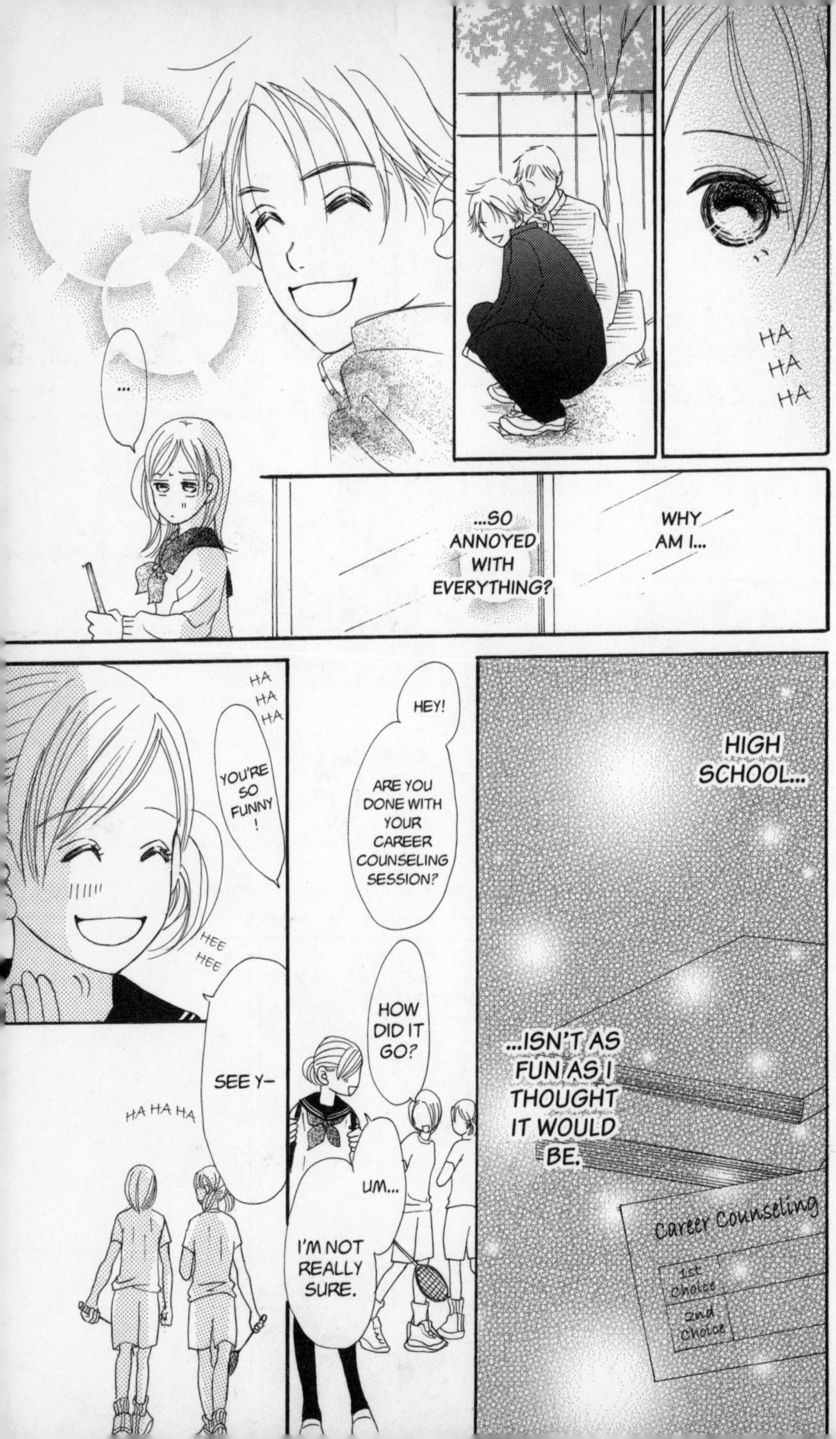
HA HA HA
...
WHY AM I...
...SO ANNOYED WITH EVERYTHING?
HIGH SCHOOL...
...ISN'T AS FUN AS I THOUGHT IT WOULD BE.
Career Counseling
1st Choice
2nd Choice
HEY!
ARE YOU DONE WITH YOUR CAREER COUNSELING SESSION?
HOW DID IT GO?
UM...
I'M NOT REALLY SURE.
HA HA HA
YOU'RE SO FUNNY!
HEE HEE
SEE Y-
HA HA HA

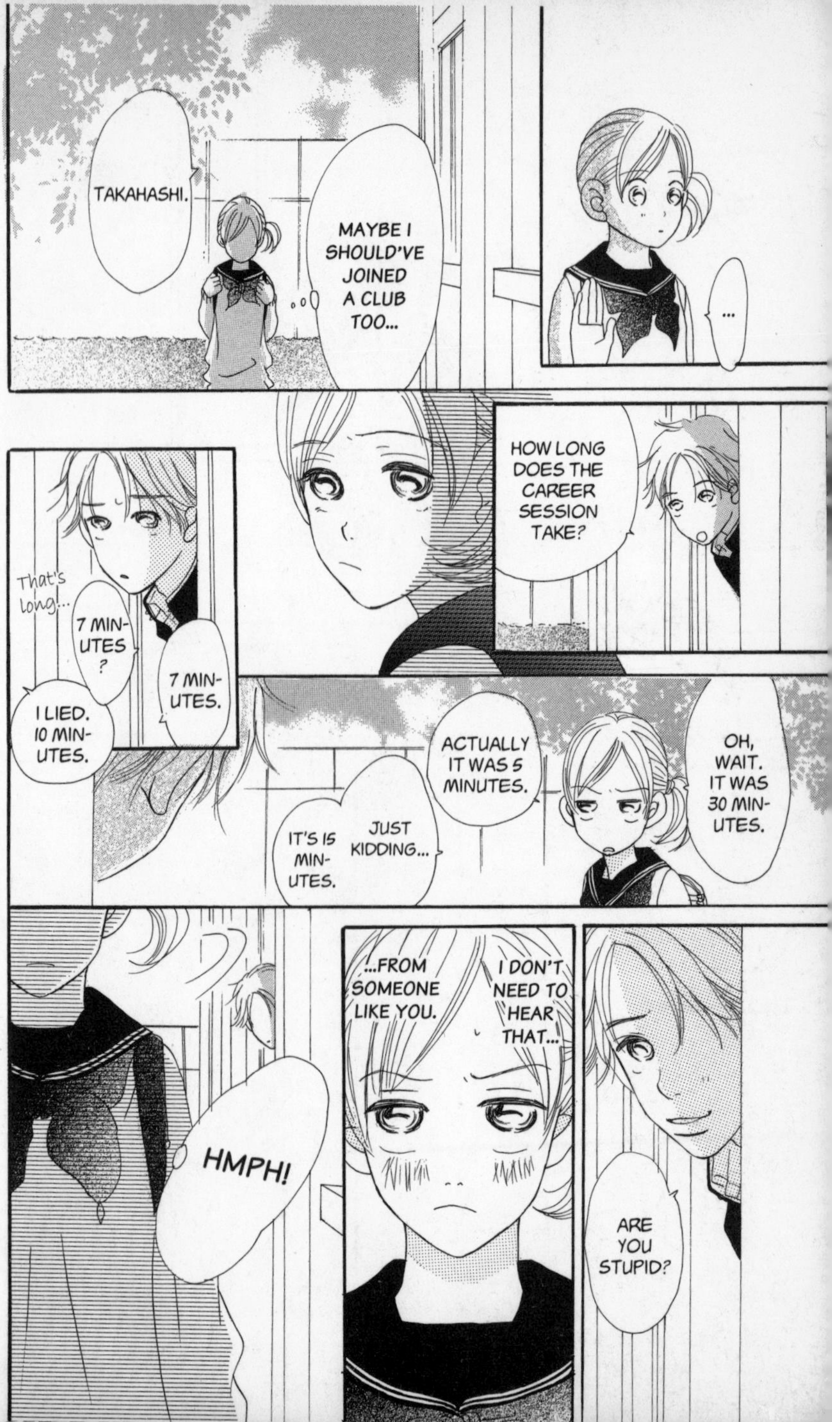
...
MAYBE I SHOULD'VE JOINED A CLUB TOO...
TAKAHASHI.
HOW LONG DOES THE CAREER SESSION TAKE?
7 MIN-UTES.
7 MIN-UTES?
That's long...
I LIED. 10 MIN-UTES.
OH, WAIT. IT WAS 30 MIN-UTES.
ACTUALLY IT WAS 5 MINUTES.
JUST KIDDING...
IT'S 15 MIN-UTES.
ARE YOU STUPID?
I DON'T NEED TO HEAR THAT...
...FROM SOMEONE LIKE YOU.
HMPH!

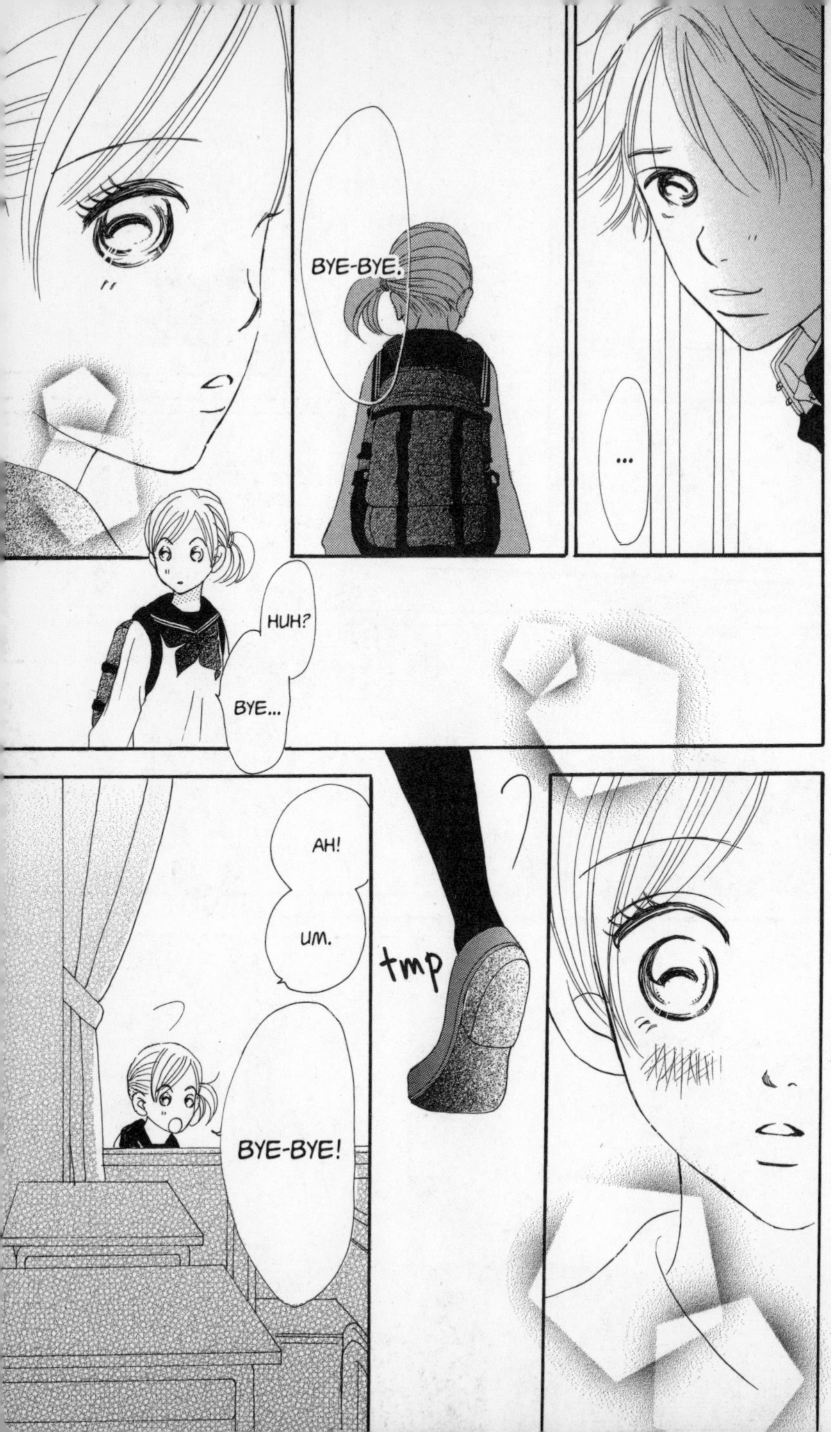
...
BYE-BYE.
HUH?
BYE...
tmp
AH!
UM.
BYE-BYE!

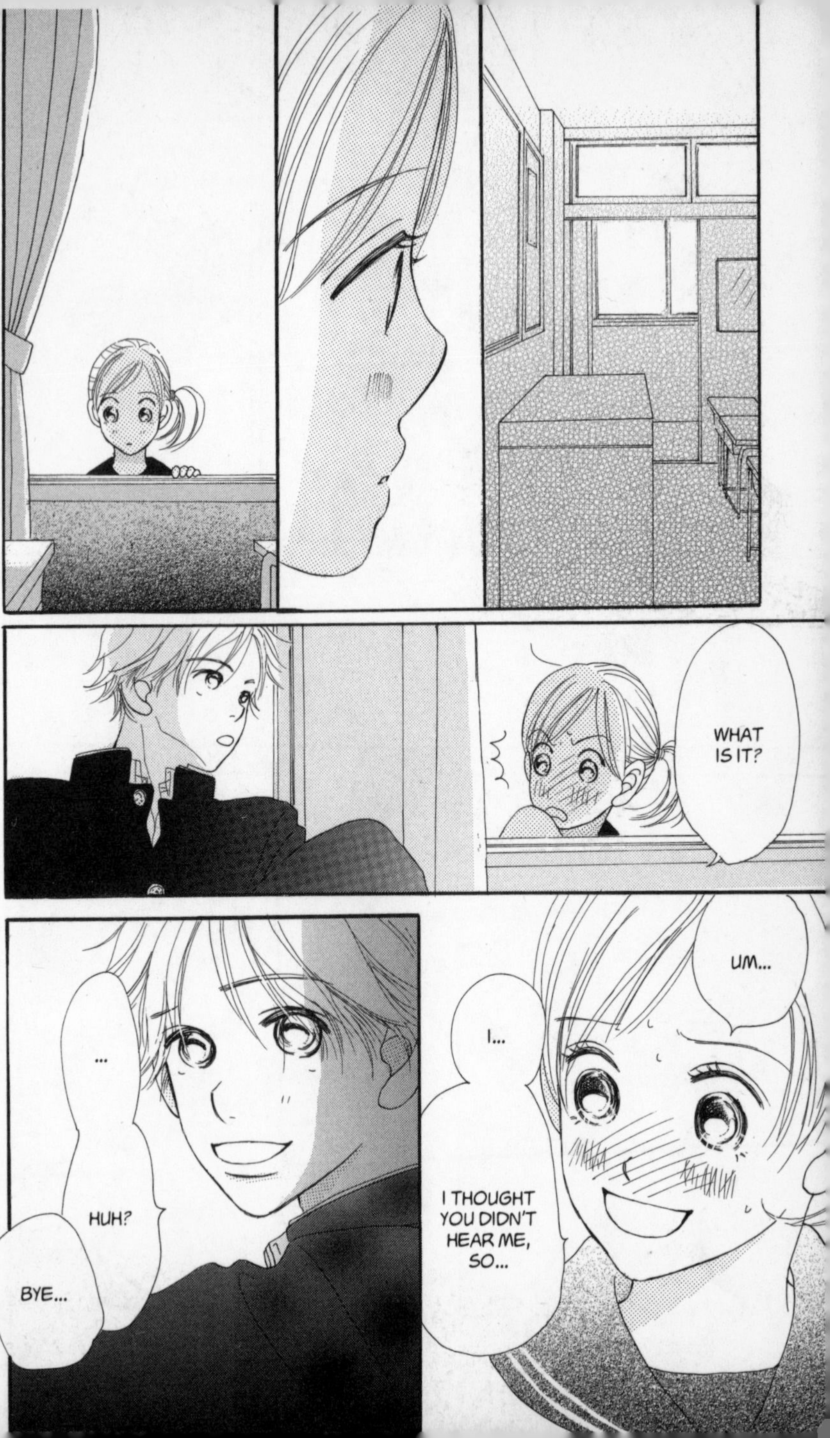
WHAT IS IT?
UM...
I...
I THOUGHT YOU DIDN'T HEAR ME, SO...
...
HUH?
BYE...

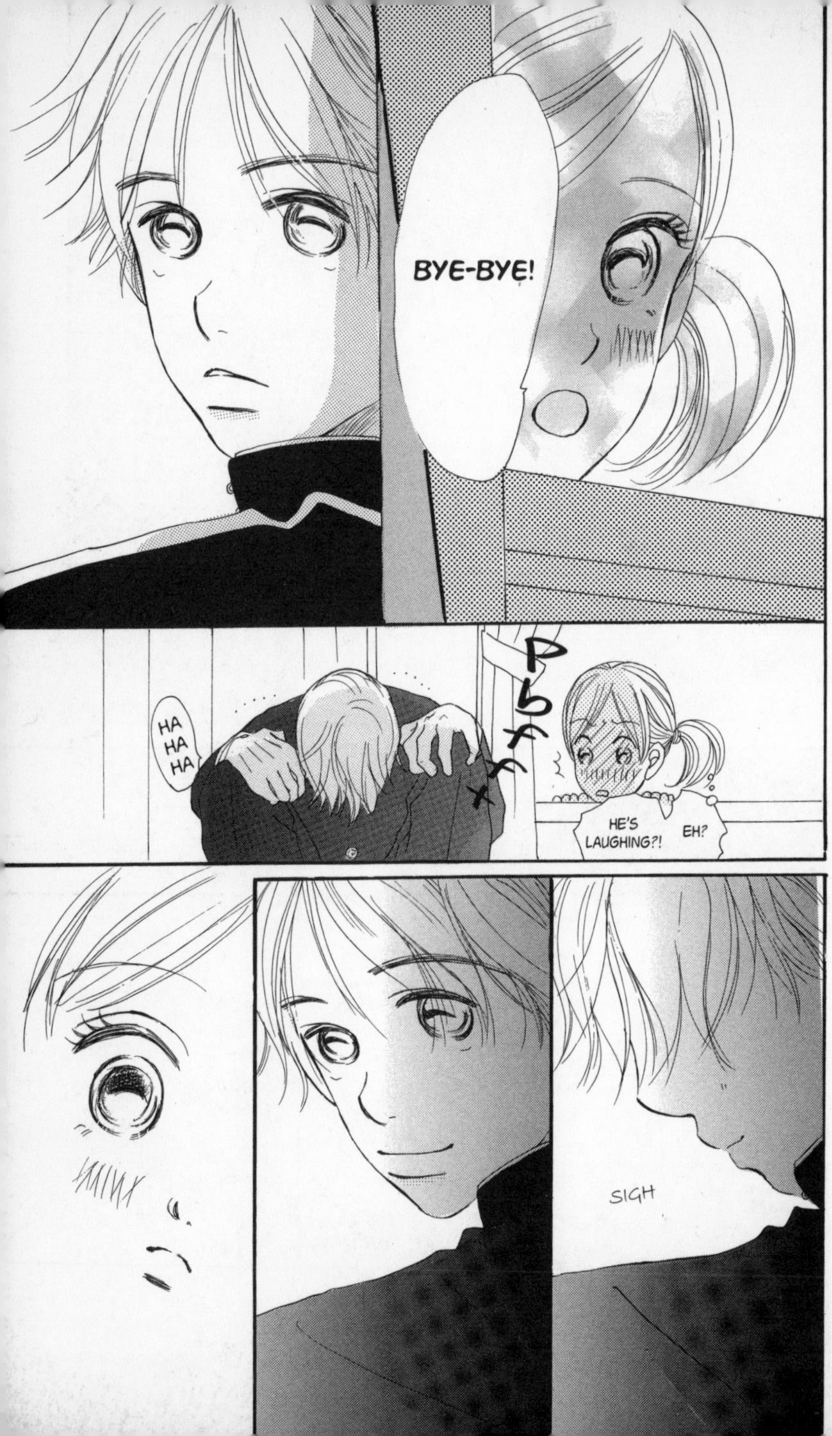
BYE-BYE!
EH?
HE'S LAUGHING?!
HA HA HA
SIGH

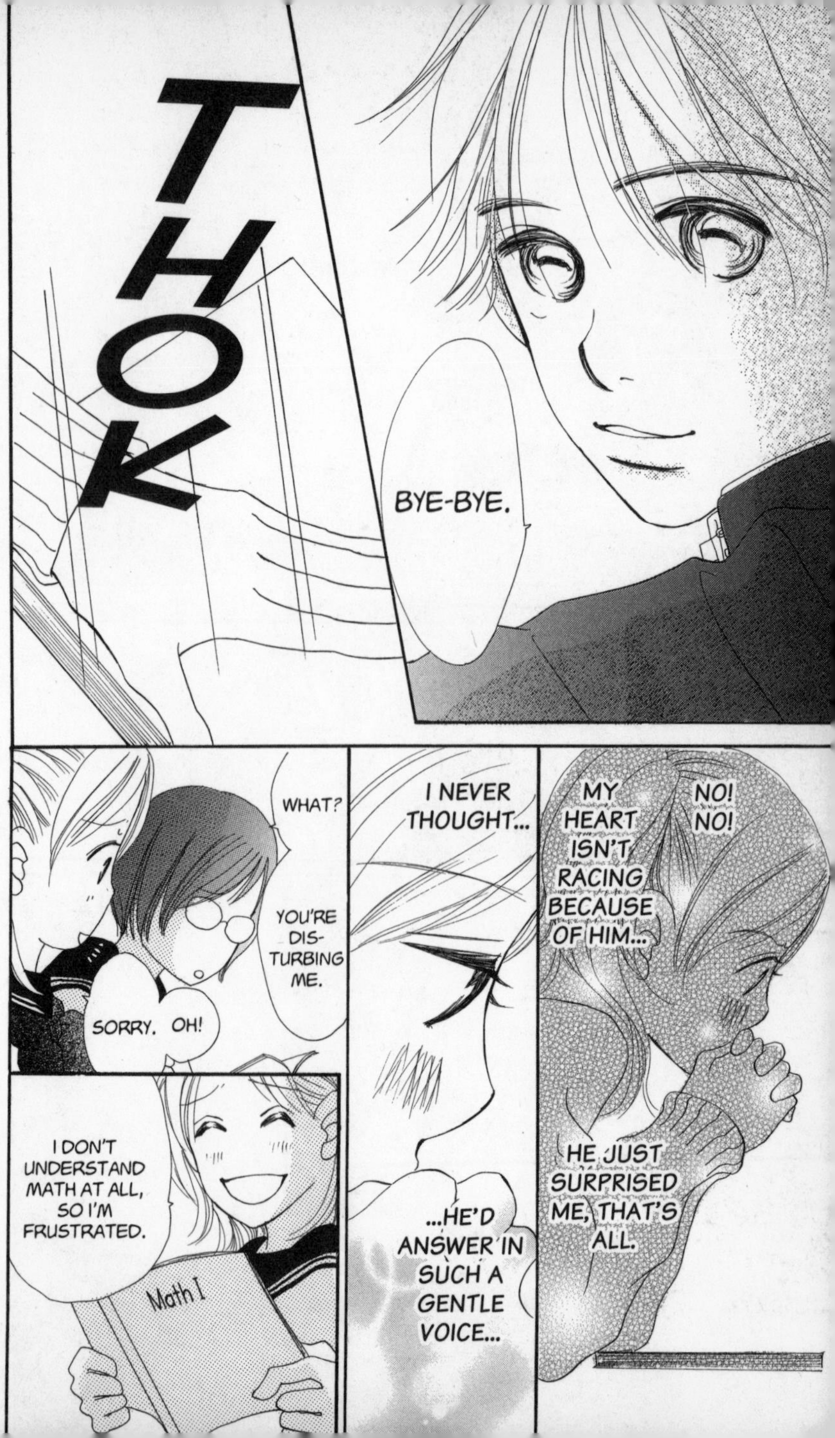
BYE-BYE.
THOK
NO! NO!
MY HEART ISN'T RACING BECAUSE OF HIM...
HE JUST SURPRISED ME, THAT'S ALL.
I NEVER THOUGHT...
...HE'D ANSWER IN SUCH A GENTLE VOICE...
WHAT?
YOU'RE DIS-TURBING ME.
SORRY. OH!
I DON'T UNDERSTAND MATH AT ALL, SO I'M FRUSTRATED.
Math I

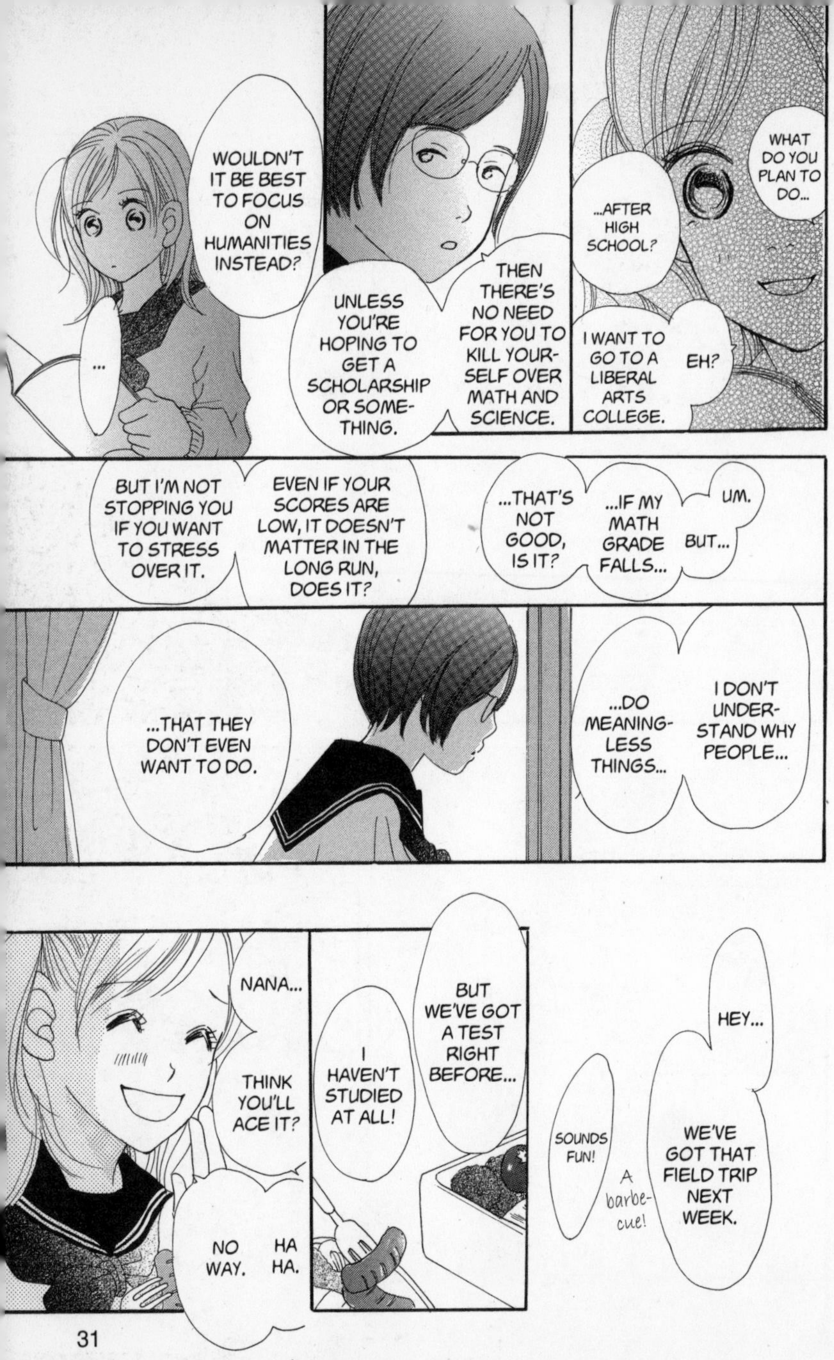
WHAT DO YOU PLAN TO DO...
...AFTER HIGH SCHOOL?
EH?
I WANT TO GO TO A LIBERAL ARTS COLLEGE.
THEN THERE'S NO NEED FOR YOU TO KILL YOURSELF OVER MATH AND SCIENCE.
UNLESS YOU'RE HOPING TO GET A SCHOLARSHIP OR SOMETHING.
WOULDN'T IT BE BEST TO FOCUS ON HUMANITIES INSTEAD?
...
UM.
BUT...
...IF MY MATH GRADE FALLS...
...THAT'S NOT GOOD, IS IT?
EVEN IF YOUR SCORES ARE LOW, IT DOESN'T MATTER IN THE LONG RUN, DOES IT?
BUT I'M NOT STOPPING YOU IF YOU WANT TO STRESS OVER IT.
I DON'T UNDERSTAND WHY PEOPLE...
...DO MEANINGLESS THINGS...
...THAT THEY DON'T EVEN WANT TO DO.
HEY...
WE'VE GOT THAT FIELD TRIP NEXT WEEK.
A barbecue!
SOUNDS FUN!
BUT WE'VE GOT A TEST RIGHT BEFORE...
I HAVEN'T STUDIED AT ALL!
NANA...
THINK YOU'LL ACE IT?
NO WAY.
HA HA.

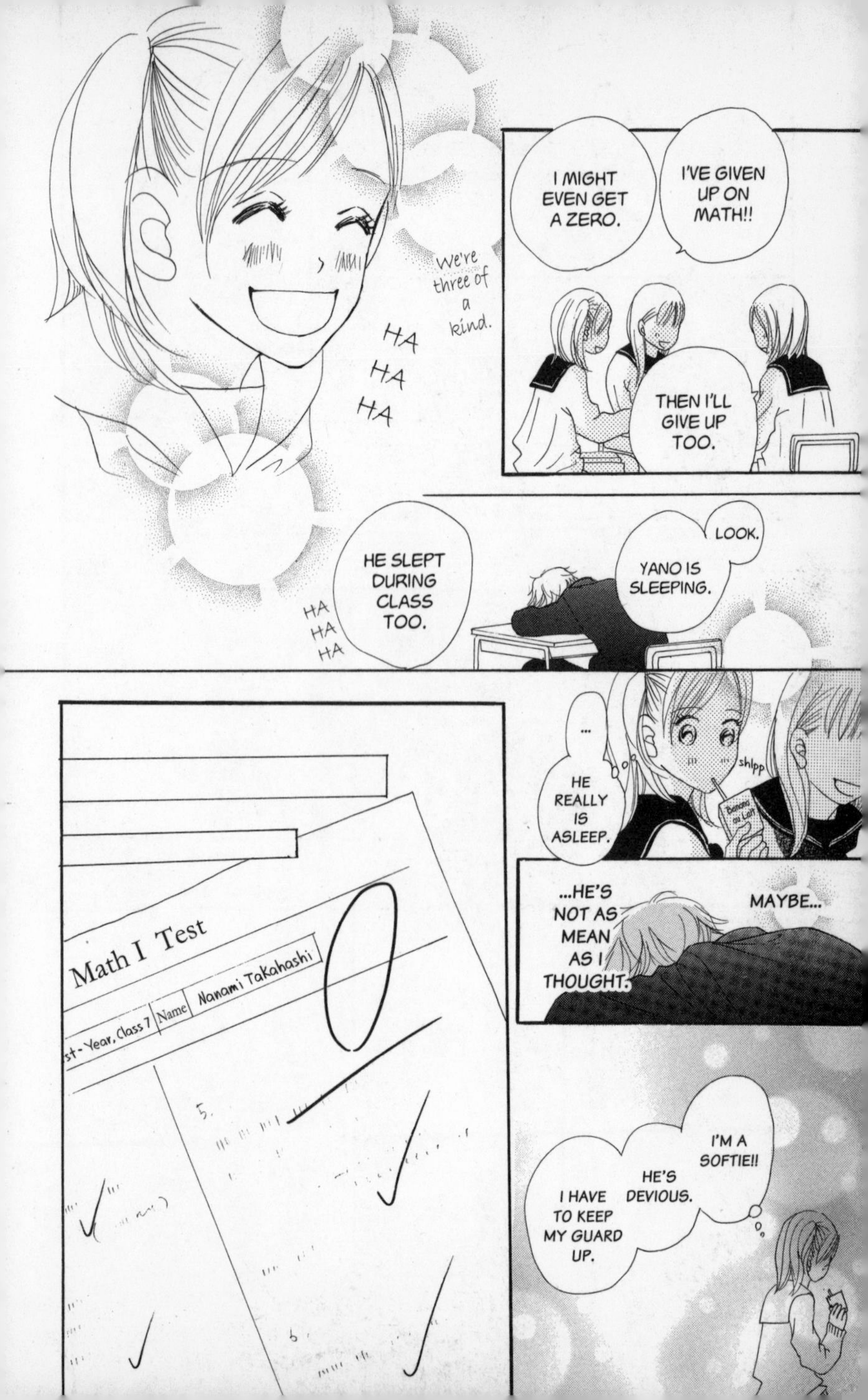

I'VE GIVEN UP ON MATH!!
I MIGHT EVEN GET A ZERO.
THEN I'LL GIVE UP TOO.
We're three of a kind.
HA HA HA
LOOK.
YANO IS SLEEPING.
HE SLEPT DURING CLASS TOO.
HA HA HA
...
HE REALLY IS ASLEEP.
shlpp
MAYBE...
...HE'S NOT AS MEAN AS I THOUGHT.
I'M A SOFTIE!!
HE'S DEVIOUS.
I HAVE TO KEEP MY GUARD UP.
Math I Test
st-Year, Class 7
Name
Nanami Takahashi
0

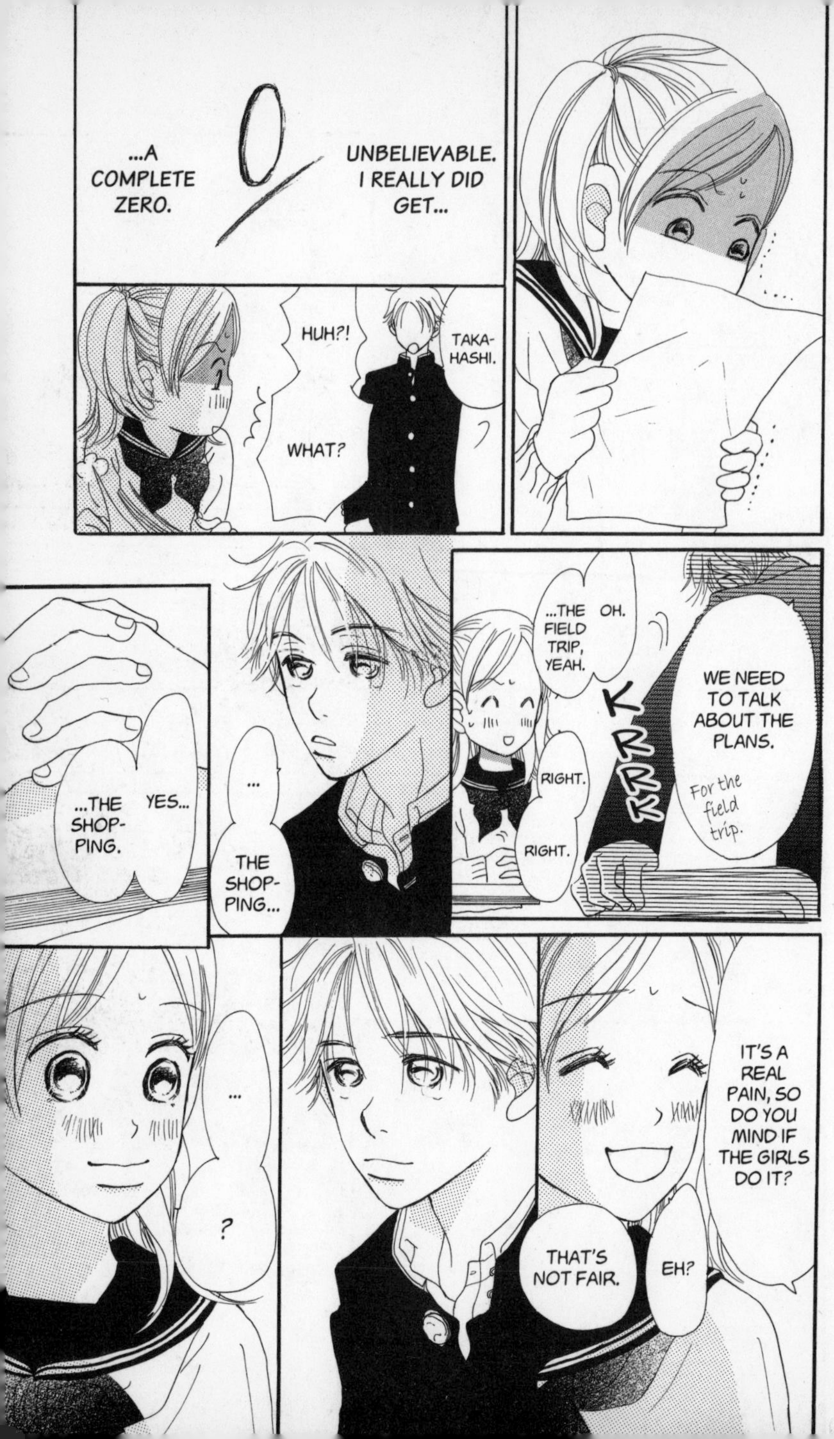
UNBELIEVABLE. I REALLY DID GET...
0
...A COMPLETE ZERO.
TAKAHASHI.
HUH?!
WHAT?
WE NEED TO TALK ABOUT THE PLANS.
For the field trip.
OH.
...THE FIELD TRIP, YEAH.
KRRR
RIGHT.
RIGHT.
...
THE SHOPPING...
YES...
...THE SHOPPING.
IT'S A REAL PAIN, SO DO YOU MIND IF THE GIRLS DO IT?
EH?
THAT'S NOT FAIR.
...
?

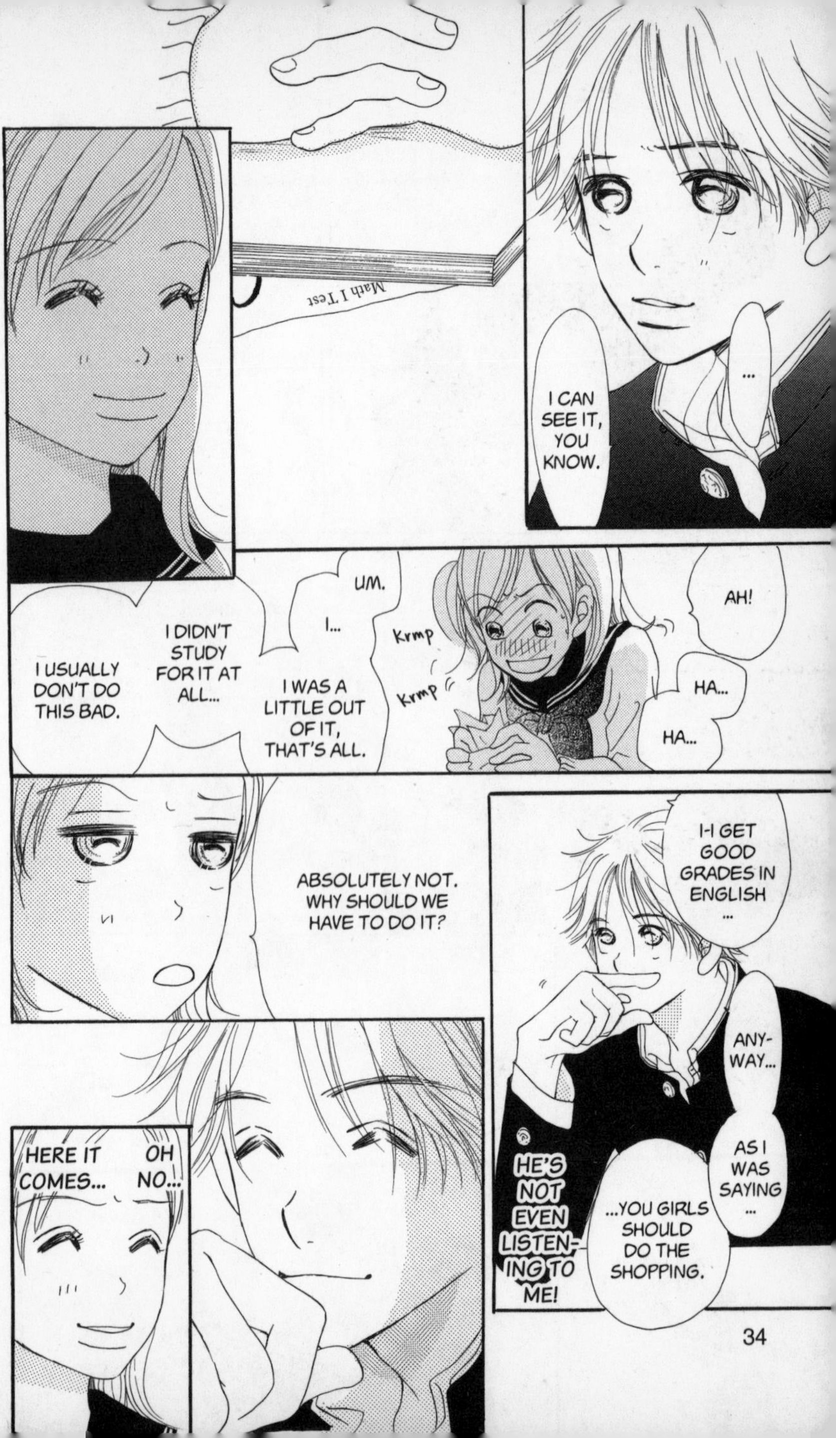
...
I CAN SEE IT, YOU KNOW.
Math I Test
AH!
HA...
HA...
Krmp
Krmp
UM.
I...
I WAS A LITTLE OUT OF IT, THAT'S ALL.
I DIDN'T STUDY FOR IT AT ALL...
I USUALLY DON'T DO THIS BAD.
I-I GET GOOD GRADES IN ENGLISH ...
ANY-WAY...
AS I WAS SAYING ...
...YOU GIRLS SHOULD DO THE SHOPPING.
HE'S NOT EVEN LISTEN-ING TO ME!
ABSOLUTELY NOT. WHY SHOULD WE HAVE TO DO IT?
OH NO...
HERE IT COMES...

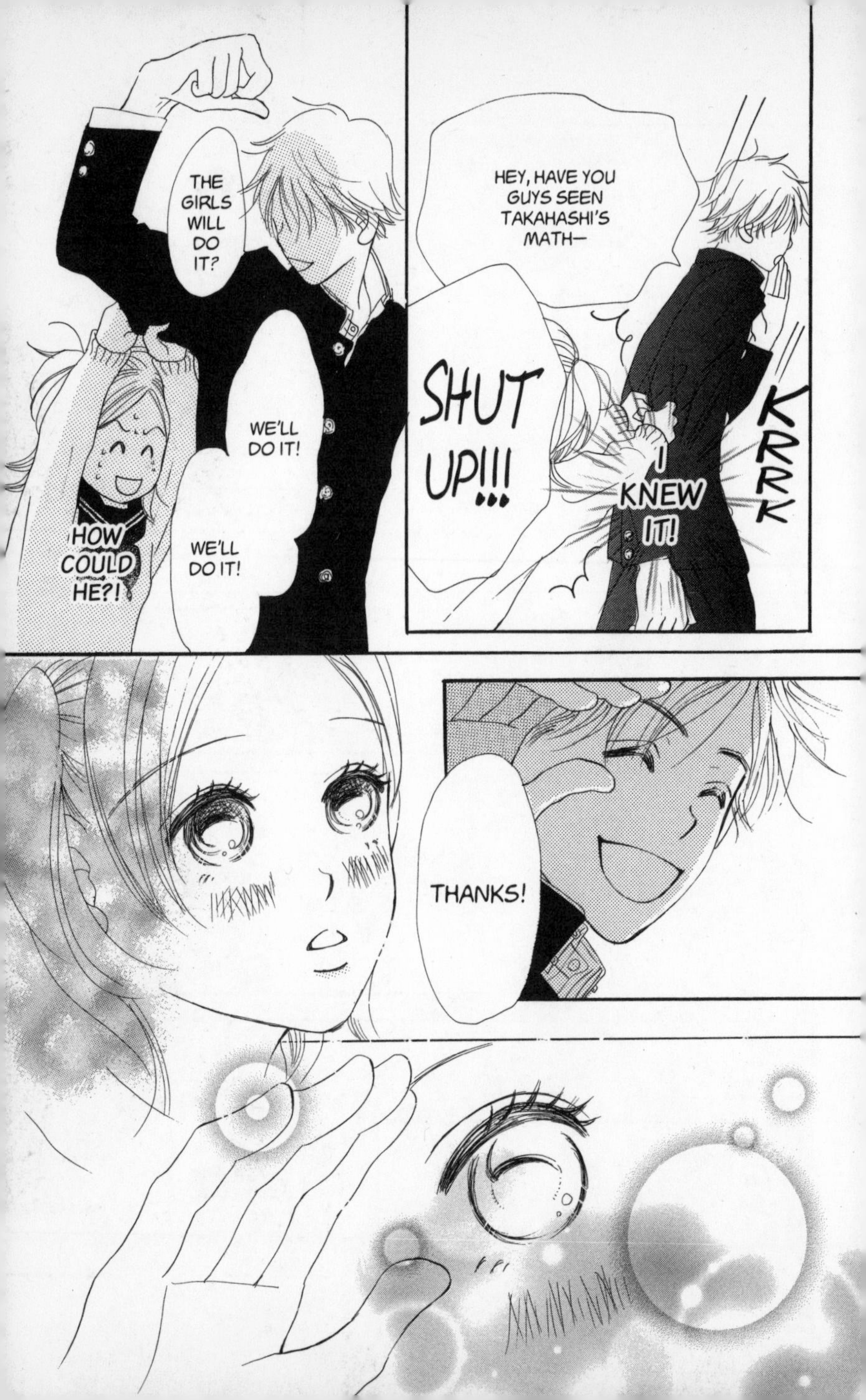
HEY, HAVE YOU GUYS SEEN TAKAHASHI'S MATH—
KRRK
I KNEW IT!
SHUT UP!!!
THE GIRLS WILL DO IT?
WE'LL DO IT!
WE'LL DO IT!
HOW COULD HE?!
THANKS!

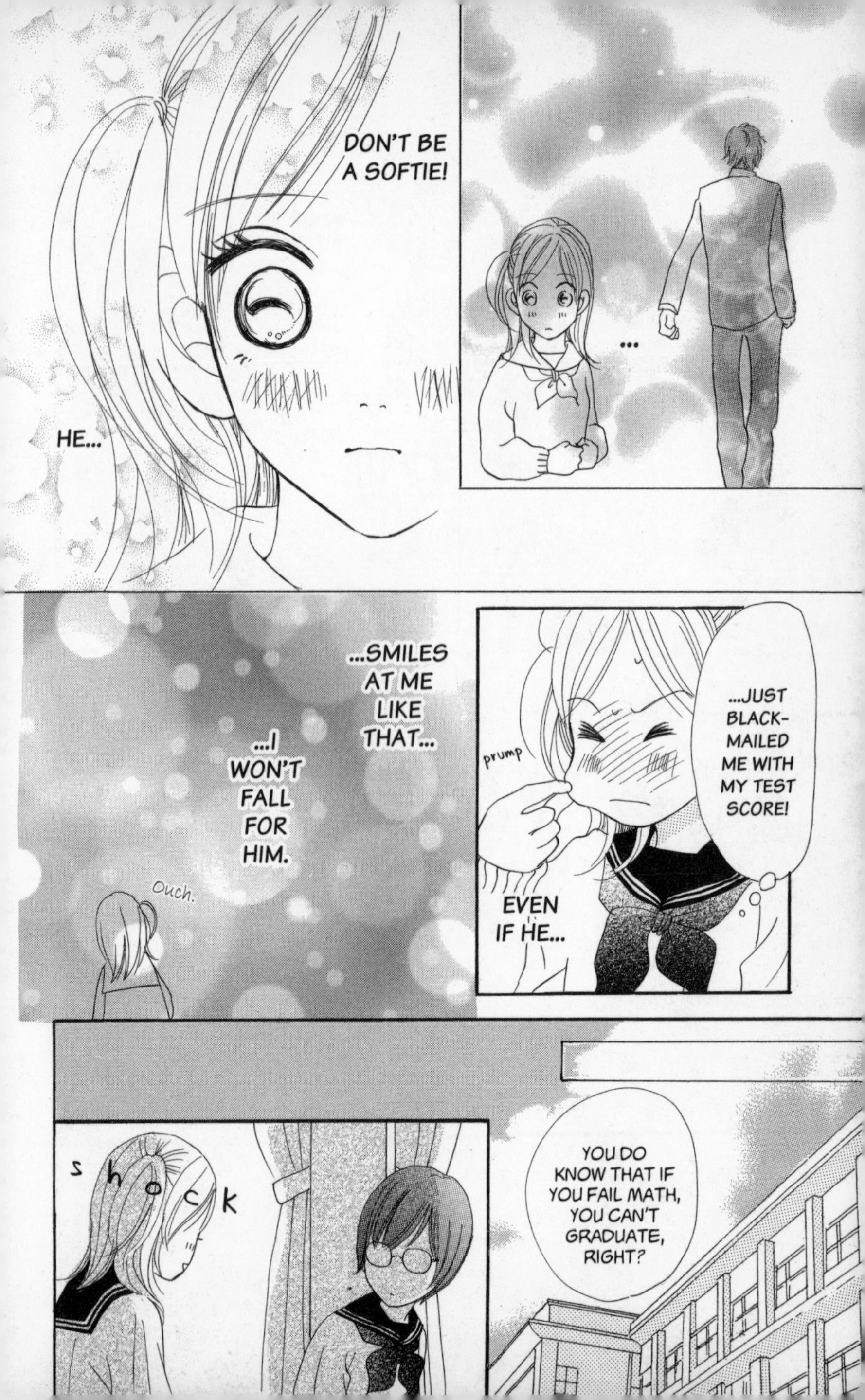
...
DON'T BE A SOFTIE!
HE...
...JUST BLACK-MAILED ME WITH MY TEST SCORE!
prump
EVEN IF HE...
...SMILES AT ME LIKE THAT...
...I WON'T FALL FOR HIM.
Ouch.
YOU DO KNOW THAT IF YOU FAIL MATH, YOU CAN'T GRADUATE, RIGHT?
shock

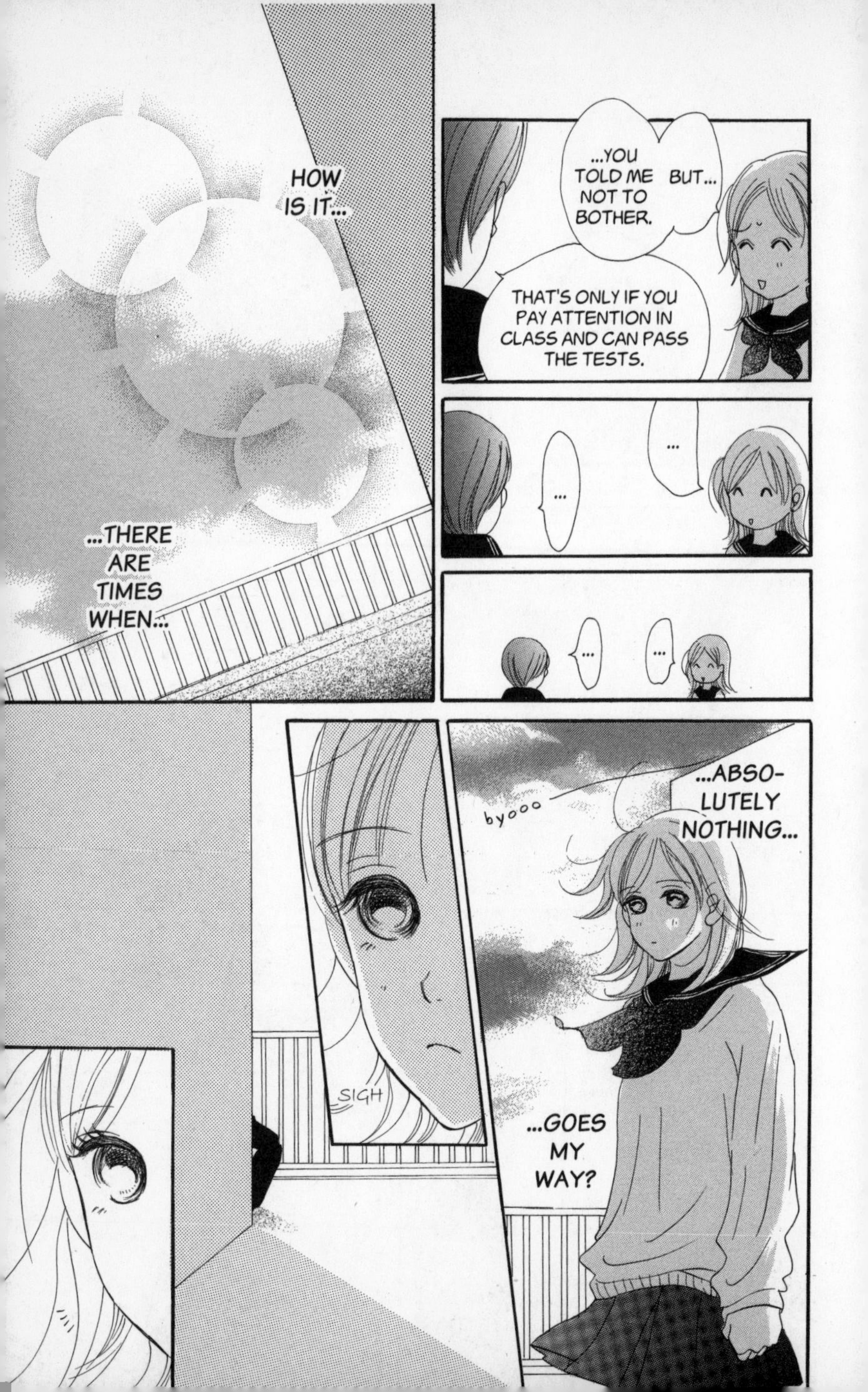

BUT...
...YOU TOLD ME NOT TO BOTHER.
THAT'S ONLY IF YOU PAY ATTENTION IN CLASS AND CAN PASS THE TESTS.
...
...
...
...
HOW IS IT...
...THERE ARE TIMES WHEN...
...ABSO-LUTELY NOTHING...
byooo
...GOES MY WAY?
SIGH

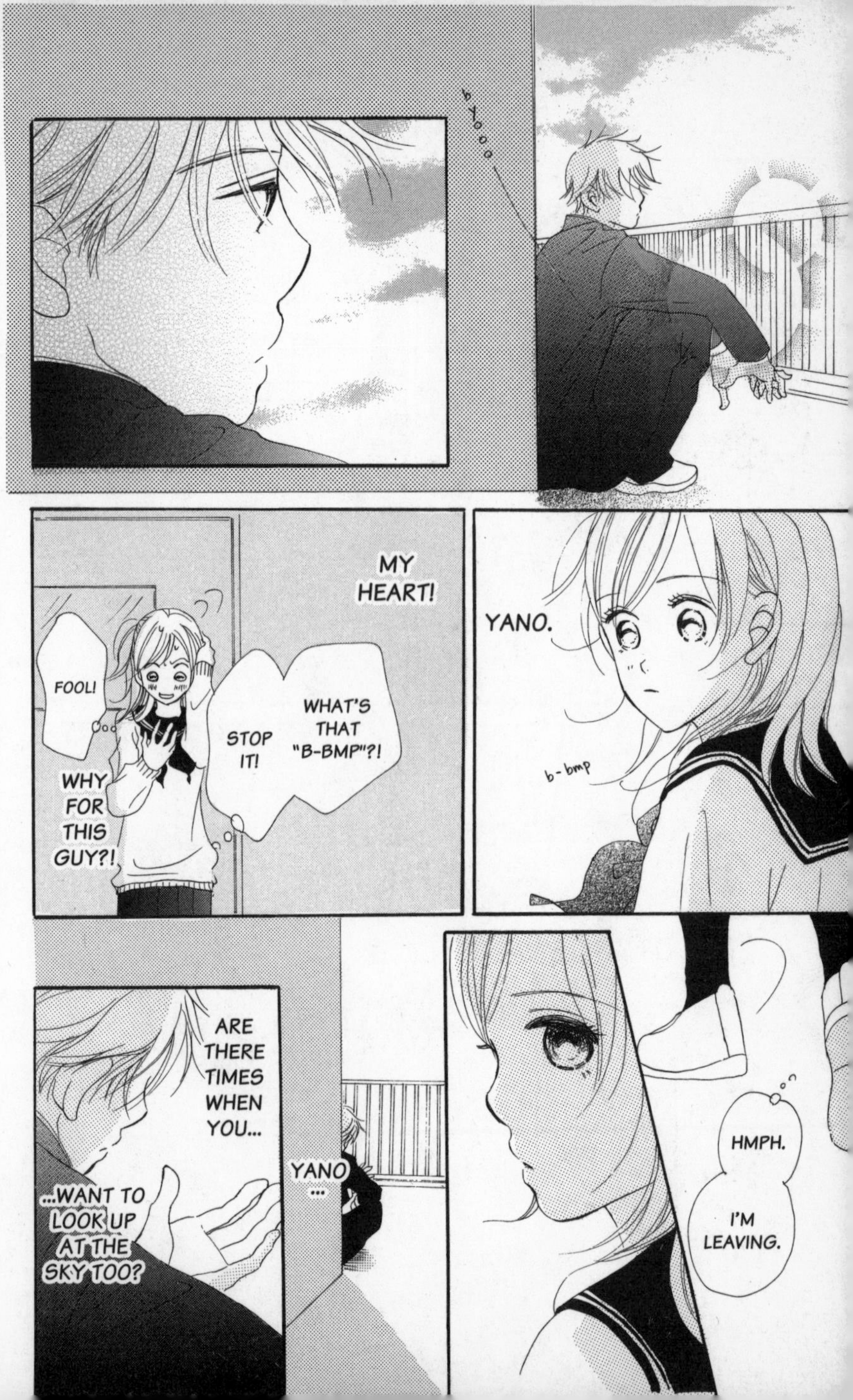
byooo
YANO.
b-bmp
MY HEART!
WHAT'S THAT "B-BMP"?!
STOP IT!
FOOL!
WHY FOR THIS GUY?!
HMPH.
I'M LEAVING.
YANO...
ARE THERE TIMES WHEN YOU...
...WANT TO LOOK UP AT THE SKY TOO?

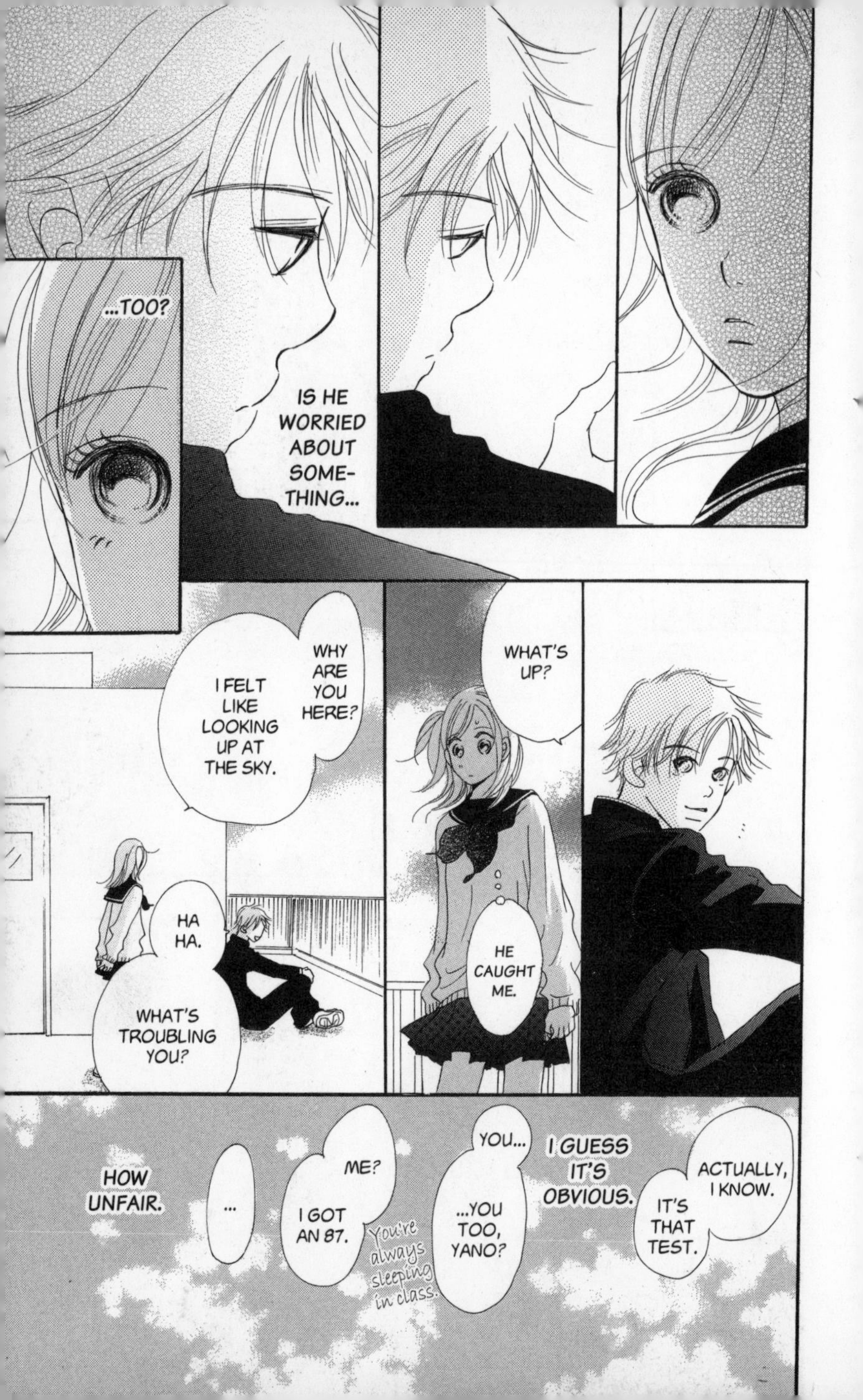
IS HE WORRIED ABOUT SOMETHING...
...TOO?
WHAT'S UP?
HE CAUGHT ME.
WHY ARE YOU HERE?
I FELT LIKE LOOKING UP AT THE SKY.
HA HA.
WHAT'S TROUBLING YOU?
ACTUALLY, I KNOW.
IT'S THAT TEST.
I GUESS IT'S OBVIOUS.
YOU...
...YOU TOO, YANO?
ME?
I GOT AN 87.
You're always sleeping in class.
...
HOW UNFAIR.

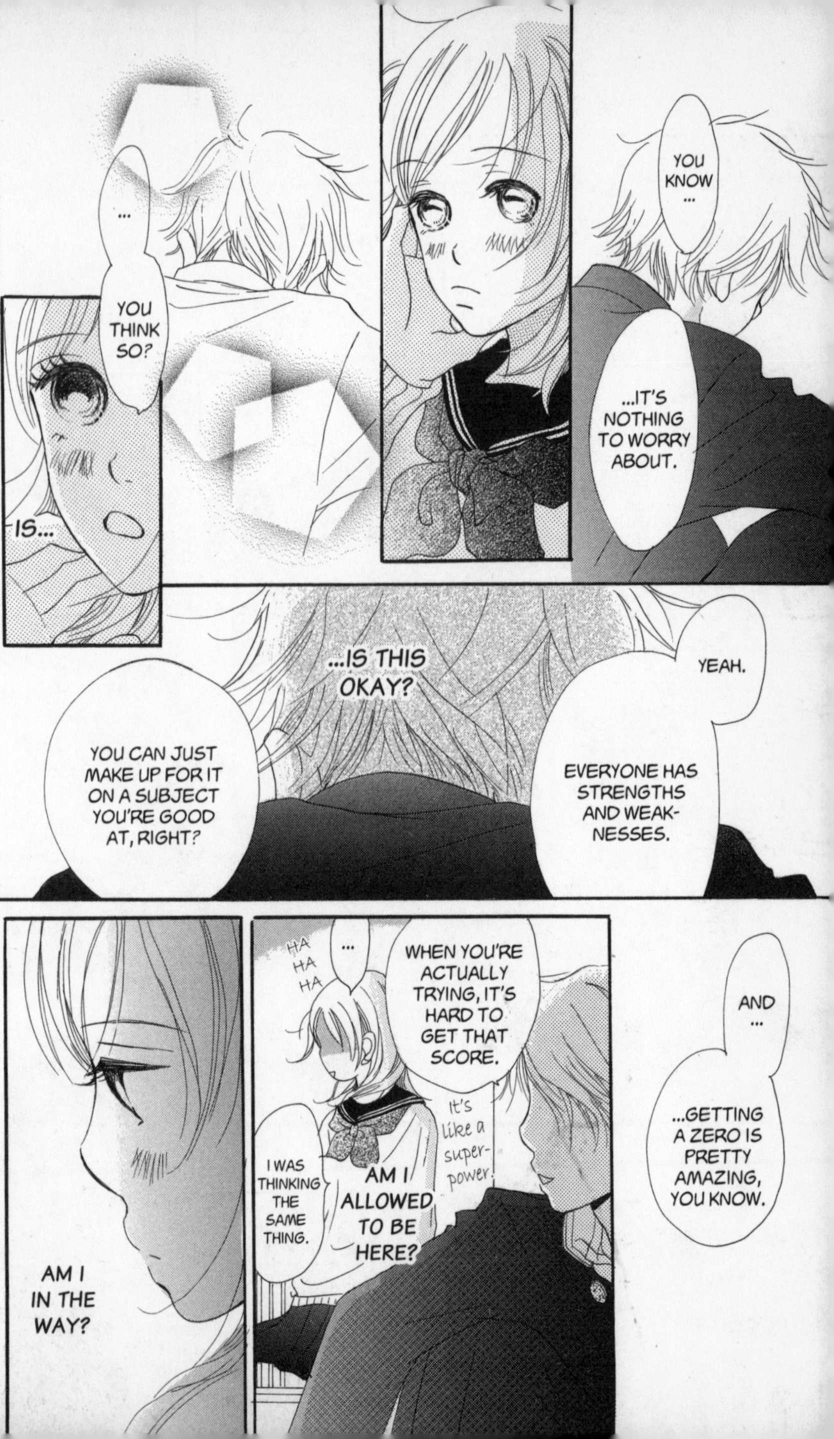
YOU KNOW ...
...IT'S NOTHING TO WORRY ABOUT.
...
YOU THINK SO?
IS...
YEAH.
...IS THIS OKAY?
EVERYONE HAS STRENGTHS AND WEAK-NESSES.
YOU CAN JUST MAKE UP FOR IT ON A SUBJECT YOU'RE GOOD AT, RIGHT?
AND ...
...GETTING A ZERO IS PRETTY AMAZING, YOU KNOW.
WHEN YOU'RE ACTUALLY TRYING, IT'S HARD TO GET THAT SCORE.
...
HA HA HA
It's like a super-power.
I WAS THINKING THE SAME THING.
AM I ALLOWED TO BE HERE?
AM I IN THE WAY?

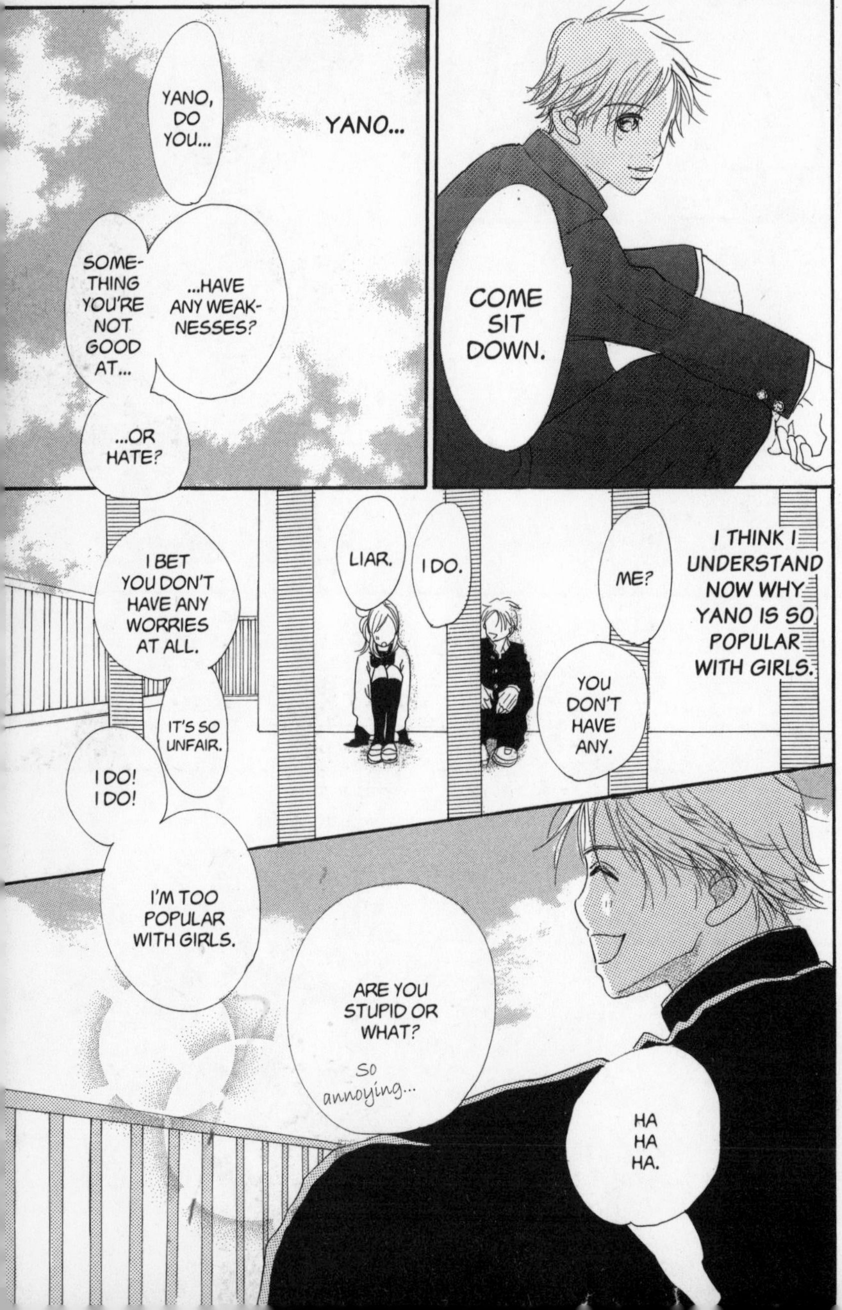
COME SIT DOWN.
YANO...
YANO, DO YOU...
...HAVE ANY WEAKNESSES?
SOMETHING YOU'RE NOT GOOD AT...
...OR HATE?
I THINK I UNDERSTAND NOW WHY YANO IS SO POPULAR WITH GIRLS.
ME?
YOU DON'T HAVE ANY.
I DO.
LIAR.
I BET YOU DON'T HAVE ANY WORRIES AT ALL.
IT'S SO UNFAIR.
I DO! I DO!
I'M TOO POPULAR WITH GIRLS.
ARE YOU STUPID OR WHAT?
So annoying...
HA HA HA.

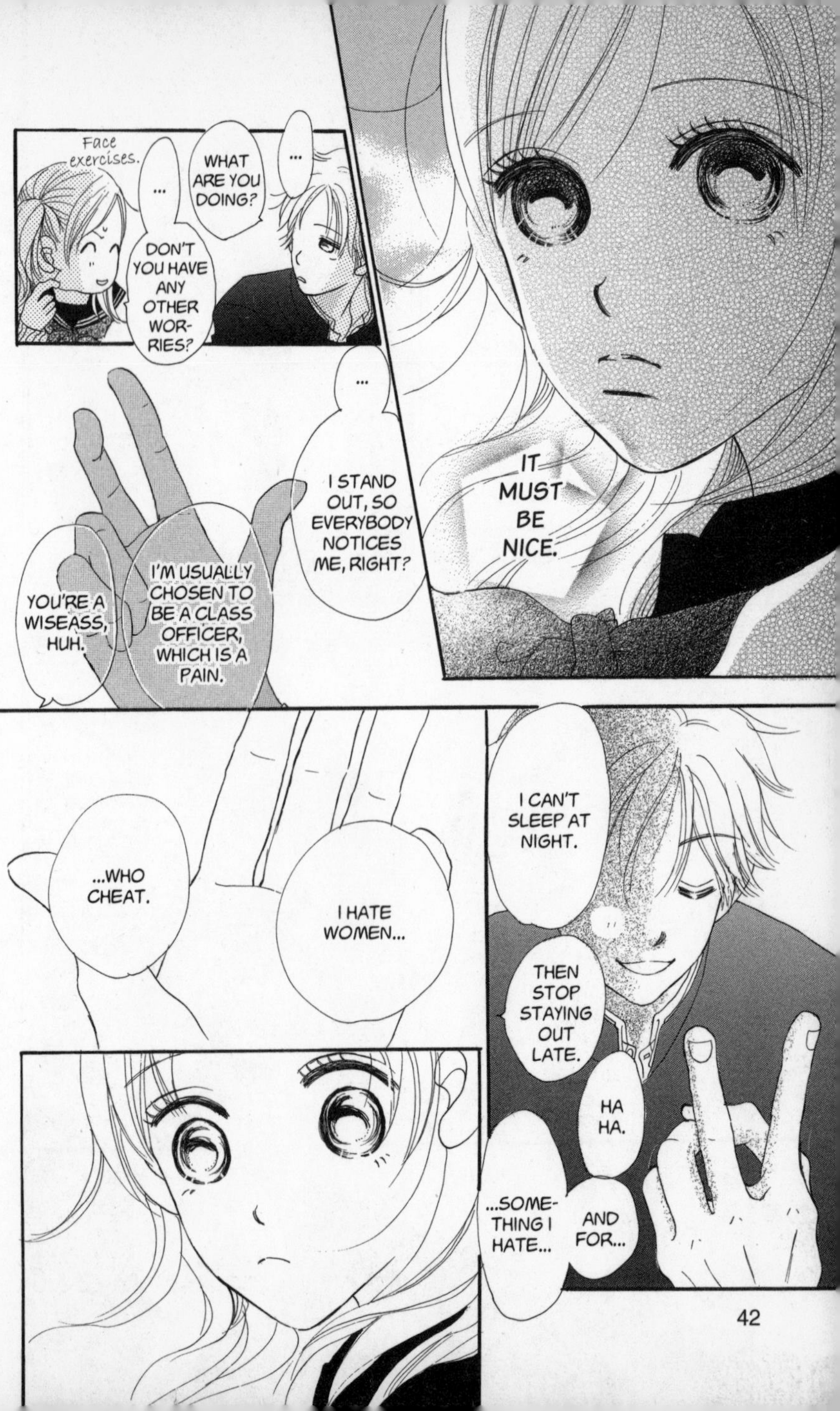
...
WHAT ARE YOU DOING?
Face exercises.
...
DON'T YOU HAVE ANY OTHER WOR-RIES?
IT MUST BE NICE.
...
I STAND OUT, SO EVERYBODY NOTICES ME, RIGHT?
I'M USUALLY CHOSEN TO BE A CLASS OFFICER, WHICH IS A PAIN.
YOU'RE A WISEASS, HUH.
I CAN'T SLEEP AT NIGHT.
THEN STOP STAYING OUT LATE.
HA HA.
AND FOR...
...SOME-THING I HATE...
I HATE WOMEN...
...WHO CHEAT.

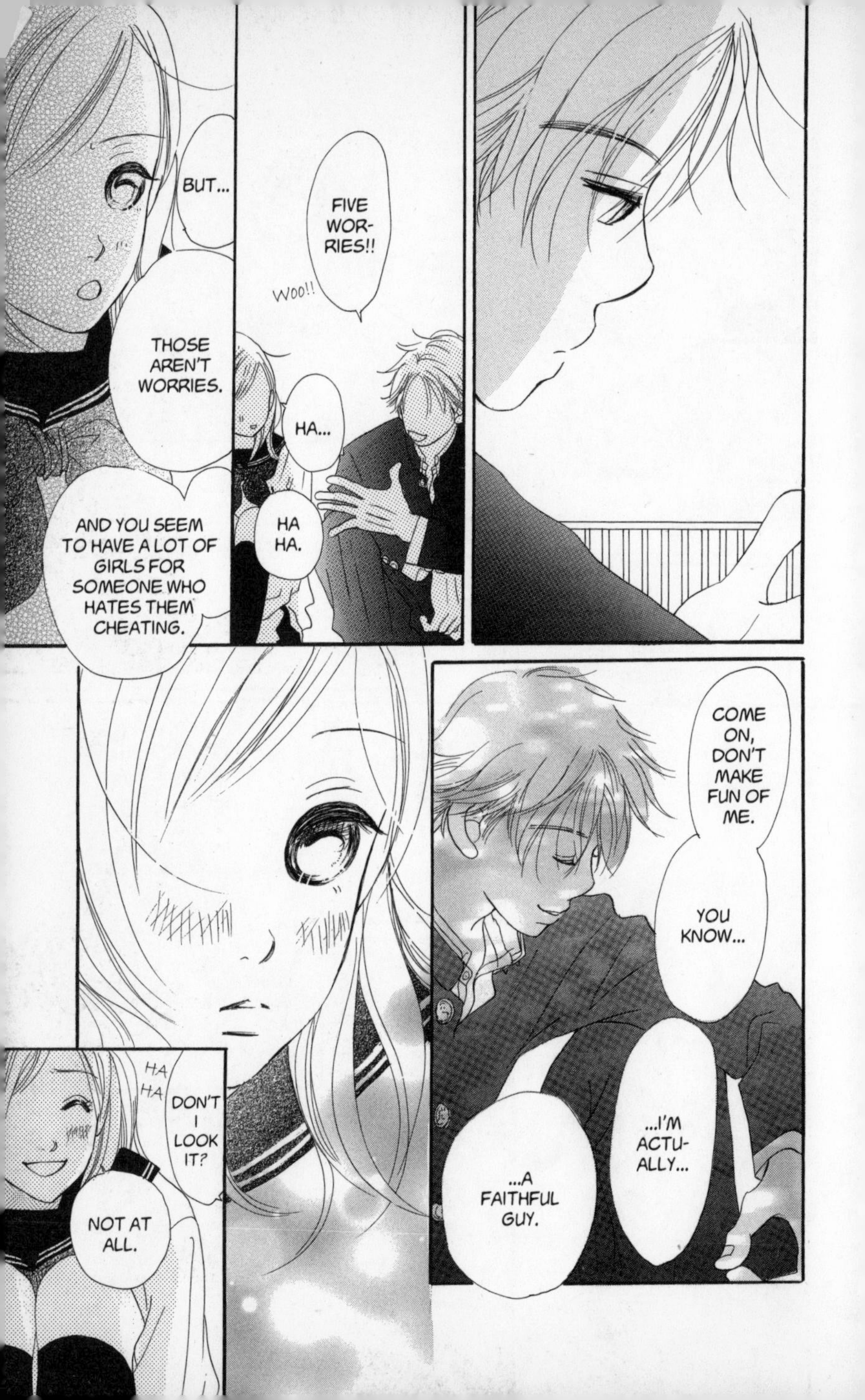
FIVE WOR-RIES!!
WOO!!
HA...
HA HA.
BUT...
THOSE AREN'T WORRIES.
AND YOU SEEM TO HAVE A LOT OF GIRLS FOR SOMEONE WHO HATES THEM CHEATING.
COME ON, DON'T MAKE FUN OF ME.
YOU KNOW...
...I'M ACTU-ALLY...
...A FAITHFUL GUY.
HA HA
DON'T I LOOK IT?
NOT AT ALL.

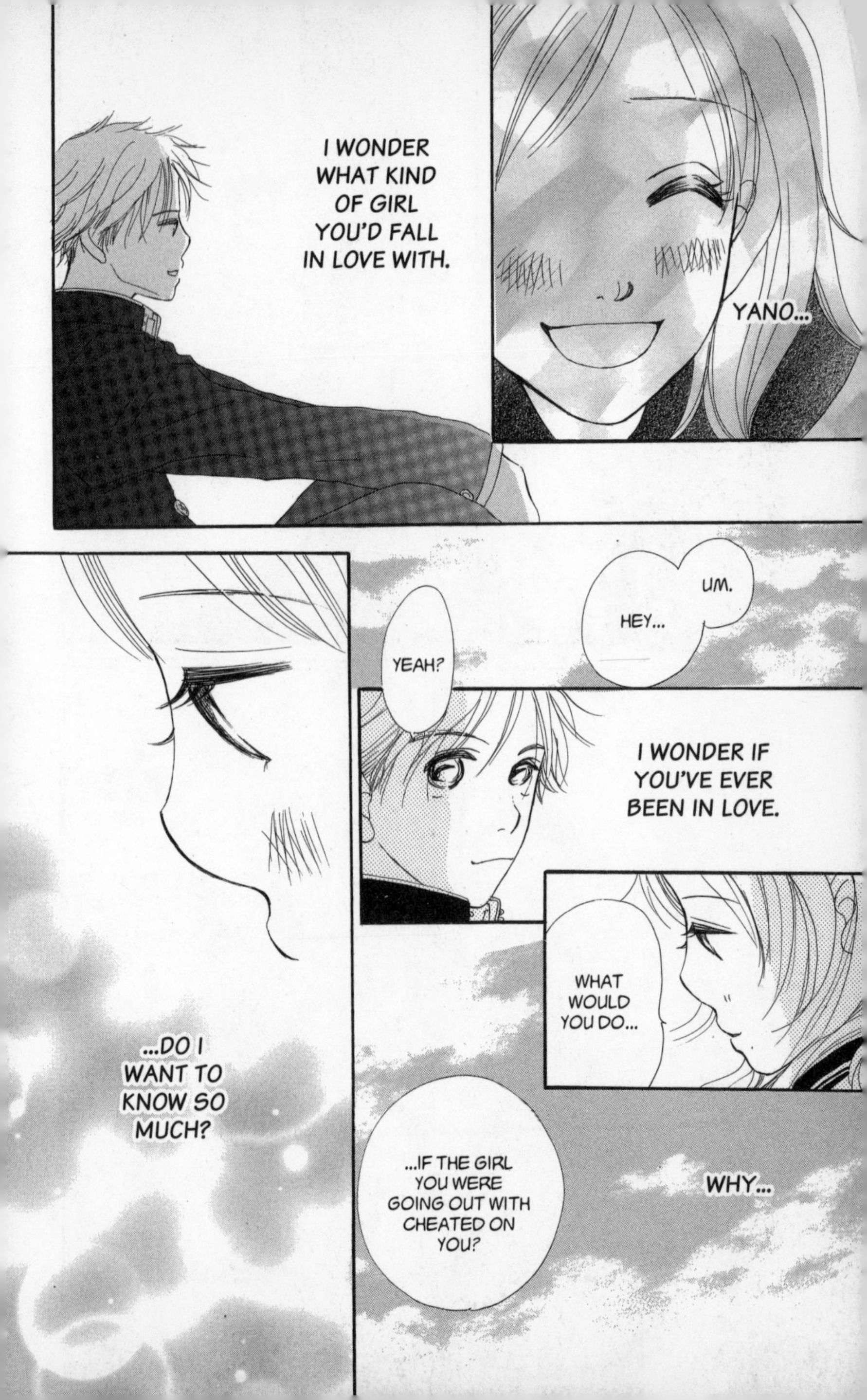
YANO...
I WONDER WHAT KIND OF GIRL YOU'D FALL IN LOVE WITH.
UM.
HEY...
YEAH?
I WONDER IF YOU'VE EVER BEEN IN LOVE.
WHAT WOULD YOU DO...
...IF THE GIRL YOU WERE GOING OUT WITH CHEATED ON YOU?
WHY...
...DO I WANT TO KNOW SO MUCH?

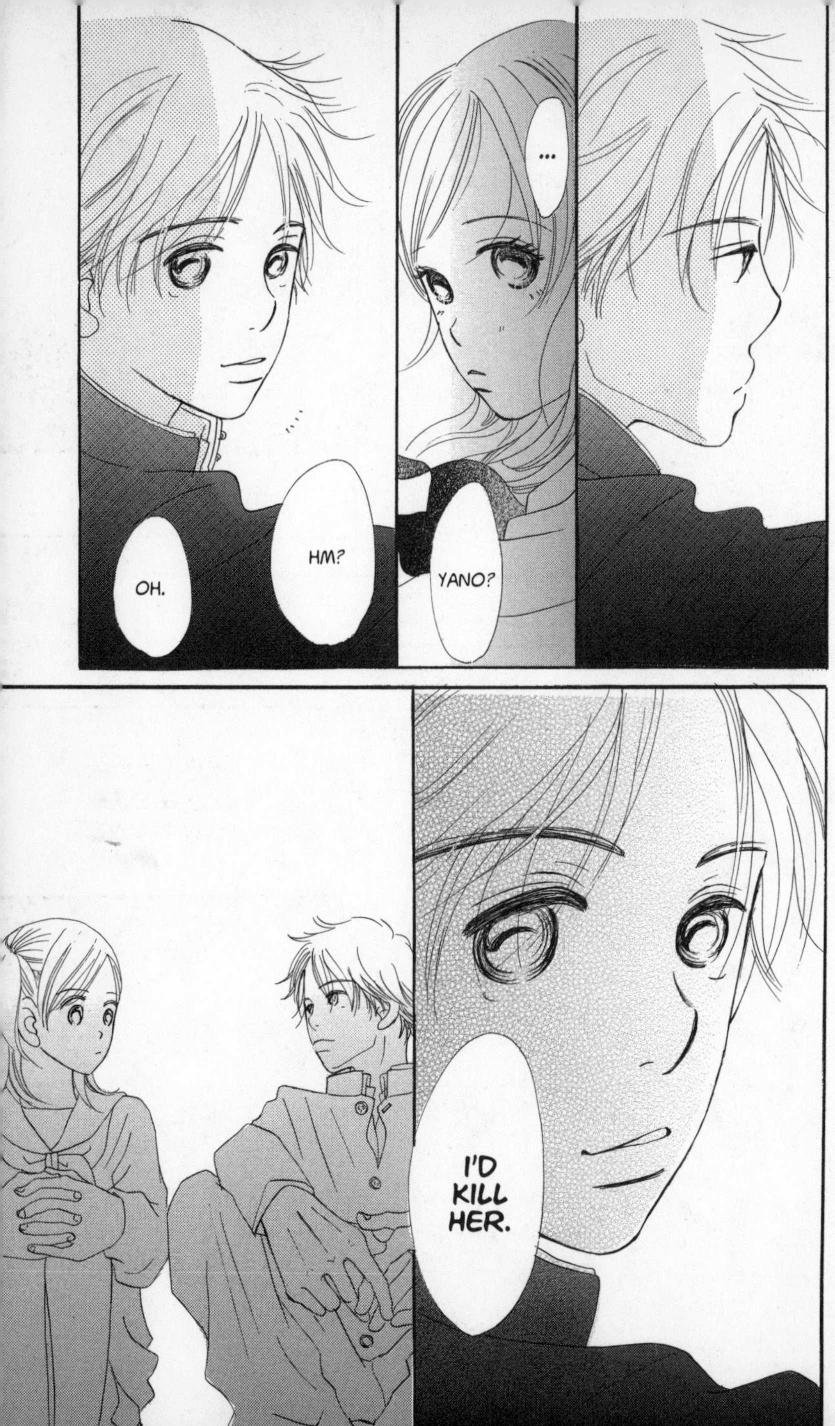
...
YANO?
HM?
OH.
I'D KILL HER.

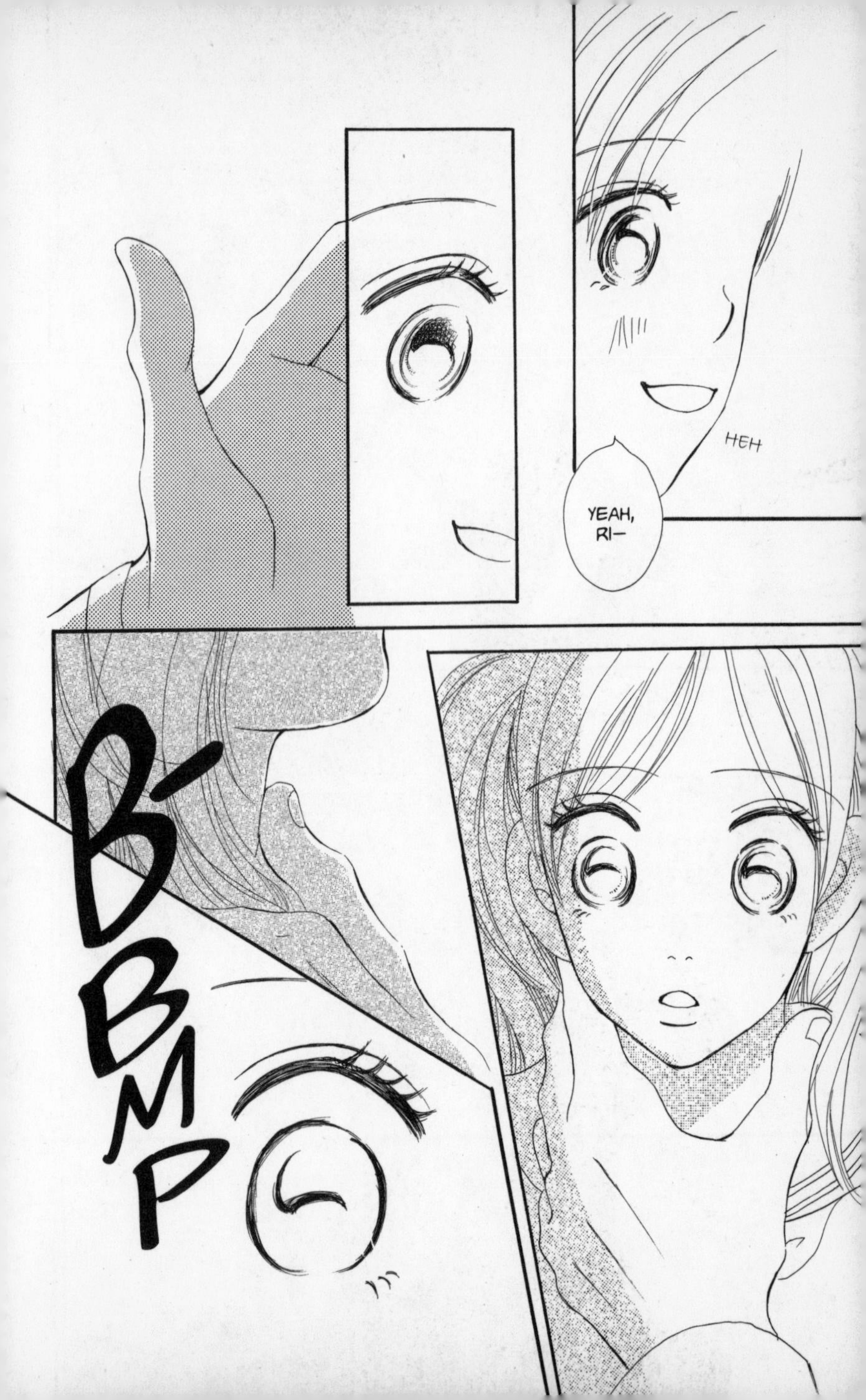
HEH
YEAH, RI—
B'BMP

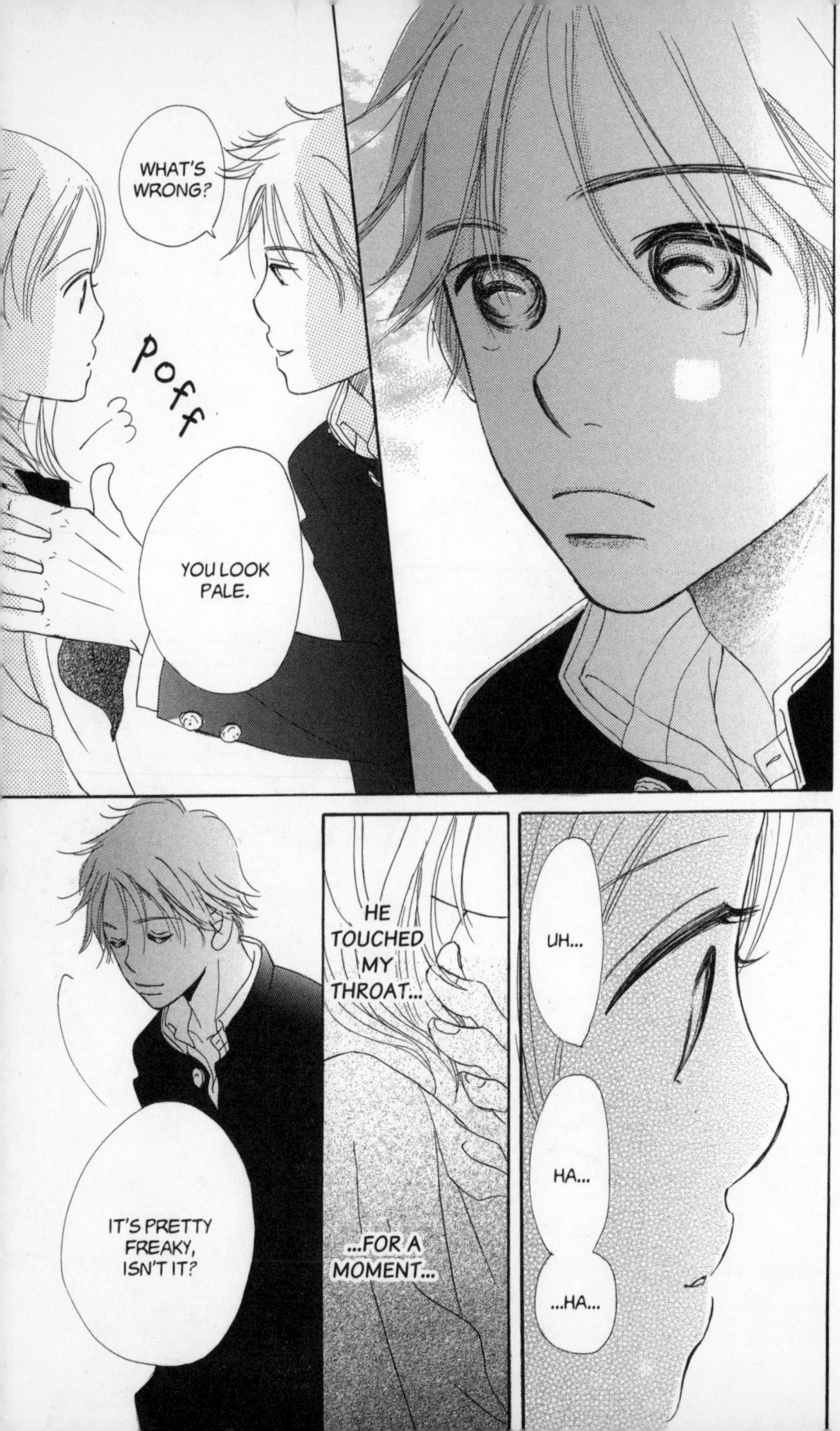
WHAT'S WRONG?
Poff
YOU LOOK PALE.
UH...
HA...
...HA...
HE TOUCHED MY THROAT...
...FOR A MOMENT...
IT'S PRETTY FREAKY, ISN'T IT?

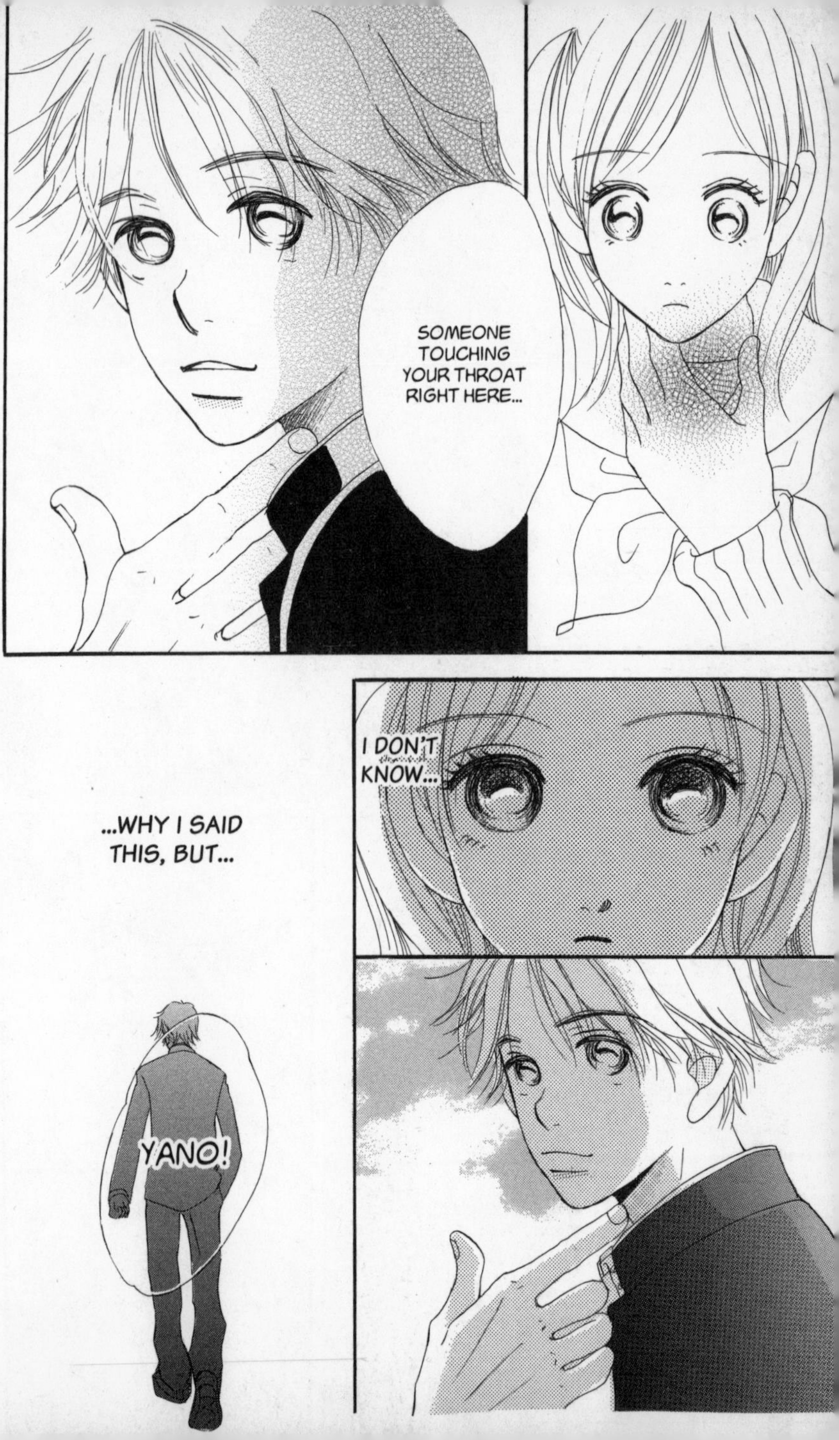
SOMEONE TOUCHING YOUR THROAT RIGHT HERE...
I DON'T KNOW...
...WHY I SAID THIS, BUT...
YANO!

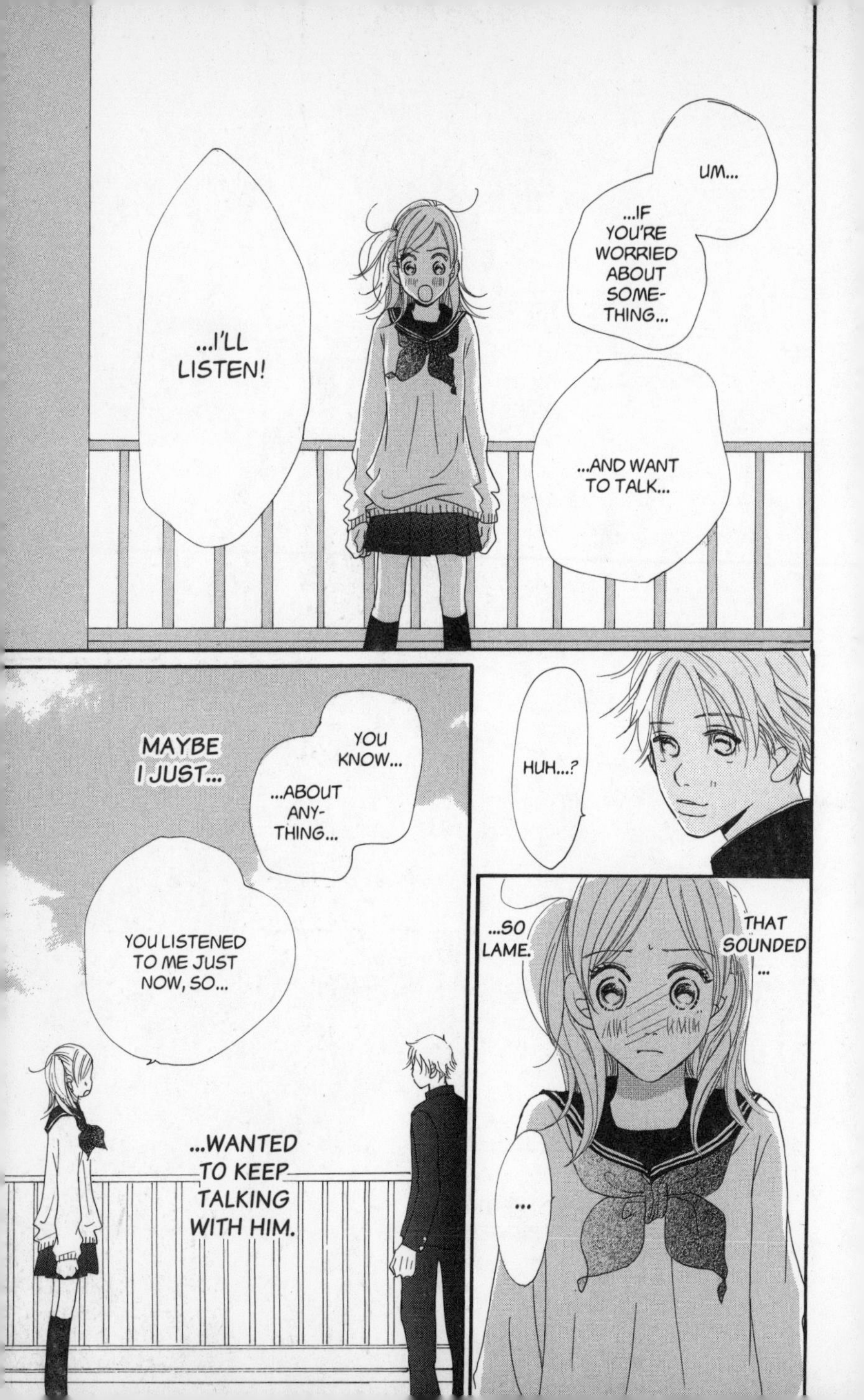
UM...
...IF YOU'RE WORRIED ABOUT SOME-THING...
...AND WANT TO TALK...
...I'LL LISTEN!
HUH...?
THAT SOUNDED...
...SO LAME.
...
YOU KNOW... ...ABOUT ANY-THING...
MAYBE I JUST...
YOU LISTENED TO ME JUST NOW, SO...
...WANTED TO KEEP TALKING WITH HIM.

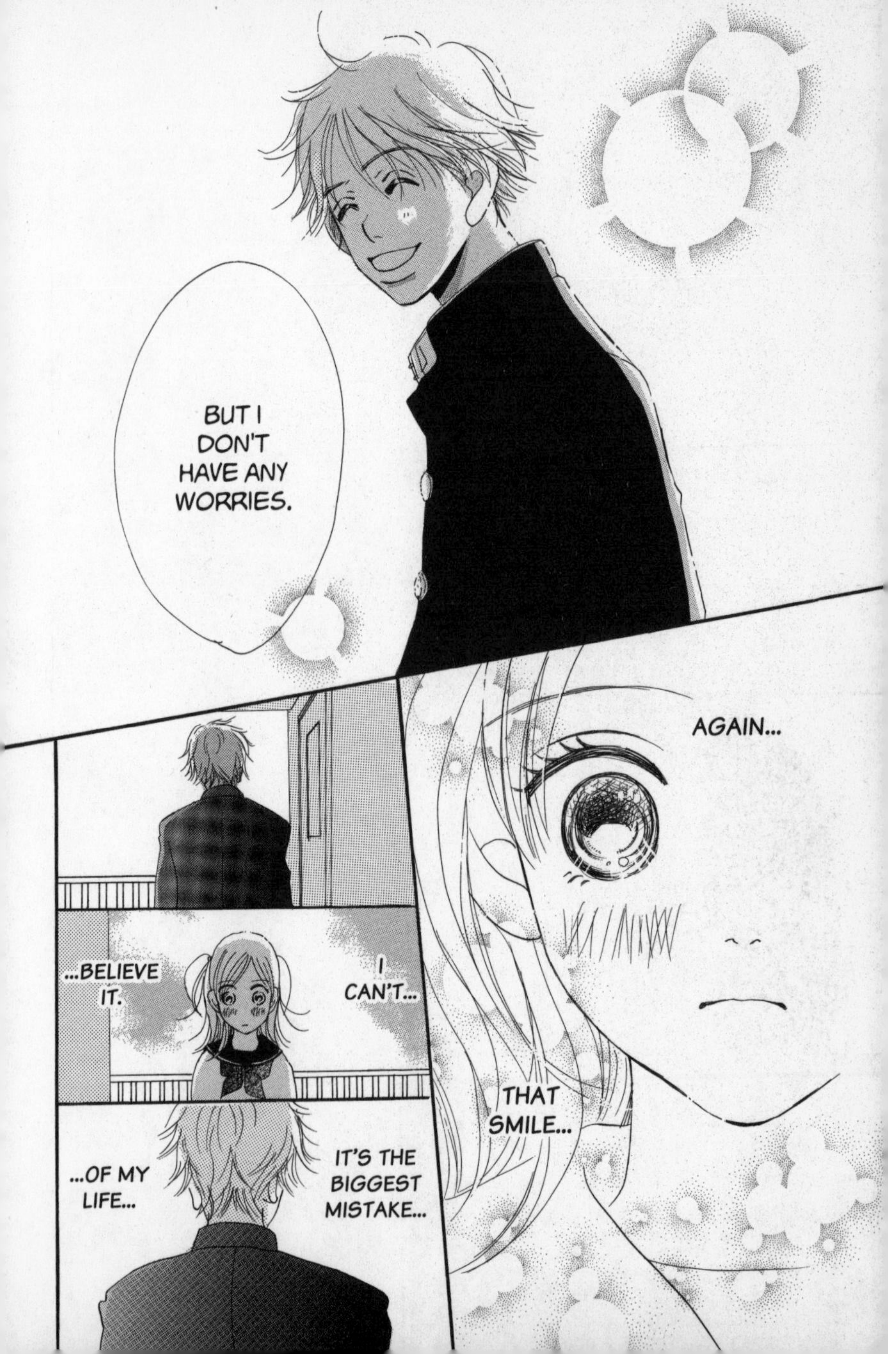
BUT I DON'T HAVE ANY WORRIES.
AGAIN...
THAT SMILE...
I CAN'T...
...BELIEVE IT.
IT'S THE BIGGEST MISTAKE...
...OF MY LIFE...

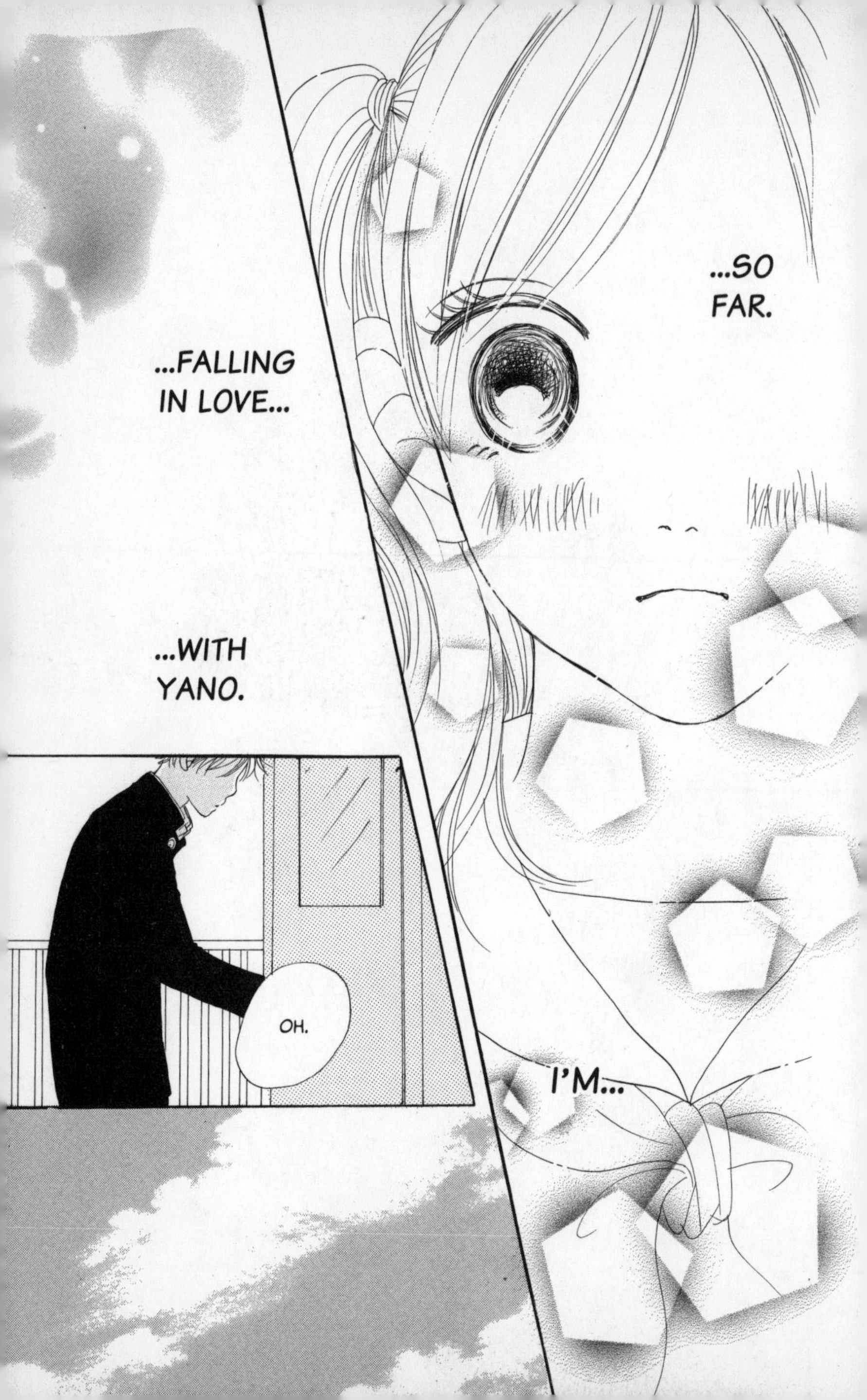
...SO FAR.
I'M...
...FALLING IN LOVE...
...WITH YANO.
OH.

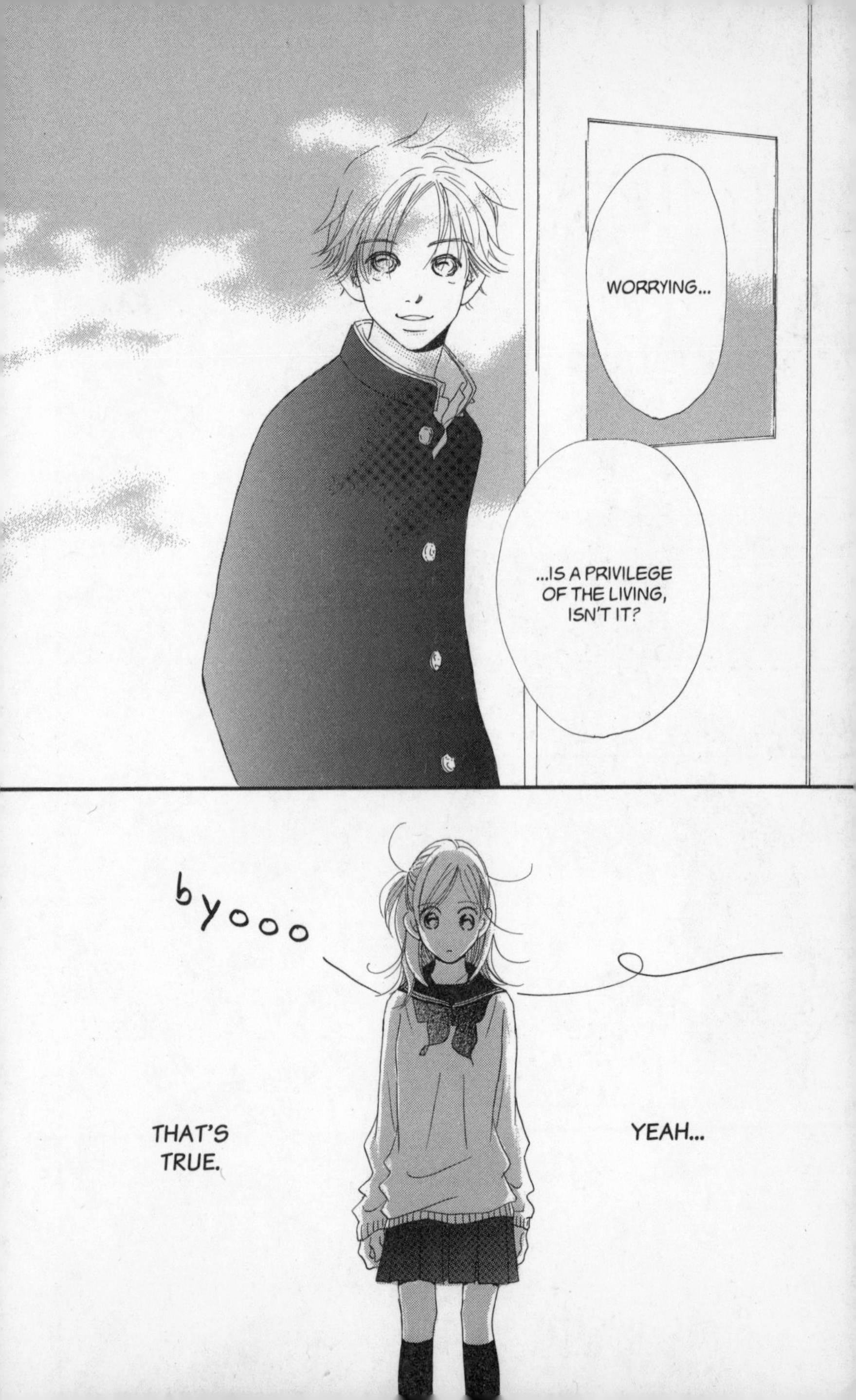
WORRYING...
...IS A PRIVILEGE OF THE LIVING, ISN'T IT?
byooo
YEAH...
THAT'S TRUE.

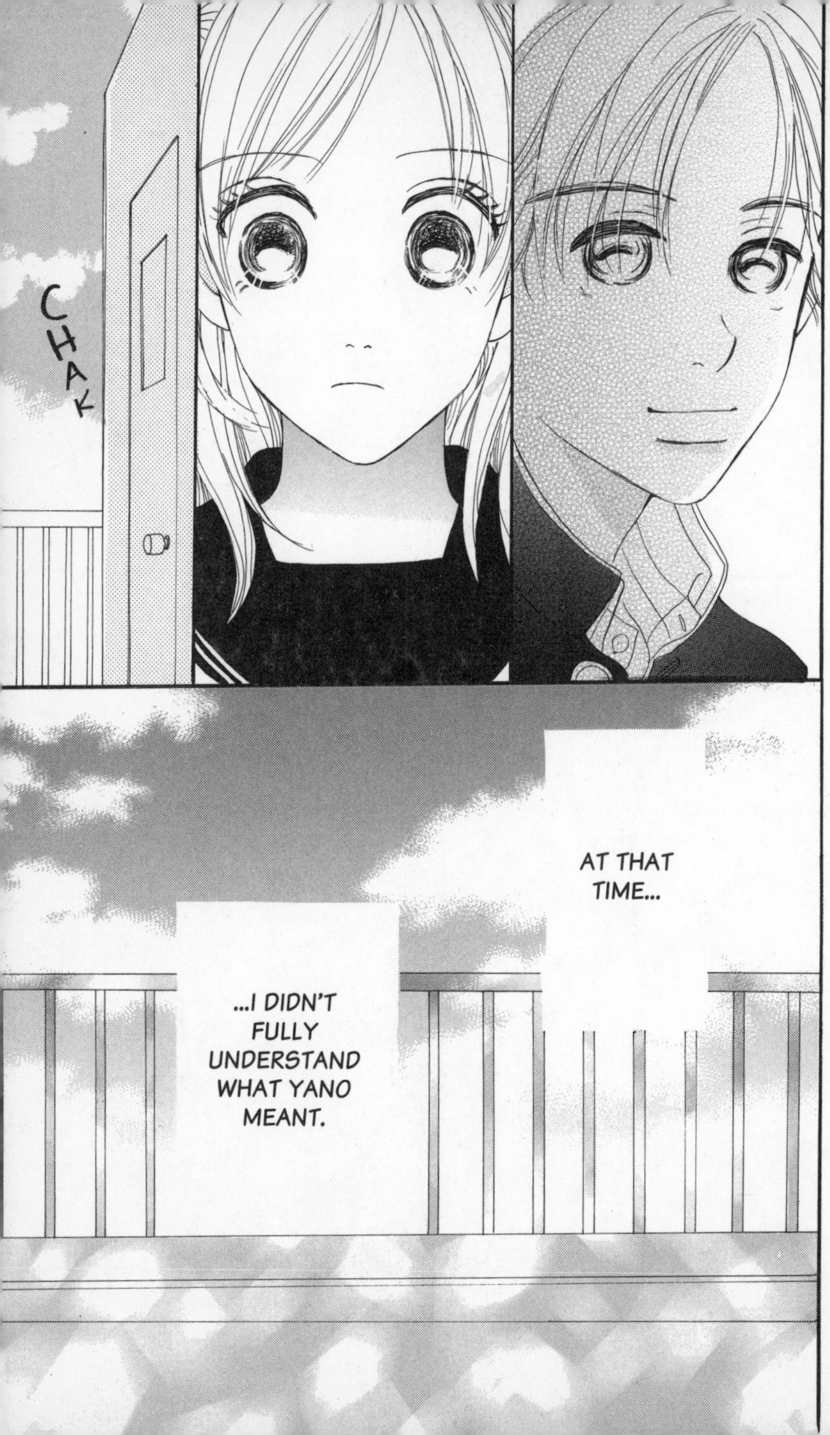
CHAK
AT THAT TIME...
...I DIDN'T FULLY UNDERSTAND WHAT YANO MEANT.

Chapter 2

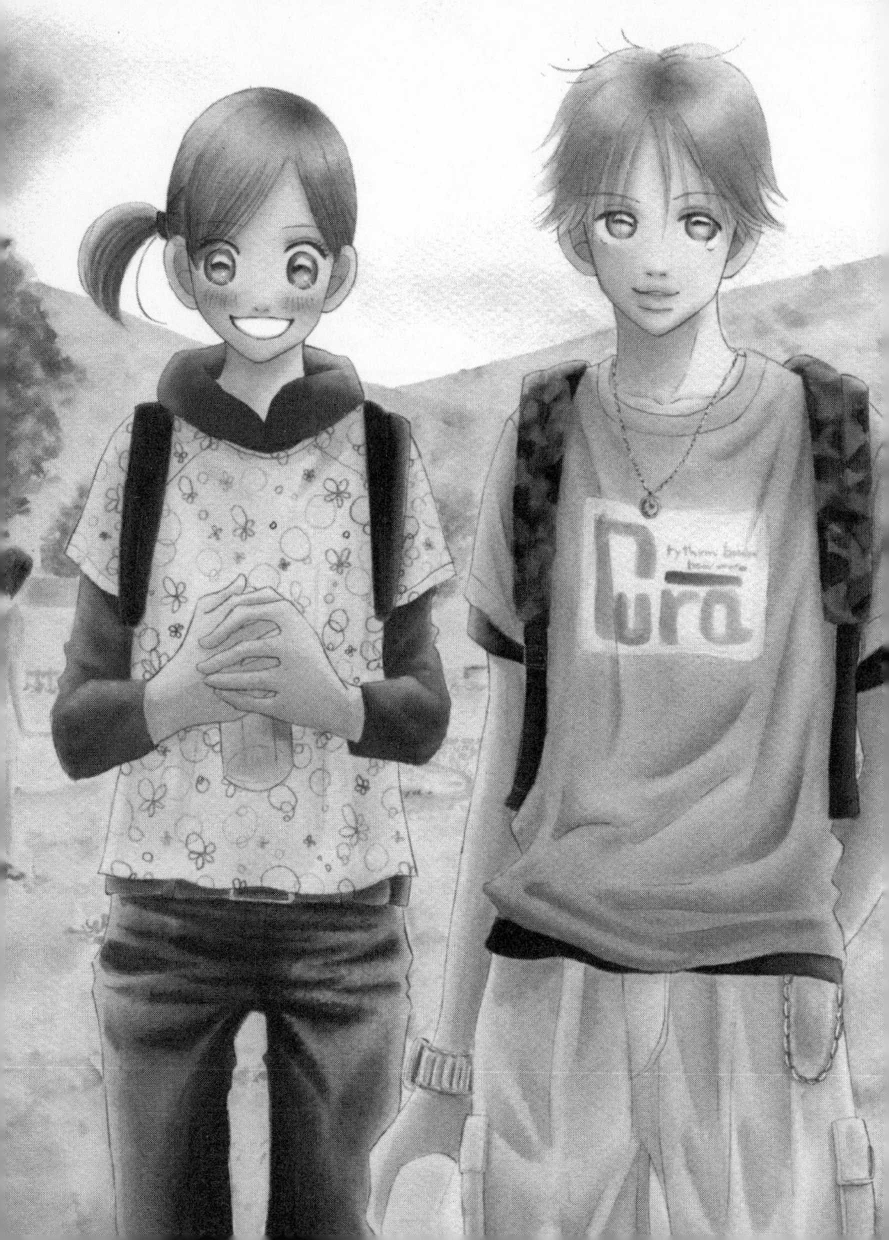

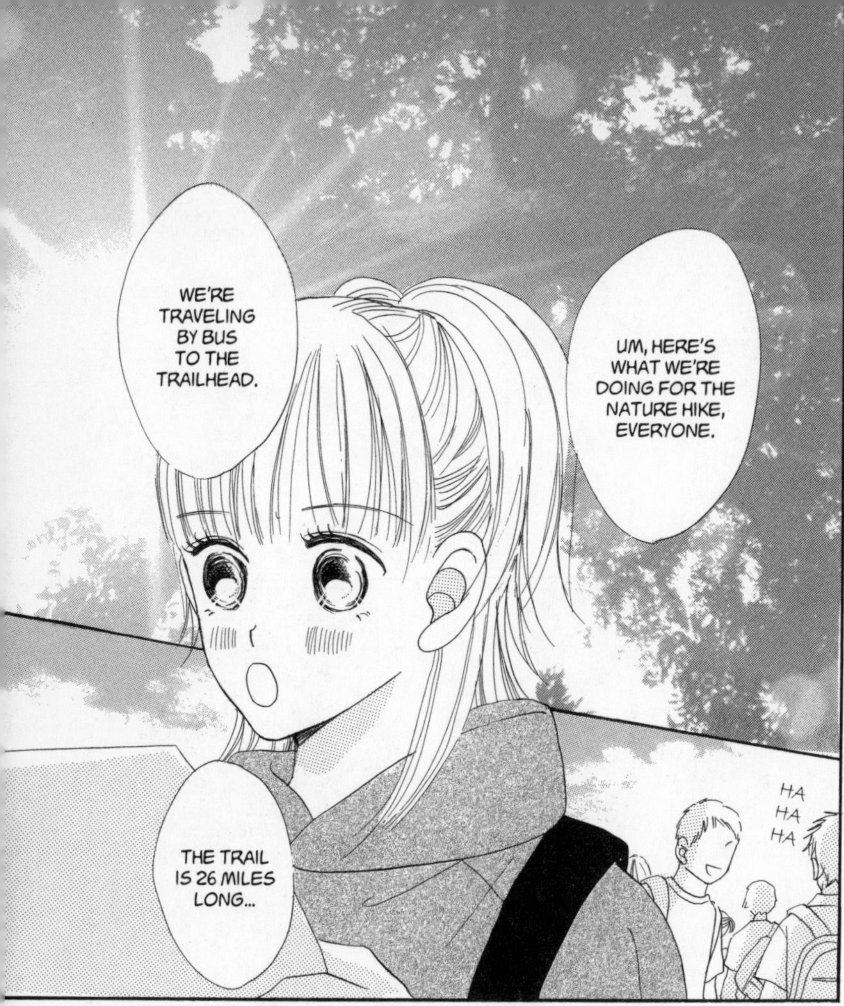
UM, HERE'S WHAT WE'RE DOING FOR THE NATURE HIKE, EVERYONE.
WE'RE TRAVELING BY BUS TO THE TRAILHEAD.
HA HA HA
THE TRAIL IS 26 MILES LONG...

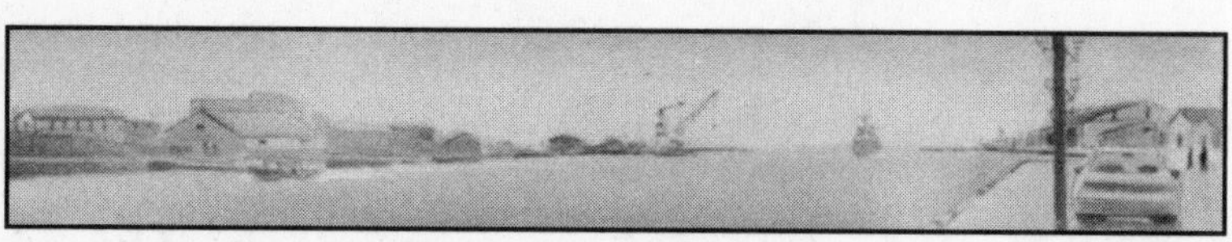

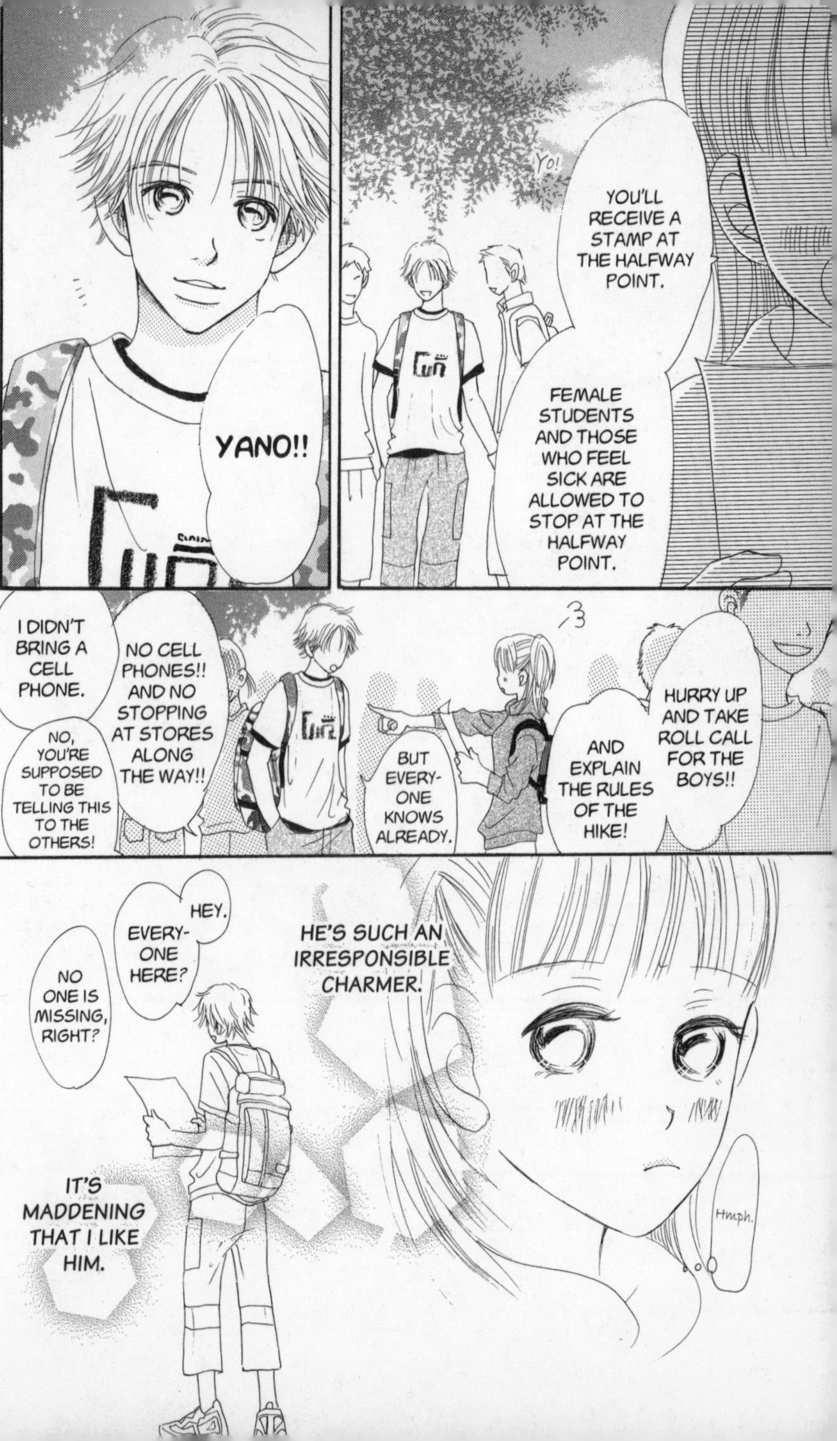
Yo!
YOU'LL RECEIVE A STAMP AT THE HALFWAY POINT.
FEMALE STUDENTS AND THOSE WHO FEEL SICK ARE ALLOWED TO STOP AT THE HALFWAY POINT.
YANO!!
HURRY UP AND TAKE ROLL CALL FOR THE BOYS!!
AND EXPLAIN THE RULES OF THE HIKE!
BUT EVERY-ONE KNOWS ALREADY.
NO CELL PHONES!! AND NO STOPPING AT STORES ALONG THE WAY!!
I DIDN'T BRING A CELL PHONE.
NO, YOU'RE SUPPOSED TO BE TELLING THIS TO THE OTHERS!
HE'S SUCH AN IRRESPONSIBLE CHARMER.
HEY. EVERY-ONE HERE?
NO ONE IS MISSING, RIGHT?
Hmph.
IT'S MADDENING THAT I LIKE HIM.

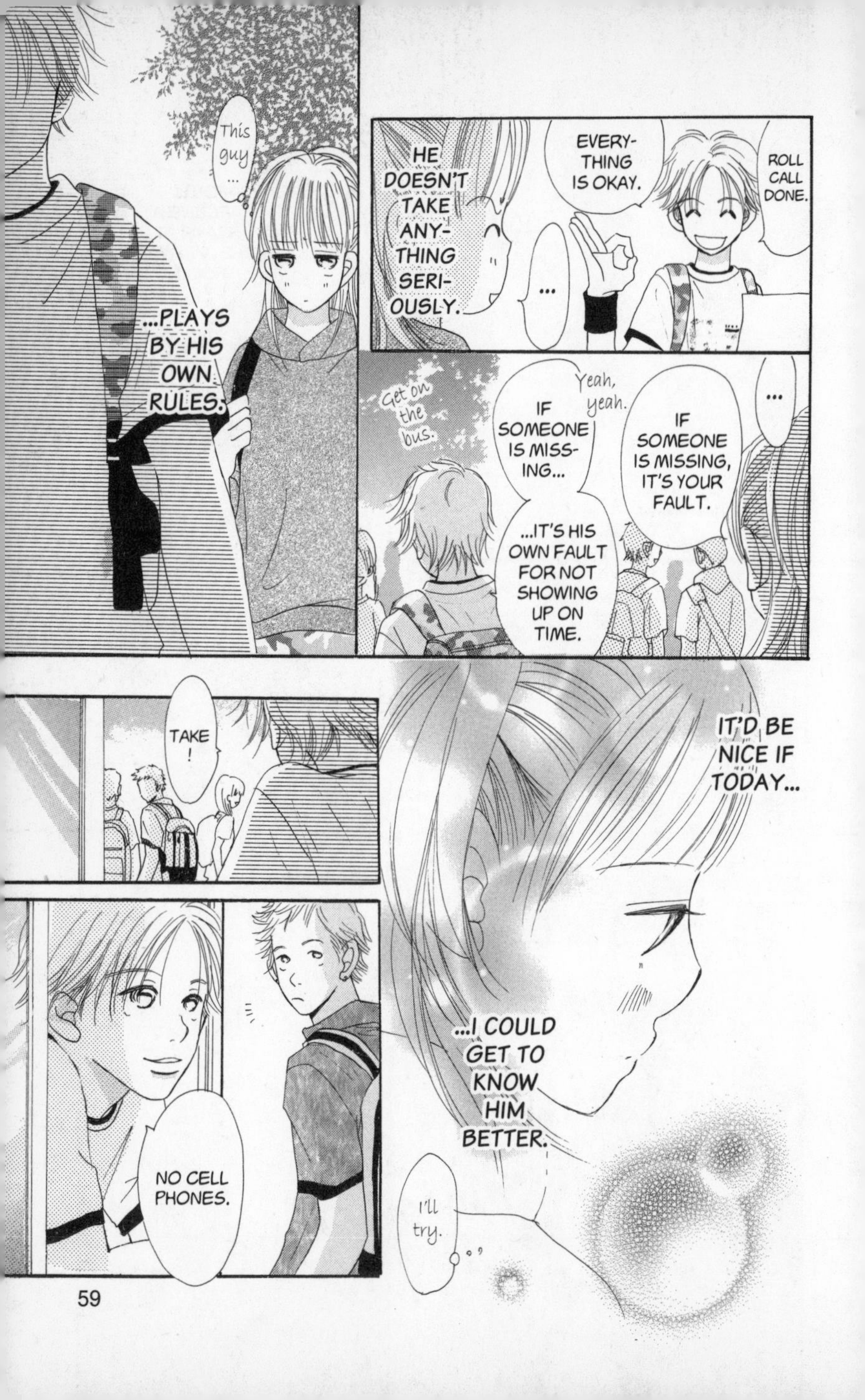
ROLL CALL DONE.
EVERYTHING IS OKAY.
...
HE DOESN'T TAKE ANYTHING SERIOUSLY.
...
IF SOMEONE IS MISSING, IT'S YOUR FAULT.
Yeah, yeah.
IF SOMEONE IS MISSING...
...IT'S HIS OWN FAULT FOR NOT SHOWING UP ON TIME.
Get on the bus.
This guy...
...PLAYS BY HIS OWN RULES.
IT'D BE NICE IF TODAY...
...I COULD GET TO KNOW HIM BETTER.
I'll try.
TAKE!
NO CELL PHONES.

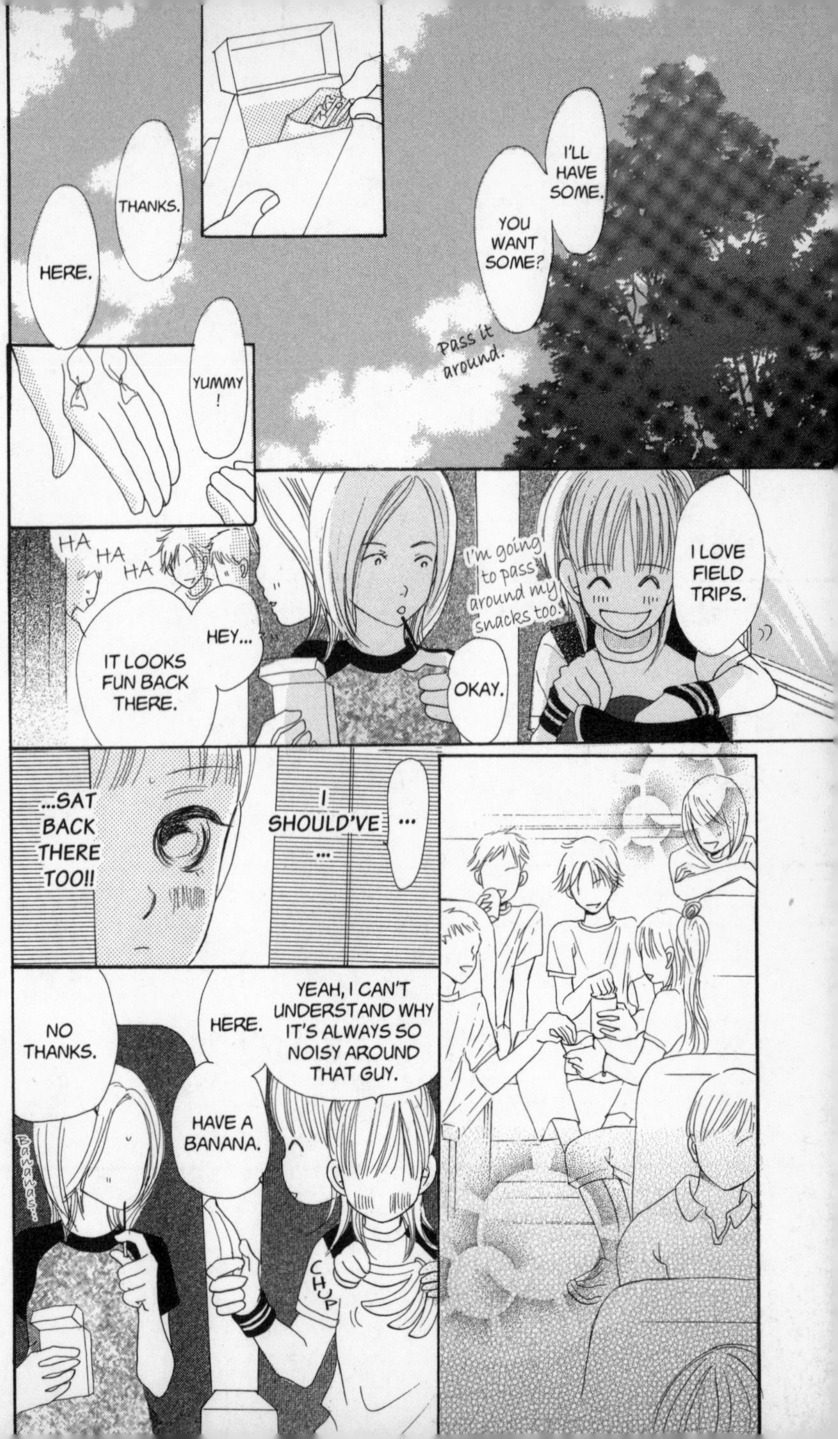
I'LL HAVE SOME.
YOU WANT SOME?
Pass it around.
HERE.
THANKS.
YUMMY!
I LOVE FIELD TRIPS.
I'm going to pass around my snacks too.
OKAY.
HEY...
IT LOOKS FUN BACK THERE.
HA HA HA
I SHOULD'VE ... ...
...SAT BACK THERE TOO!!
YEAH, I CAN'T UNDERSTAND WHY IT'S ALWAYS SO NOISY AROUND THAT GUY.
HERE.
HAVE A BANANA.
CHUP
NO THANKS.
Bananas...

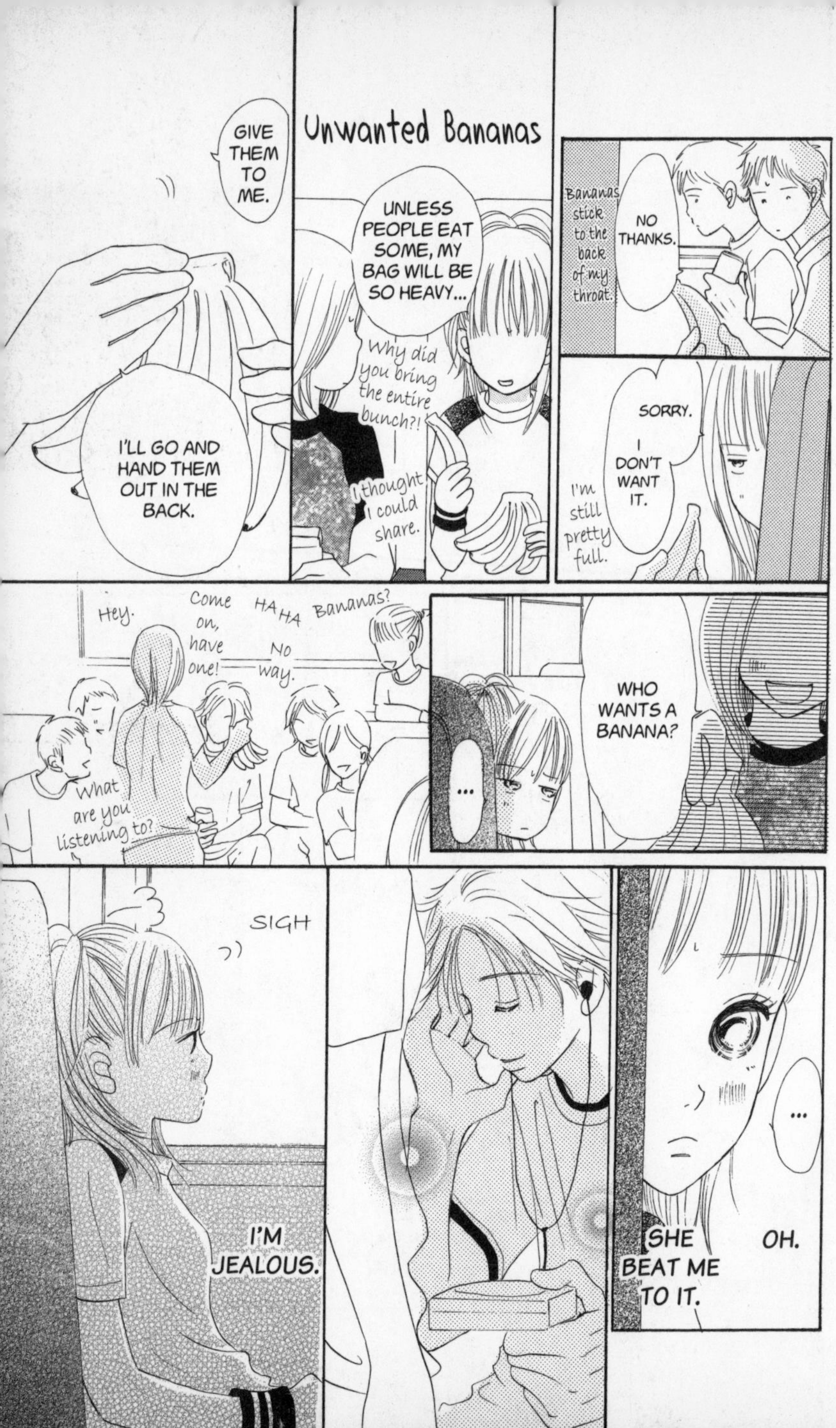
Bananas stick to the back of my throat.
NO THANKS.
SORRY.
I DON'T WANT IT.
I'm still pretty full.
Unwanted Bananas
UNLESS PEOPLE EAT SOME, MY BAG WILL BE SO HEAVY...
Why did you bring the entire bunch?!
I thought I could share.
GIVE THEM TO ME.
I'LL GO AND HAND THEM OUT IN THE BACK.
WHO WANTS A BANANA?
...
Bananas?
HA HA
Come on, have one!
No way.
Hey.
What are you listening to?
OH.
...
SHE BEAT ME TO IT.
SIGH
I'M JEALOUS.

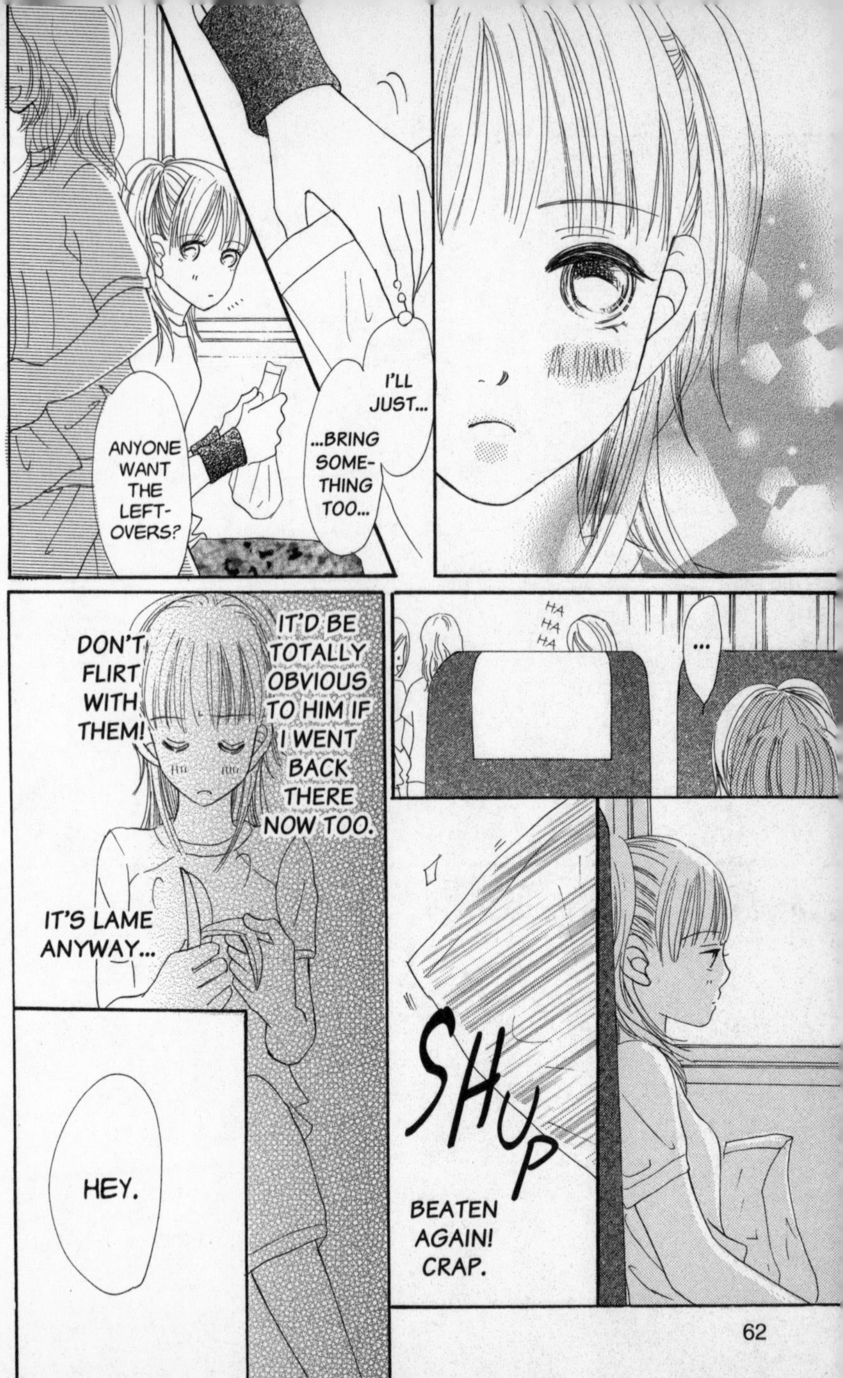
I'LL JUST...
...BRING SOMETHING TOO...
ANYONE WANT THE LEFTOVERS?
HA HA HA
...
SHUP
BEATEN AGAIN! CRAP.
IT'D BE TOTALLY OBVIOUS TO HIM IF I WENT BACK THERE NOW TOO.
DON'T FLIRT WITH THEM!
IT'S LAME ANYWAY...
HEY.

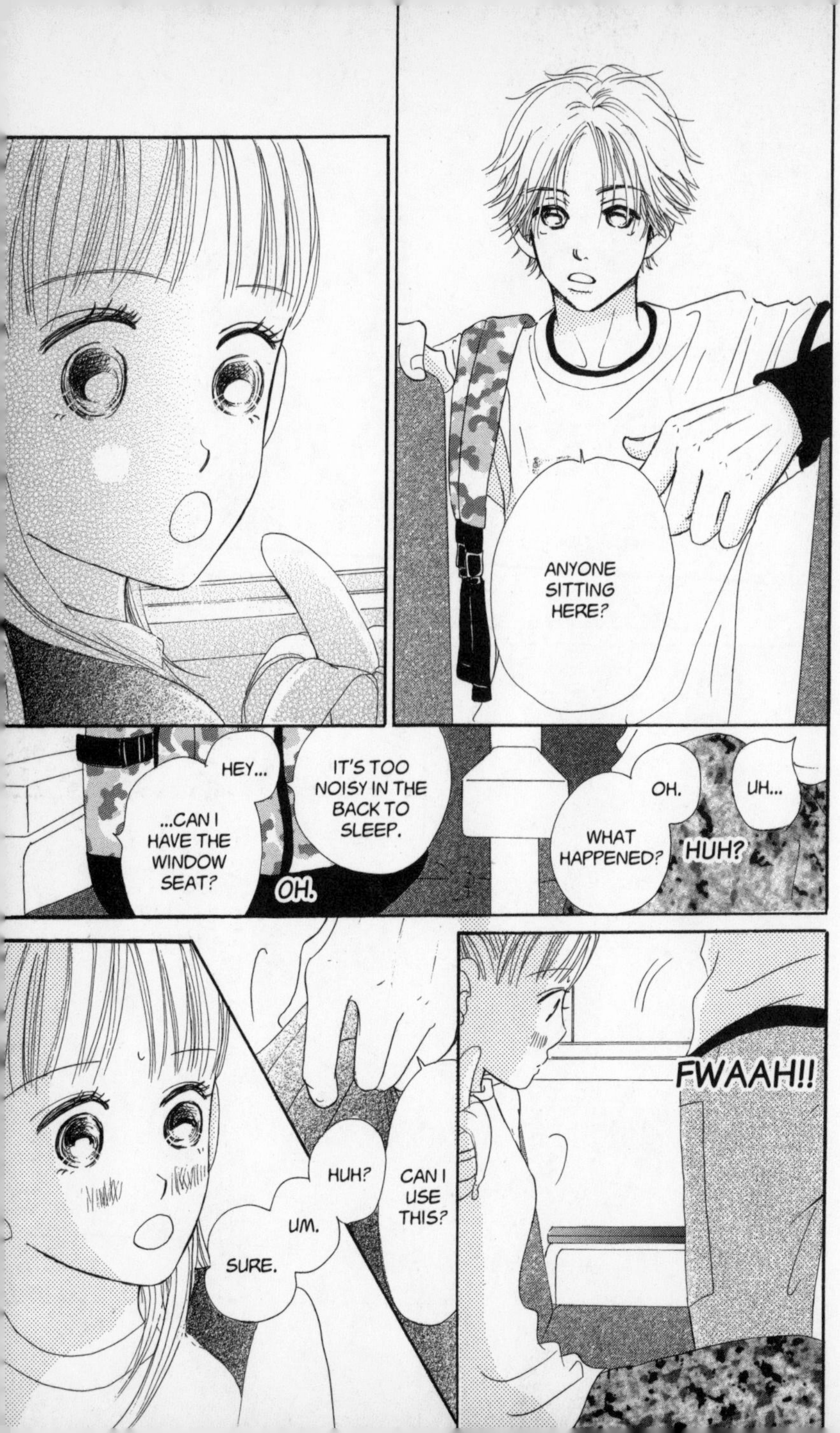
ANYONE SITTING HERE?
UH...
HUH?
OH.
WHAT HAPPENED?
IT'S TOO NOISY IN THE BACK TO SLEEP.
HEY...
...CAN I HAVE THE WINDOW SEAT?
OH.
FWAAH!!
CAN I USE THIS?
HUH?
UM.
SURE.

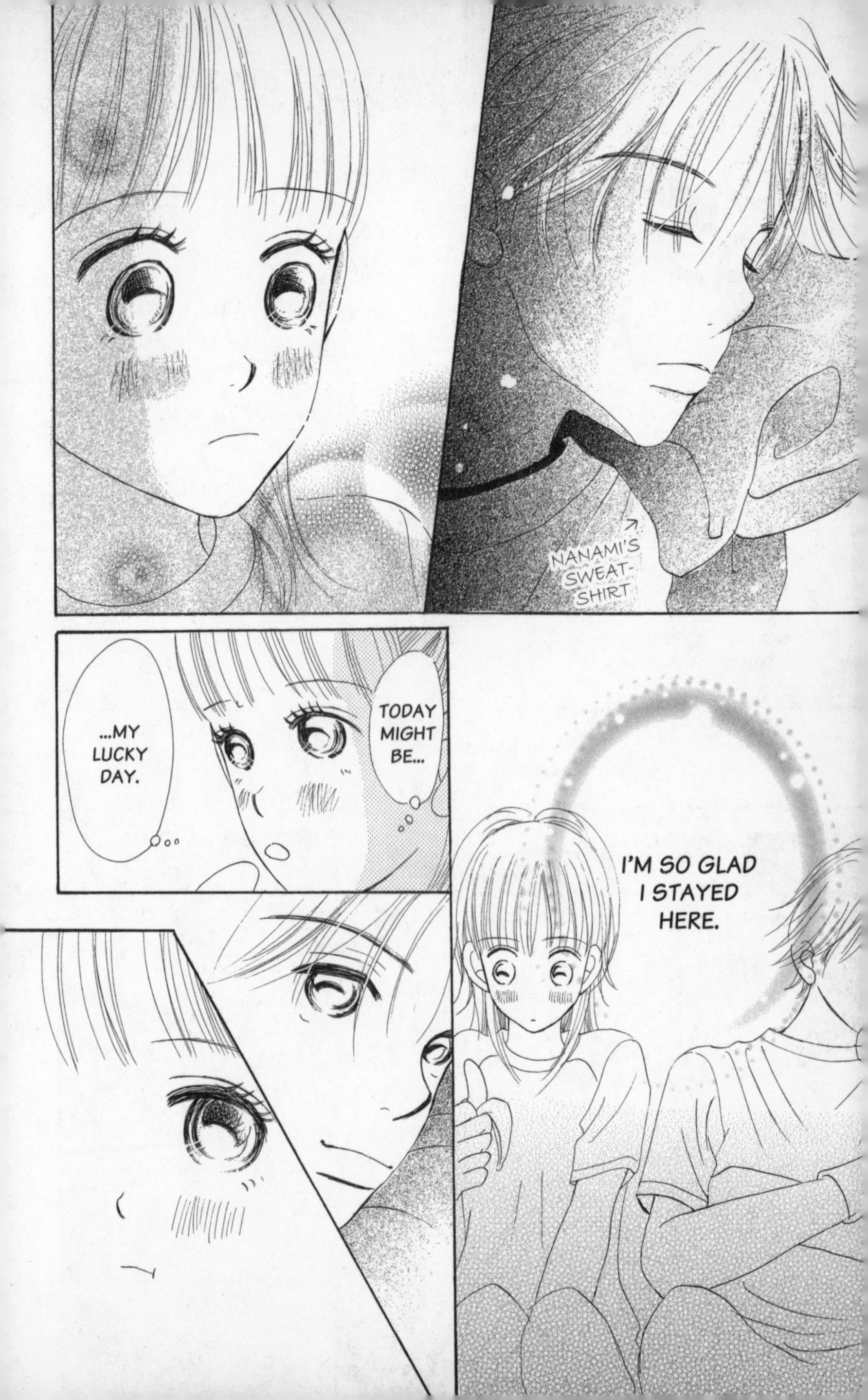
NANAMI'S SWEAT-SHIRT
I'M SO GLAD I STAYED HERE.
TODAY MIGHT BE...
...MY LUCKY DAY.

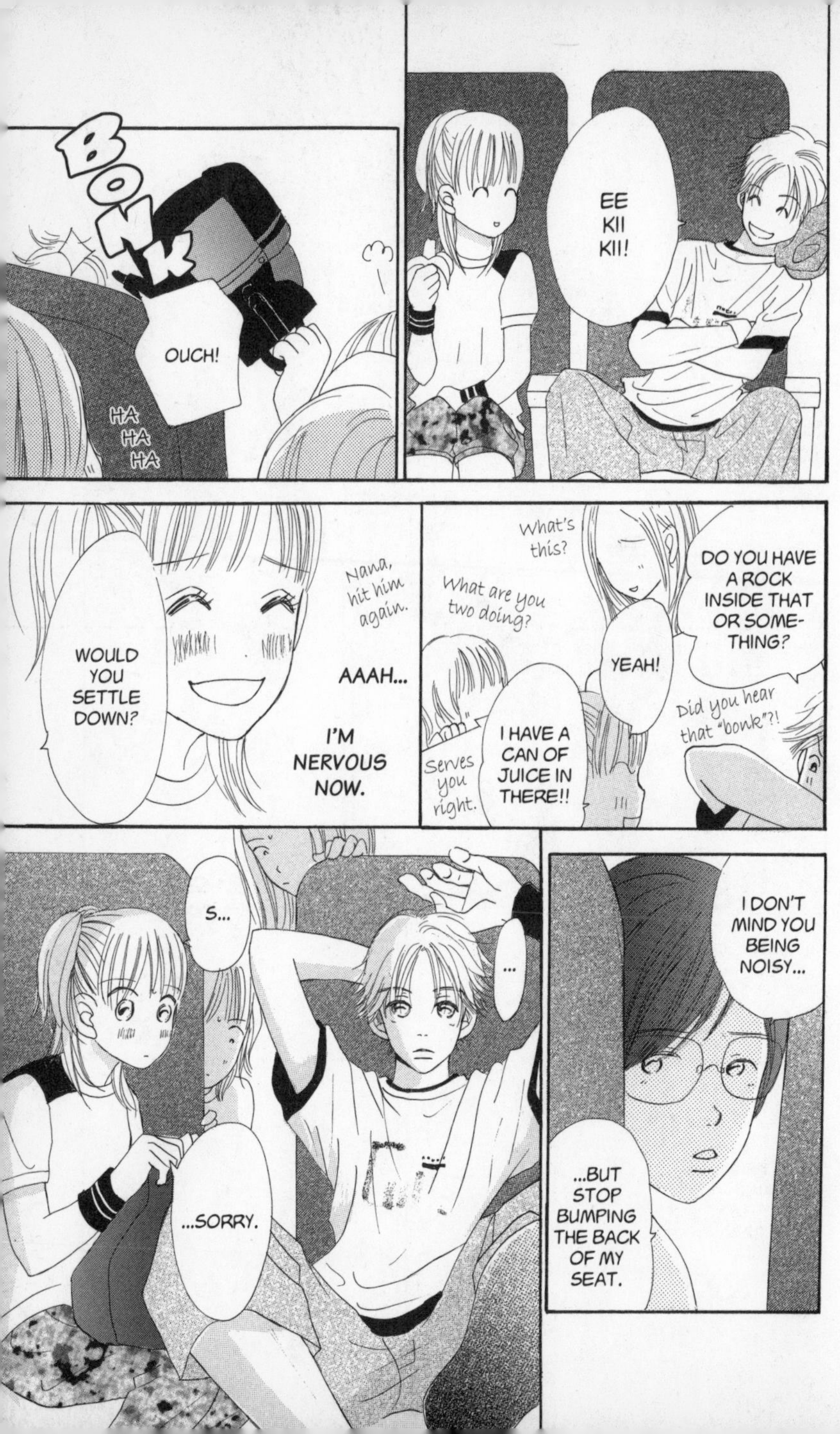
EE KII KII!
BONK
OUCH!
HA HA HA
What's this?
DO YOU HAVE A ROCK INSIDE THAT OR SOMETHING?
YEAH!
What are you two doing?
Did you hear that "bonk"?!
I HAVE A CAN OF JUICE IN THERE!!
Serves you right.
Nana, hit him again.
AAAH... I'M NERVOUS NOW.
WOULD YOU SETTLE DOWN?
I DON'T MIND YOU BEING NOISY...
...BUT STOP BUMPING THE BACK OF MY SEAT.
...
S...
...SORRY.

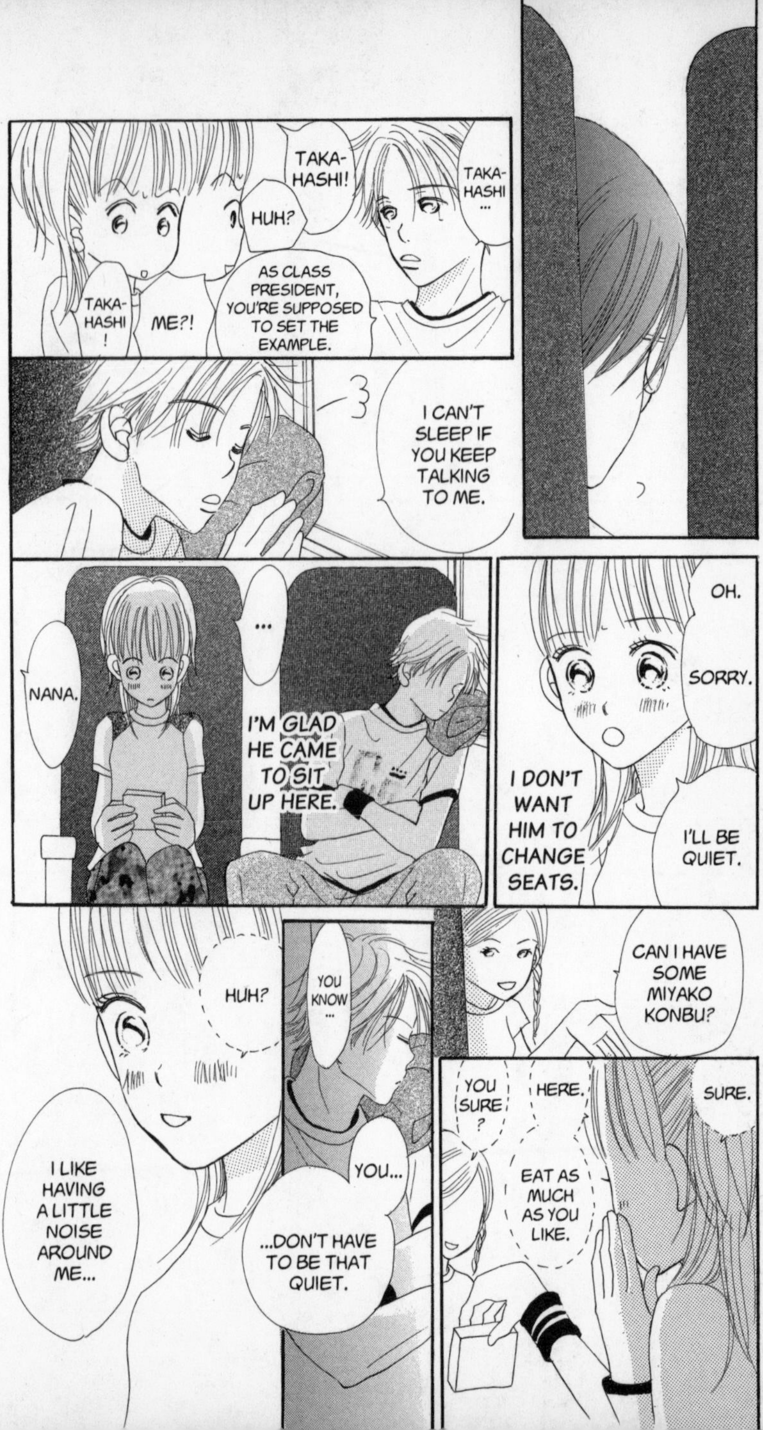
TAKA-HASHI ...
TAKA-HASHI!
HUH?
AS CLASS PRESIDENT, YOU'RE SUPPOSED TO SET THE EXAMPLE.
ME?!
TAKA-HASHI!
I CAN'T SLEEP IF YOU KEEP TALKING TO ME.
OH.
SORRY.
I'LL BE QUIET.
I DON'T WANT HIM TO CHANGE SEATS.
...
NANA.
I'M GLAD HE CAME TO SIT UP HERE.
CAN I HAVE SOME MIYAKO KONBU?
SURE.
HERE.
YOU SURE?
EAT AS MUCH AS YOU LIKE.
YOU KNOW ...
YOU...
...DON'T HAVE TO BE THAT QUIET.
HUH?
I LIKE HAVING A LITTLE NOISE AROUND ME...

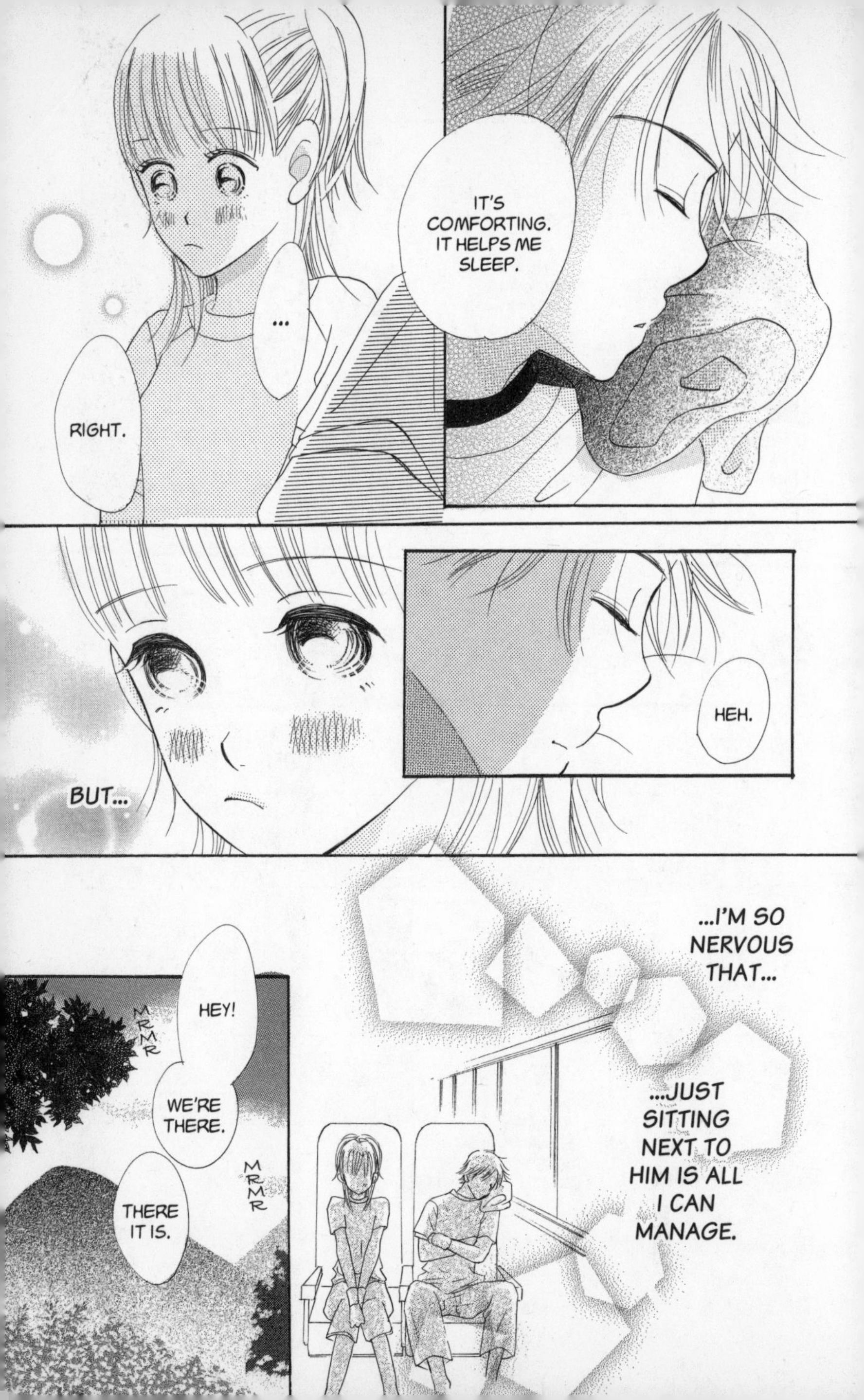
IT'S COMFORTING. IT HELPS ME SLEEP.
...
RIGHT.
HEH.
BUT...
...I'M SO NERVOUS THAT...
...JUST SITTING NEXT TO HIM IS ALL I CAN MANAGE.
HEY!
MRMR
WE'RE THERE.
MRMR
THERE IT IS.

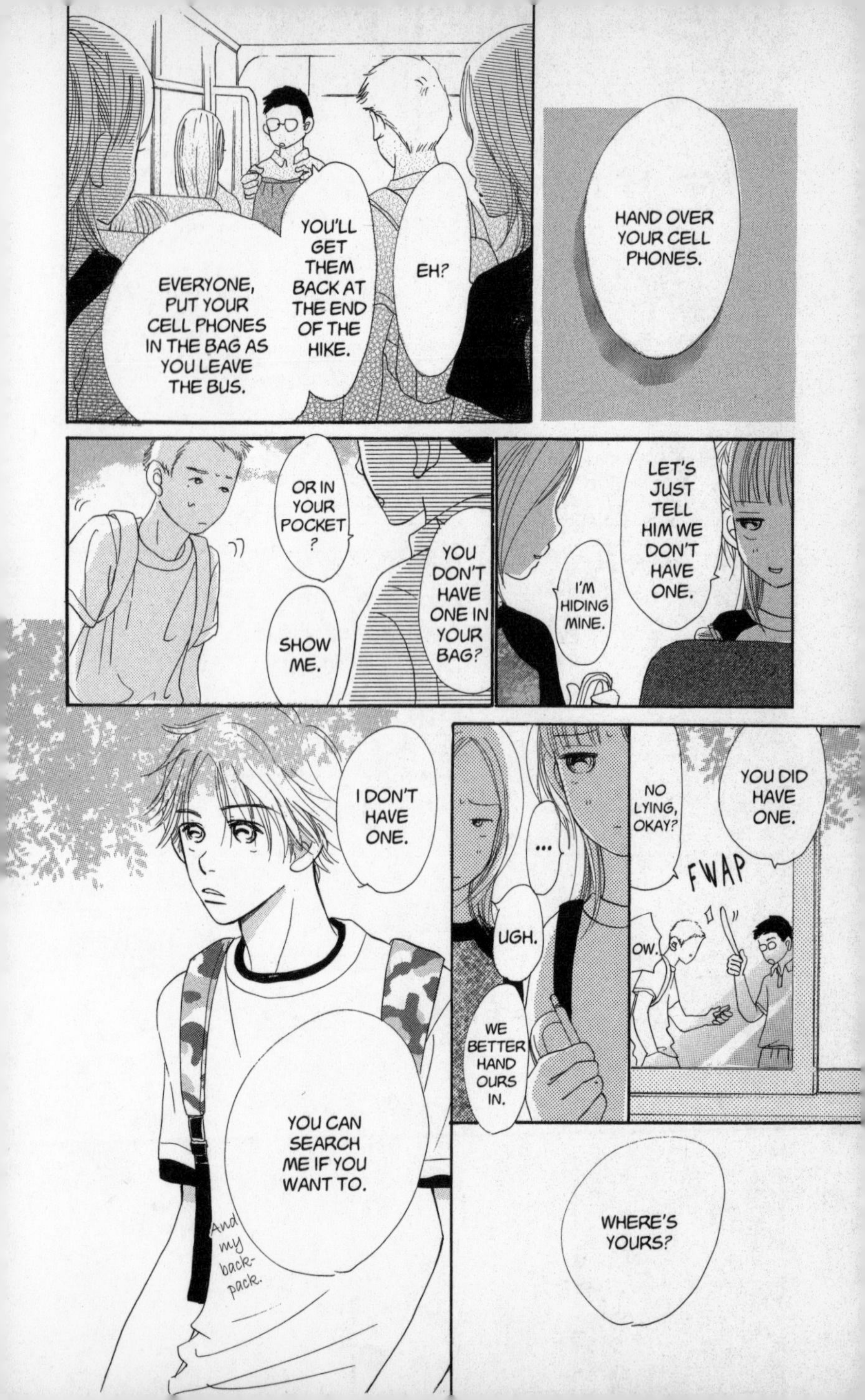
HAND OVER YOUR CELL PHONES.
EH?
YOU'LL GET THEM BACK AT THE END OF THE HIKE.
EVERYONE, PUT YOUR CELL PHONES IN THE BAG AS YOU LEAVE THE BUS.
LET'S JUST TELL HIM WE DON'T HAVE ONE.
I'M HIDING MINE.
YOU DON'T HAVE ONE IN YOUR BAG?
OR IN YOUR POCKET?
SHOW ME.
YOU DID HAVE ONE.
NO LYING, OKAY?
FWAP
OW.
...
UGH.
WE BETTER HAND OURS IN.
WHERE'S YOURS?
I DON'T HAVE ONE.
YOU CAN SEARCH ME IF YOU WANT TO.
And my back-pack.

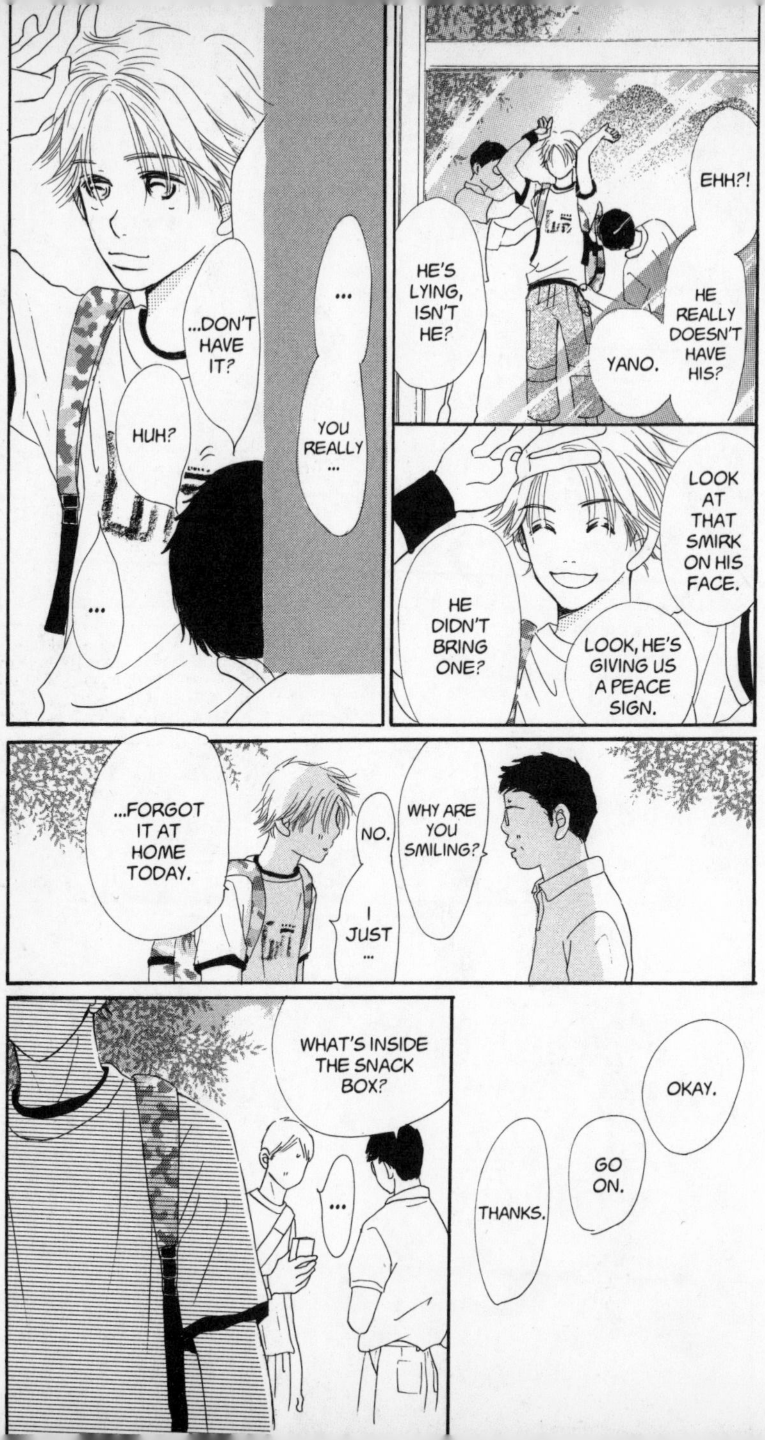
EHH?!
HE REALLY DOESN'T HAVE HIS?
YANO.
HE'S LYING, ISN'T HE?
LOOK AT THAT SMIRK ON HIS FACE.
LOOK, HE'S GIVING US A PEACE SIGN.
HE DIDN'T BRING ONE?
... YOU REALLY ...
...DON'T HAVE IT?
HUH?
...
WHY ARE YOU SMILING?
NO. I JUST ...
...FORGOT IT AT HOME TODAY.
OKAY.
GO ON.
THANKS.
WHAT'S INSIDE THE SNACK BOX?
...

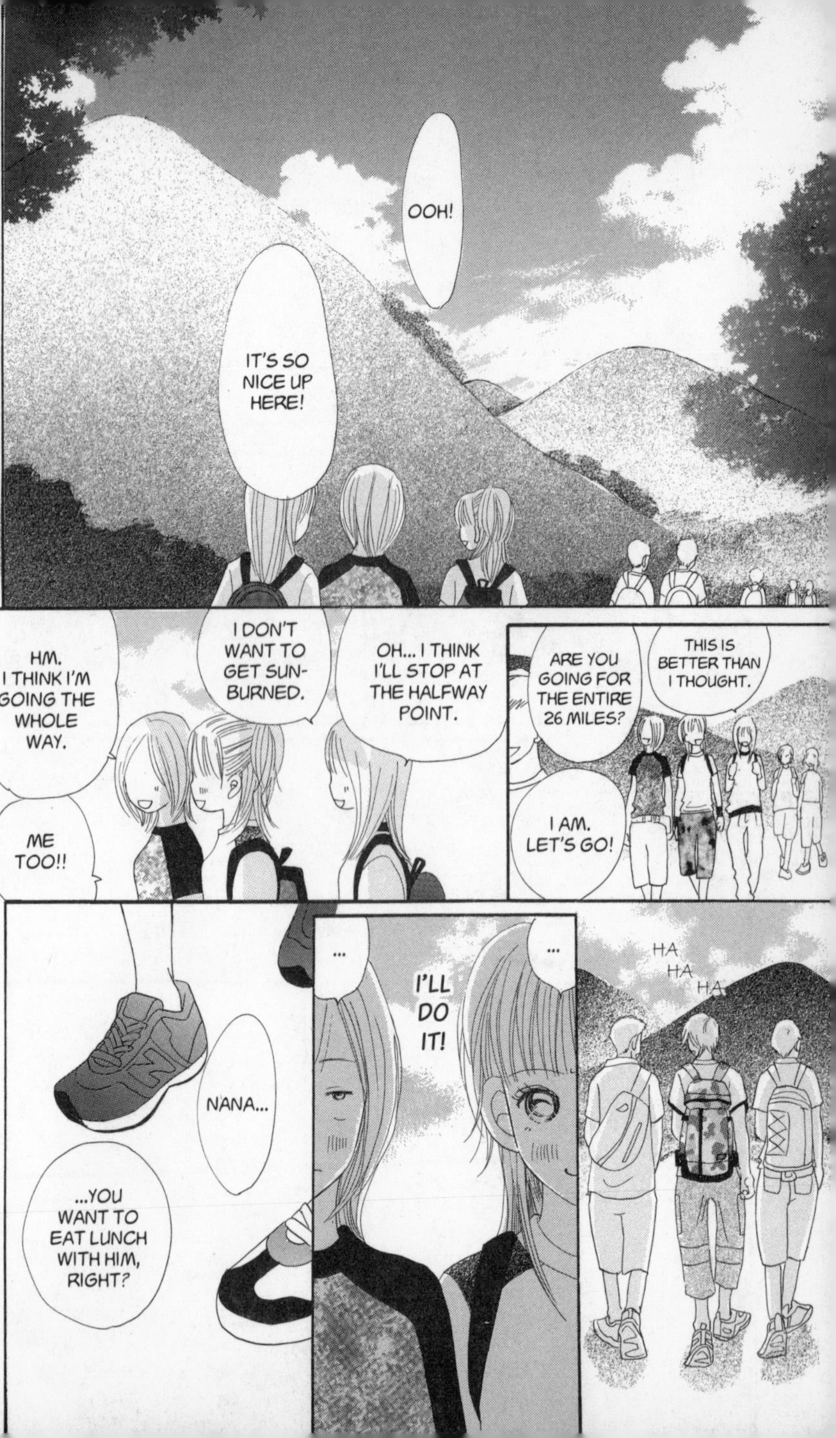
OOH!
IT'S SO NICE UP HERE!
THIS IS BETTER THAN I THOUGHT.
ARE YOU GOING FOR THE ENTIRE 26 MILES?
I AM. LET'S GO!
OH... I THINK I'LL STOP AT THE HALFWAY POINT.
I DON'T WANT TO GET SUN-BURNED.
HM. I THINK I'M GOING THE WHOLE WAY.
ME TOO!!
HA HA HA
...
I'LL DO IT!
...
NANA...
...YOU WANT TO EAT LUNCH WITH HIM, RIGHT?

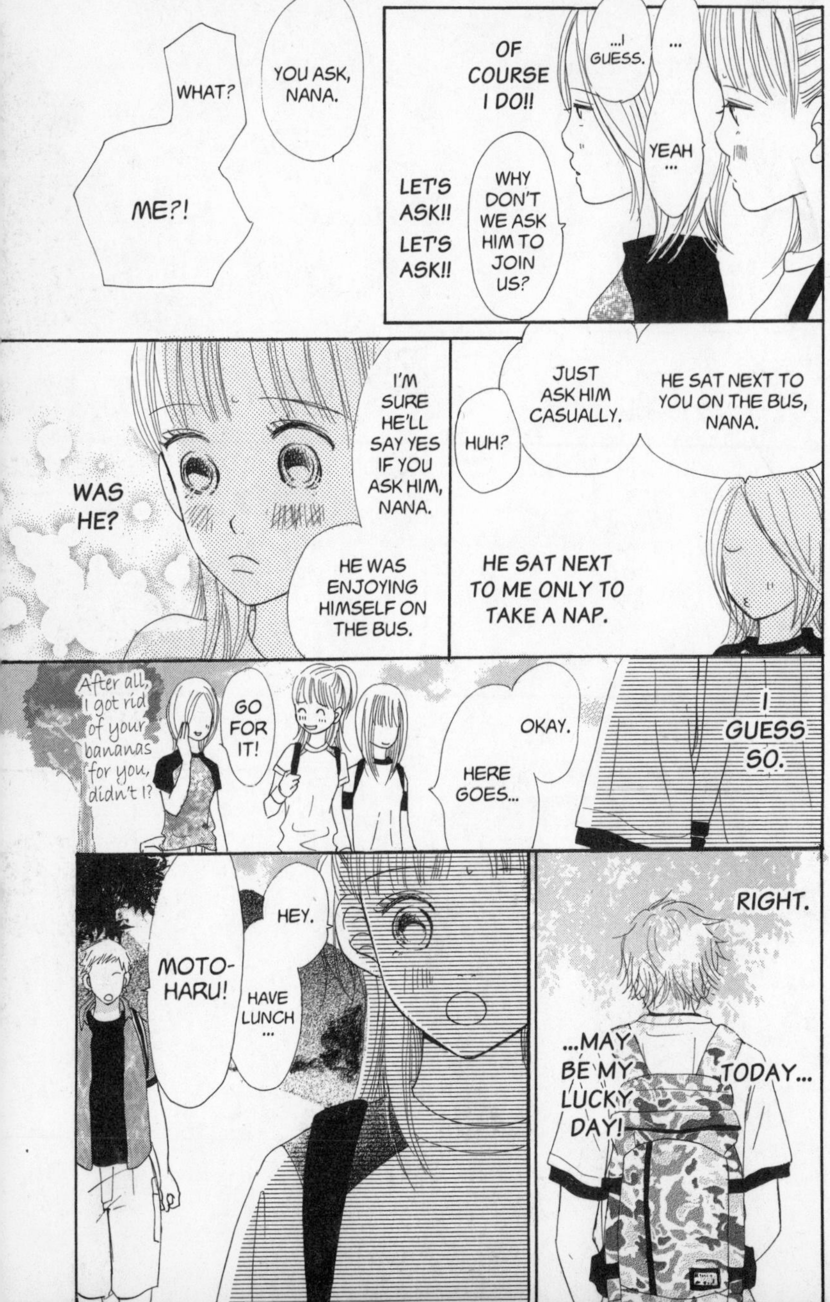
...
...I GUESS.
OF COURSE I DO!!
YEAH...
WHY DON'T WE ASK HIM TO JOIN US?
LET'S ASK!! LET'S ASK!!
YOU ASK, NANA.
WHAT?
ME?!
HE SAT NEXT TO YOU ON THE BUS, NANA.
JUST ASK HIM CASUALLY.
HUH?
HE SAT NEXT TO ME ONLY TO TAKE A NAP.
I'M SURE HE'LL SAY YES IF YOU ASK HIM, NANA.
HE WAS ENJOYING HIMSELF ON THE BUS.
WAS HE?
I GUESS SO.
OKAY.
HERE GOES...
GO FOR IT!
After all, I got rid of your bananas for you, didn't I?
RIGHT.
TODAY...
...MAY BE MY LUCKY DAY!
HEY.
HAVE LUNCH ...
MOTO-HARU!

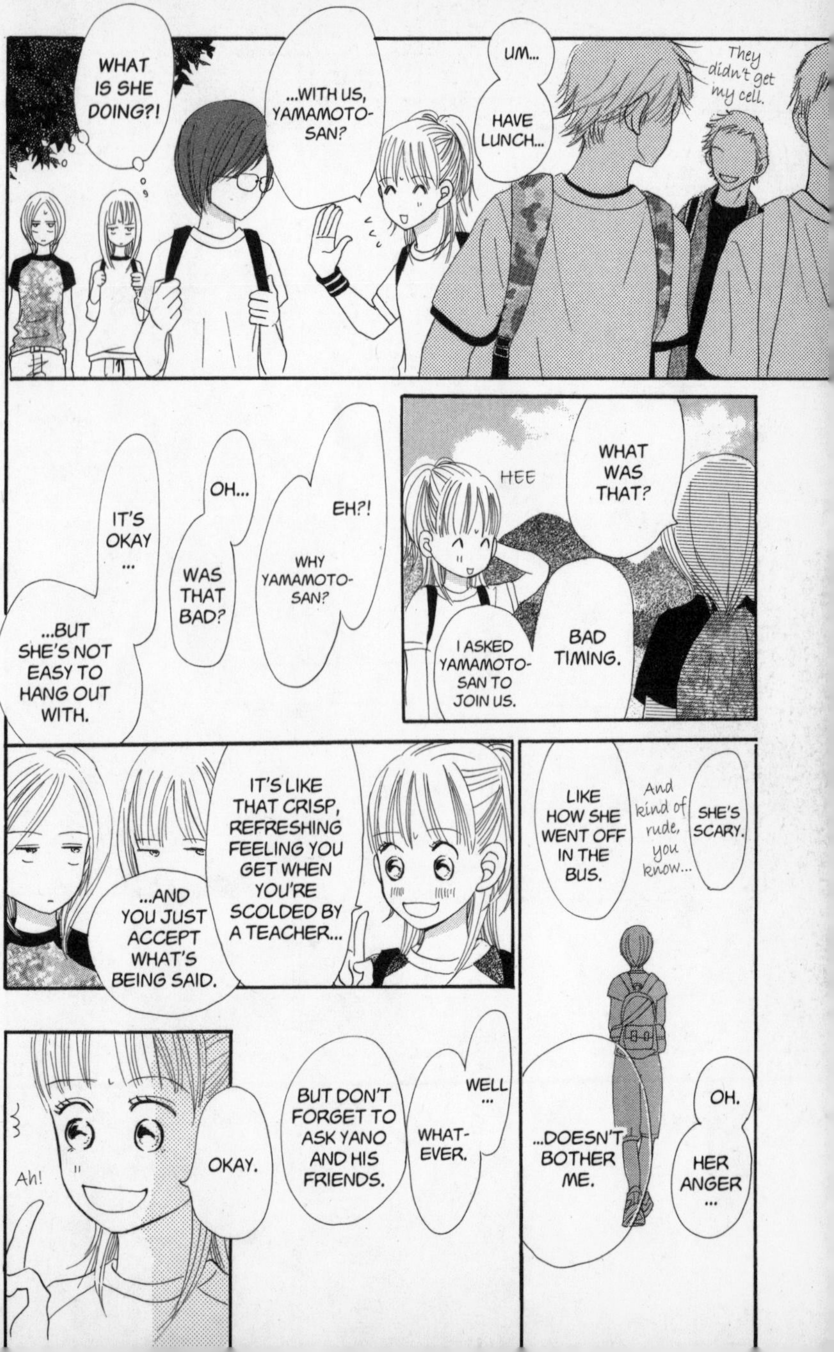
They didn't get my cell.
UM...
HAVE LUNCH...
...WITH US, YAMAMOTO-SAN?
WHAT IS SHE DOING?!
WHAT WAS THAT?
HEE
BAD TIMING.
I ASKED YAMAMOTO-SAN TO JOIN US.
EH?!
WHY YAMAMOTO-SAN?
OH...
WAS THAT BAD?
IT'S OKAY ...
...BUT SHE'S NOT EASY TO HANG OUT WITH.
SHE'S SCARY.
And kind of rude, you know...
LIKE HOW SHE WENT OFF IN THE BUS.
OH.
HER ANGER ...
...DOESN'T BOTHER ME.
IT'S LIKE THAT CRISP, REFRESHING FEELING YOU GET WHEN YOU'RE SCOLDED BY A TEACHER...
...AND YOU JUST ACCEPT WHAT'S BEING SAID.
WELL ...
WHAT-EVER.
BUT DON'T FORGET TO ASK YANO AND HIS FRIENDS.
OKAY.
Ah!

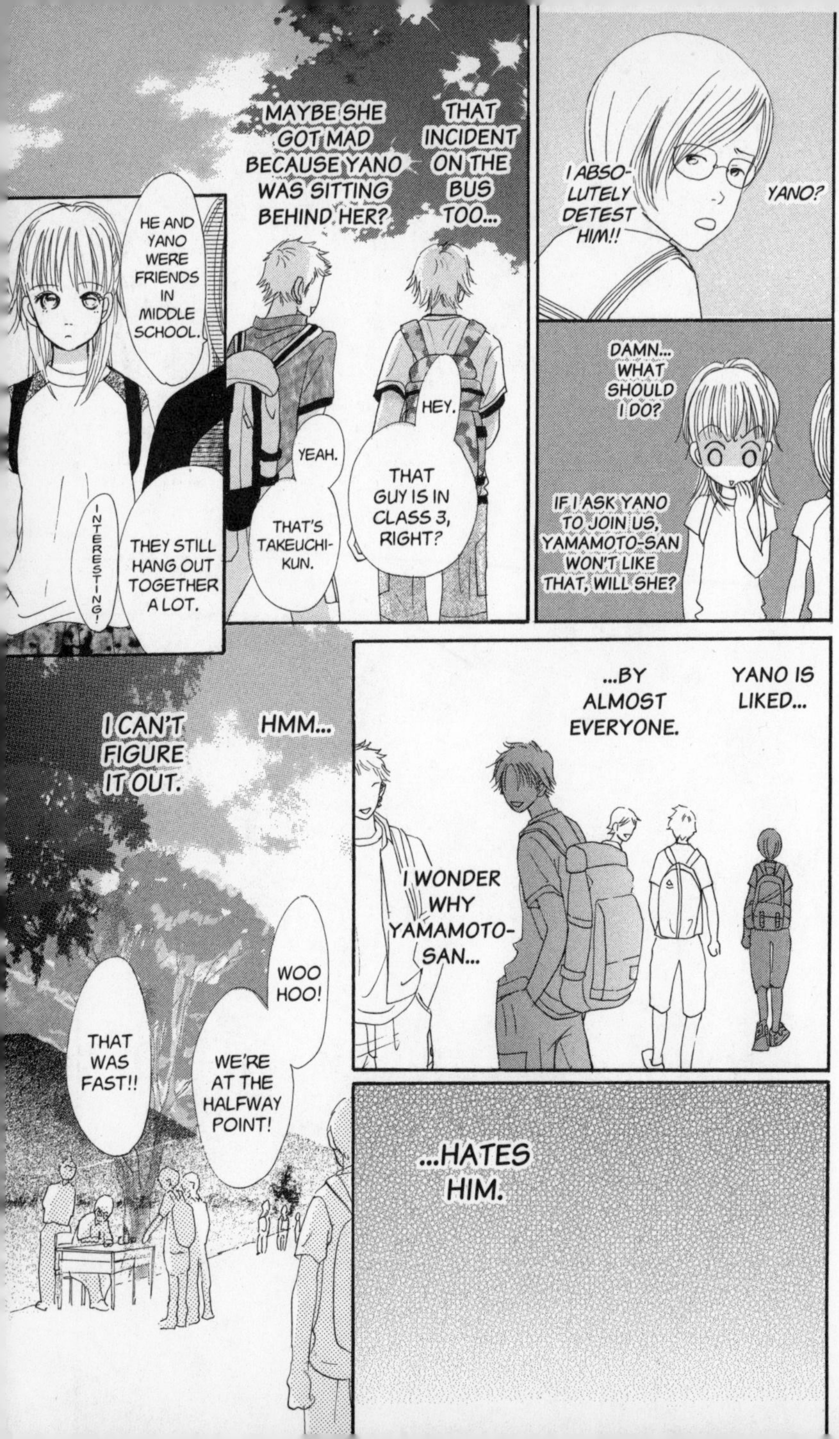
YANO?
I ABSO-LUTELY DETEST HIM!!
DAMN... WHAT SHOULD I DO?
IF I ASK YANO TO JOIN US, YAMAMOTO-SAN WON'T LIKE THAT, WILL SHE?
THAT INCIDENT ON THE BUS TOO...
MAYBE SHE GOT MAD BECAUSE YANO WAS SITTING BEHIND HER?
HEY.
THAT GUY IS IN CLASS 3, RIGHT?
YEAH.
THAT'S TAKEUCHI-KUN.
HE AND YANO WERE FRIENDS IN MIDDLE SCHOOL.
THEY STILL HANG OUT TOGETHER A LOT.
INTERESTING!
YANO IS LIKED...
...BY ALMOST EVERYONE.
I WONDER WHY YAMAMOTO-SAN...
...HATES HIM.
HMM...
I CAN'T FIGURE IT OUT.
WOO HOO!
WE'RE AT THE HALFWAY POINT!
THAT WAS FAST!!

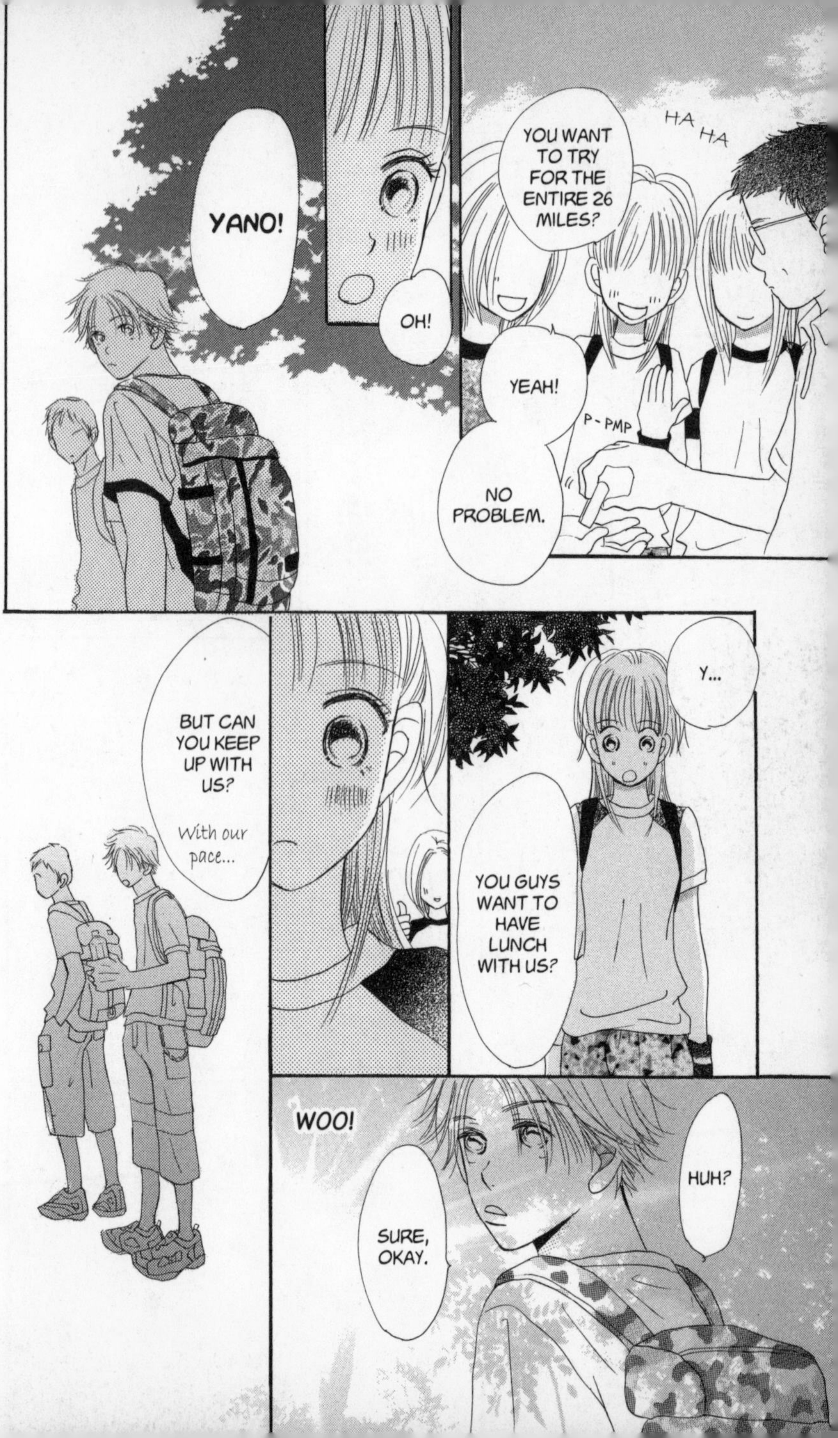
HA HA
YOU WANT TO TRY FOR THE ENTIRE 26 MILES?
YEAH!
P-PMP
NO PROBLEM.
OH!
YANO!
Y...
YOU GUYS WANT TO HAVE LUNCH WITH US?
HUH?
SURE, OKAY.
WOO!
BUT CAN YOU KEEP UP WITH US?
With our pace...

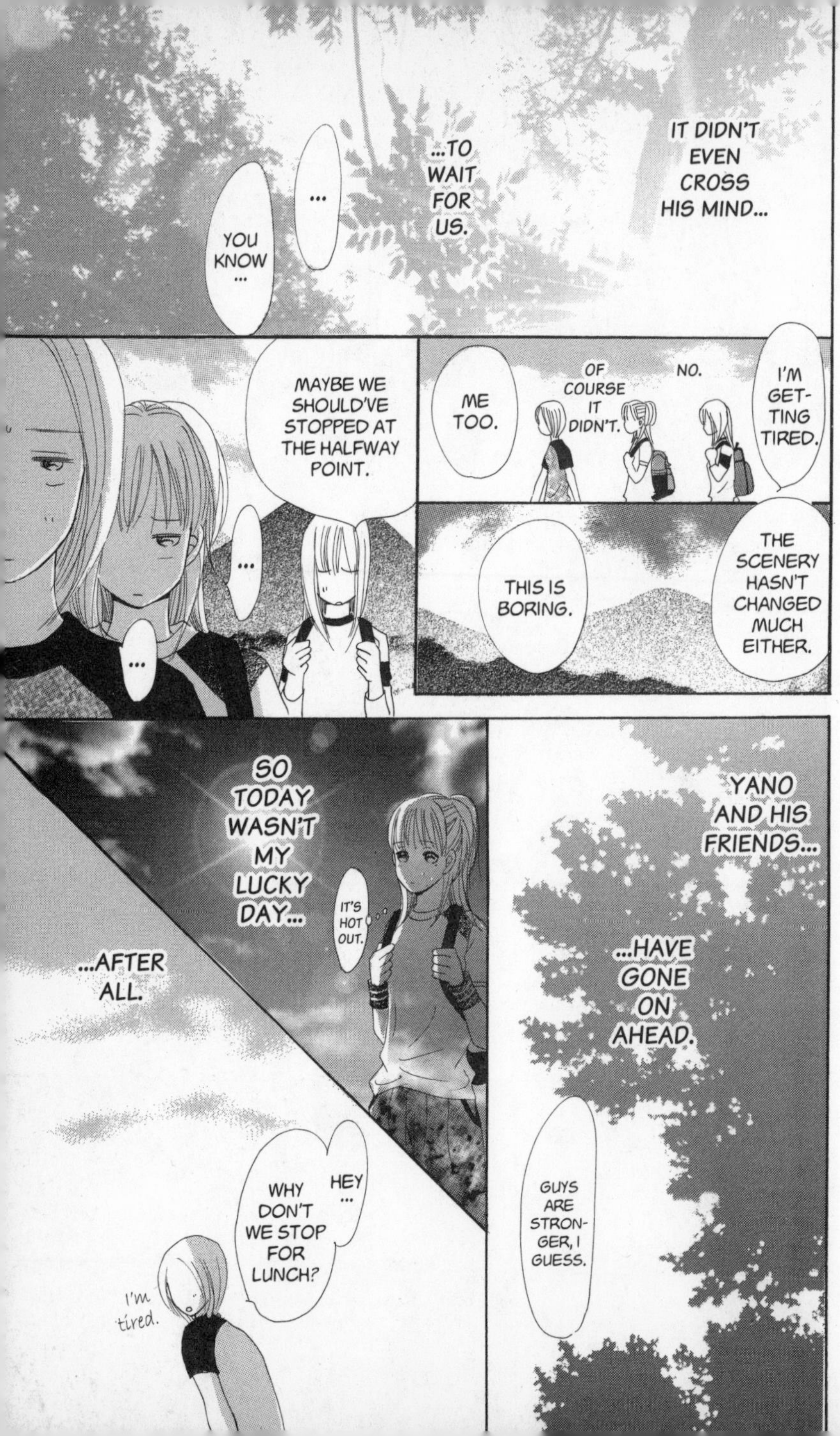
IT DIDN'T EVEN CROSS HIS MIND...
...TO WAIT FOR US.
...
YOU KNOW ...
I'M GET-TING TIRED.
NO.
OF COURSE IT DIDN'T.
ME TOO.
THE SCENERY HASN'T CHANGED MUCH EITHER.
THIS IS BORING.
MAYBE WE SHOULD'VE STOPPED AT THE HALFWAY POINT.
...
...
YANO AND HIS FRIENDS...
...HAVE GONE ON AHEAD.
GUYS ARE STRON-GER, I GUESS.
SO TODAY WASN'T MY LUCKY DAY...
IT'S HOT OUT.
...AFTER ALL.
HEY ...
WHY DON'T WE STOP FOR LUNCH?
I'm tired.

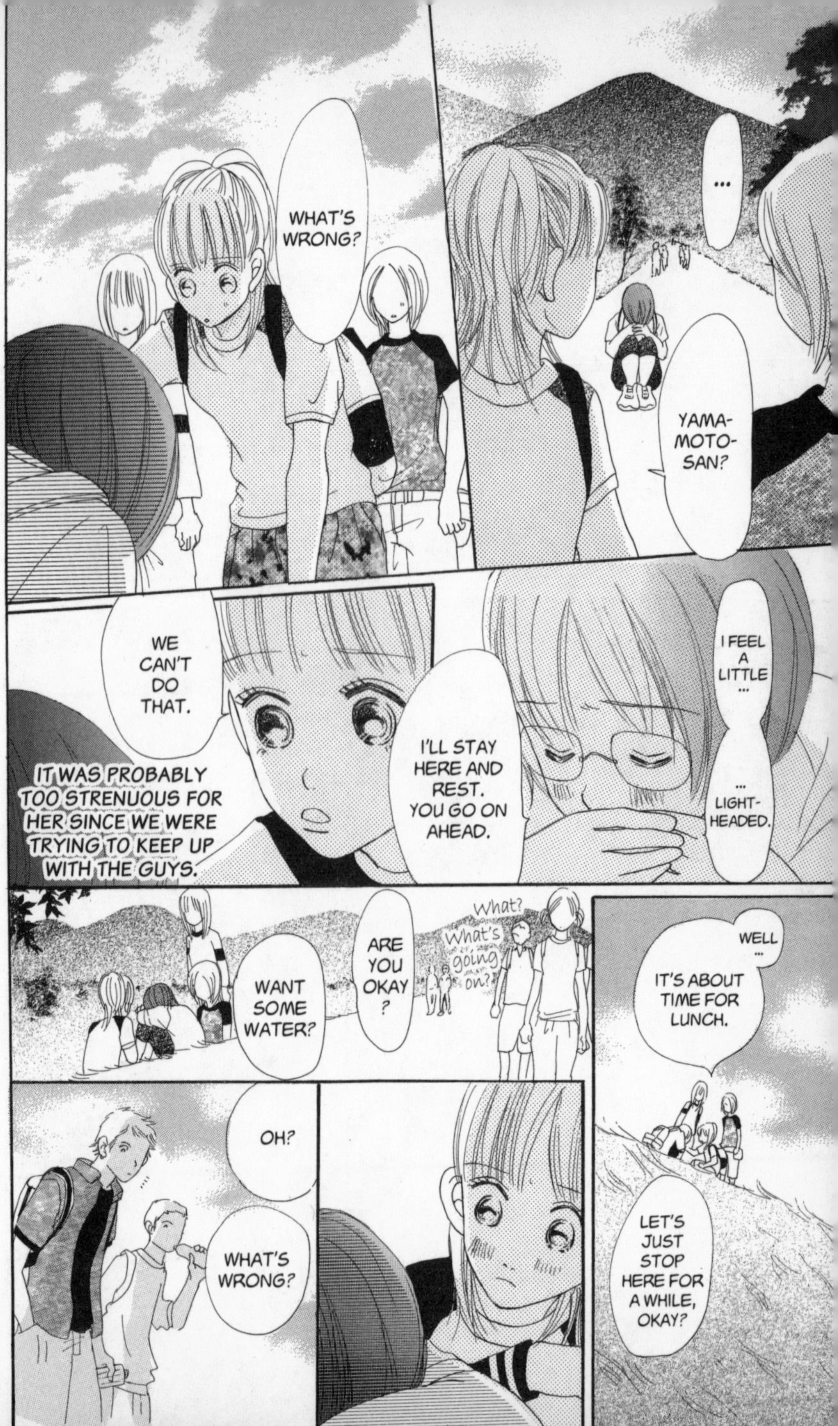
...
YAMAMOTO-SAN?
WHAT'S WRONG?
I FEEL A LITTLE ... ... LIGHT-HEADED.
I'LL STAY HERE AND REST. YOU GO ON AHEAD.
WE CAN'T DO THAT.
IT WAS PROBABLY TOO STRENUOUS FOR HER SINCE WE WERE TRYING TO KEEP UP WITH THE GUYS.
WELL ...
IT'S ABOUT TIME FOR LUNCH.
LET'S JUST STOP HERE FOR A WHILE, OKAY?
What?
What's going on?
ARE YOU OKAY?
WANT SOME WATER?
OH?
WHAT'S WRONG?

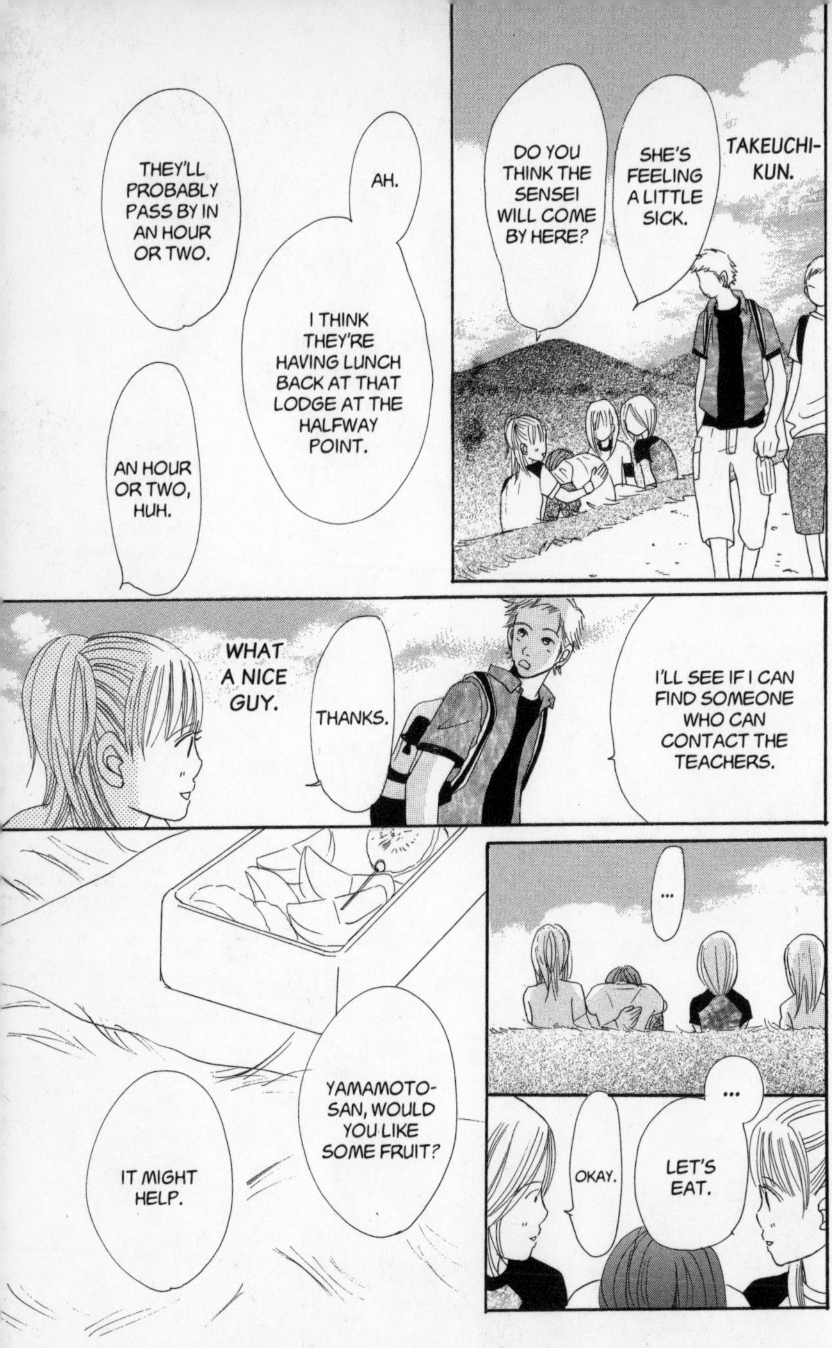
TAKEUCHI-KUN.
SHE'S FEELING A LITTLE SICK.
DO YOU THINK THE SENSEI WILL COME BY HERE?
AH.
I THINK THEY'RE HAVING LUNCH BACK AT THAT LODGE AT THE HALFWAY POINT.
THEY'LL PROBABLY PASS BY IN AN HOUR OR TWO.
AN HOUR OR TWO, HUH.
I'LL SEE IF I CAN FIND SOMEONE WHO CAN CONTACT THE TEACHERS.
THANKS.
WHAT A NICE GUY.
...
...
LET'S EAT.
OKAY.
YAMAMOTO-SAN, WOULD YOU LIKE SOME FRUIT?
IT MIGHT HELP.

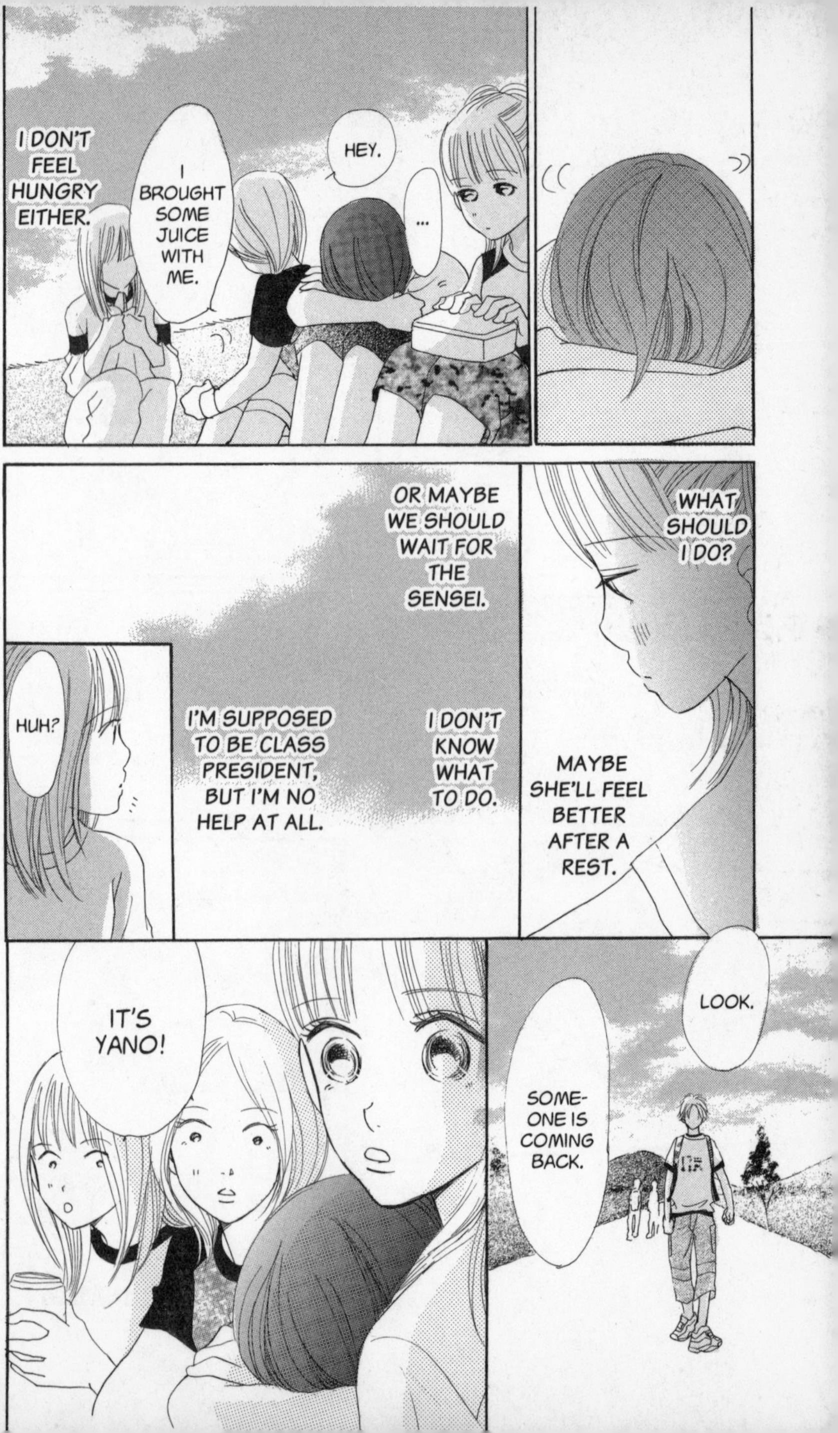
HEY.
...
I BROUGHT SOME JUICE WITH ME.
I DON'T FEEL HUNGRY EITHER.
WHAT SHOULD I DO?
MAYBE SHE'LL FEEL BETTER AFTER A REST.
OR MAYBE WE SHOULD WAIT FOR THE SENSEI.
I DON'T KNOW WHAT TO DO.
I'M SUPPOSED TO BE CLASS PRESIDENT, BUT I'M NO HELP AT ALL.
HUH?
LOOK.
SOME-ONE IS COMING BACK.
IT'S YANO!

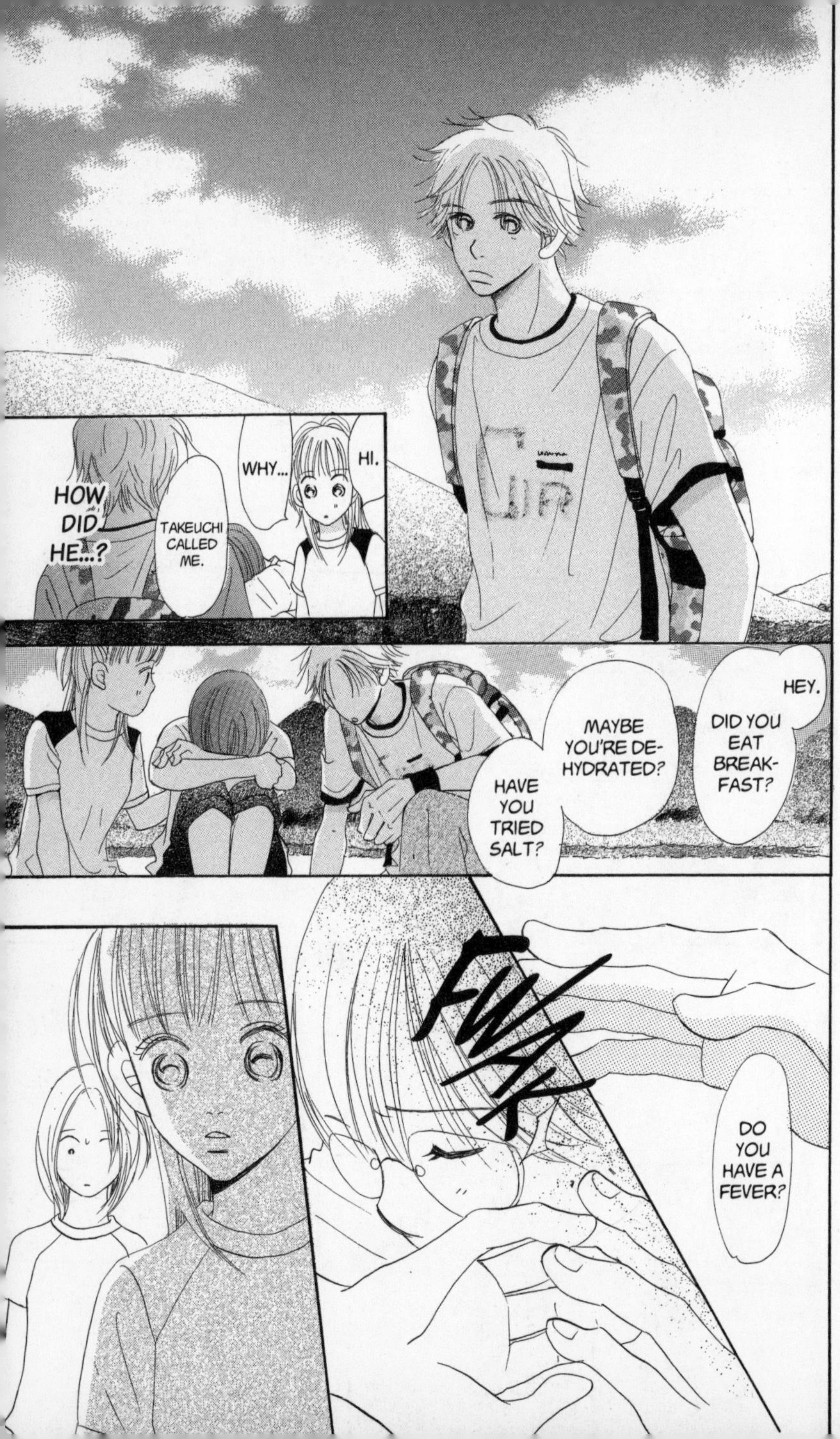
HI.
WHY...
TAKEUCHI CALLED ME.
HOW DID HE...?
HEY.
DID YOU EAT BREAKFAST?
MAYBE YOU'RE DE-HYDRATED?
HAVE YOU TRIED SALT?
FWAK
DO YOU HAVE A FEVER?

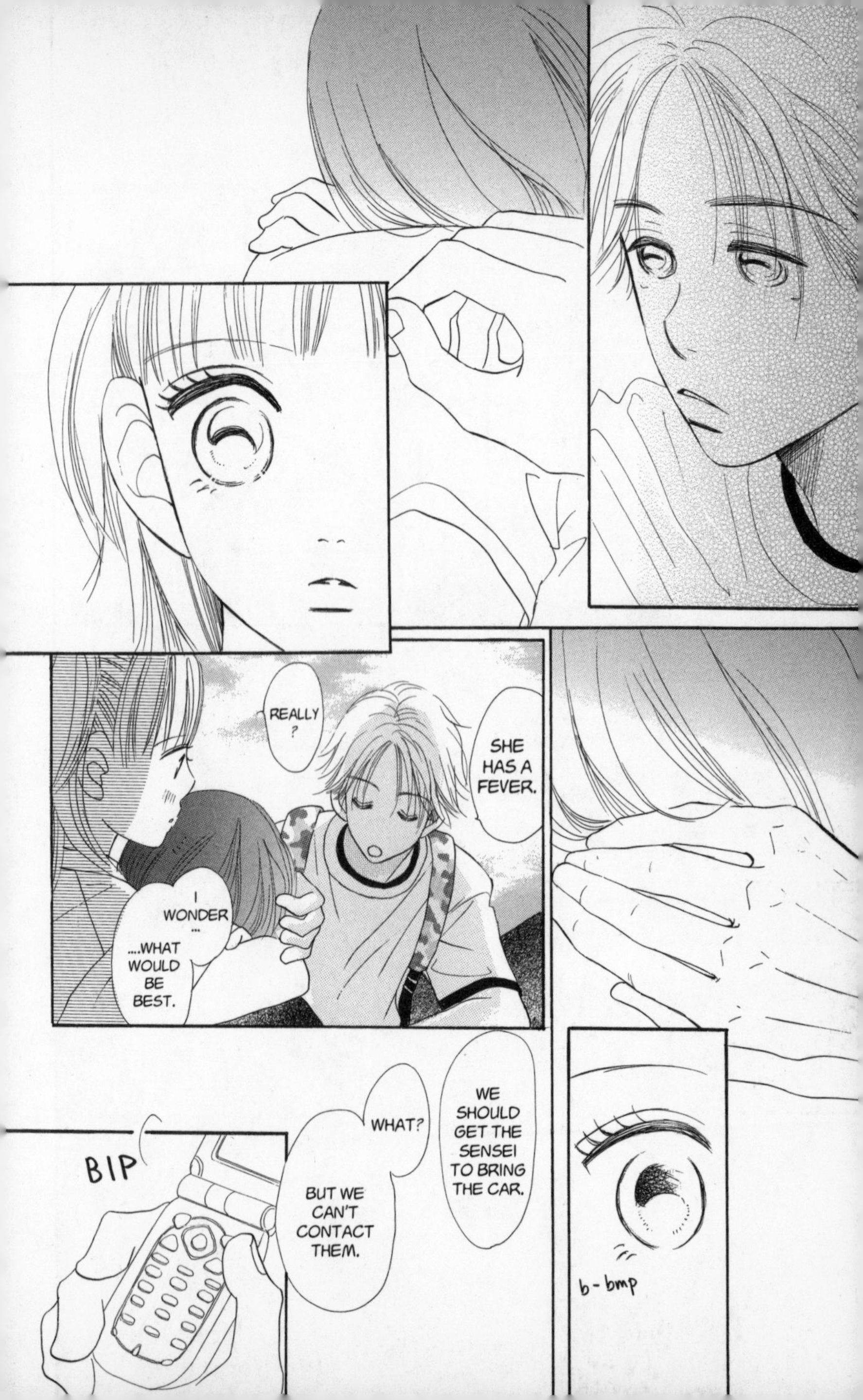
SHE HAS A FEVER.
REALLY?
I WONDER... ....WHAT WOULD BE BEST.
b-bmp
WE SHOULD GET THE SENSEI TO BRING THE CAR.
WHAT?
BUT WE CAN'T CONTACT THEM.
BIP

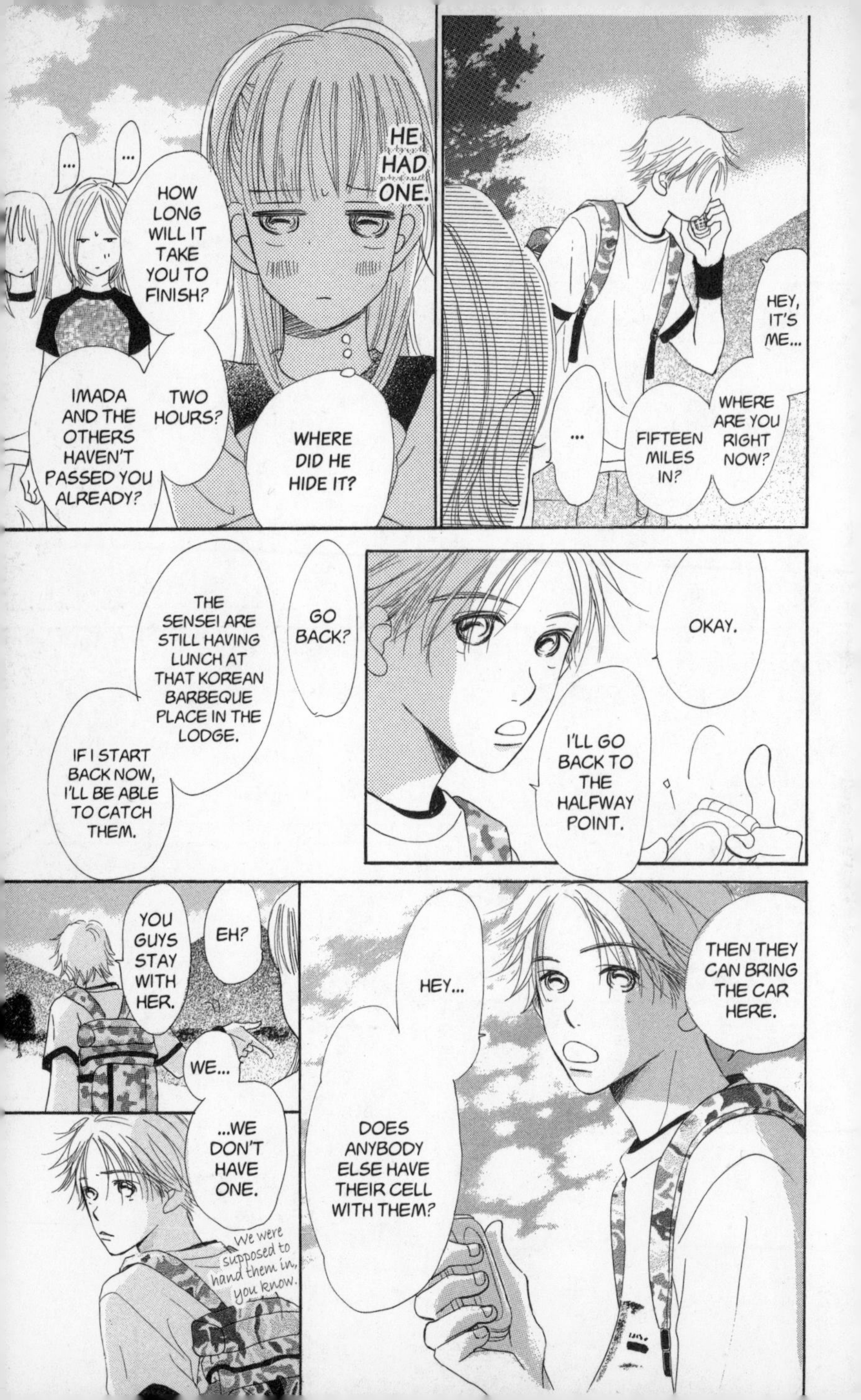
HEY, IT'S ME...
WHERE ARE YOU RIGHT NOW?
FIFTEEN MILES IN?
...
HE HAD ONE.
...
...
HOW LONG WILL IT TAKE YOU TO FINISH?
TWO HOURS?
WHERE DID HE HIDE IT?
IMADA AND THE OTHERS HAVEN'T PASSED YOU ALREADY?
OKAY.
I'LL GO BACK TO THE HALFWAY POINT.
GO BACK?
THE SENSEI ARE STILL HAVING LUNCH AT THAT KOREAN BARBEQUE PLACE IN THE LODGE.
IF I START BACK NOW, I'LL BE ABLE TO CATCH THEM.
THEN THEY CAN BRING THE CAR HERE.
HEY...
DOES ANYBODY ELSE HAVE THEIR CELL WITH THEM?
EH?
YOU GUYS STAY WITH HER.
WE...
...WE DON'T HAVE ONE.
We were supposed to hand them in, you know.

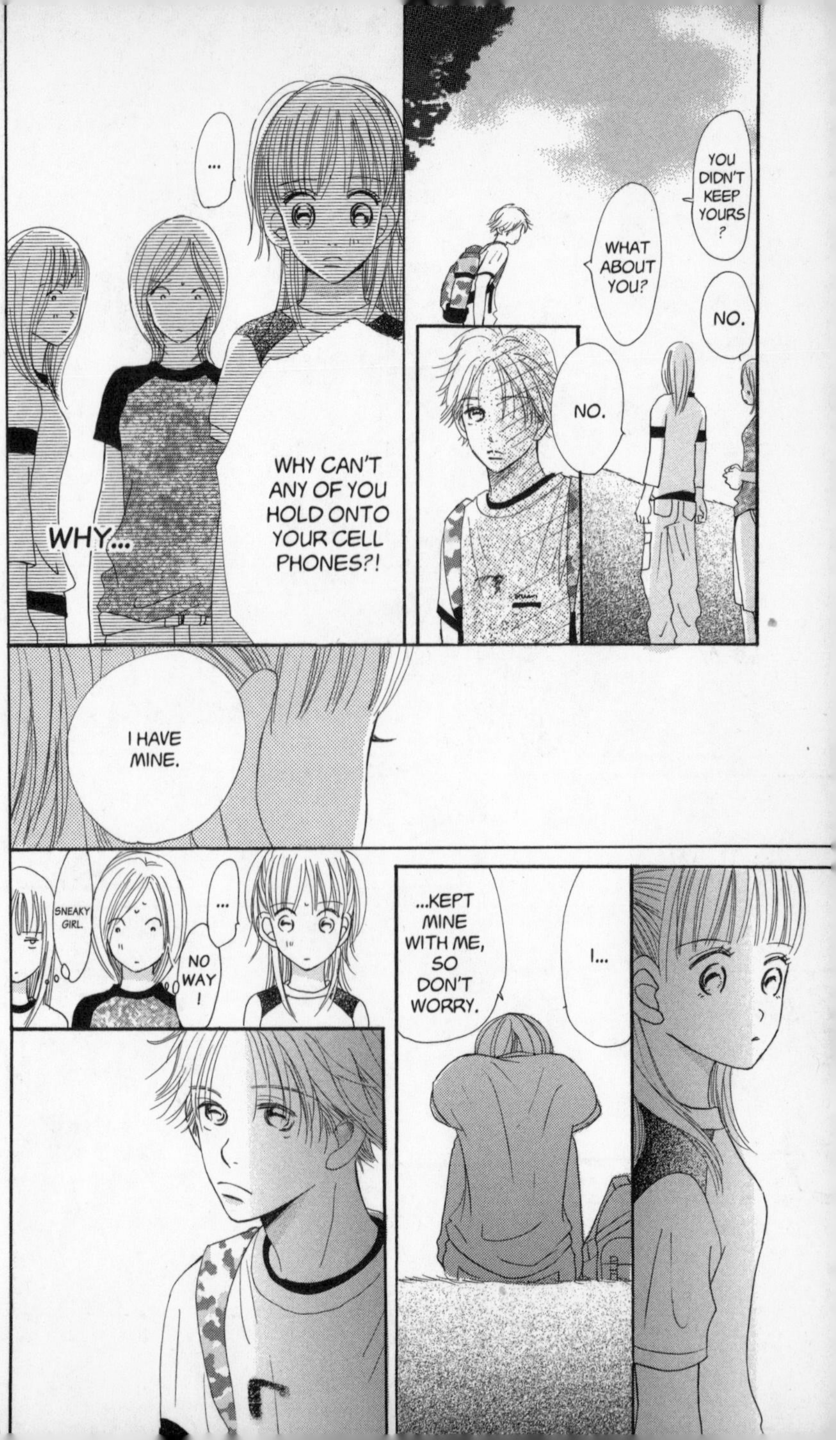
YOU DIDN'T KEEP YOURS?
NO.
WHAT ABOUT YOU?
NO.
...
WHY...
WHY CAN'T ANY OF YOU HOLD ONTO YOUR CELL PHONES?!
I HAVE MINE.
I...
...KEPT MINE WITH ME, SO DON'T WORRY.
...
NO WAY!
SNEAKY GIRL.

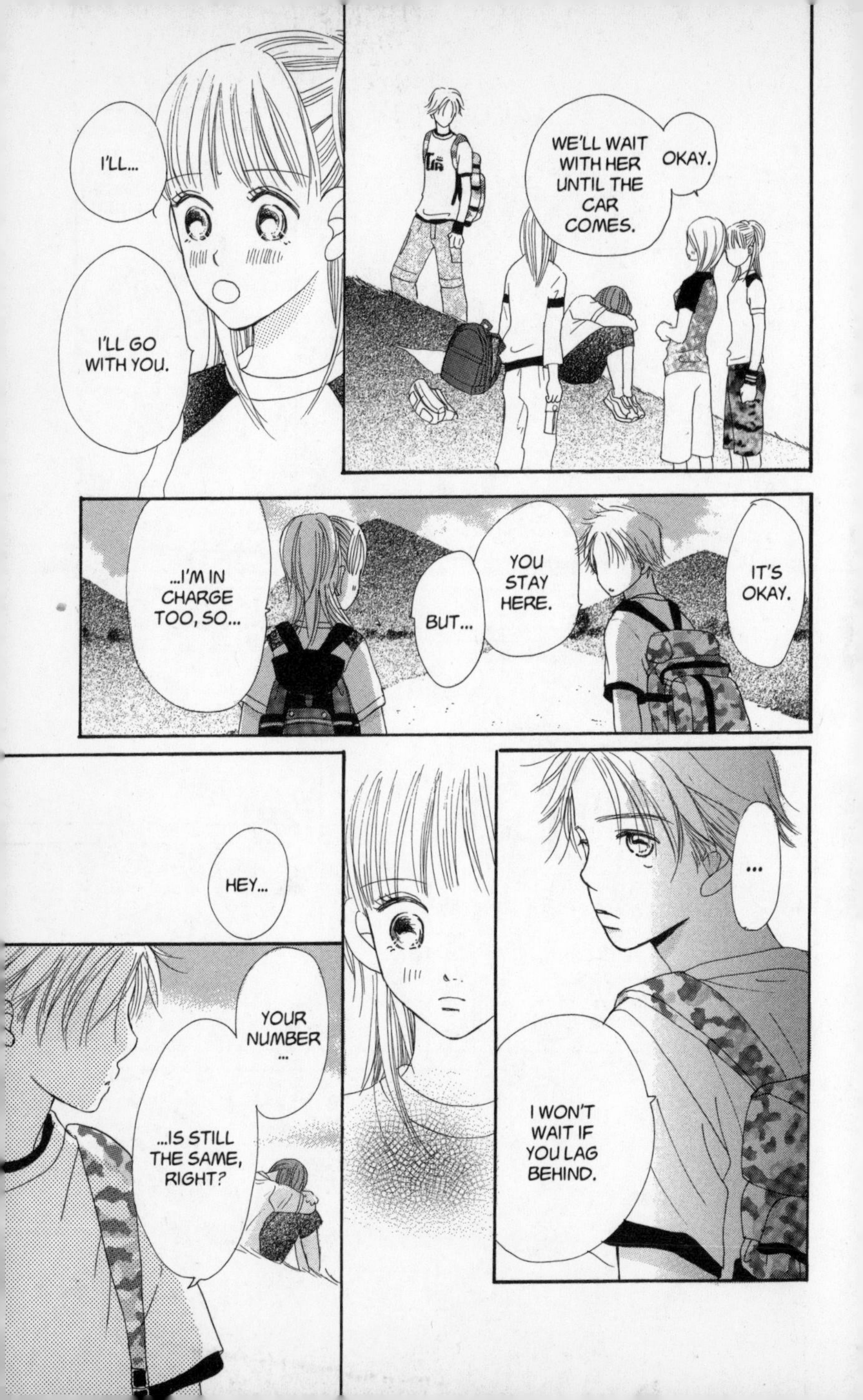
WE'LL WAIT WITH HER UNTIL THE CAR COMES.
OKAY.
I'LL...
I'LL GO WITH YOU.
IT'S OKAY.
YOU STAY HERE.
BUT...
...I'M IN CHARGE TOO, SO...
...
I WON'T WAIT IF YOU LAG BEHIND.
HEY...
YOUR NUMBER ...
...IS STILL THE SAME, RIGHT?

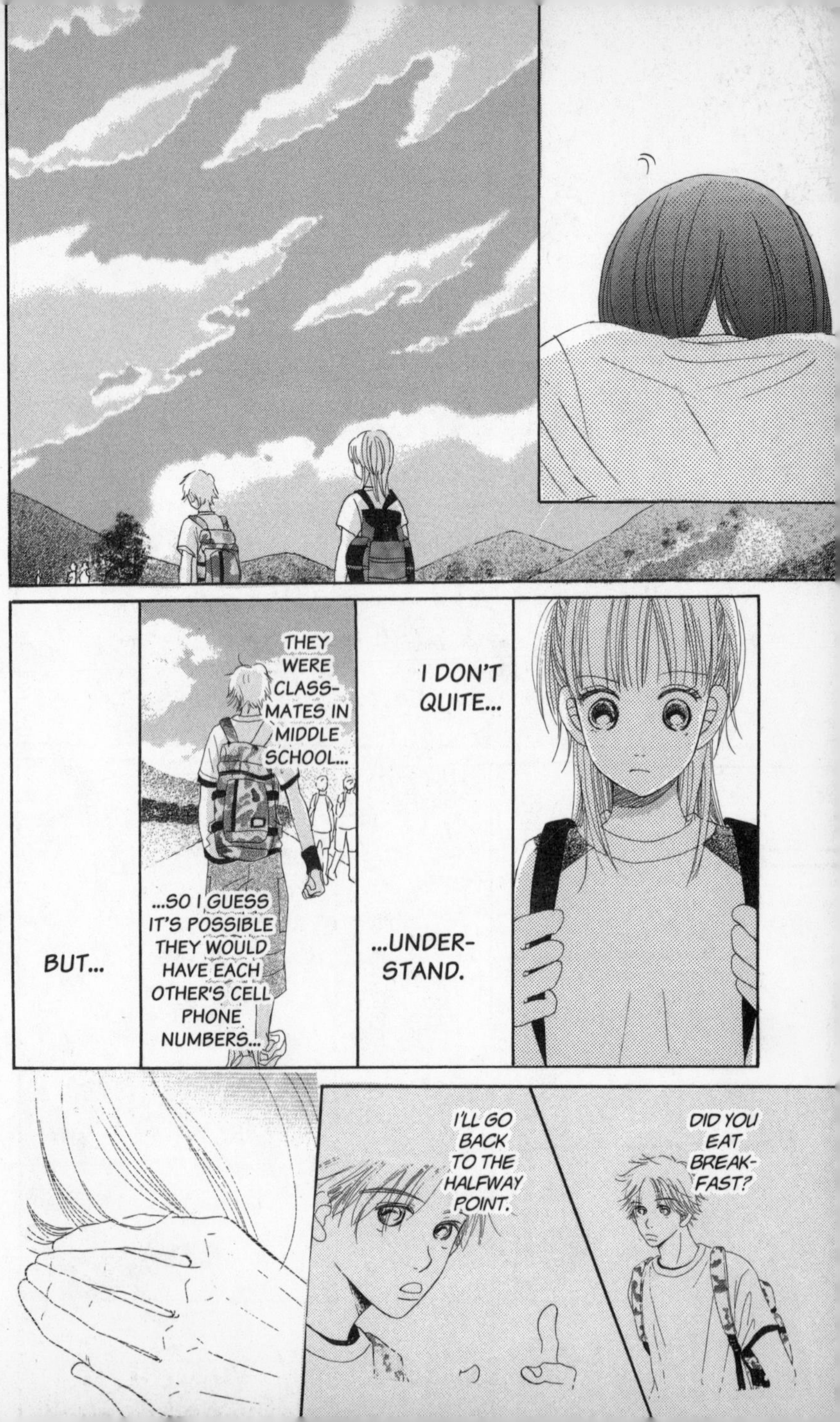
I DON'T QUITE...
...UNDER-STAND.
THEY WERE CLASS-MATES IN MIDDLE SCHOOL...
...SO I GUESS IT'S POSSIBLE THEY WOULD HAVE EACH OTHER'S CELL PHONE NUMBERS...
BUT...
DID YOU EAT BREAK-FAST?
I'LL GO BACK TO THE HALFWAY POINT.

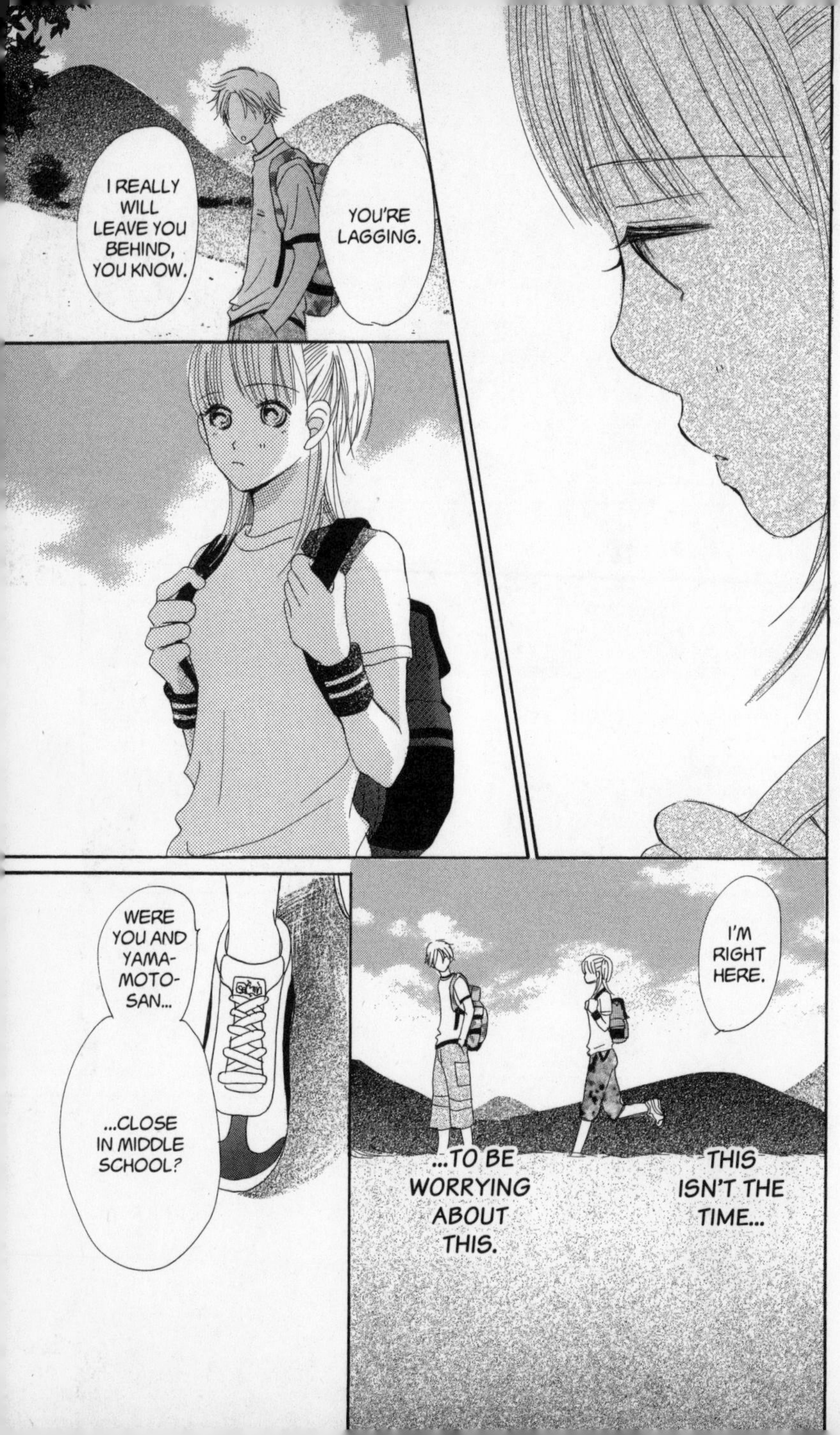
YOU'RE LAGGING.
I REALLY WILL LEAVE YOU BEHIND, YOU KNOW.
I'M RIGHT HERE.
THIS ISN'T THE TIME...
...TO BE WORRYING ABOUT THIS.
WERE YOU AND YAMA-MOTO-SAN...
...CLOSE IN MIDDLE SCHOOL?

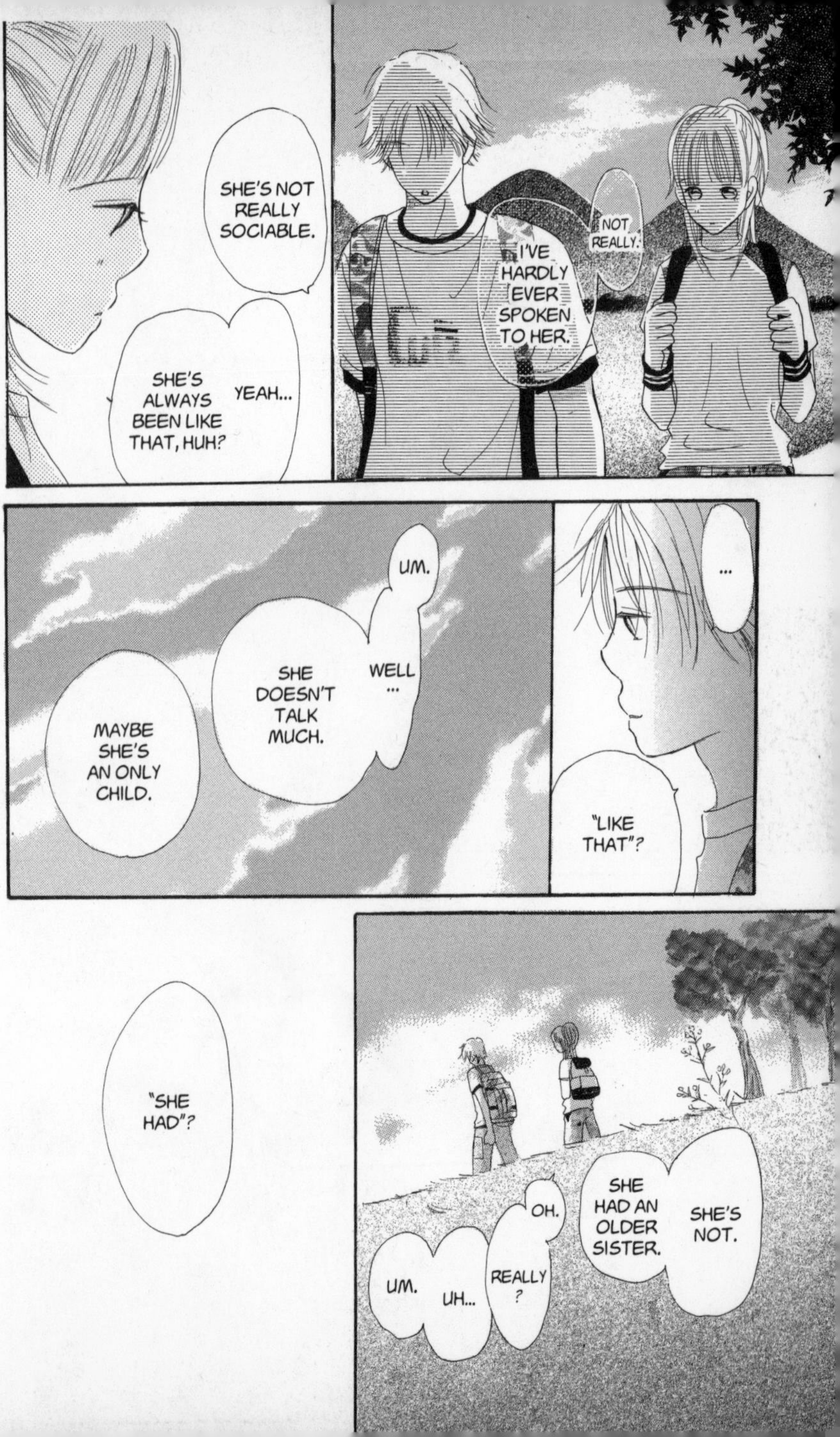
NOT REALLY.
I'VE HARDLY EVER SPOKEN TO HER.
SHE'S NOT REALLY SOCIABLE.
YEAH...
SHE'S ALWAYS BEEN LIKE THAT, HUH?
...
"LIKE THAT"?
UM.
WELL...
SHE DOESN'T TALK MUCH.
MAYBE SHE'S AN ONLY CHILD.
SHE'S NOT.
SHE HAD AN OLDER SISTER.
OH.
REALLY?
UH...
UM.
"SHE HAD"?

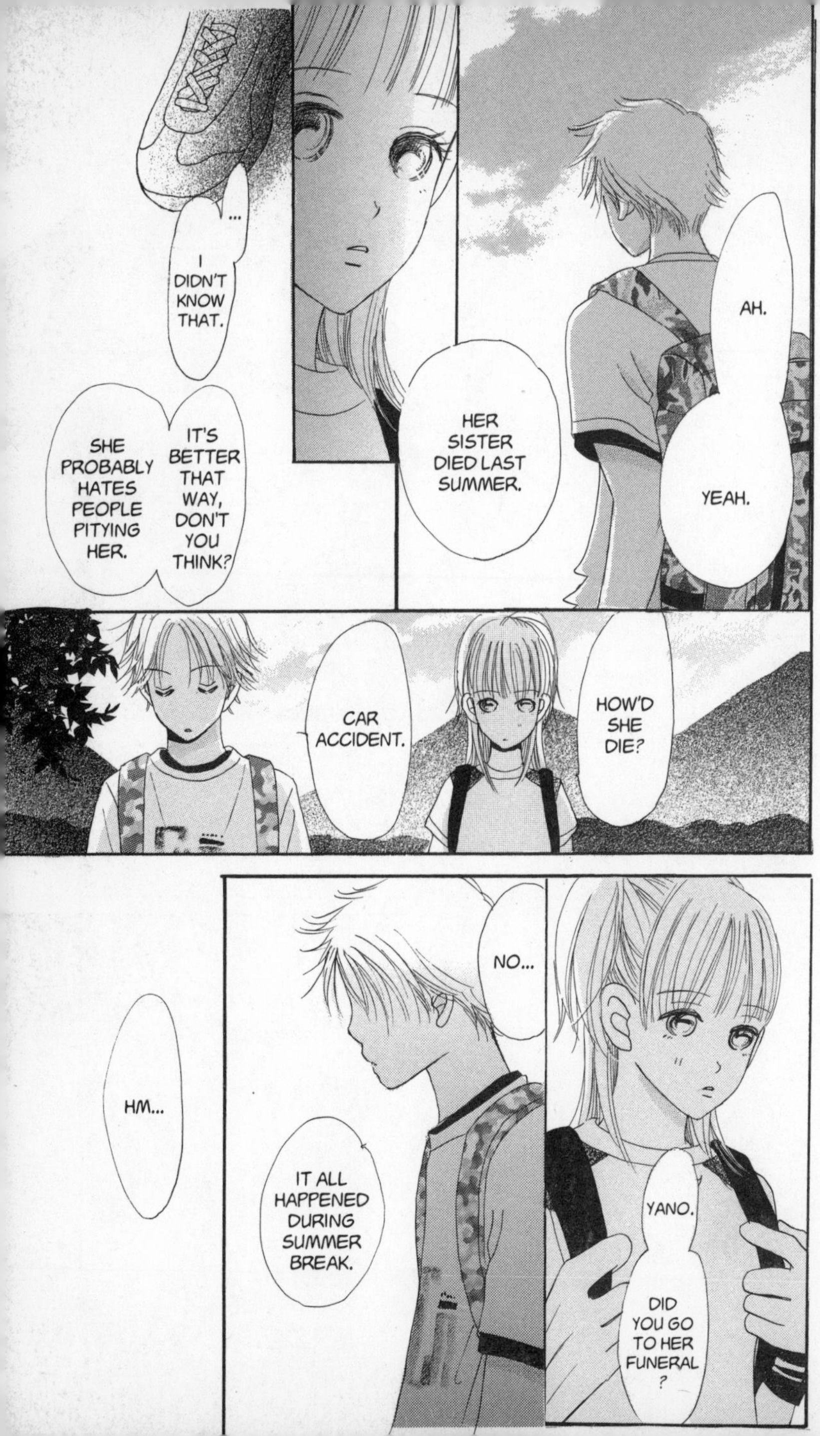
AH.
YEAH.
HER SISTER DIED LAST SUMMER.
...
I DIDN'T KNOW THAT.
IT'S BETTER THAT WAY, DON'T YOU THINK?
SHE PROBABLY HATES PEOPLE PITYING HER.
HOW'D SHE DIE?
CAR ACCIDENT.
YANO.
DID YOU GO TO HER FUNERAL?
NO...
IT ALL HAPPENED DURING SUMMER BREAK.
HM...

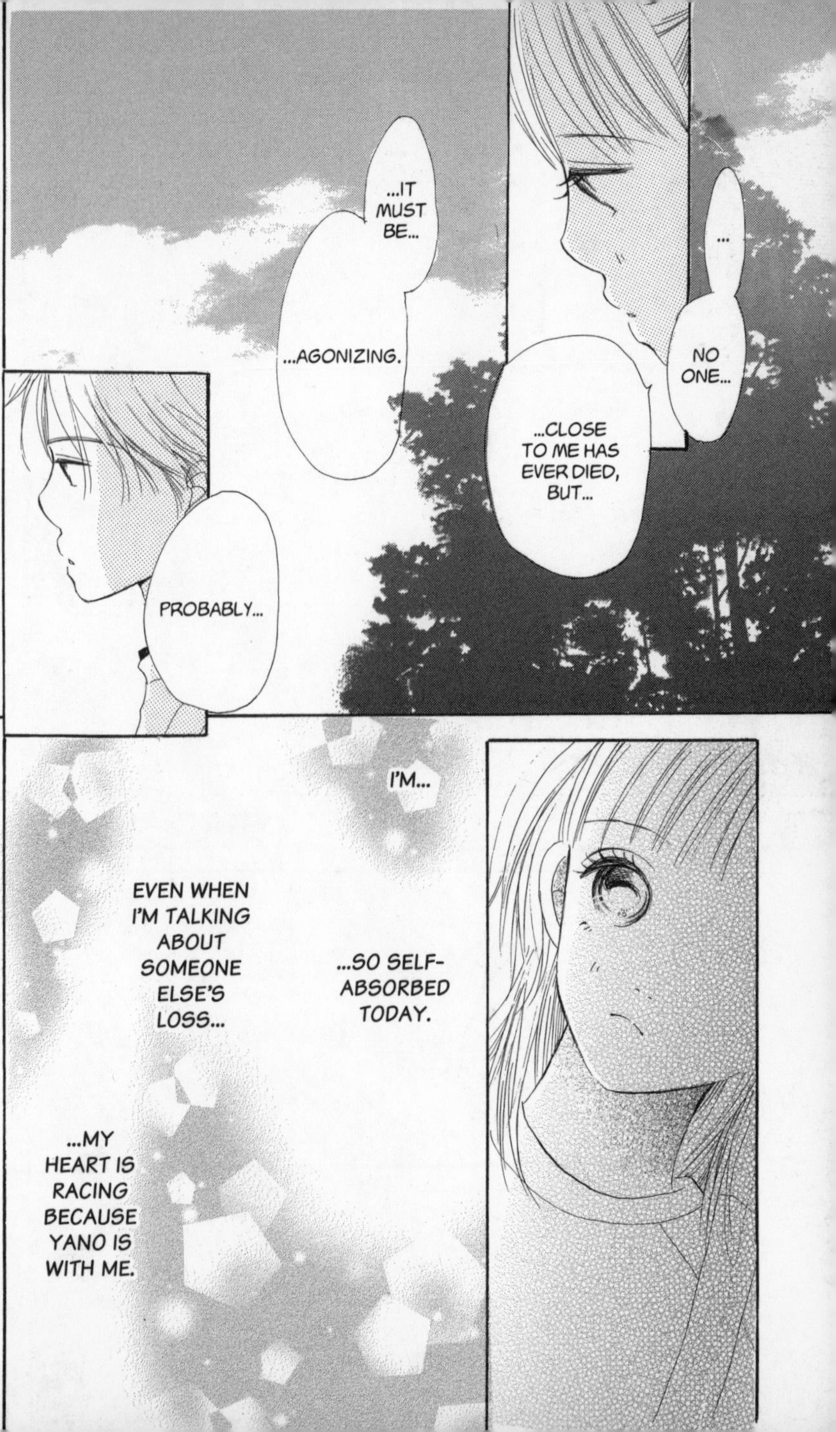
...
NO ONE...
...CLOSE TO ME HAS EVER DIED, BUT...
...IT MUST BE...
...AGONIZING.
PROBABLY...
I'M...
...SO SELF-ABSORBED TODAY.
EVEN WHEN I'M TALKING ABOUT SOMEONE ELSE'S LOSS...
...MY HEART IS RACING BECAUSE YANO IS WITH ME.

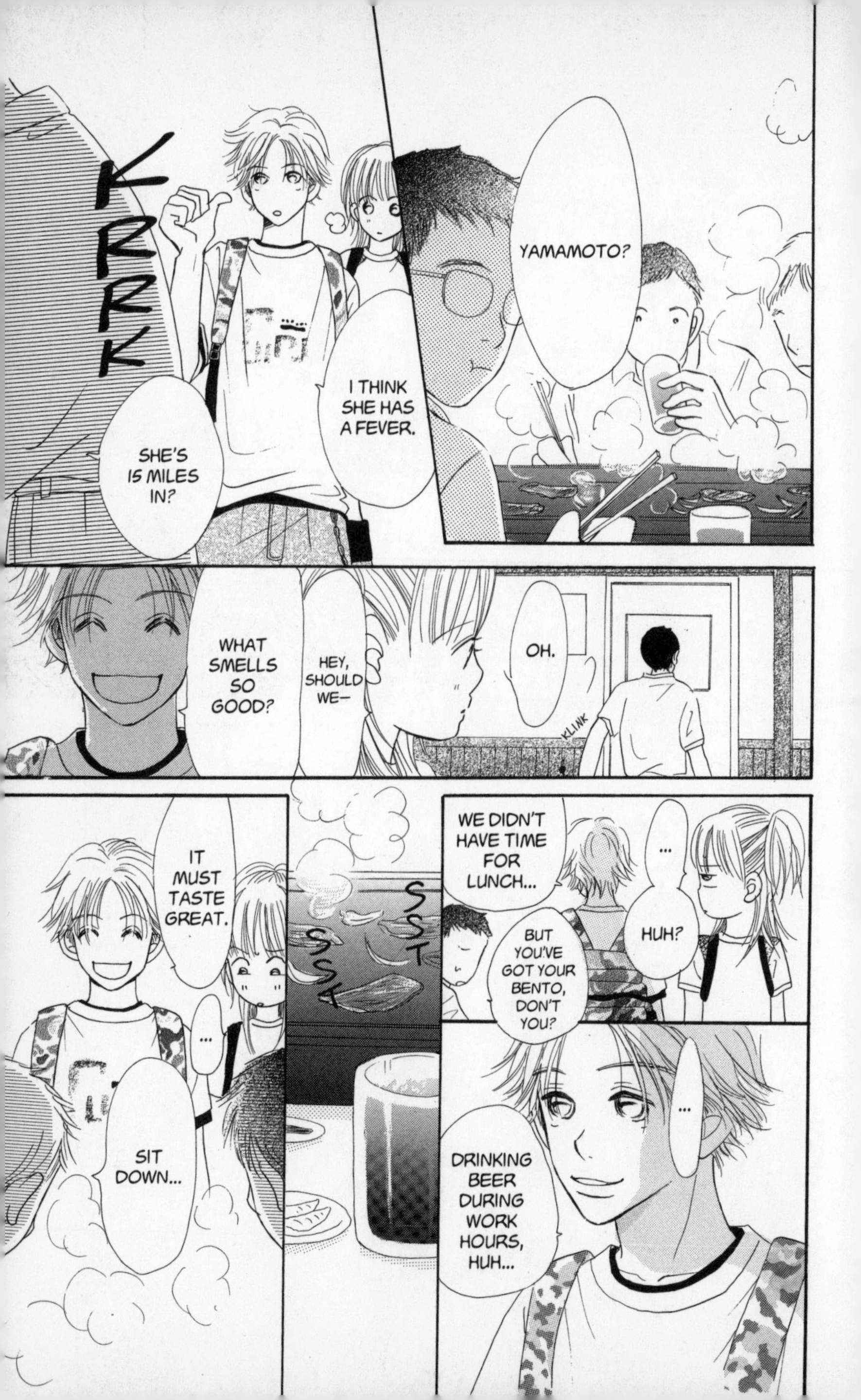
YAMAMOTO?
I THINK SHE HAS A FEVER.
SHE'S 15 MILES IN?
KRRK
OH.
KLINK
HEY, SHOULD WE—
WHAT SMELLS SO GOOD?
...
WE DIDN'T HAVE TIME FOR LUNCH...
HUH?
BUT YOU'VE GOT YOUR BENTO, DON'T YOU?
...
DRINKING BEER DURING WORK HOURS, HUH...
SSST
SSSA
IT MUST TASTE GREAT.
...
SIT DOWN...

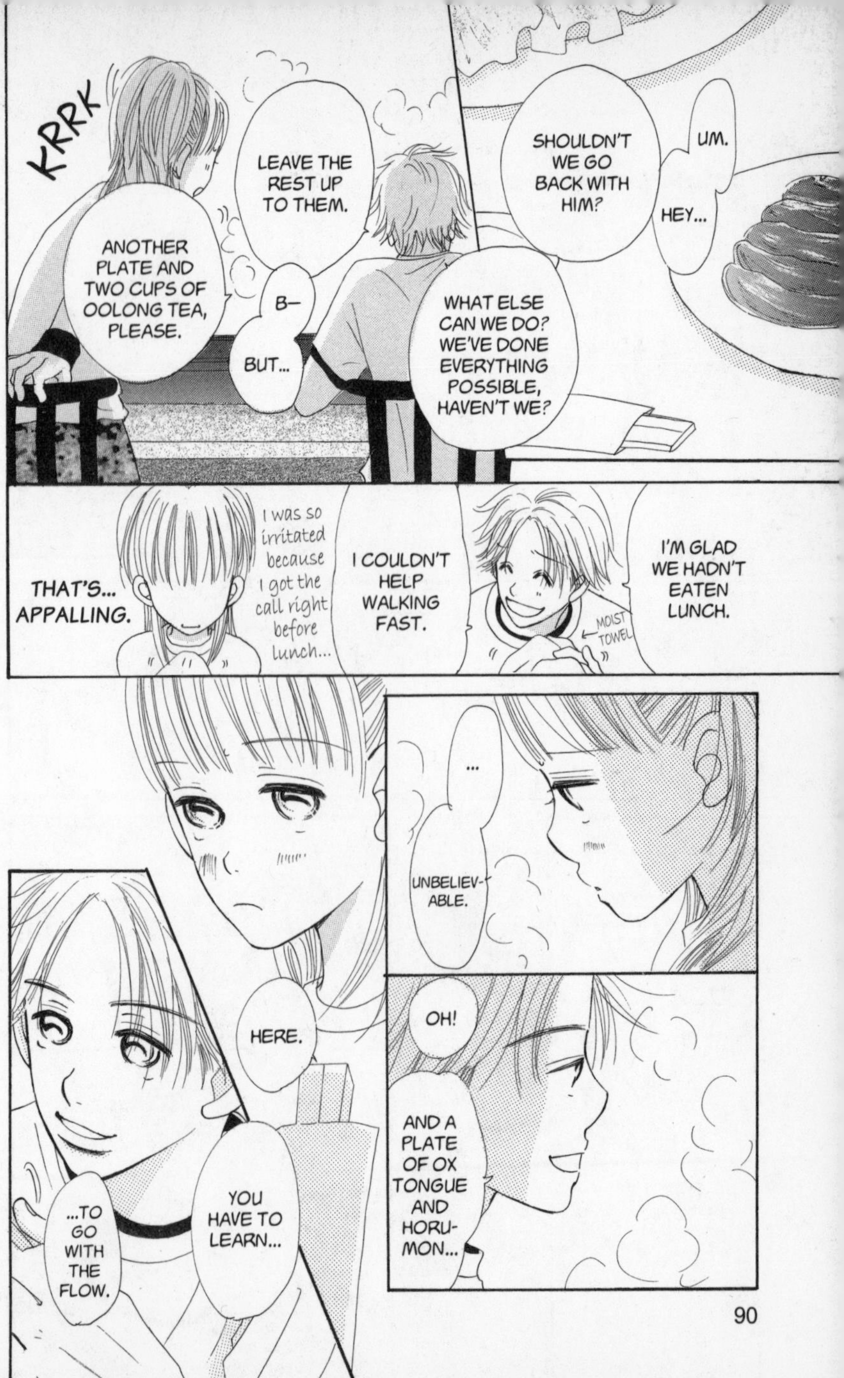
UM.
HEY...
SHOULDN'T WE GO BACK WITH HIM?
WHAT ELSE CAN WE DO? WE'VE DONE EVERYTHING POSSIBLE, HAVEN'T WE?
LEAVE THE REST UP TO THEM.
KRRK
ANOTHER PLATE AND TWO CUPS OF OOLONG TEA, PLEASE.
B—
BUT...
I'M GLAD WE HADN'T EATEN LUNCH.
MOIST TOWEL
I COULDN'T HELP WALKING FAST.
I was so irritated because I got the call right before lunch...
THAT'S... APPALLING.
...
UNBELIEVABLE.
OH!
AND A PLATE OF OX TONGUE AND HORUMON...
HERE.
YOU HAVE TO LEARN...
...TO GO WITH THE FLOW.

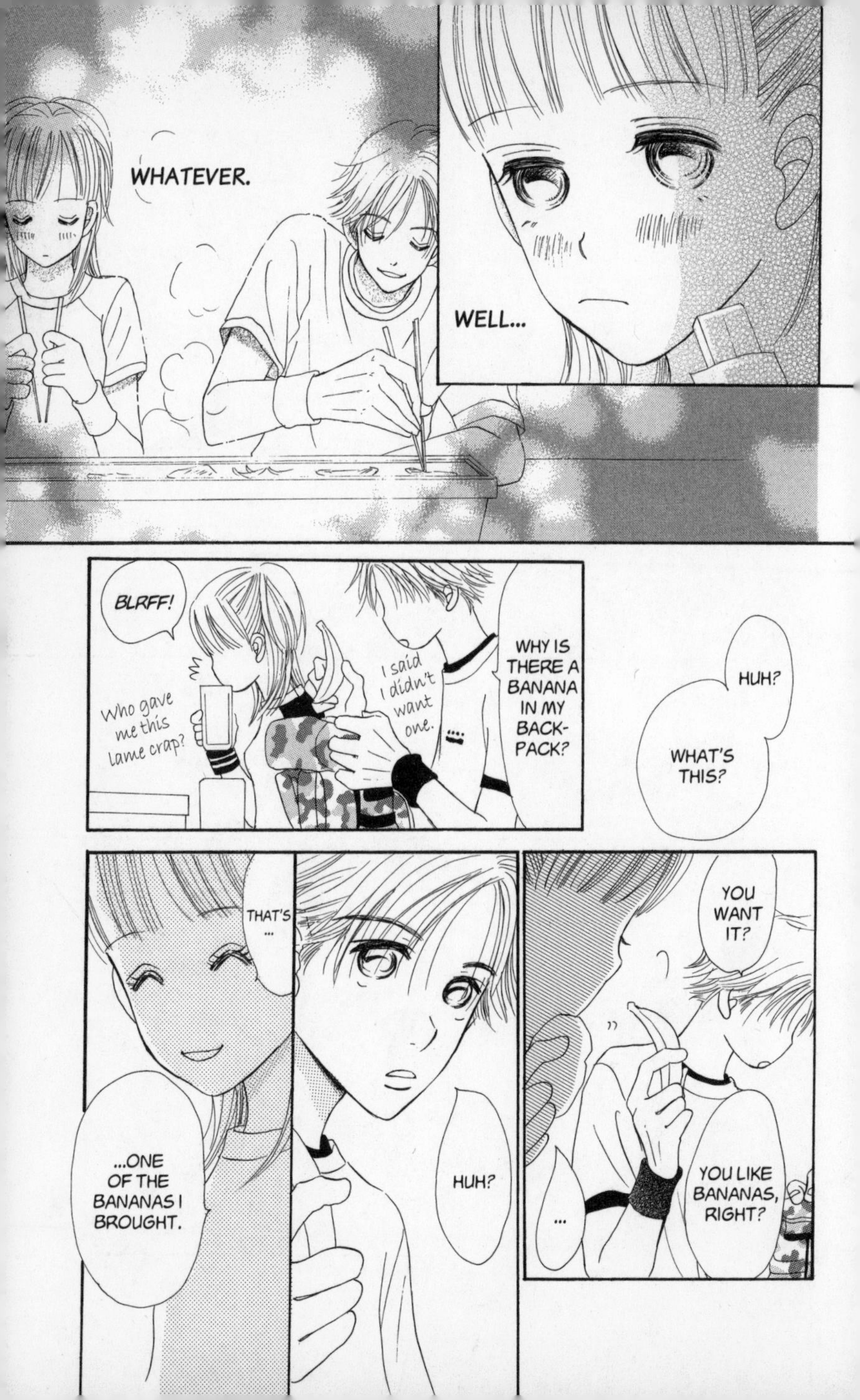
WELL...
WHATEVER.
HUH?
WHAT'S THIS?
WHY IS THERE A BANANA IN MY BACKPACK?
I said I didn't want one.
...
Who gave me this lame crap?
BLRFF!
YOU WANT IT?
YOU LIKE BANANAS, RIGHT?
...
HUH?
THAT'S...
...ONE OF THE BANANAS I BROUGHT.

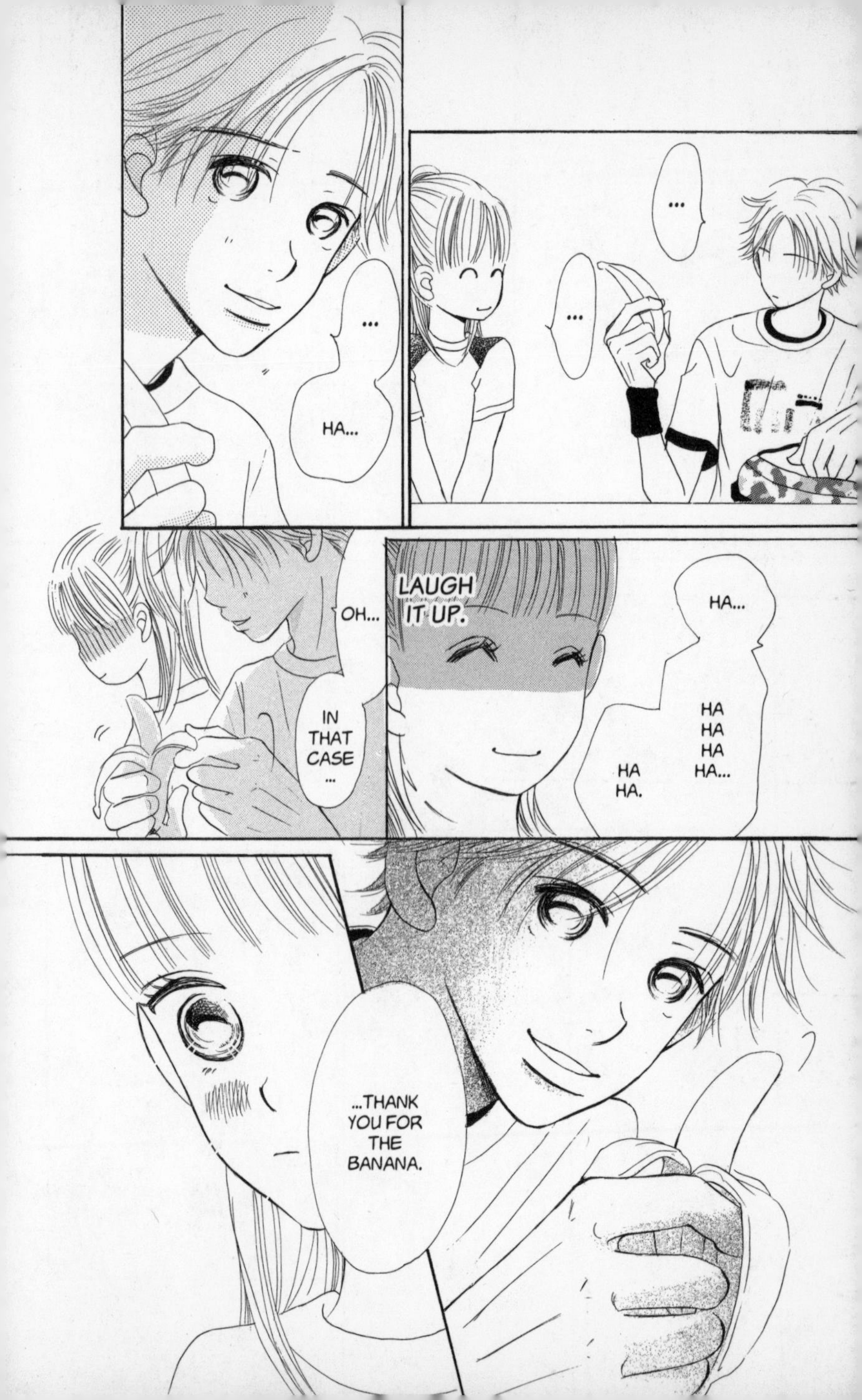
...
...
...
HA...
HA...
HA HA HA HA...
HA HA.
LAUGH IT UP.
OH...
IN THAT CASE ...
...THANK YOU FOR THE BANANA.

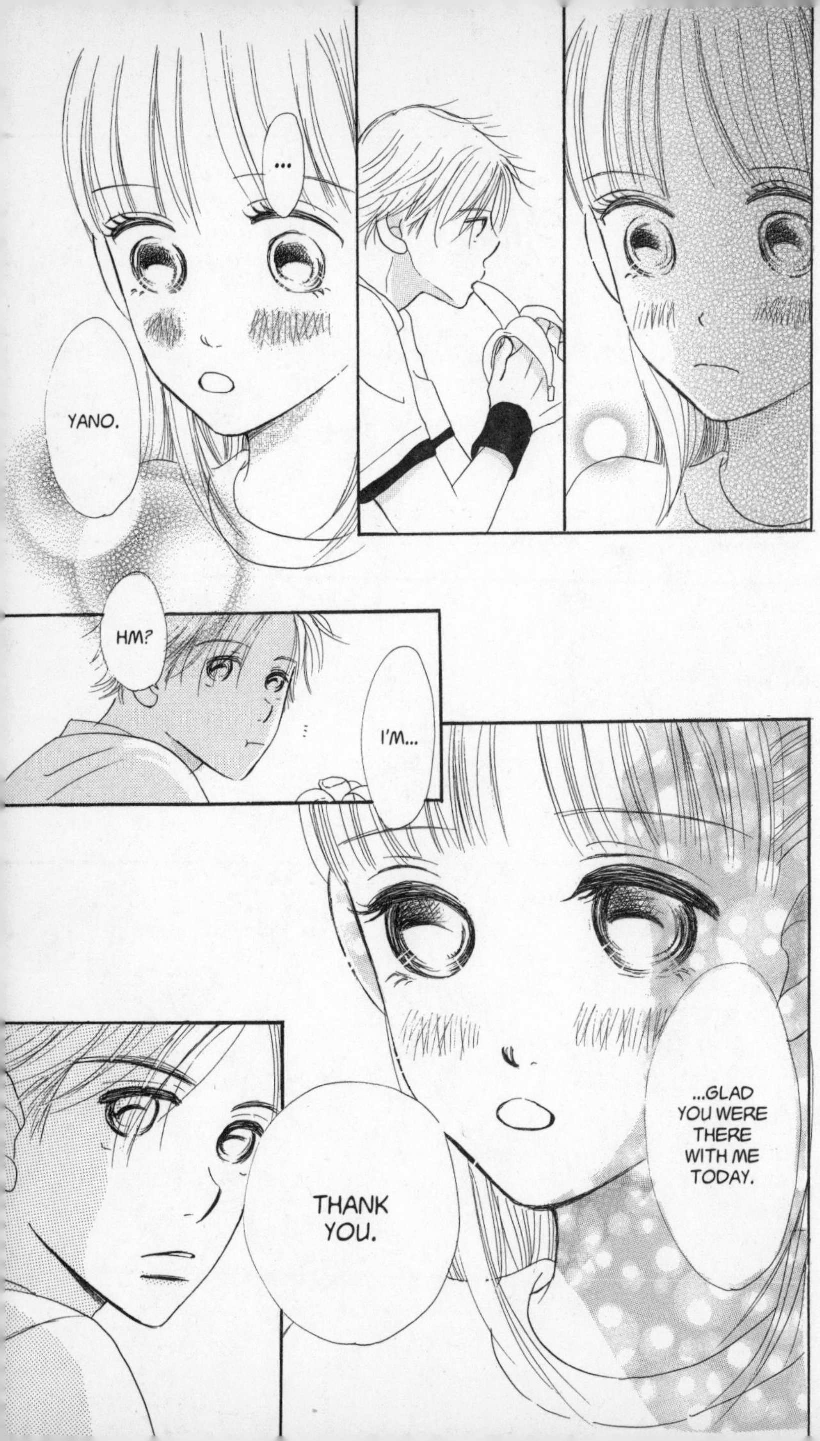
...
YANO.
HM?
I'M...
...GLAD YOU WERE THERE WITH ME TODAY.
THANK YOU.

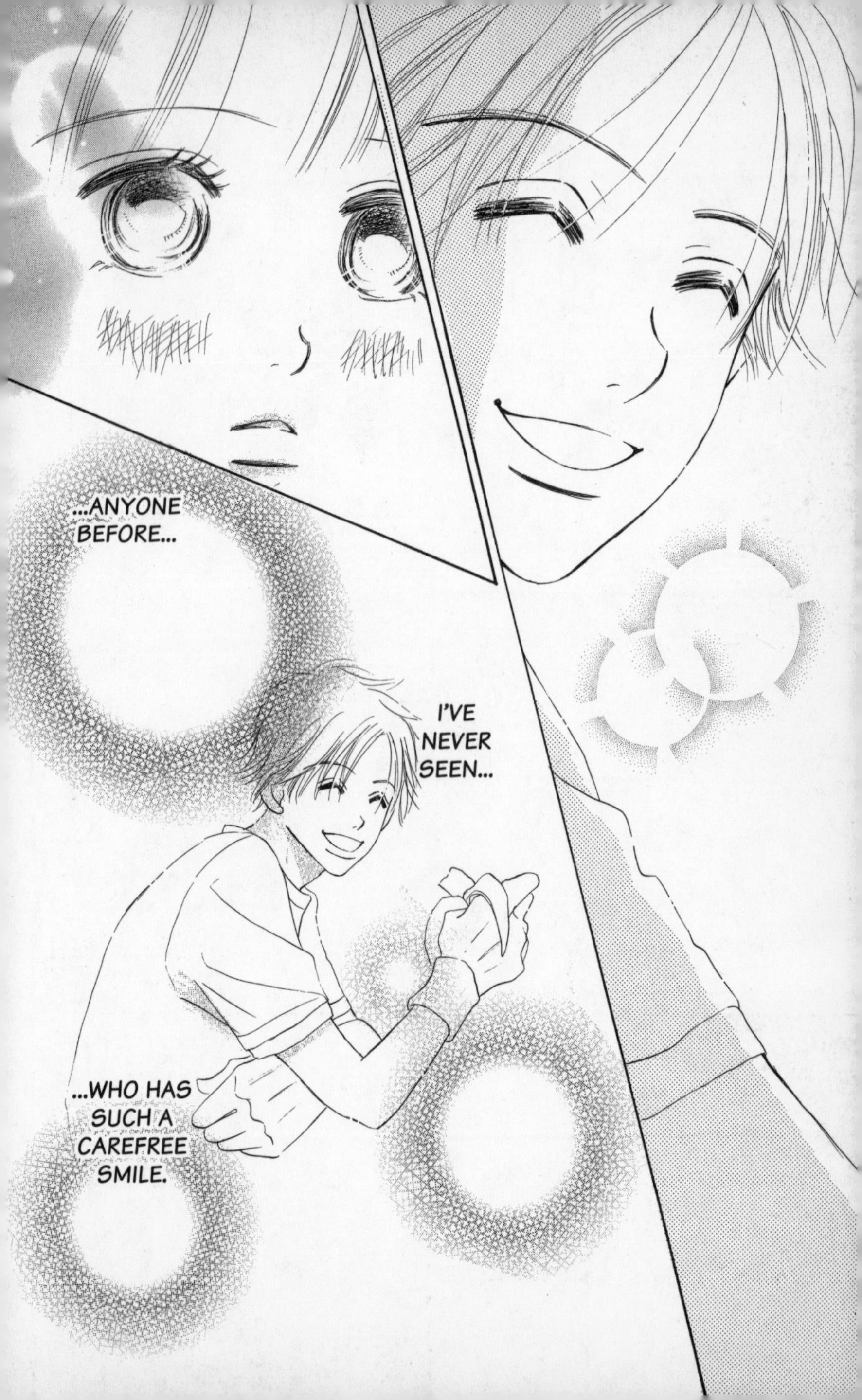
I'VE NEVER SEEN...
...ANYONE BEFORE...
...WHO HAS SUCH A CAREFREE SMILE.

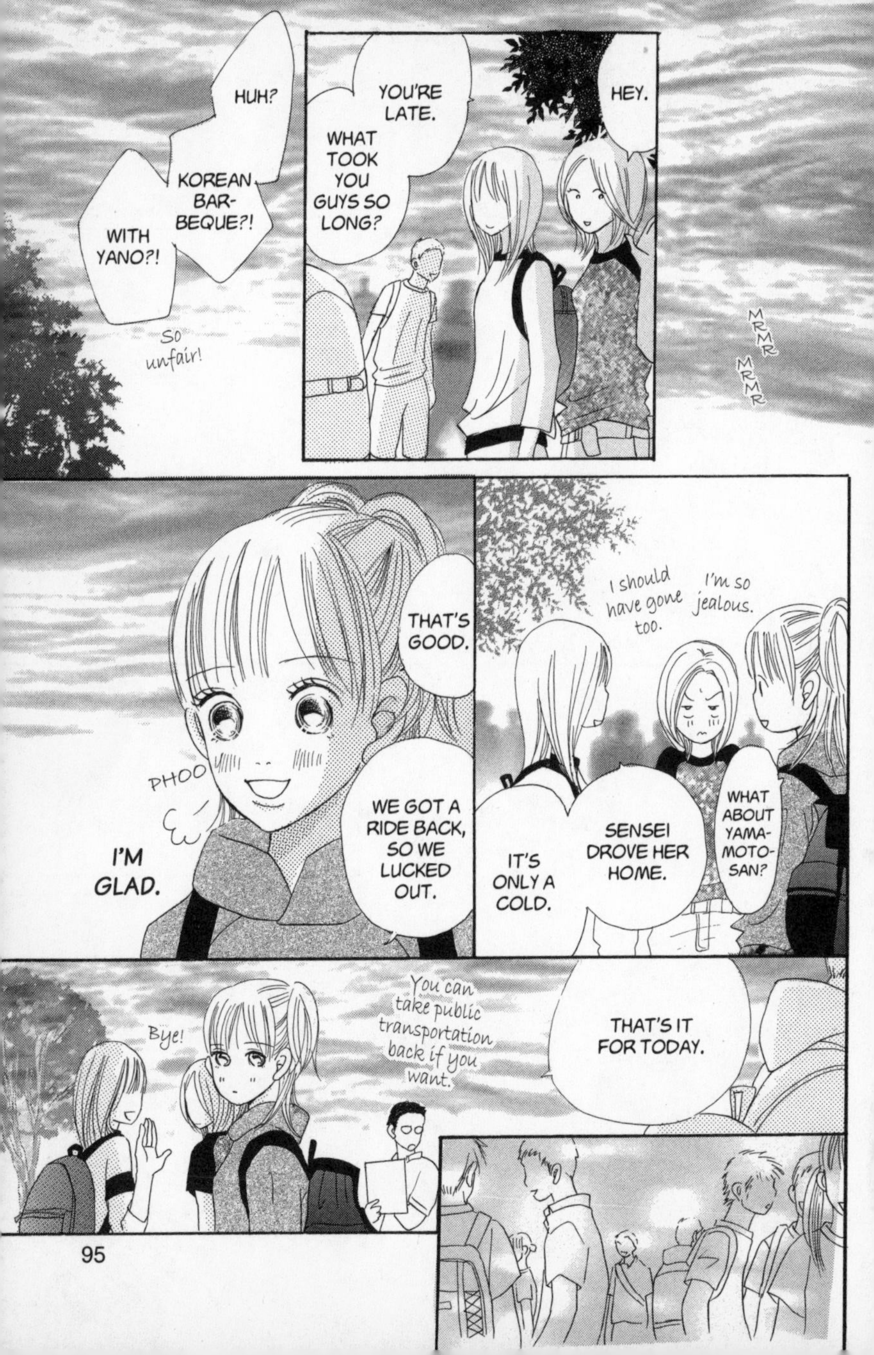
MRMR
MRMR
HEY.
YOU'RE LATE.
WHAT TOOK YOU GUYS SO LONG?
HUH?
KOREAN BAR-BEQUE?!
WITH YANO?!
So unfair!
I'm so jealous.
I should have gone too.
WHAT ABOUT YAMA-MOTO-SAN?
SENSEI DROVE HER HOME.
IT'S ONLY A COLD.
THAT'S GOOD.
WE GOT A RIDE BACK, SO WE LUCKED OUT.
PHOO
I'M GLAD.
THAT'S IT FOR TODAY.
You can take public transportation back if you want.
Bye!

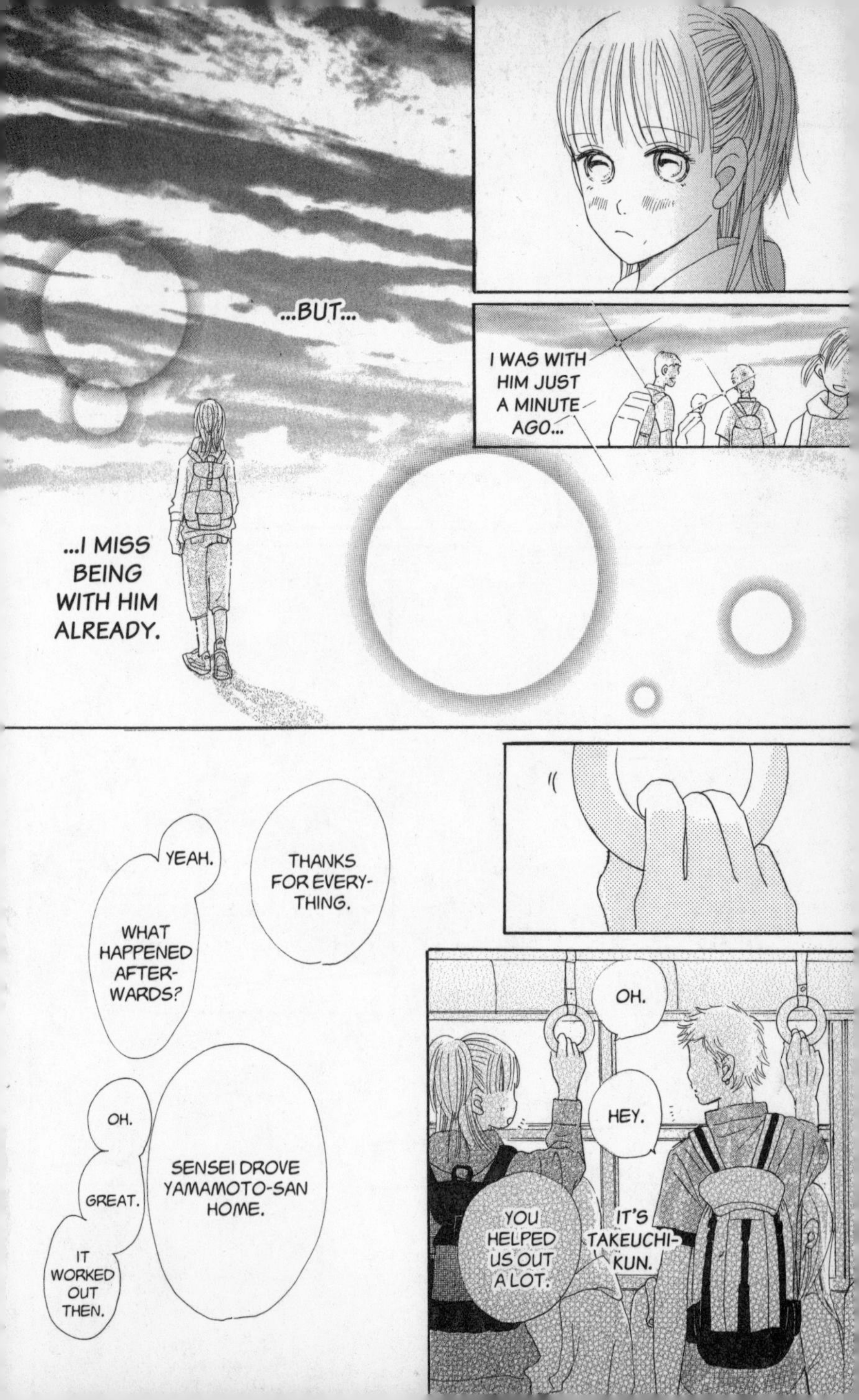
I WAS WITH HIM JUST A MINUTE AGO...
...BUT...
...I MISS BEING WITH HIM ALREADY.
OH.
HEY.
IT'S TAKEUCHI-KUN.
YOU HELPED US OUT A LOT.
THANKS FOR EVERYTHING.
YEAH.
WHAT HAPPENED AFTERWARDS?
SENSEI DROVE YAMAMOTO-SAN HOME.
OH.
GREAT.
IT WORKED OUT THEN.

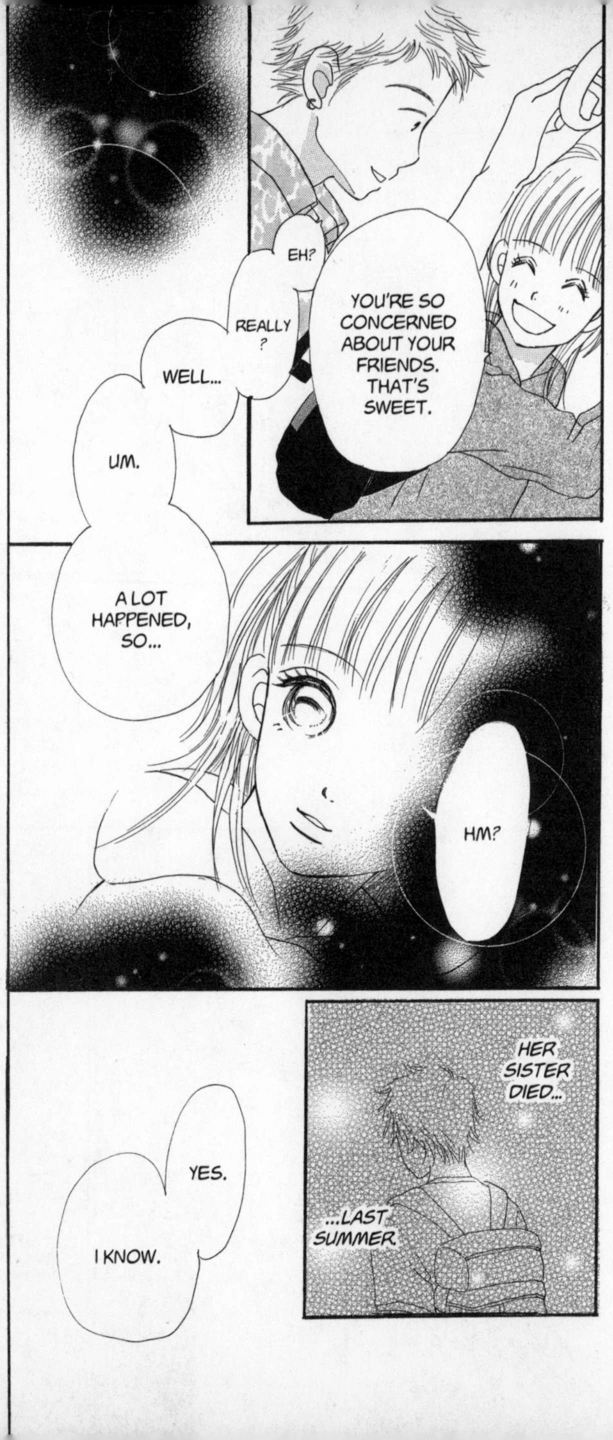
YOU'RE SO CONCERNED ABOUT YOUR FRIENDS. THAT'S SWEET.
EH?
REALLY?
WELL...
UM.
A LOT HAPPENED, SO...
HM?
HER SISTER DIED...
...LAST SUMMER.
YES.
I KNOW.

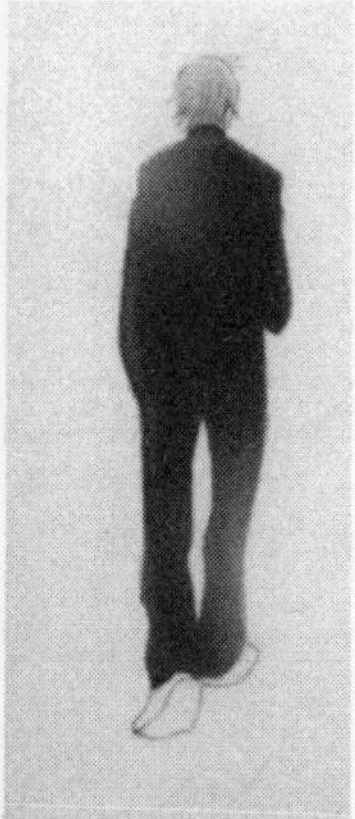

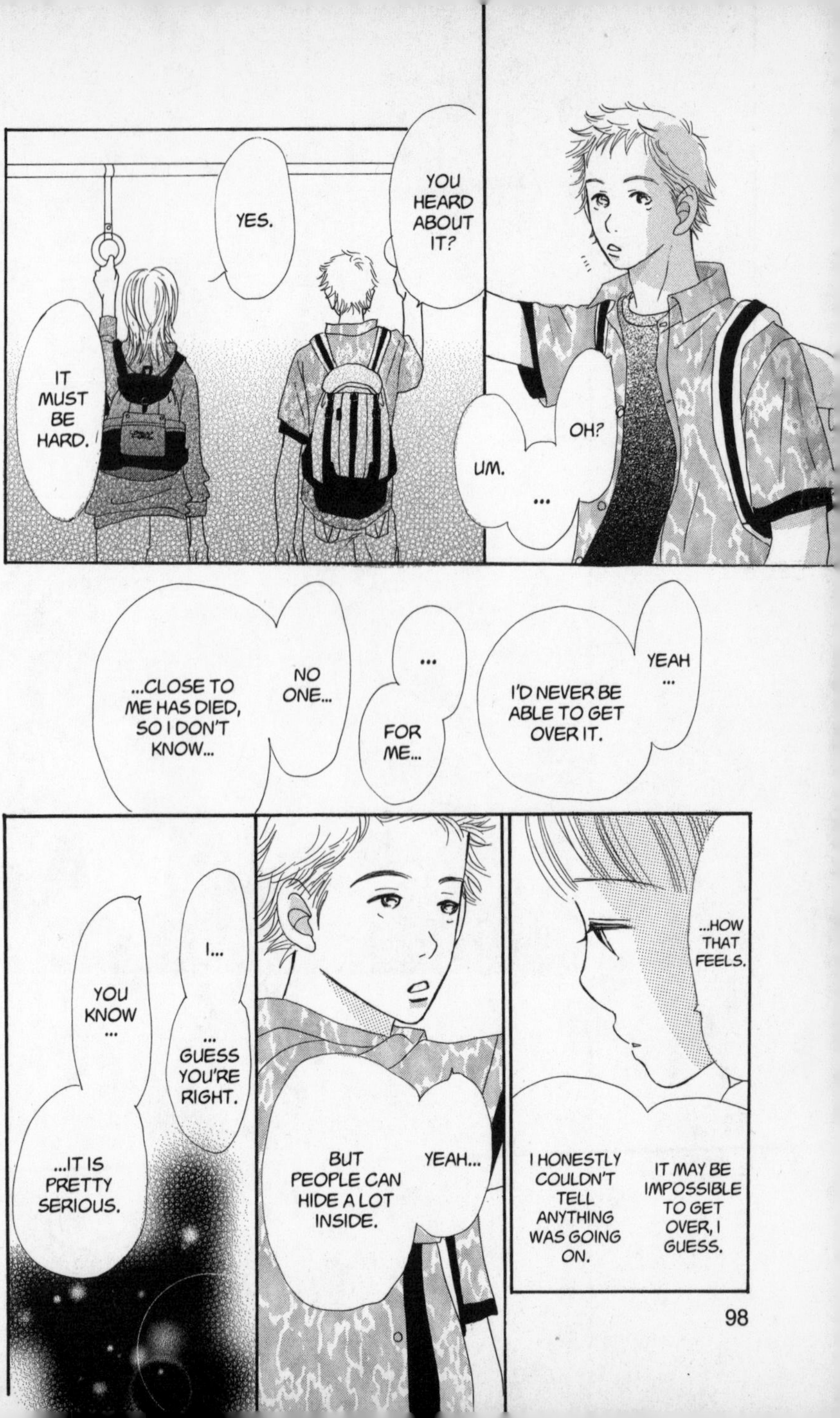
OH?
UM.
...
YOU HEARD ABOUT IT?
YES.
IT MUST BE HARD.
YEAH...
I'D NEVER BE ABLE TO GET OVER IT.
...
FOR ME...
NO ONE...
...CLOSE TO ME HAS DIED, SO I DON'T KNOW...
...HOW THAT FEELS.
IT MAY BE IMPOSSIBLE TO GET OVER, I GUESS.
I HONESTLY COULDN'T TELL ANYTHING WAS GOING ON.
YEAH...
BUT PEOPLE CAN HIDE A LOT INSIDE.
I...
...GUESS YOU'RE RIGHT.
YOU KNOW...
...IT IS PRETTY SERIOUS.

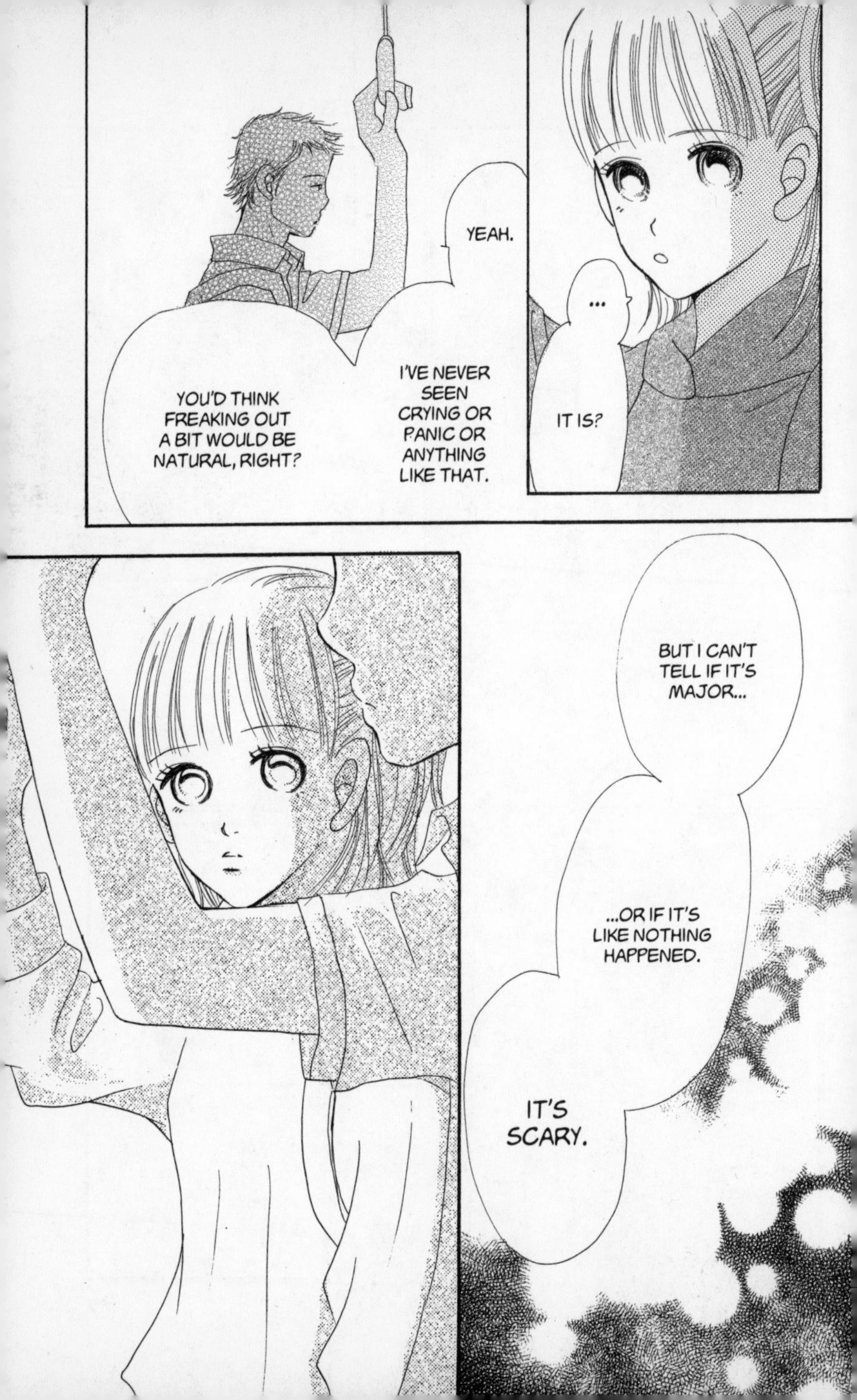
...
IT IS?
YEAH.
I'VE NEVER SEEN CRYING OR PANIC OR ANYTHING LIKE THAT.
YOU'D THINK FREAKING OUT A BIT WOULD BE NATURAL, RIGHT?
BUT I CAN'T TELL IF IT'S MAJOR...
...OR IF IT'S LIKE NOTHING HAPPENED.
IT'S SCARY.

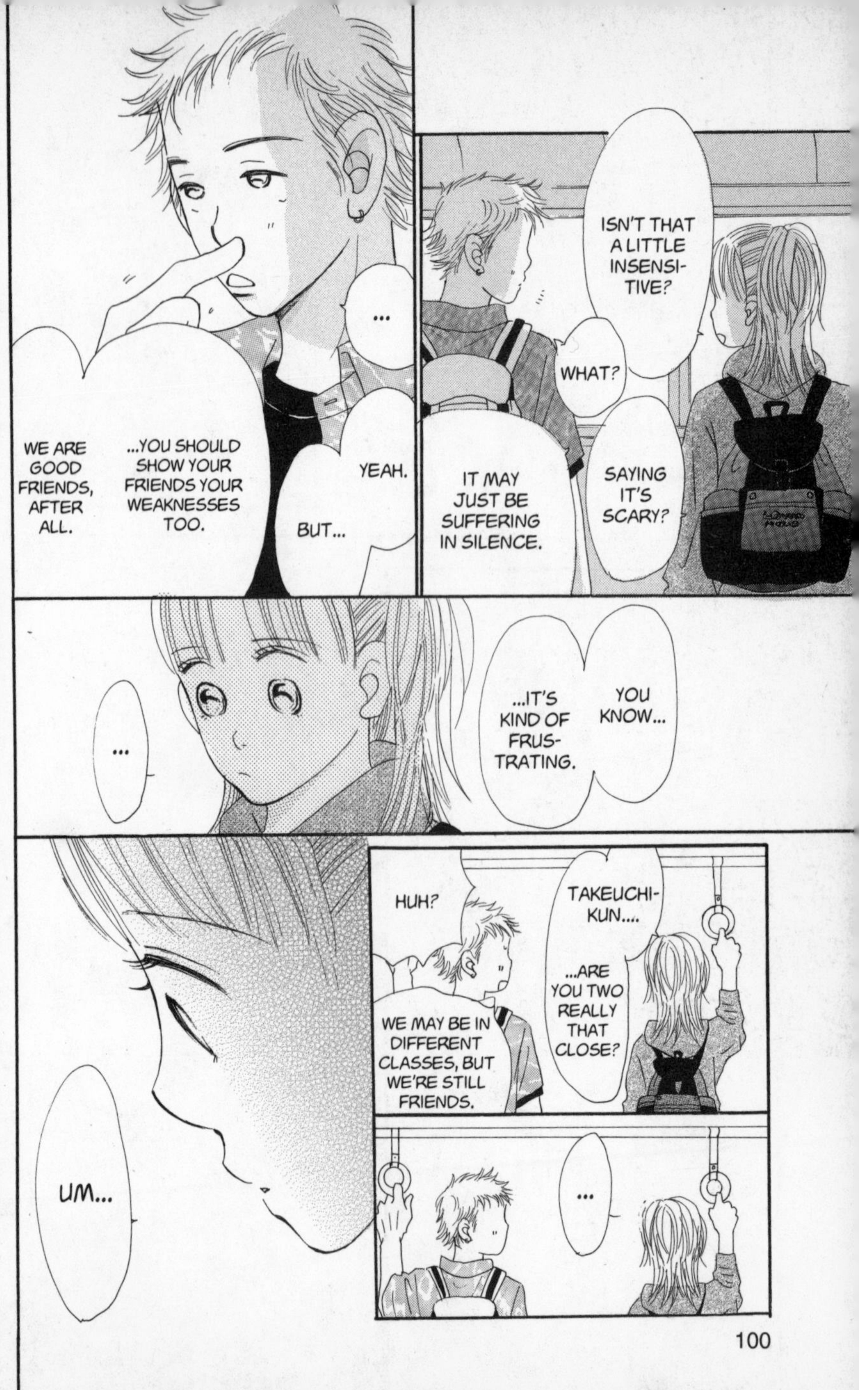
ISN'T THAT A LITTLE INSENSI-TIVE?
WHAT?
SAYING IT'S SCARY?
IT MAY JUST BE SUFFERING IN SILENCE.
...
YEAH.
BUT...
...YOU SHOULD SHOW YOUR FRIENDS YOUR WEAKNESSES TOO.
WE ARE GOOD FRIENDS, AFTER ALL.
YOU KNOW...
...IT'S KIND OF FRUS-TRATING.
...
TAKEUCHI-KUN....
...ARE YOU TWO REALLY THAT CLOSE?
HUH?
WE MAY BE IN DIFFERENT CLASSES, BUT WE'RE STILL FRIENDS.
...
UM...

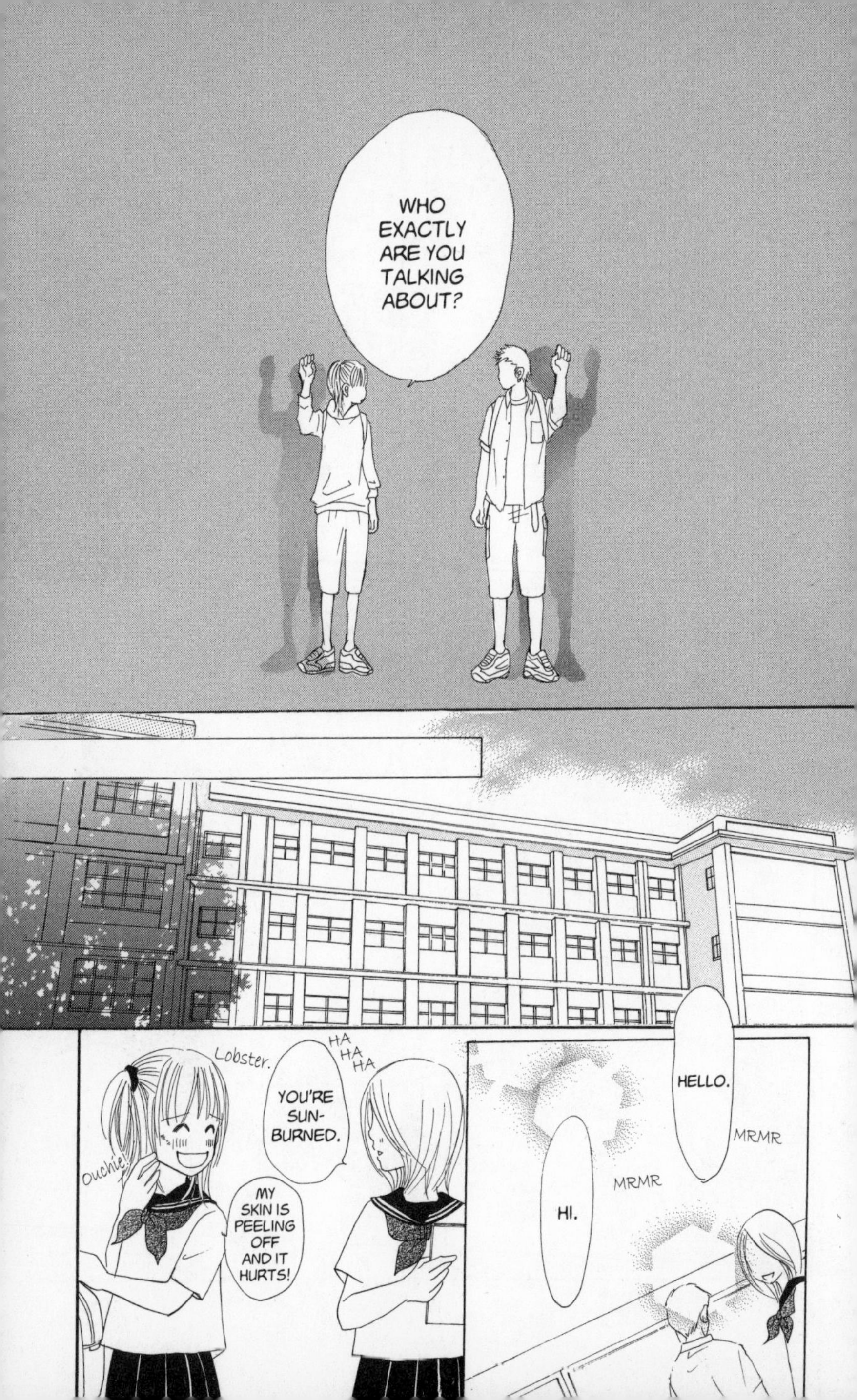
WHO EXACTLY ARE YOU TALKING ABOUT?
HELLO.
MRMR
HI.
MRMR
HA HA HA
YOU'RE SUN-BURNED.
Lobster.
Ouchie!
MY SKIN IS PEELING OFF AND IT HURTS!

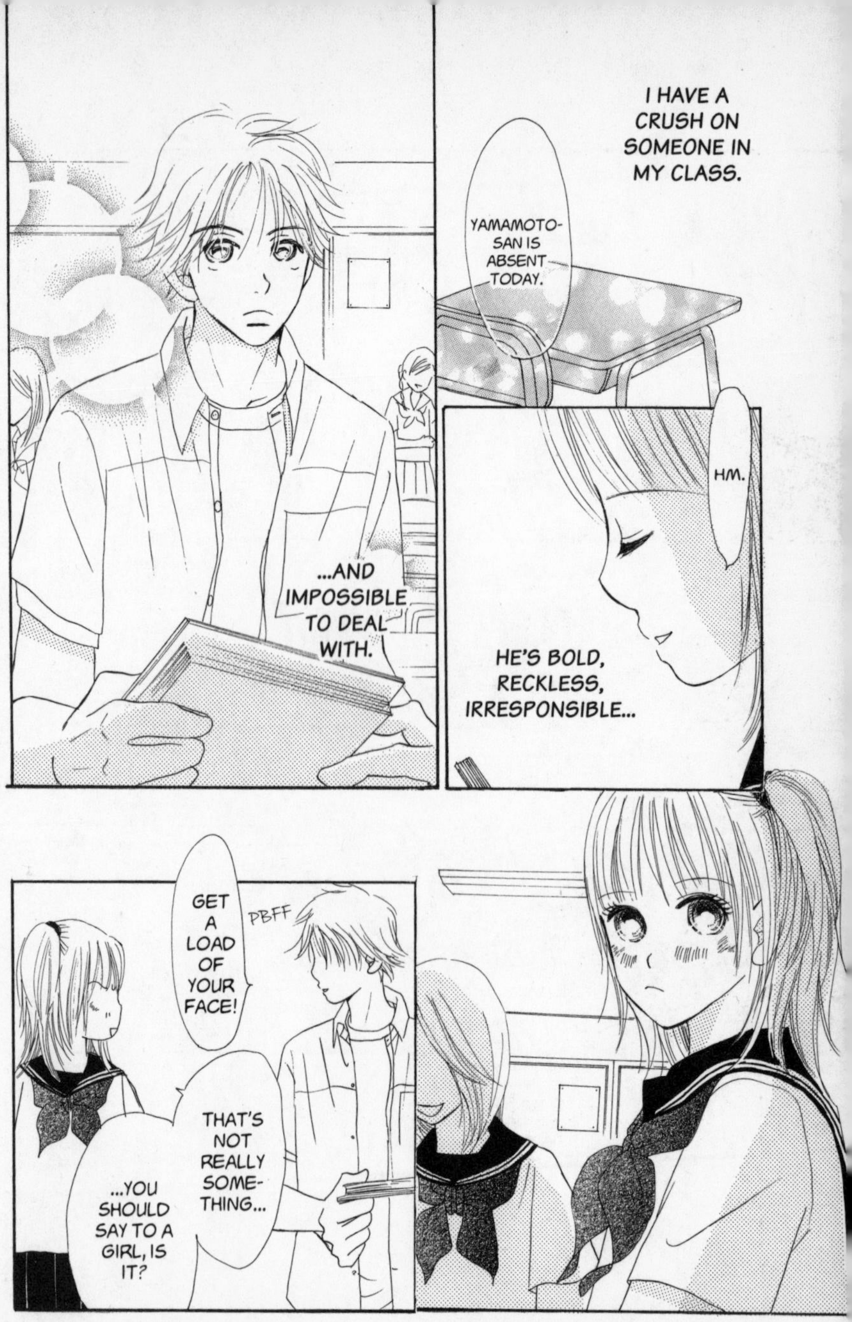
I HAVE A CRUSH ON SOMEONE IN MY CLASS.
YAMAMOTO-SAN IS ABSENT TODAY.
HM.
HE'S BOLD, RECKLESS, IRRESPONSIBLE...
...AND IMPOSSIBLE TO DEAL WITH.
GET A LOAD OF YOUR FACE!
PBFF
THAT'S NOT REALLY SOMETHING...
...YOU SHOULD SAY TO A GIRL, IS IT?

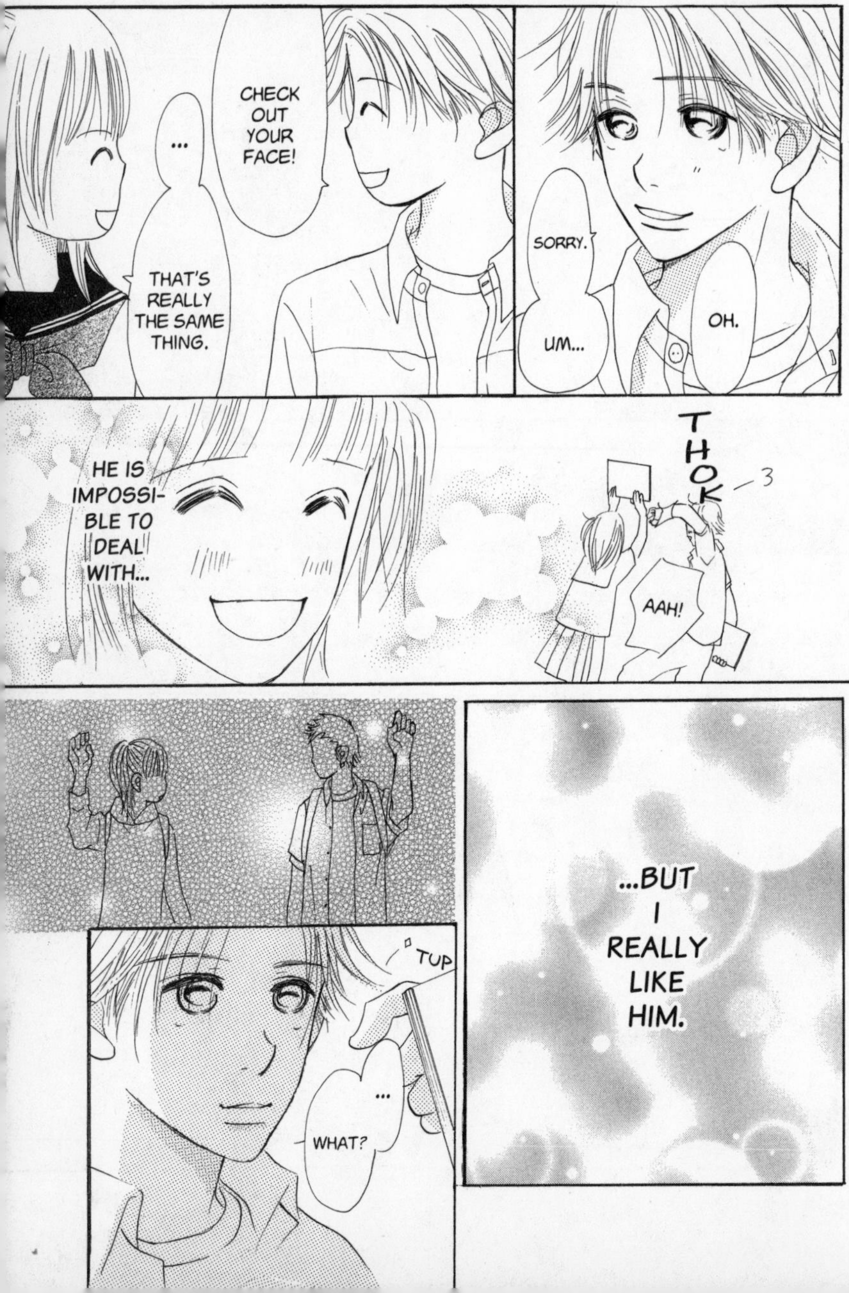
OH.
SORRY.
UM...
CHECK OUT YOUR FACE!
...
THAT'S REALLY THE SAME THING.
THOK
AAH!
HE IS IMPOSSI-BLE TO DEAL WITH...
...BUT I REALLY LIKE HIM.
TUP
...
WHAT?

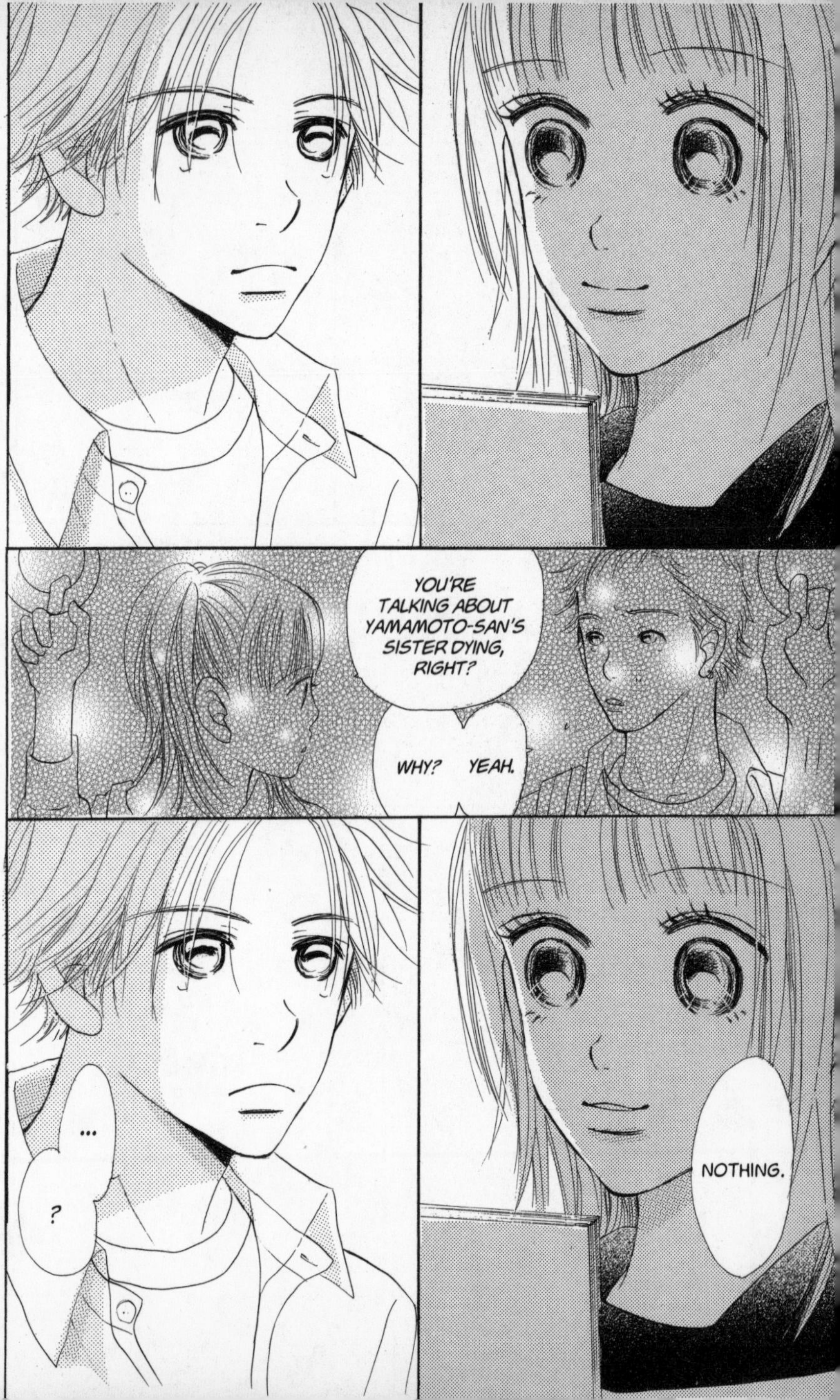
YOU'RE TALKING ABOUT YAMAMOTO-SAN'S SISTER DYING, RIGHT?
YEAH.
WHY?
NOTHING.
...
?

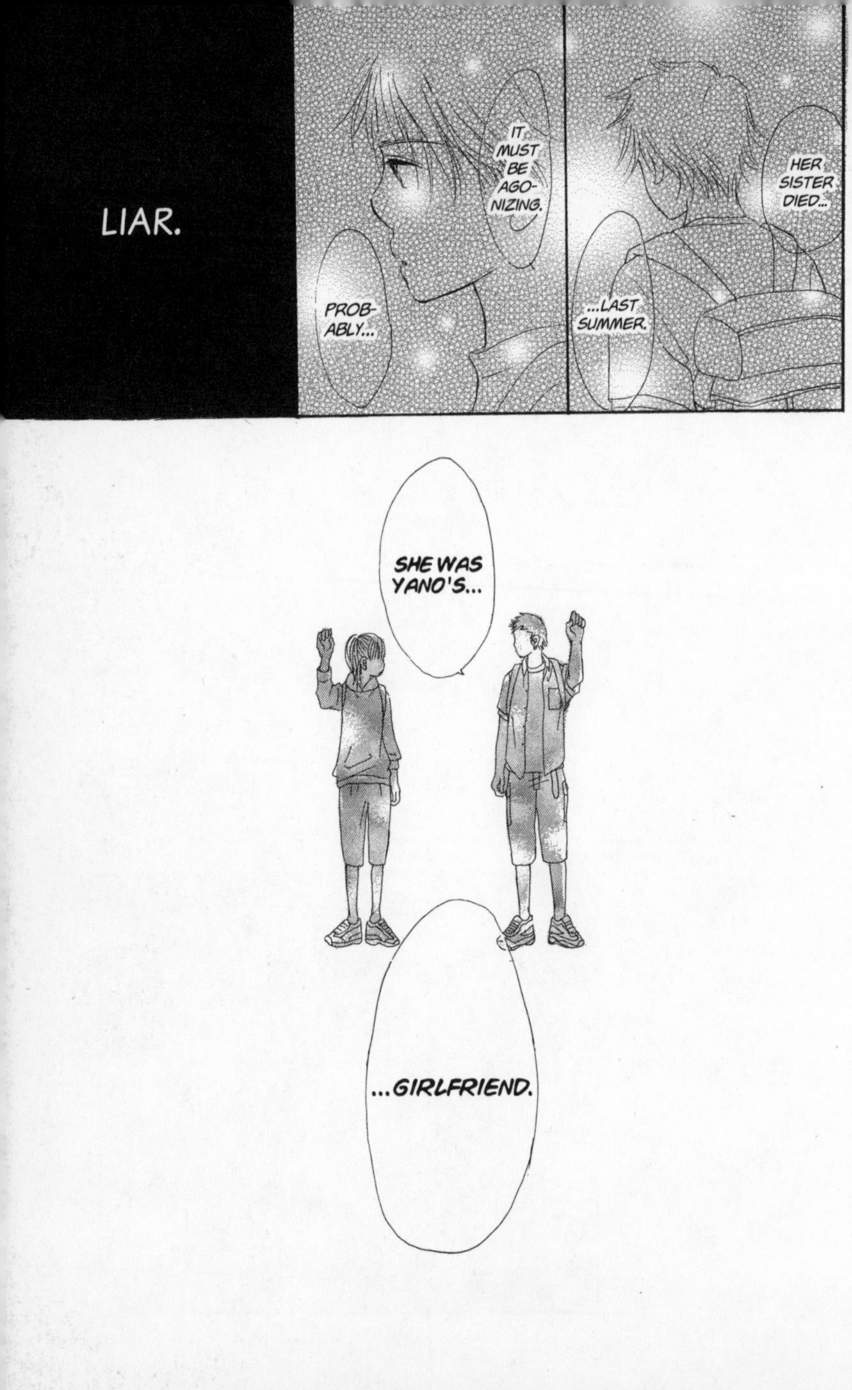
HER SISTER DIED...
...LAST SUMMER.
IT MUST BE AGO-NIZING.
PROB-ABLY...
LIAR.
SHE WAS YANO'S...
...GIRLFRIEND.

Chapter 3

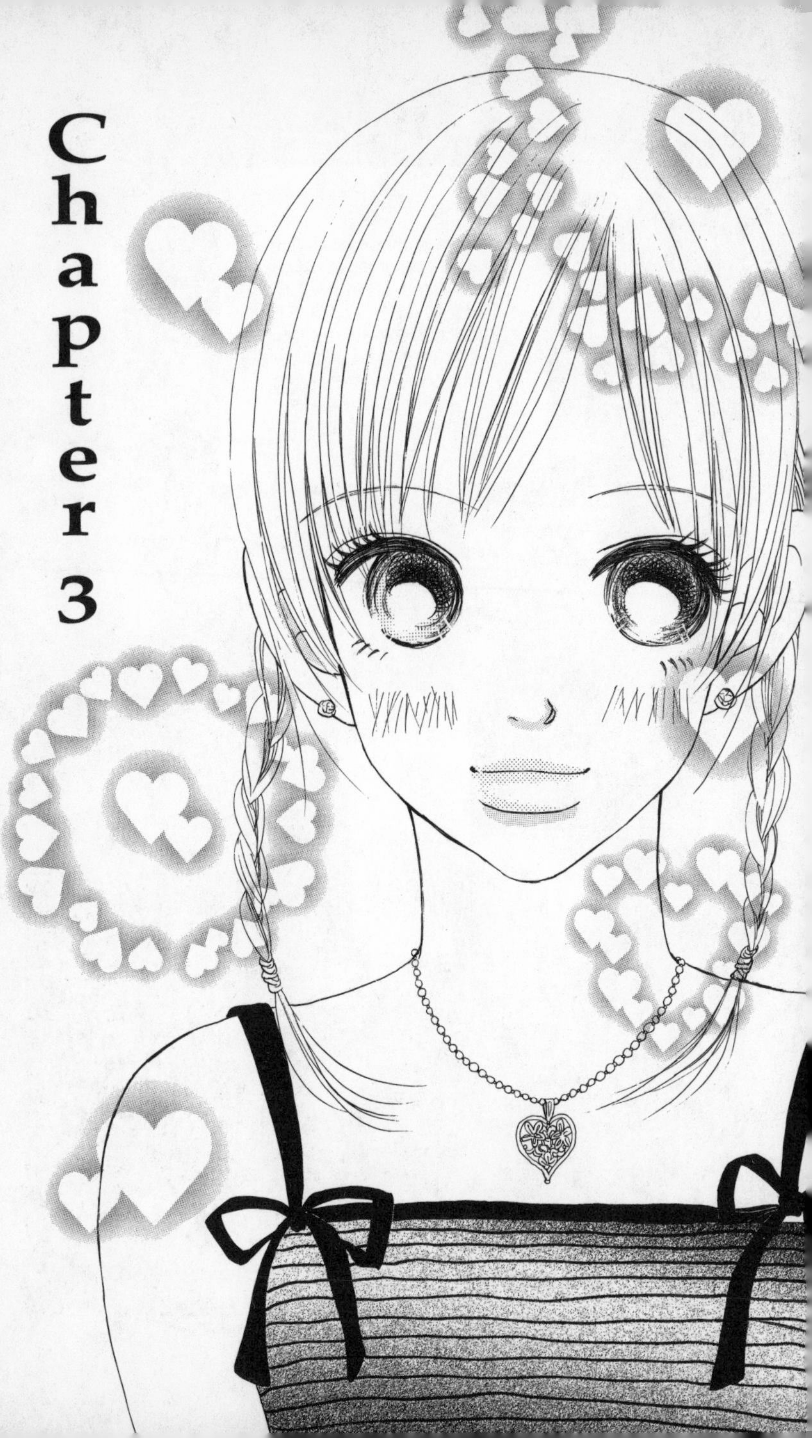

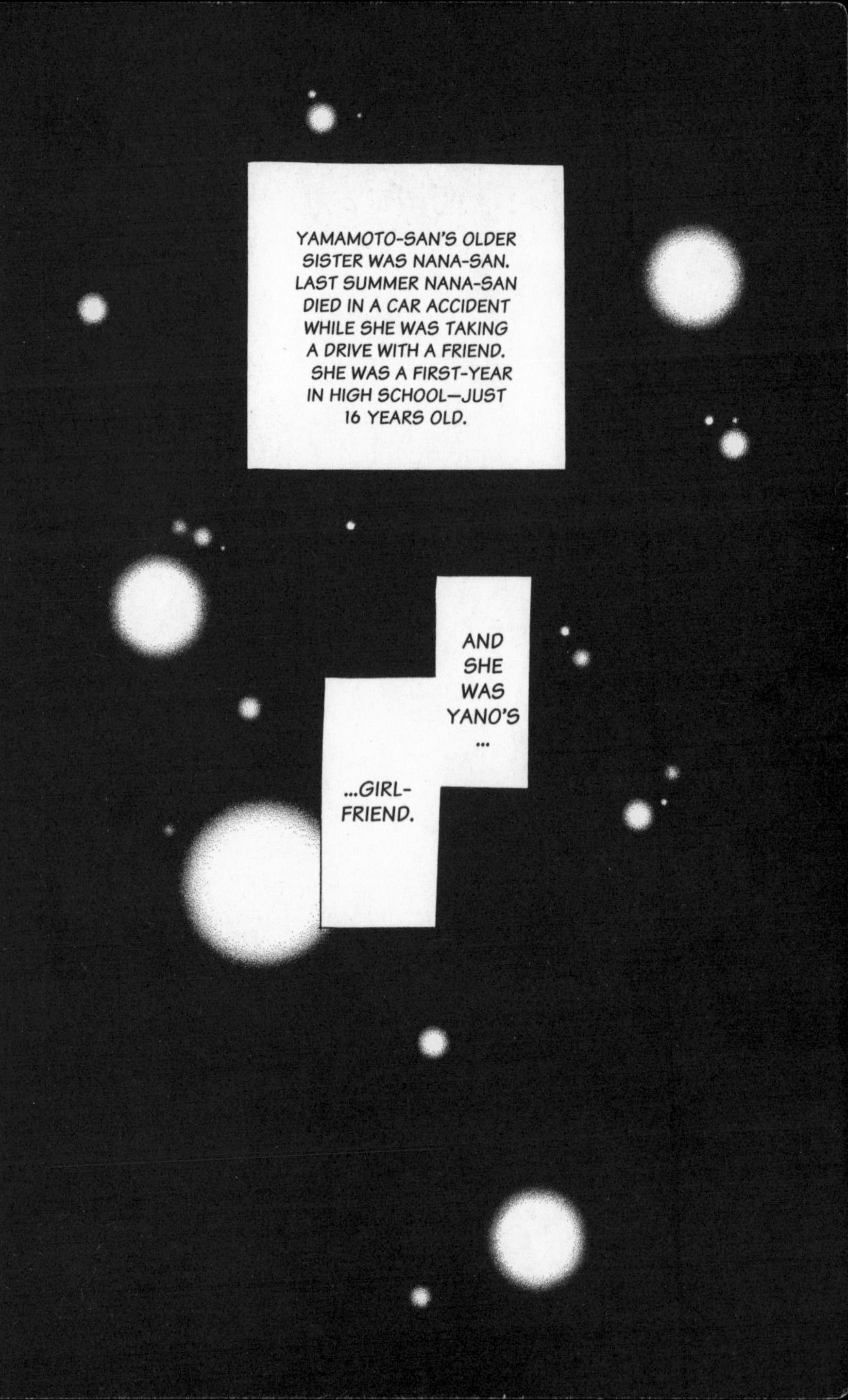
YAMAMOTO-SAN'S OLDER SISTER WAS NANA-SAN. LAST SUMMER NANA-SAN DIED IN A CAR ACCIDENT WHILE SHE WAS TAKING A DRIVE WITH A FRIEND. SHE WAS A FIRST-YEAR IN HIGH SCHOOL—JUST 16 YEARS OLD.
AND SHE WAS YANO'S ...
...GIRL-FRIEND.

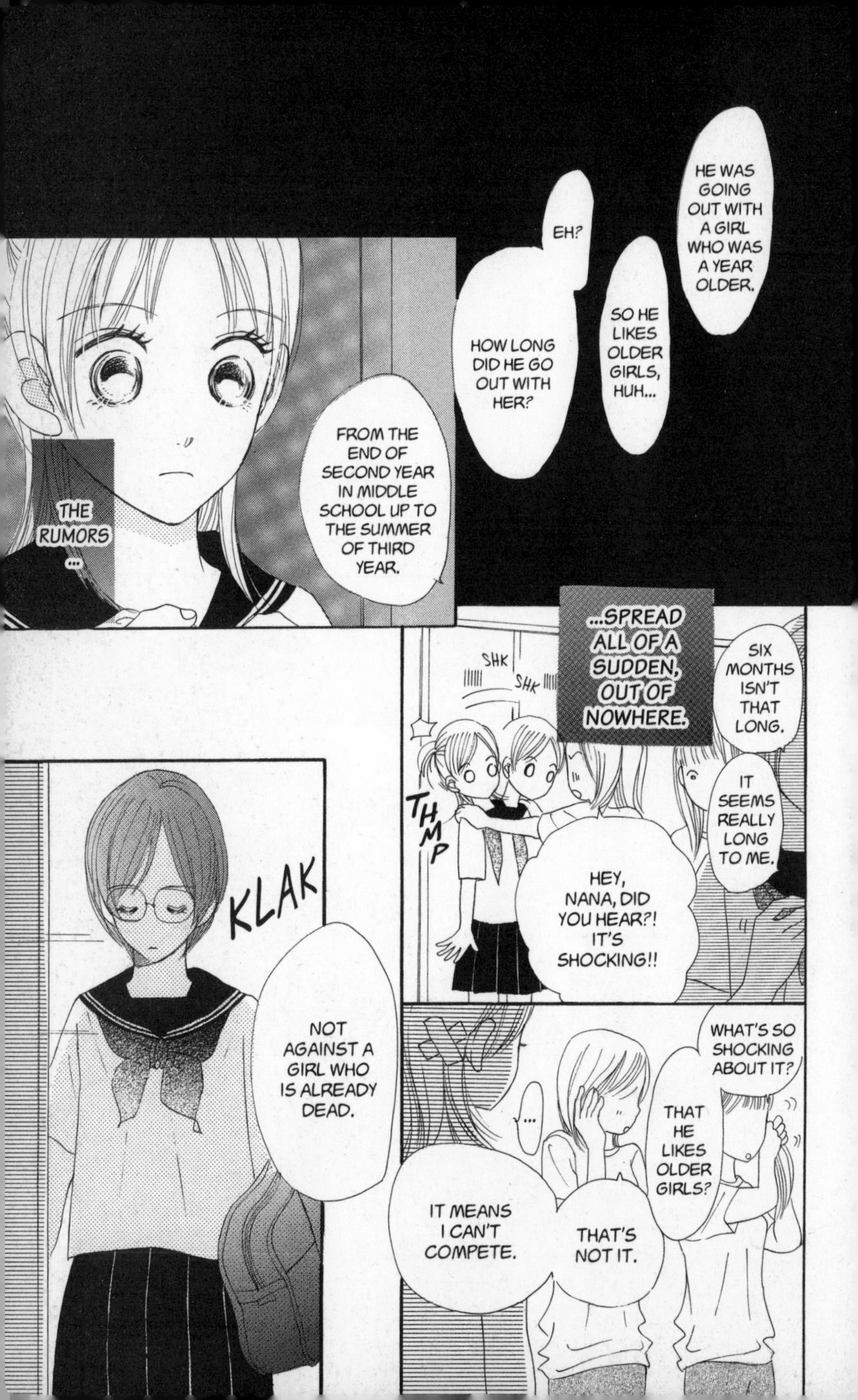
HE WAS GOING OUT WITH A GIRL WHO WAS A YEAR OLDER.
SO HE LIKES OLDER GIRLS, HUH...
EH?
HOW LONG DID HE GO OUT WITH HER?
FROM THE END OF SECOND YEAR IN MIDDLE SCHOOL UP TO THE SUMMER OF THIRD YEAR.
THE RUMORS ...
...SPREAD ALL OF A SUDDEN, OUT OF NOWHERE.
SIX MONTHS ISN'T THAT LONG.
IT SEEMS REALLY LONG TO ME.
SHK
SHK
THMP
HEY, NANA, DID YOU HEAR?! IT'S SHOCKING!!
WHAT'S SO SHOCKING ABOUT IT?
THAT HE LIKES OLDER GIRLS?
THAT'S NOT IT.
...
IT MEANS I CAN'T COMPETE.
KLAK
NOT AGAINST A GIRL WHO IS ALREADY DEAD.

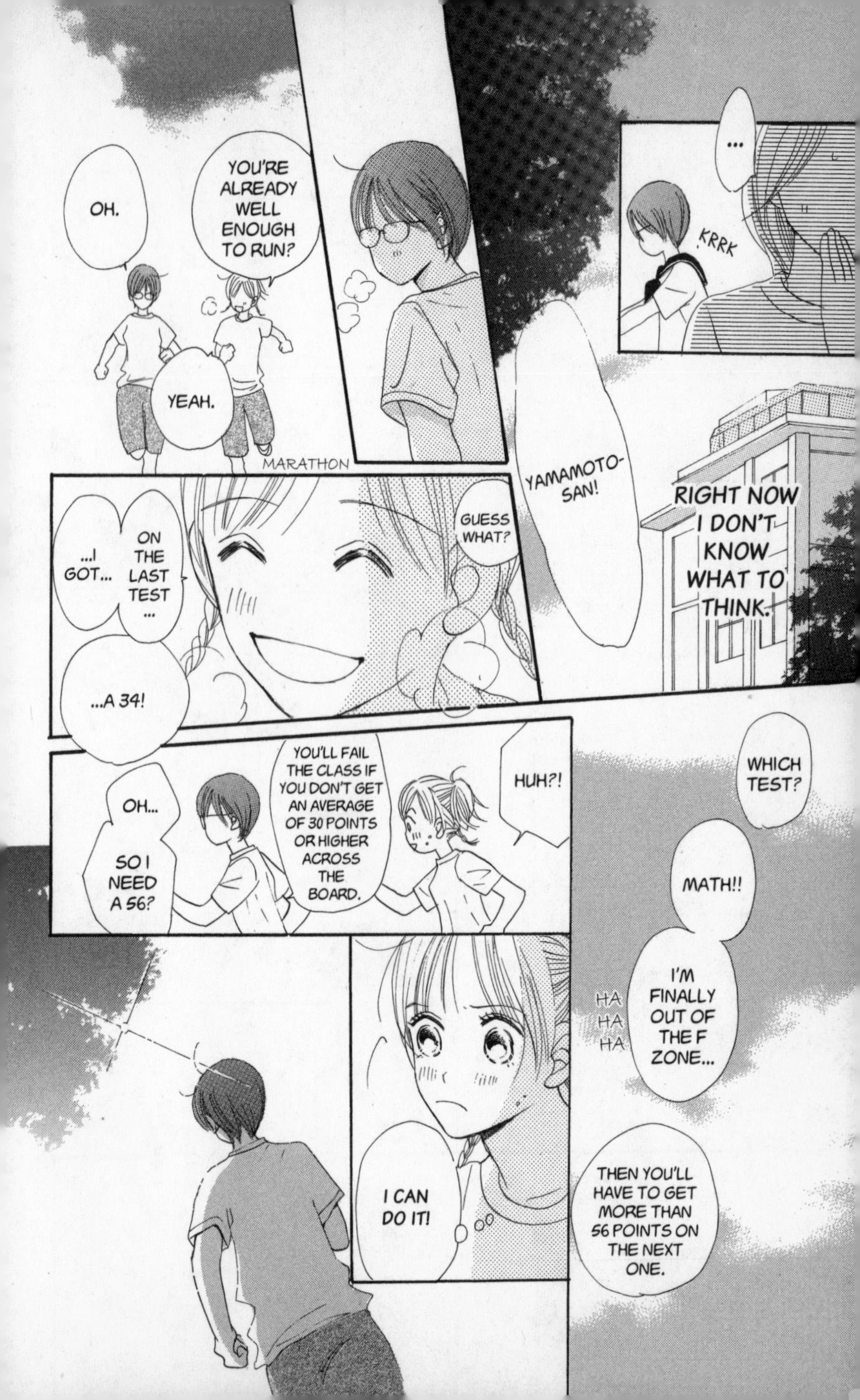
...
KRRK
RIGHT NOW I DON'T KNOW WHAT TO THINK.
YAMAMOTO-SAN!
YOU'RE ALREADY WELL ENOUGH TO RUN?
OH.
YEAH.
MARATHON
GUESS WHAT?
ON THE LAST TEST...
...I GOT...
...A 34!
WHICH TEST?
MATH!!
HA HA HA
I'M FINALLY OUT OF THE F ZONE...
HUH?!
YOU'LL FAIL THE CLASS IF YOU DON'T GET AN AVERAGE OF 30 POINTS OR HIGHER ACROSS THE BOARD.
OH...
SO I NEED A 56?
THEN YOU'LL HAVE TO GET MORE THAN 56 POINTS ON THE NEXT ONE.
I CAN DO IT!

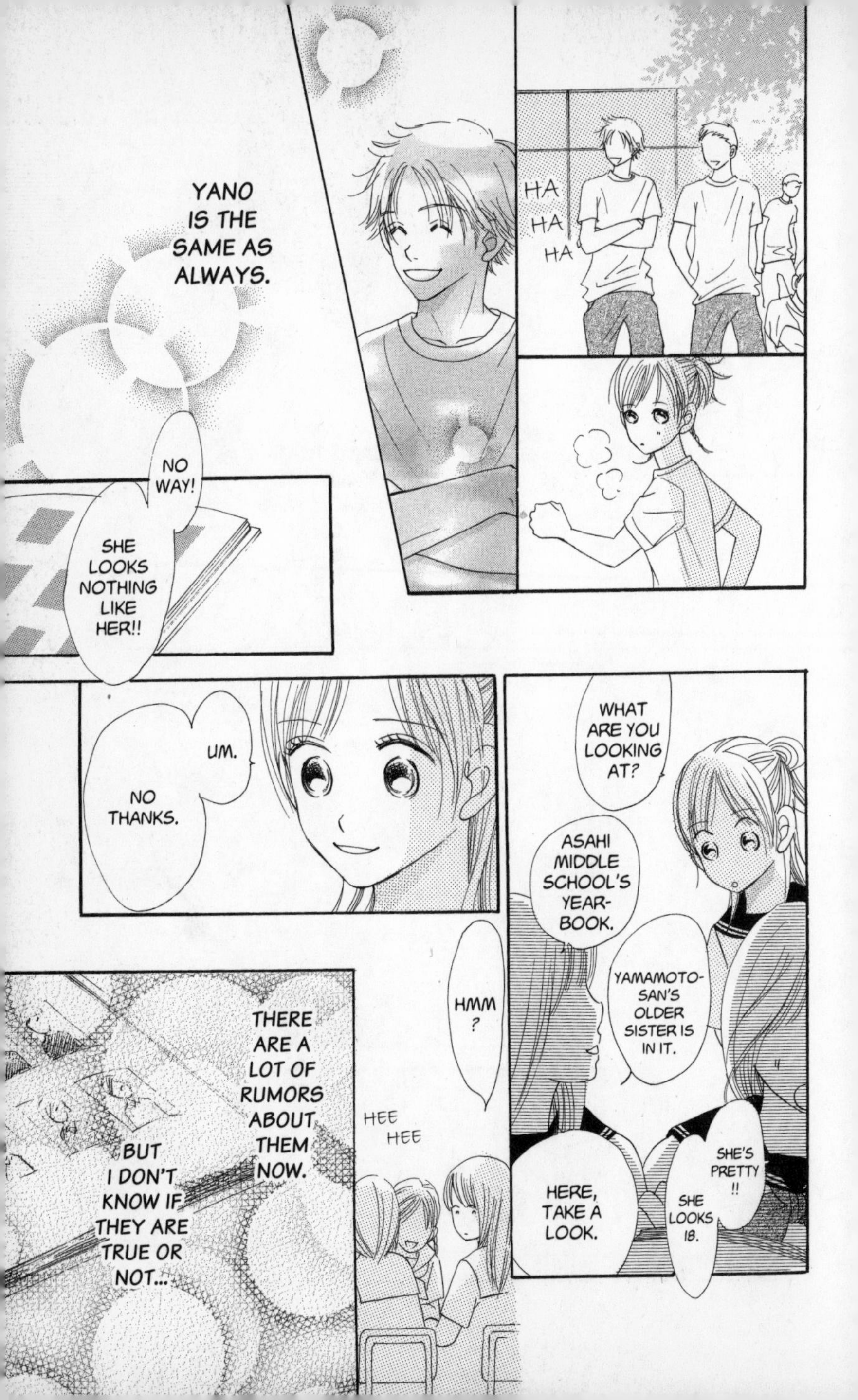
HA HA HA
YANO IS THE SAME AS ALWAYS.
WHAT ARE YOU LOOKING AT?
ASAHI MIDDLE SCHOOL'S YEAR-BOOK.
YAMAMOTO-SAN'S OLDER SISTER IS IN IT.
HERE, TAKE A LOOK.
SHE'S PRETTY!!
SHE LOOKS 18.
HMM?
HEE HEE
NO WAY!
SHE LOOKS NOTHING LIKE HER!!
UM.
NO THANKS.
THERE ARE A LOT OF RUMORS ABOUT THEM NOW.
BUT I DON'T KNOW IF THEY ARE TRUE OR NOT...

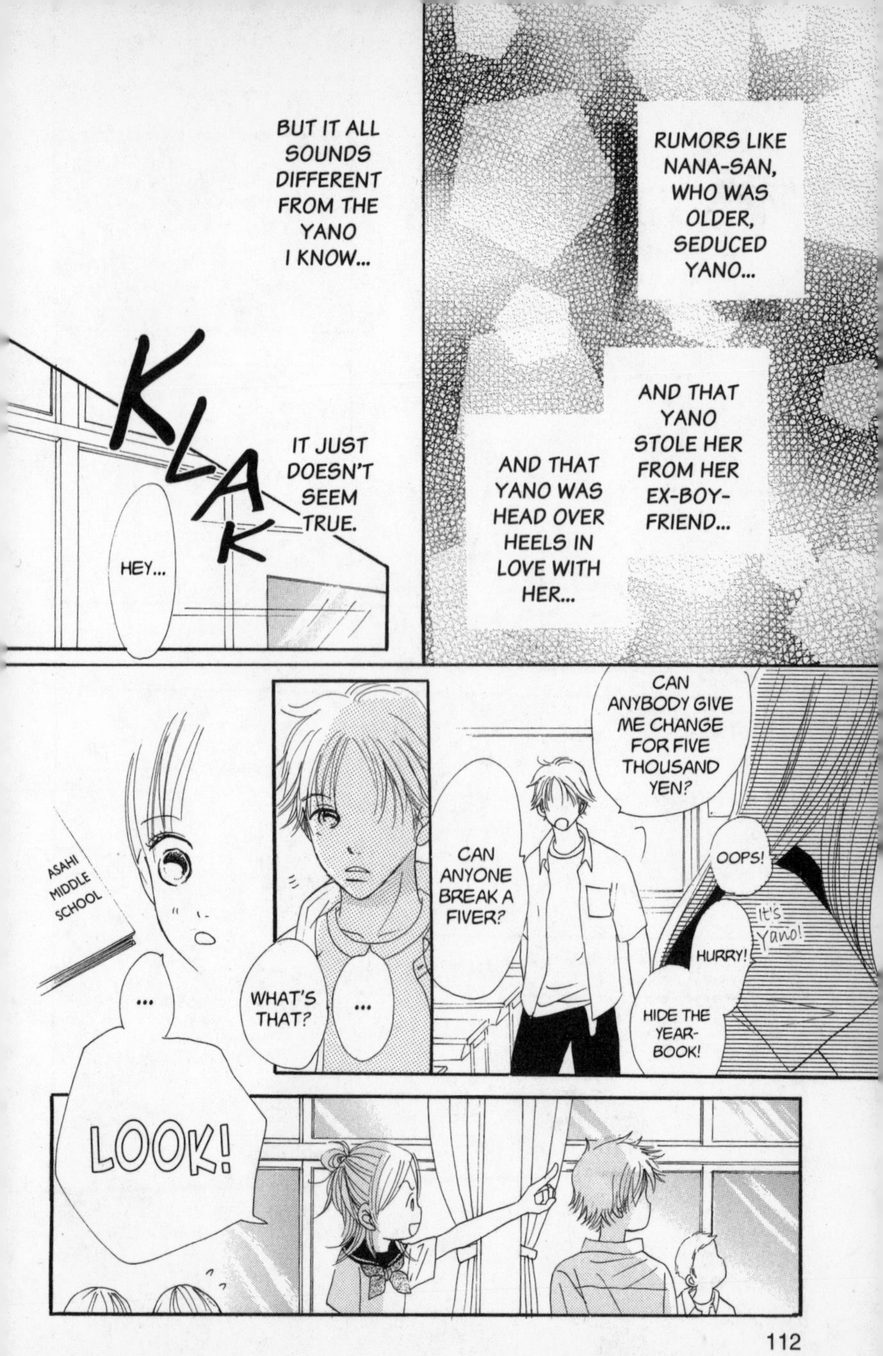
RUMORS LIKE NANA-SAN, WHO WAS OLDER, SEDUCED YANO...
AND THAT YANO STOLE HER FROM HER EX-BOY-FRIEND...
AND THAT YANO WAS HEAD OVER HEELS IN LOVE WITH HER...
BUT IT ALL SOUNDS DIFFERENT FROM THE YANO I KNOW...
IT JUST DOESN'T SEEM TRUE.
KLAK
HEY...
CAN ANYBODY GIVE ME CHANGE FOR FIVE THOUSAND YEN?
OOPS!
It's Yano!
HURRY!
HIDE THE YEAR-BOOK!
CAN ANYONE BREAK A FIVER?
...
WHAT'S THAT?
ASAHI MIDDLE SCHOOL
...
LOOK!

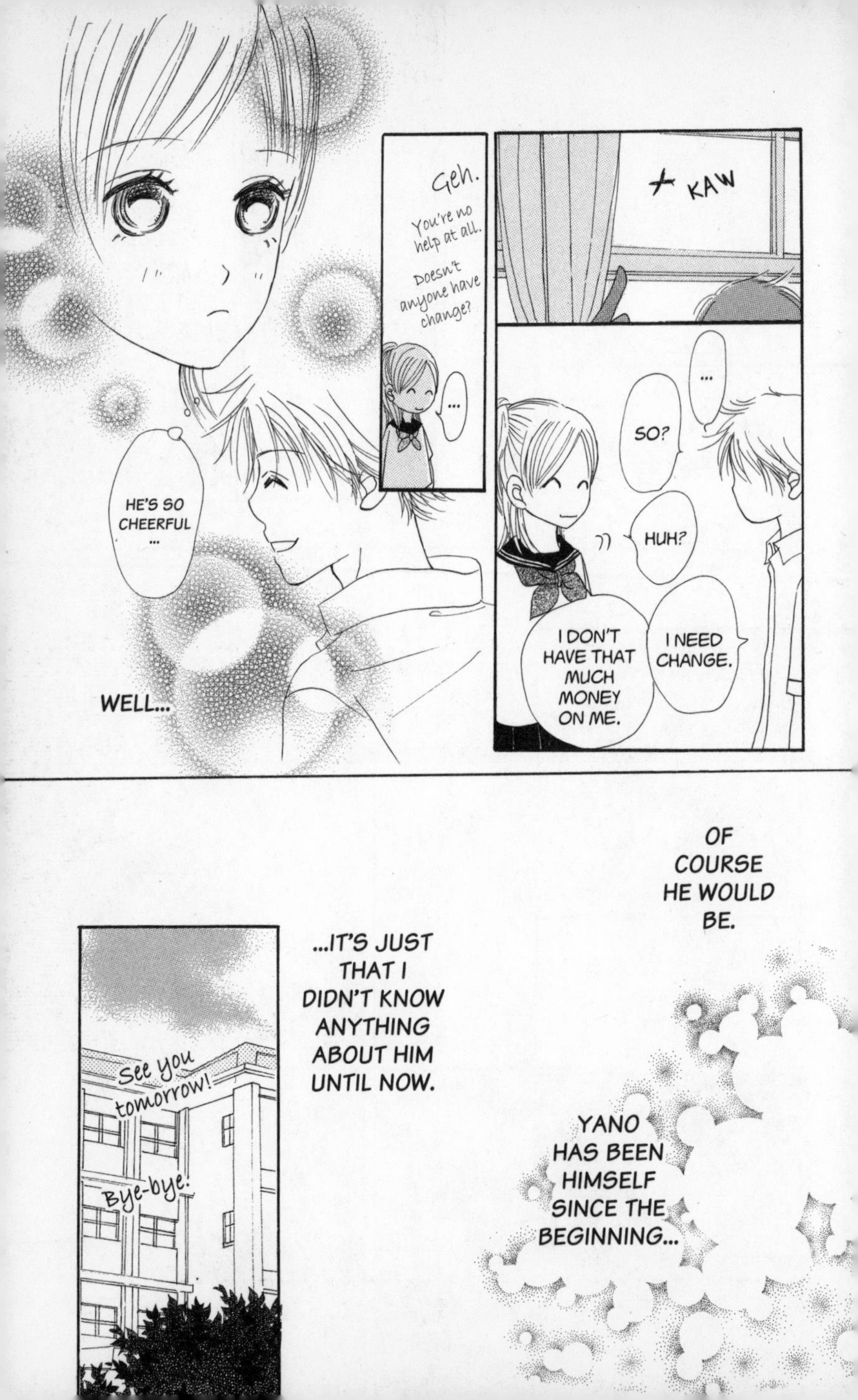
KAW
...
SO?
HUH?
I NEED CHANGE.
I DON'T HAVE THAT MUCH MONEY ON ME.
Geh.
You're no help at all.
Doesn't anyone have change?
...
HE'S SO CHEERFUL ...
WELL...
OF COURSE HE WOULD BE.
YANO HAS BEEN HIMSELF SINCE THE BEGINNING...
...IT'S JUST THAT I DIDN'T KNOW ANYTHING ABOUT HIM UNTIL NOW.
See you tomorrow!
Bye-bye!

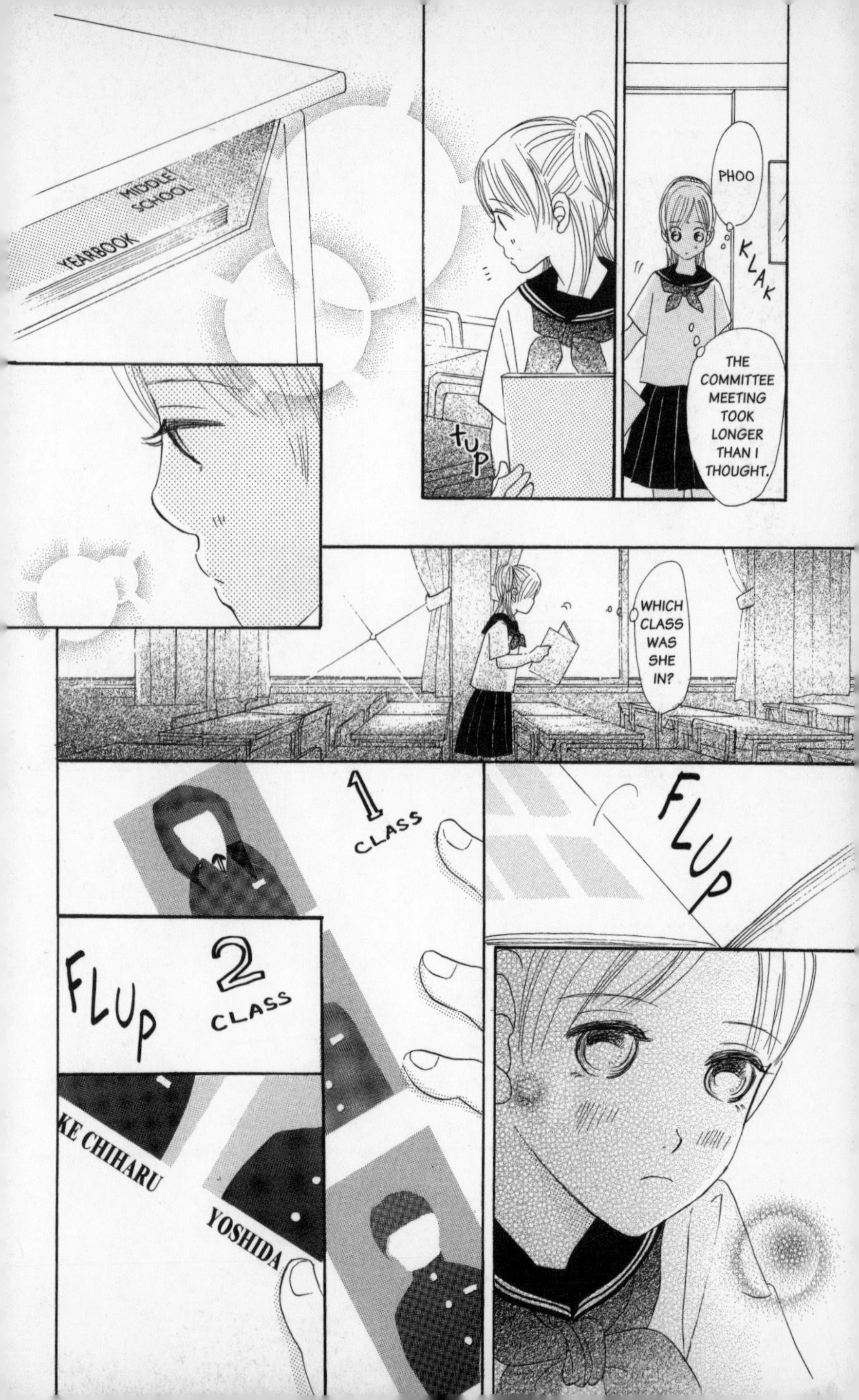
PHOO
KLAK
THE COMMITTEE MEETING TOOK LONGER THAN I THOUGHT.
TUP
MIDDLE SCHOOL
YEARBOOK
WHICH CLASS WAS SHE IN?
FLUP
1 CLASS
2 CLASS
FLUP
KE CHIHARU
YOSHIDA

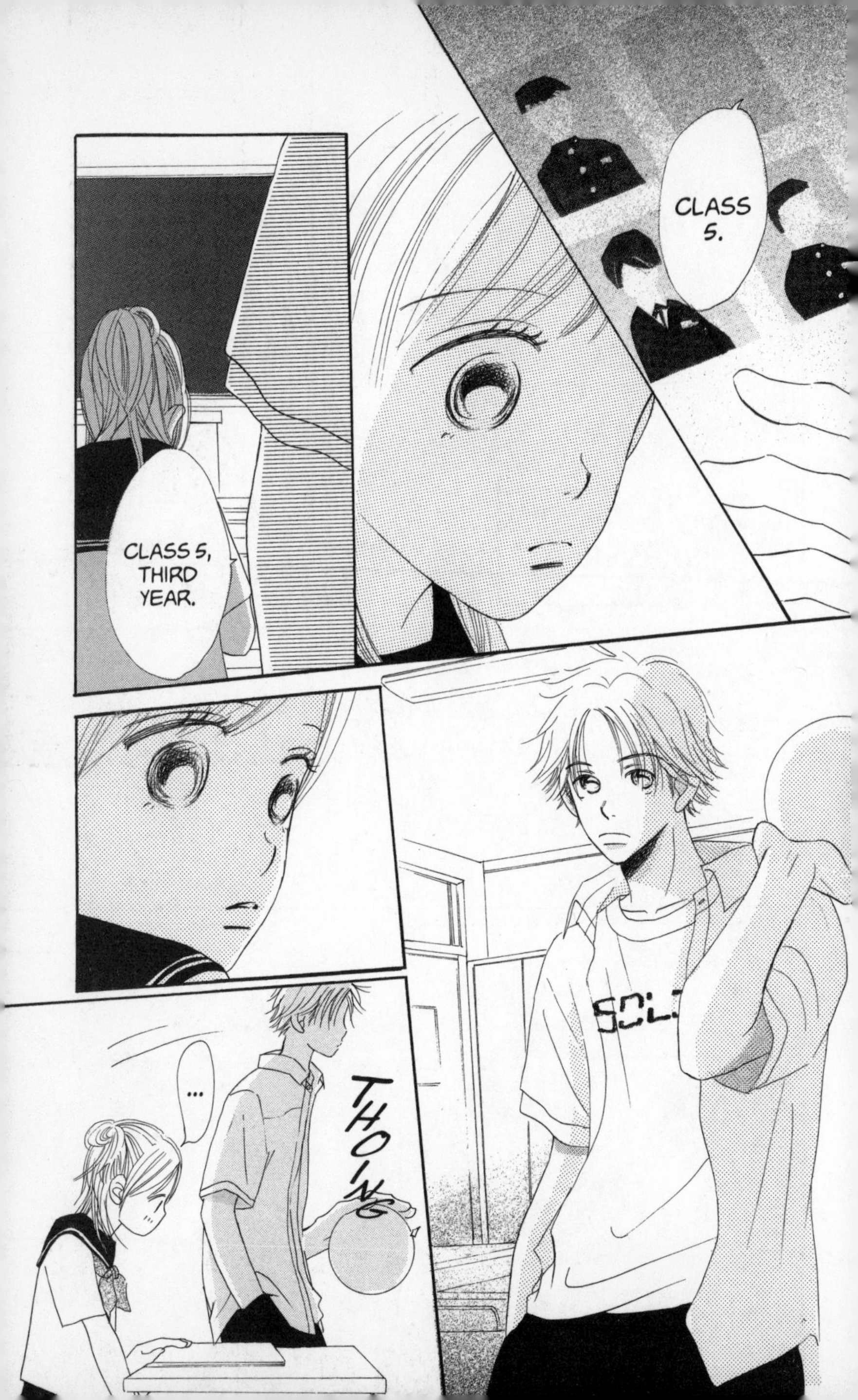
CLASS 5.
CLASS 5, THIRD YEAR.
...
THOING

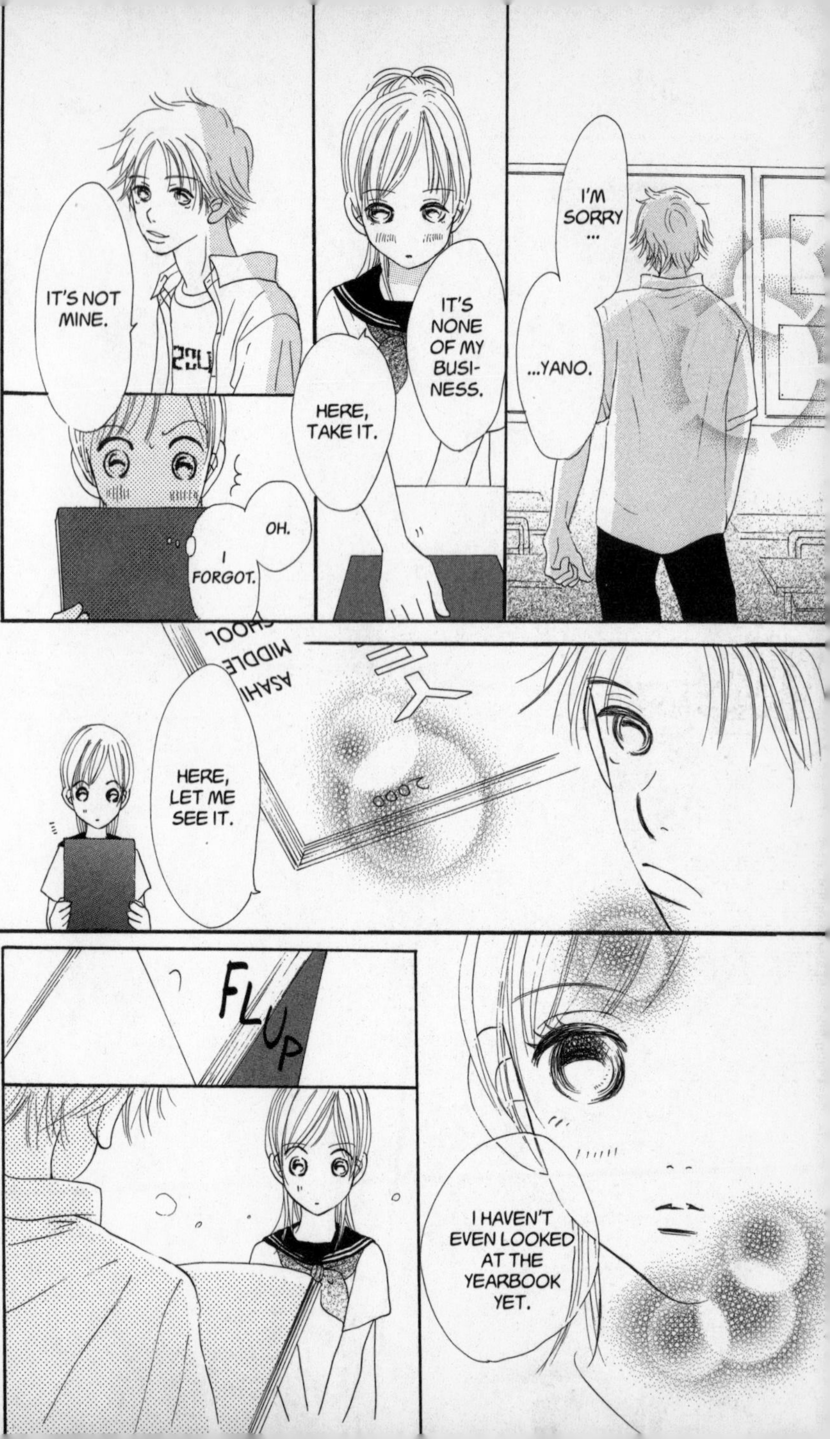
I'M SORRY...
...YANO.
IT'S NONE OF MY BUSINESS.
HERE, TAKE IT.
IT'S NOT MINE.
OH. I FORGOT.
ASAHI MIDDLE
HERE, LET ME SEE IT.
I HAVEN'T EVEN LOOKED AT THE YEARBOOK YET.
FLUP

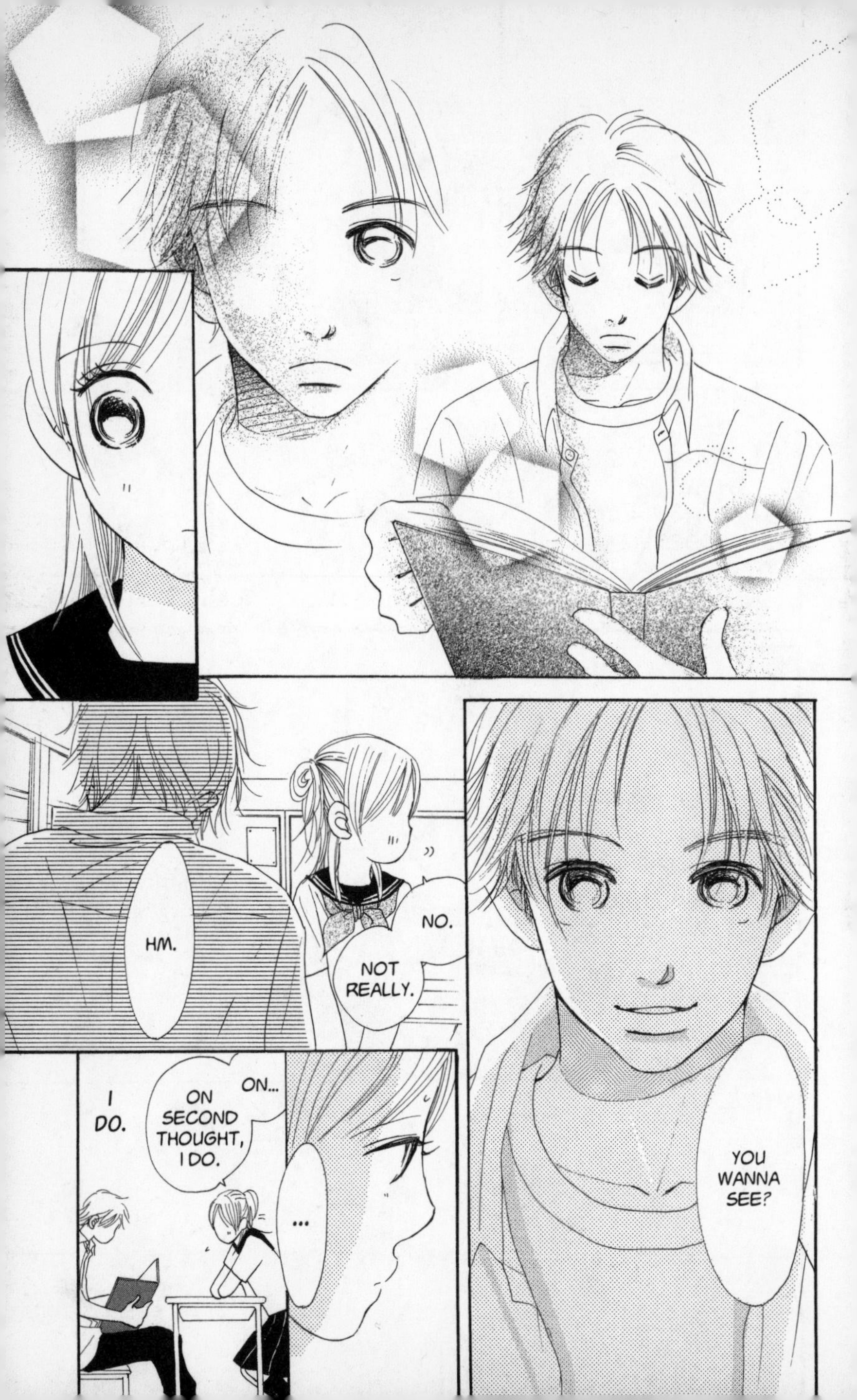
YOU WANNA SEE?
NO.
NOT REALLY.
HM.
ON...
ON SECOND THOUGHT, I DO.
I DO.
...

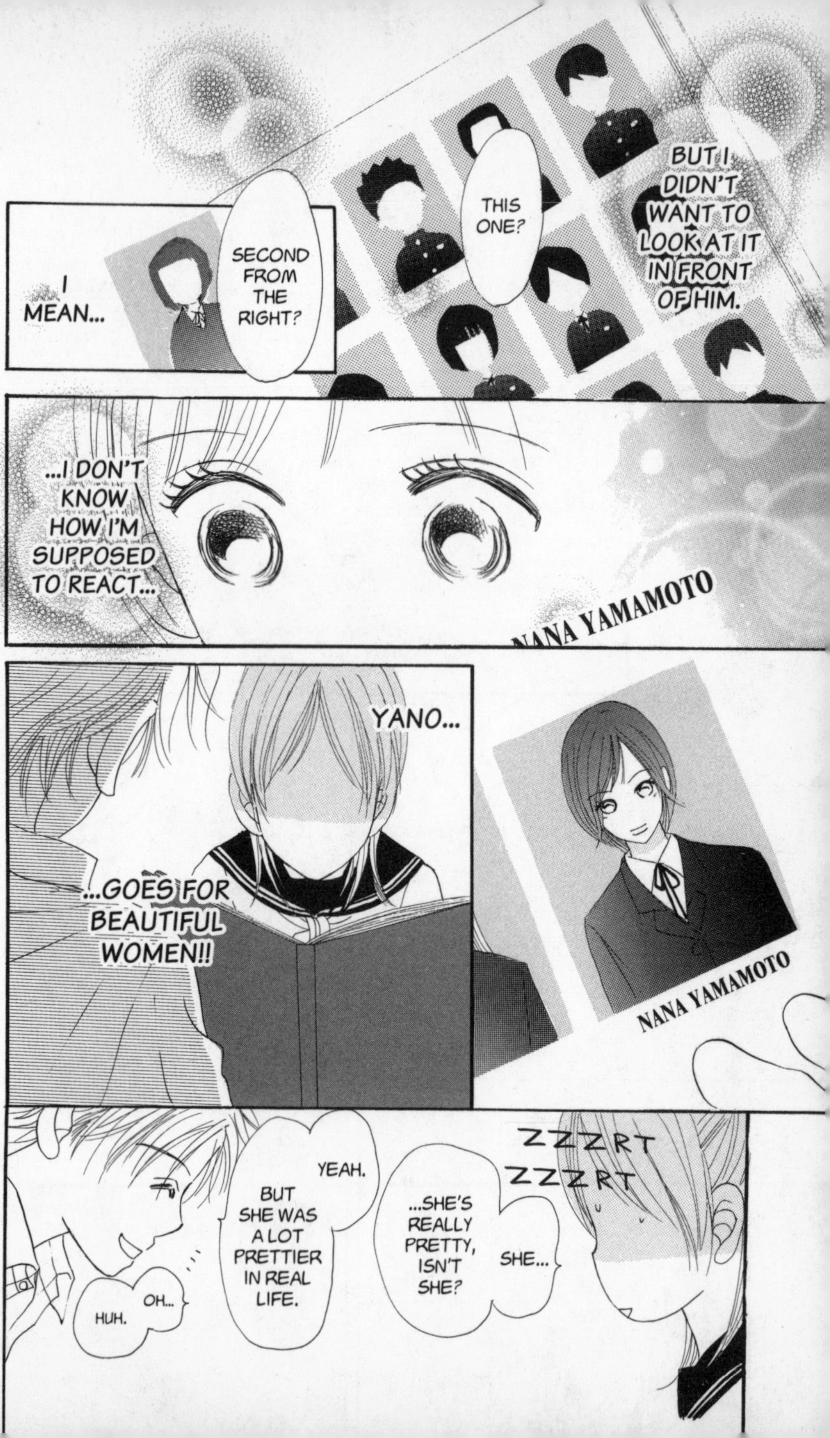
BUT I DIDN'T WANT TO LOOK AT IT IN FRONT OF HIM.
THIS ONE?
SECOND FROM THE RIGHT?
I MEAN...
NANA YAMAMOTO
...I DON'T KNOW HOW I'M SUPPOSED TO REACT...
NANA YAMAMOTO
YANO...
...GOES FOR BEAUTIFUL WOMEN!!
ZZZRT
ZZZRT
SHE...
...SHE'S REALLY PRETTY, ISN'T SHE?
YEAH.
BUT SHE WAS A LOT PRETTIER IN REAL LIFE.
OH... HUH.

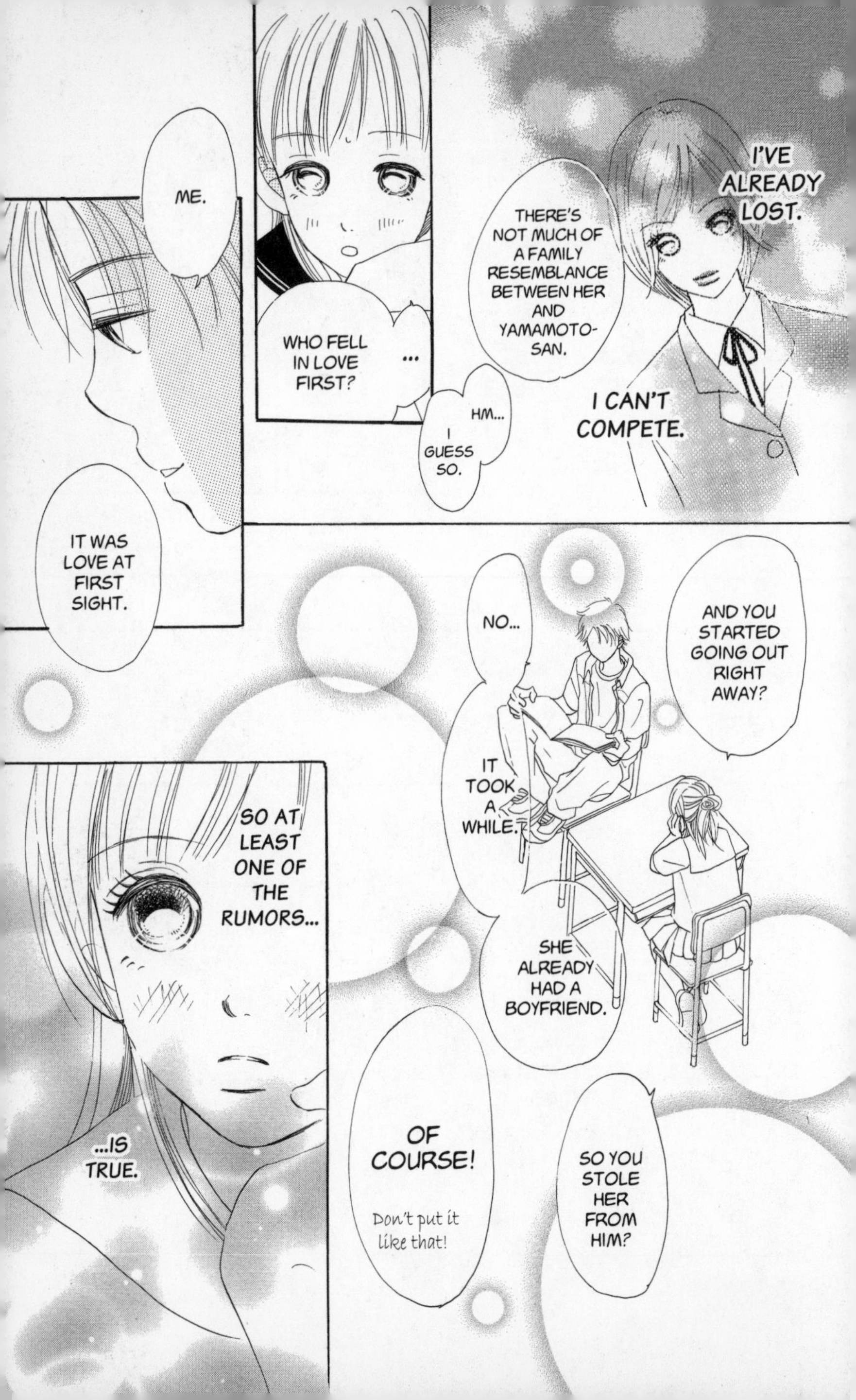
I'VE ALREADY LOST.
THERE'S NOT MUCH OF A FAMILY RESEMBLANCE BETWEEN HER AND YAMAMOTO-SAN.
I CAN'T COMPETE.
HM... I GUESS SO.
WHO FELL IN LOVE FIRST?
...
ME.
IT WAS LOVE AT FIRST SIGHT.
AND YOU STARTED GOING OUT RIGHT AWAY?
NO... IT TOOK A WHILE.
SHE ALREADY HAD A BOYFRIEND.
SO YOU STOLE HER FROM HIM?
OF COURSE!
Don't put it like that!
SO AT LEAST ONE OF THE RUMORS...
...IS TRUE.

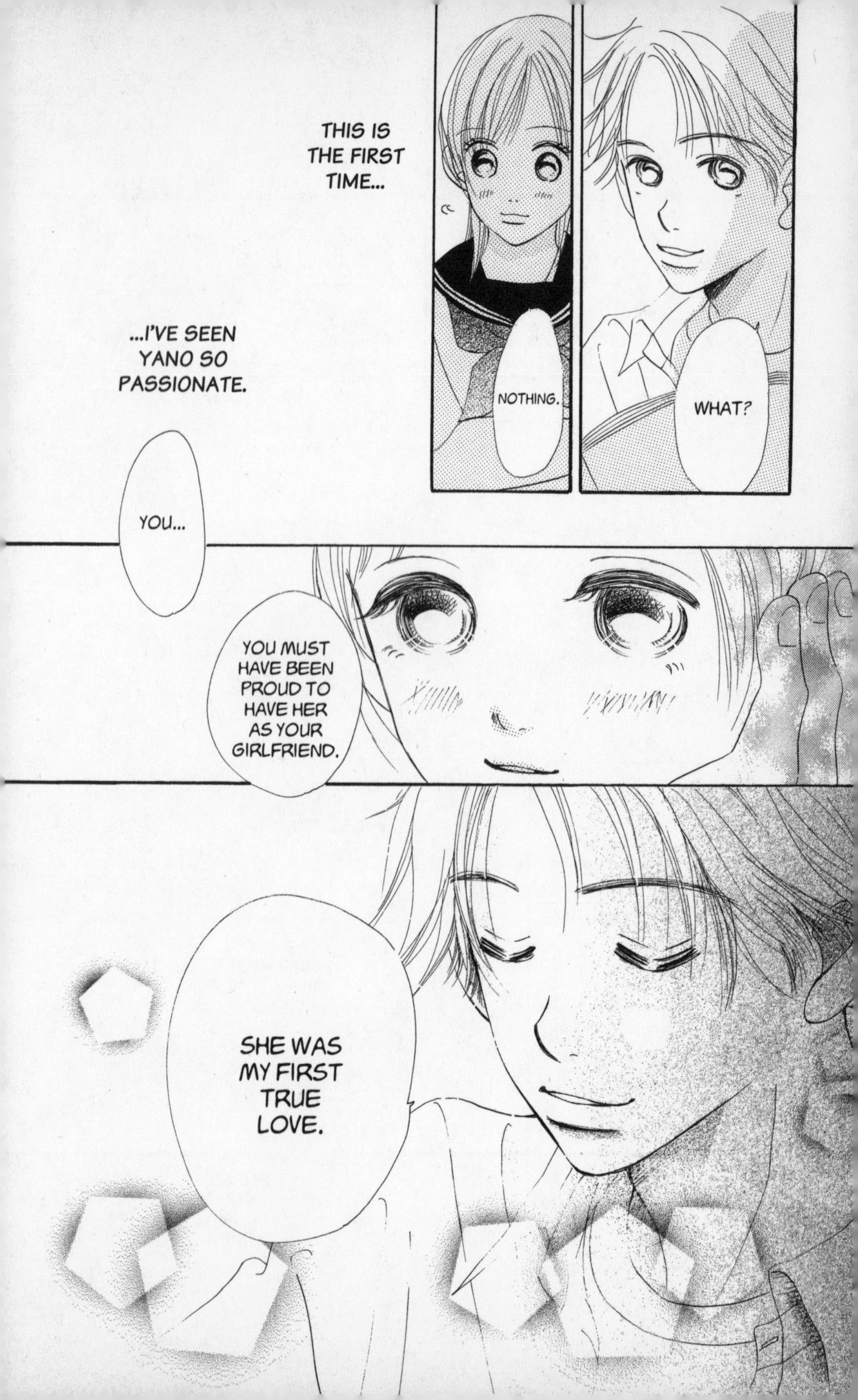
WHAT?
NOTHING.
THIS IS THE FIRST TIME...
...I'VE SEEN YANO SO PASSIONATE.
YOU...
YOU MUST HAVE BEEN PROUD TO HAVE HER AS YOUR GIRLFRIEND.
SHE WAS MY FIRST TRUE LOVE.

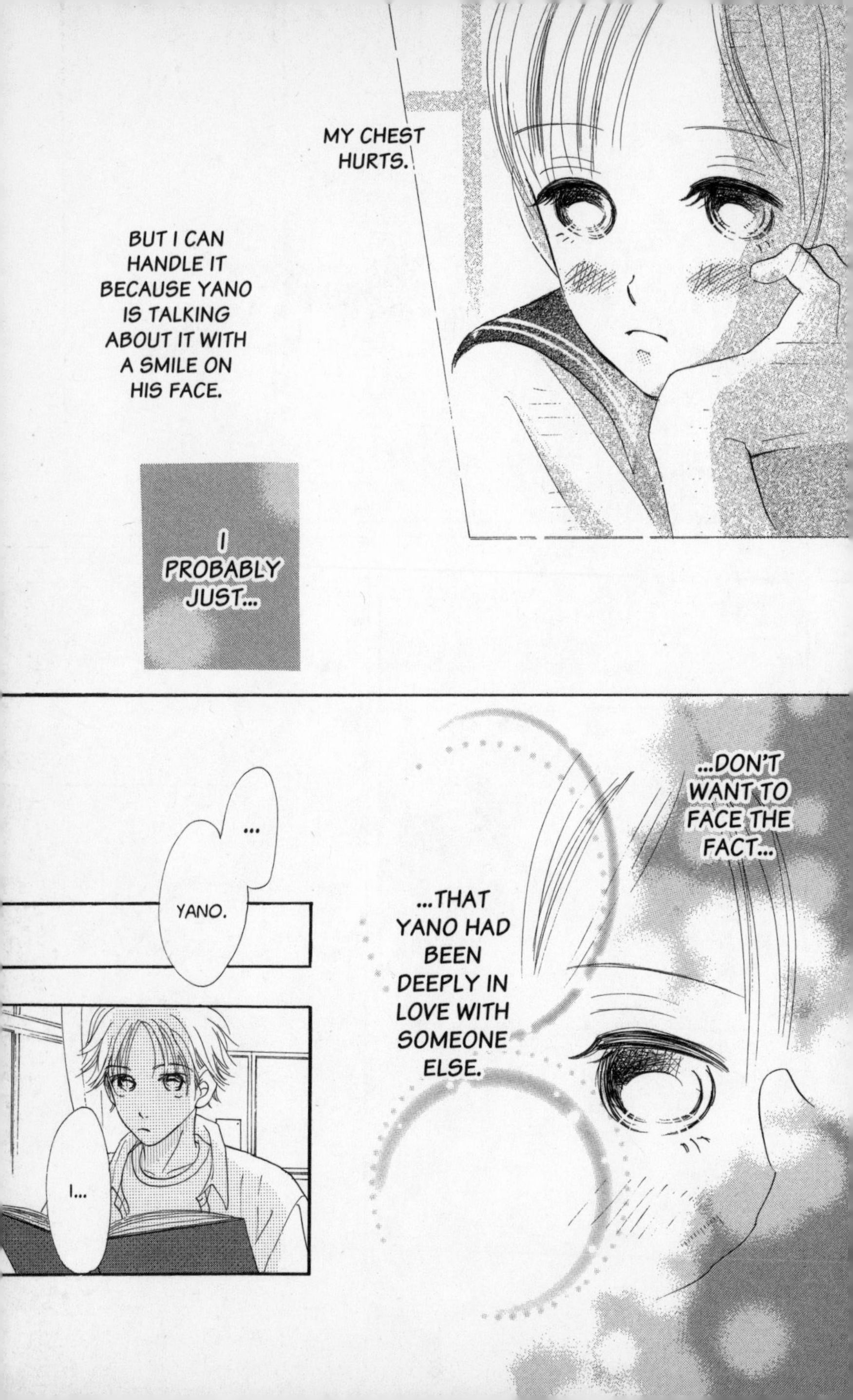
MY CHEST HURTS.
BUT I CAN HANDLE IT BECAUSE YANO IS TALKING ABOUT IT WITH A SMILE ON HIS FACE.
I PROBABLY JUST...
...DON'T WANT TO FACE THE FACT...
...THAT YANO HAD BEEN DEEPLY IN LOVE WITH SOMEONE ELSE.
...
YANO.
I...

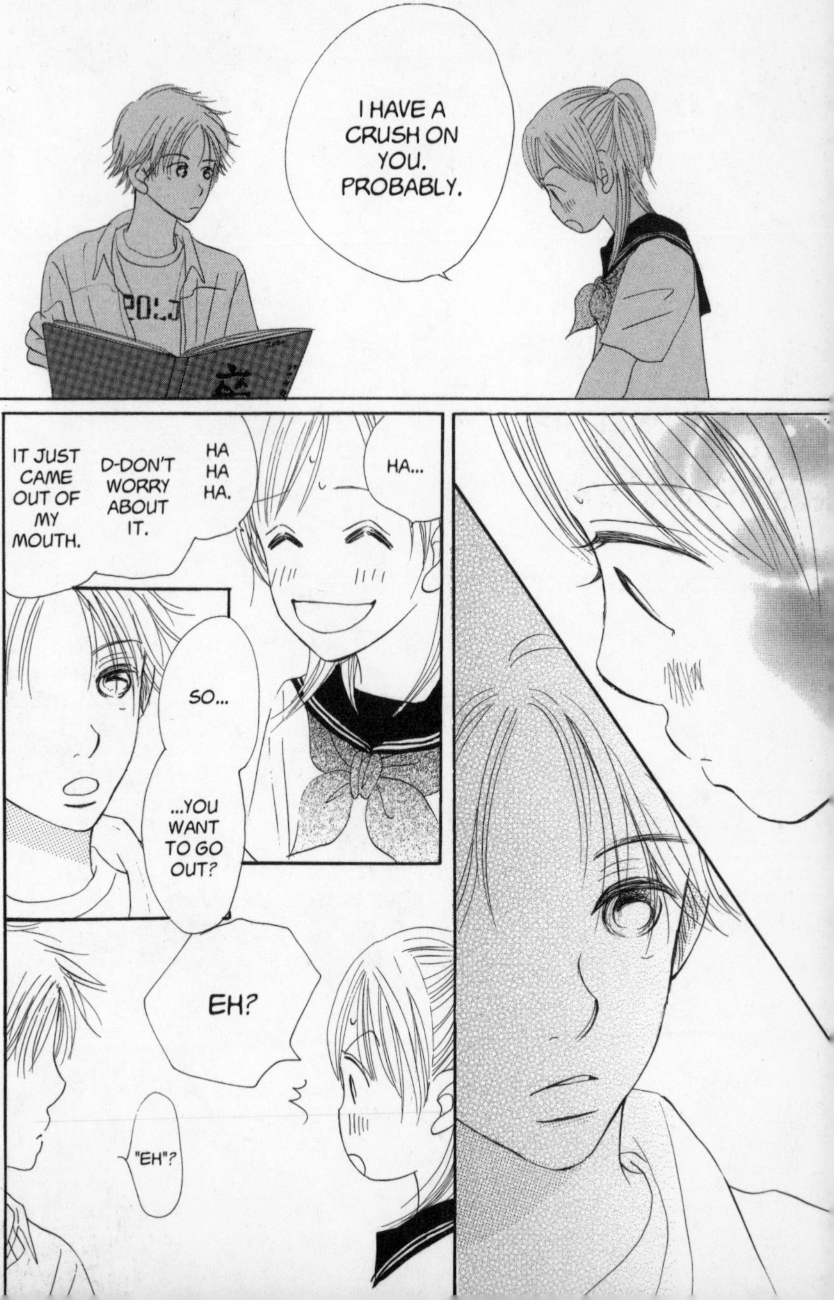
I HAVE A CRUSH ON YOU. PROBABLY.
HA...
HA HA HA.
D-DON'T WORRY ABOUT IT.
IT JUST CAME OUT OF MY MOUTH.
SO...
...YOU WANT TO GO OUT?
EH?
"EH"?

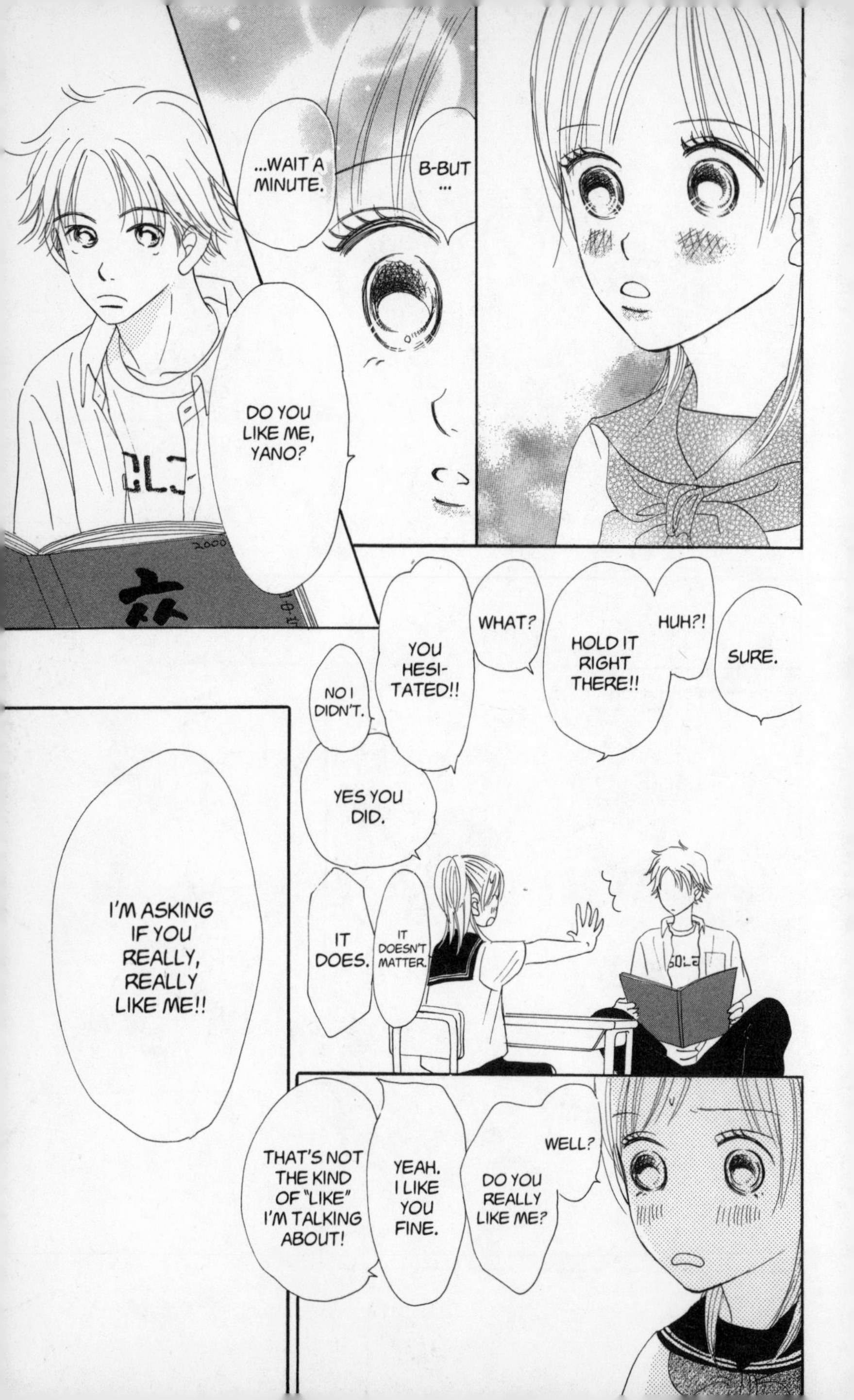
B-BUT ...
...WAIT A MINUTE.
DO YOU LIKE ME, YANO?
SURE.
HUH?!
HOLD IT RIGHT THERE!!
WHAT?
YOU HESI-TATED!!
NO I DIDN'T.
YES YOU DID.
IT DOESN'T MATTER.
IT DOES.
WELL?
DO YOU REALLY LIKE ME?
YEAH. I LIKE YOU FINE.
THAT'S NOT THE KIND OF "LIKE" I'M TALKING ABOUT!
I'M ASKING IF YOU REALLY, REALLY LIKE ME!!

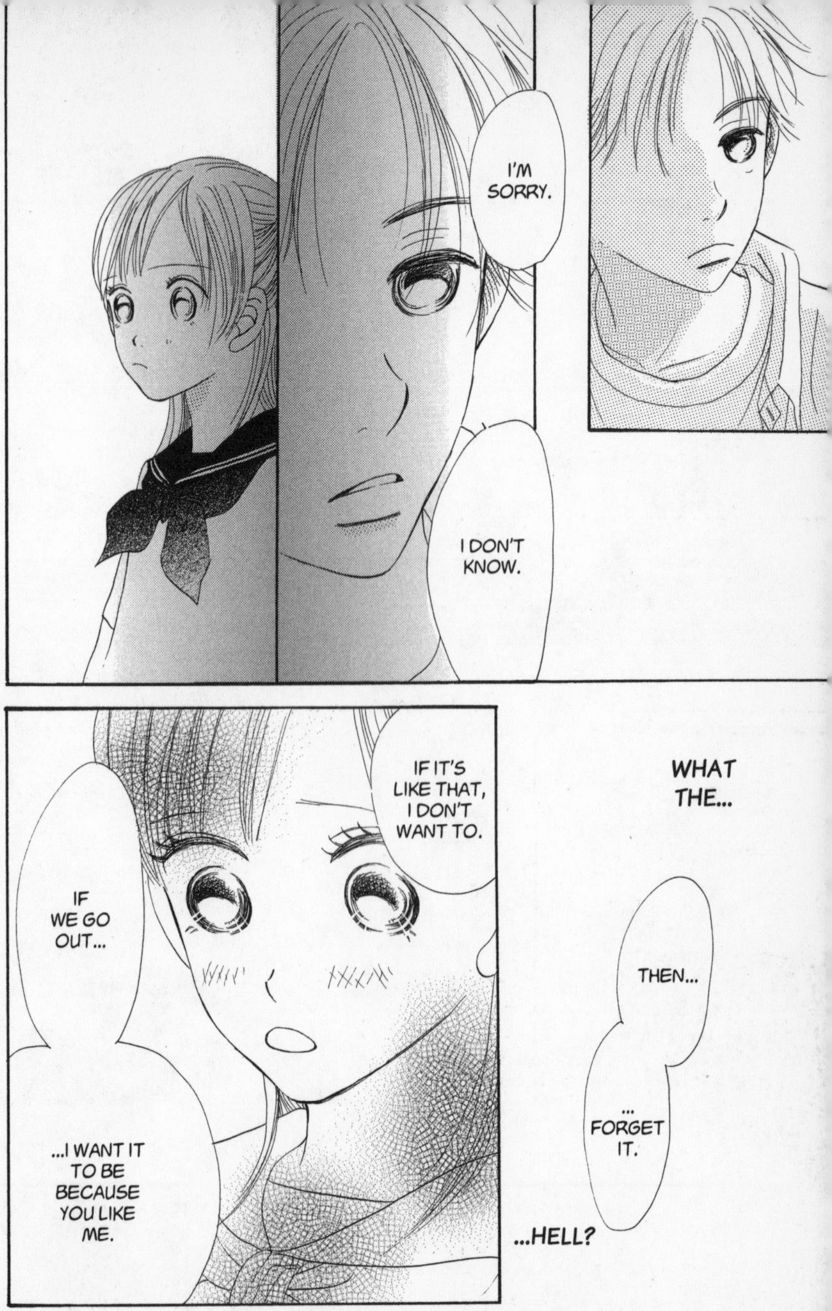
I'M SORRY.
I DON'T KNOW.
WHAT THE...
THEN...
...FORGET IT.
...HELL?
IF IT'S LIKE THAT, I DON'T WANT TO.
IF WE GO OUT...
...I WANT IT TO BE BECAUSE YOU LIKE ME.

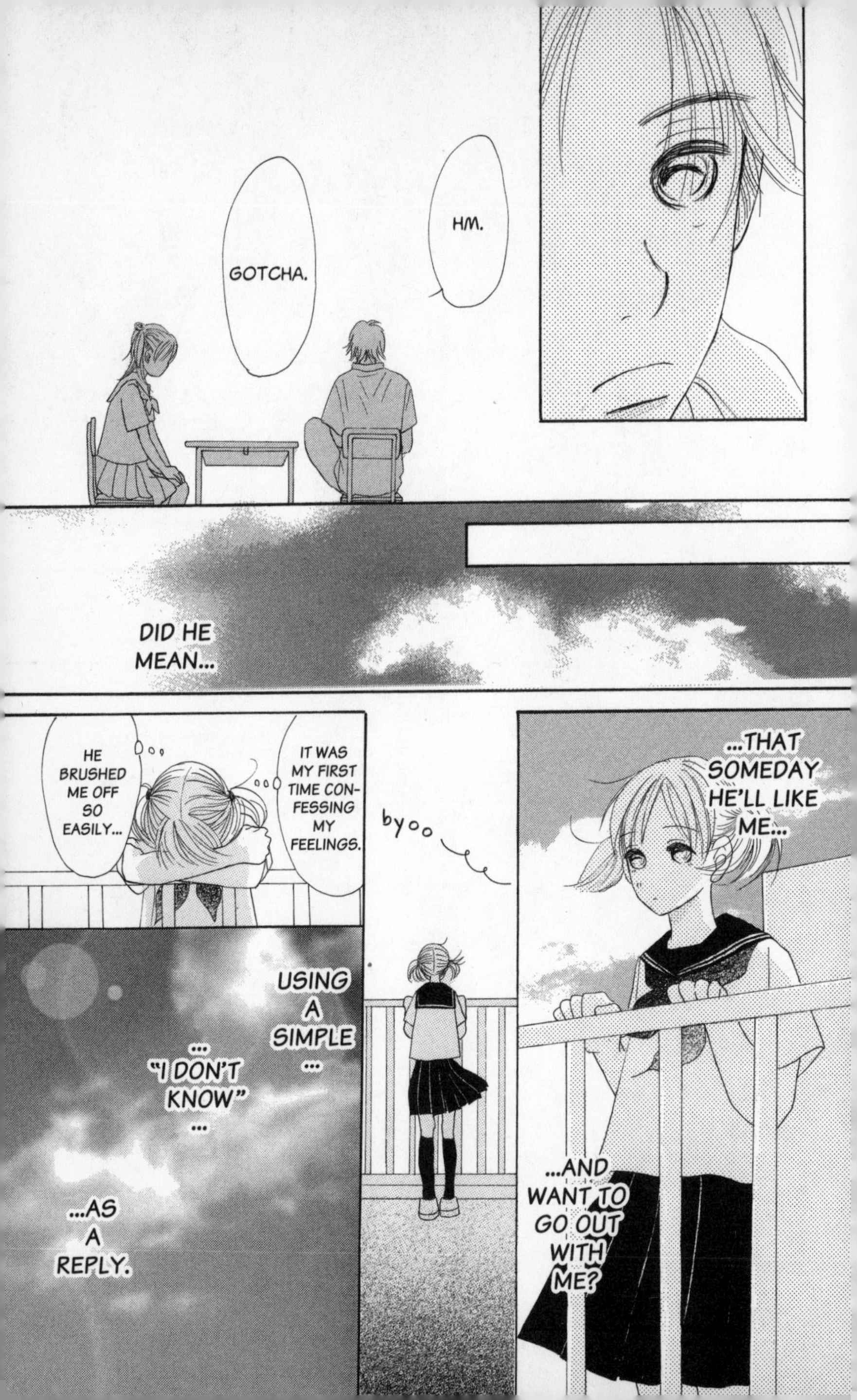
HM.
GOTCHA.
DID HE MEAN...
...THAT SOMEDAY HE'LL LIKE ME...
...AND WANT TO GO OUT WITH ME?
byoo
IT WAS MY FIRST TIME CON-FESSING MY FEELINGS.
HE BRUSHED ME OFF SO EASILY...
USING A SIMPLE ...
... "I DON'T KNOW" ...
...AS A REPLY.

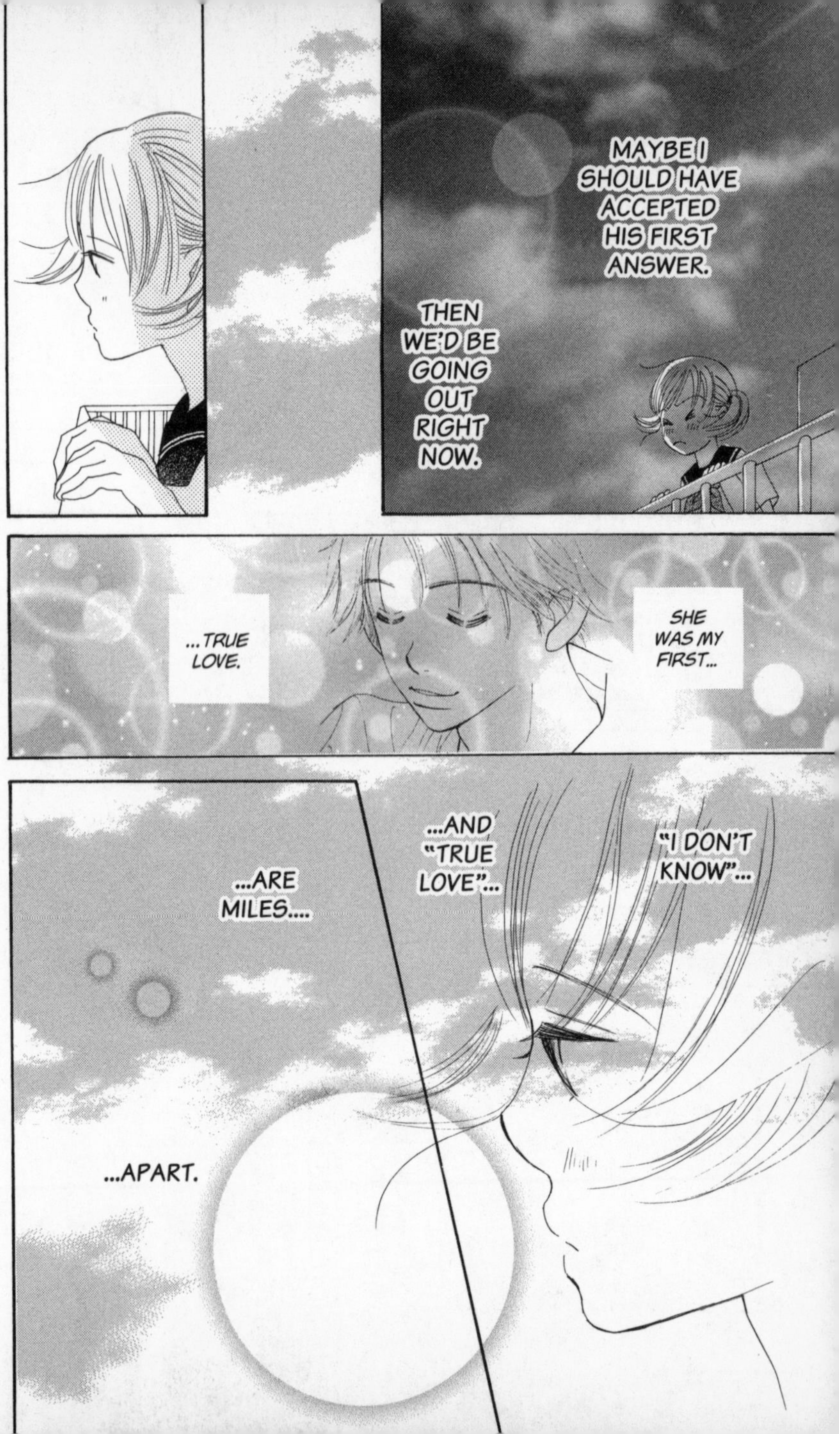
MAYBE I SHOULD HAVE ACCEPTED HIS FIRST ANSWER.
THEN WE'D BE GOING OUT RIGHT NOW.
SHE WAS MY FIRST...
...TRUE LOVE.
"I DON'T KNOW"...
...AND "TRUE LOVE"...
...ARE MILES....
...APART.

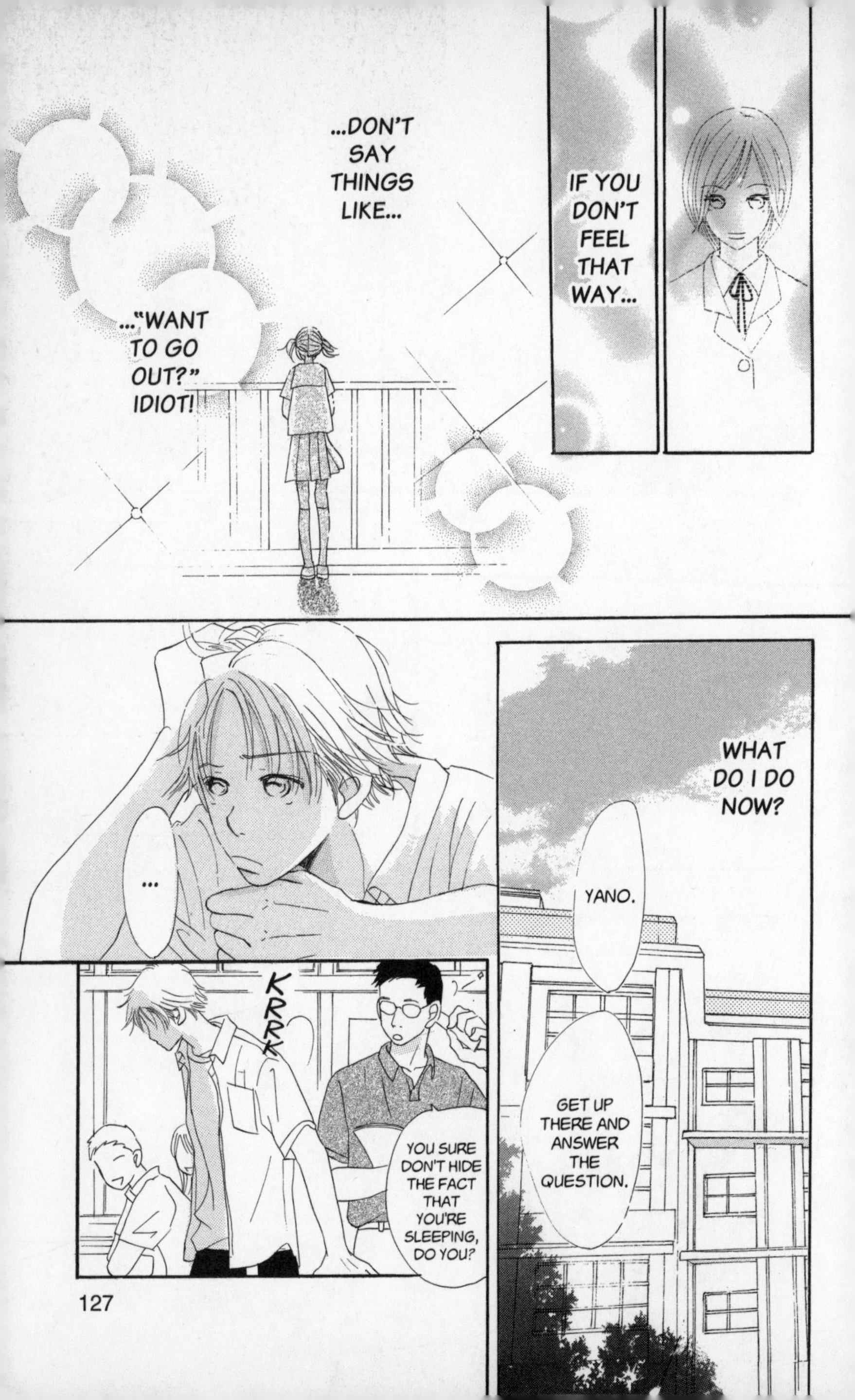
IF YOU DON'T FEEL THAT WAY...
...DON'T SAY THINGS LIKE...
..."WANT TO GO OUT?" IDIOT!
WHAT DO I DO NOW?
YANO.
GET UP THERE AND ANSWER THE QUESTION.
...
KRRK
YOU SURE DON'T HIDE THE FACT THAT YOU'RE SLEEPING, DO YOU?

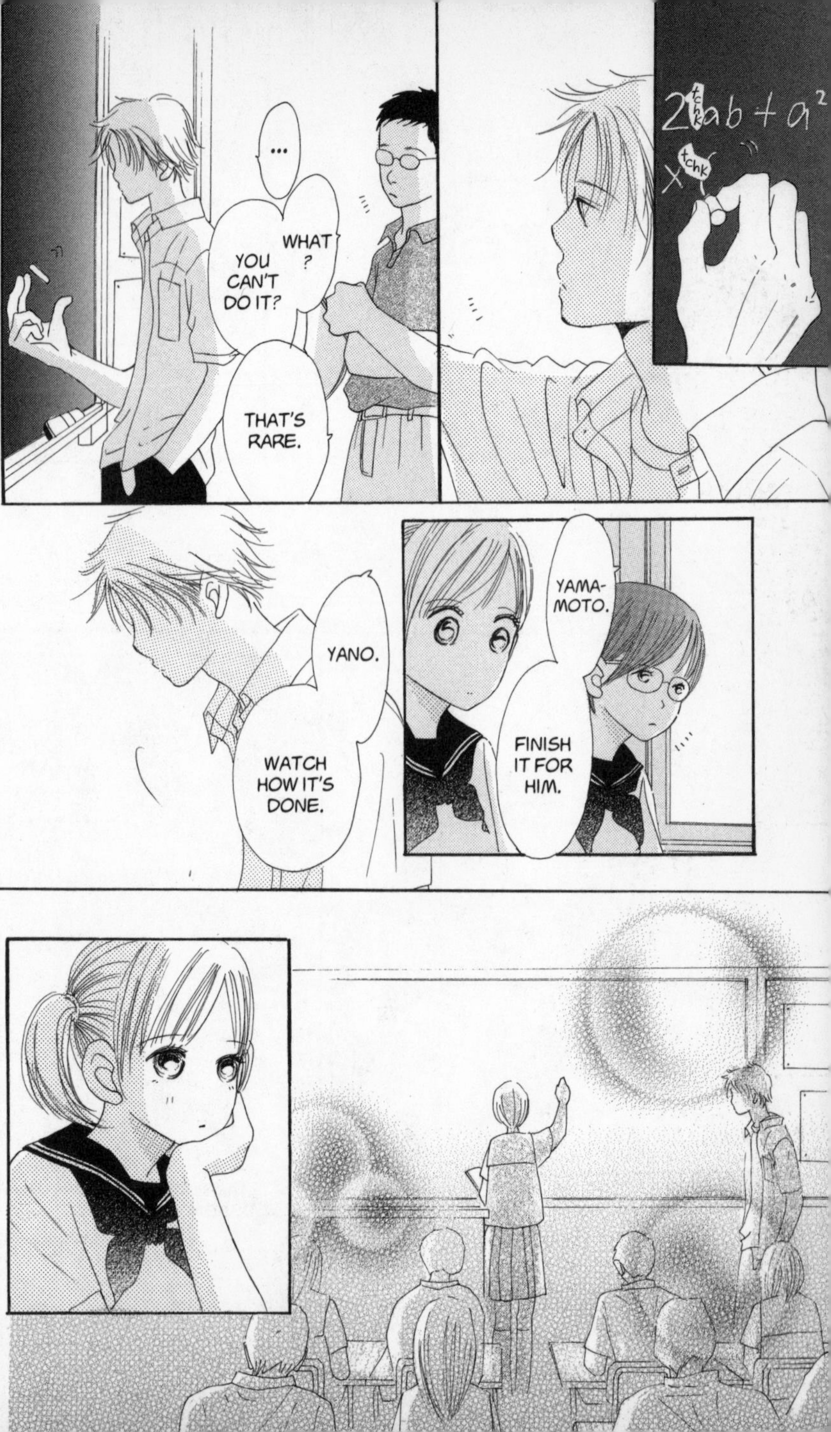
2ab + a²
tchk
tchk
...
WHAT?
YOU CAN'T DO IT?
THAT'S RARE.
YAMA-MOTO.
FINISH IT FOR HIM.
YANO.
WATCH HOW IT'S DONE.

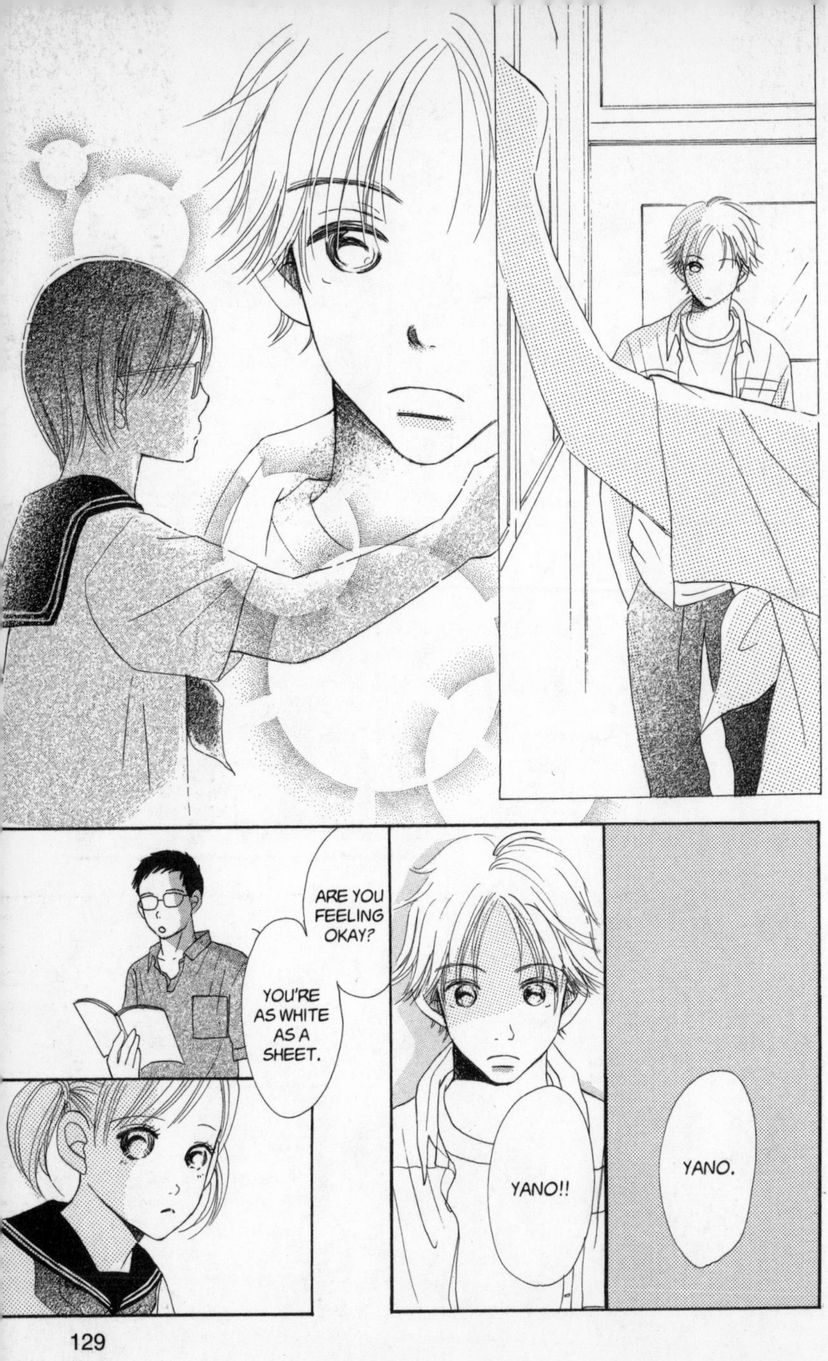
YANO.
YANO!!
ARE YOU FEELING OKAY?
YOU'RE AS WHITE AS A SHEET.

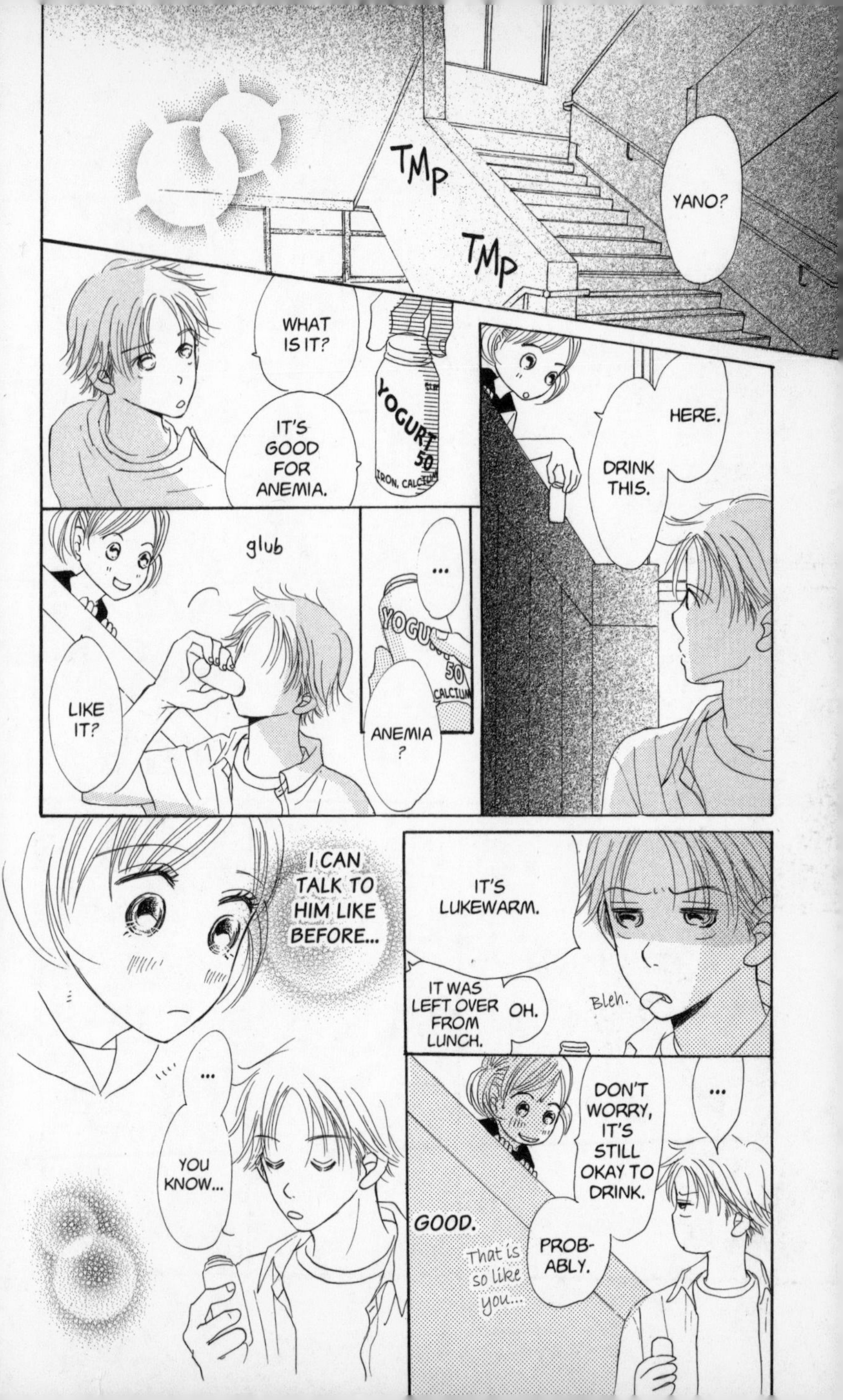
YANO?
TMP
TMP
HERE.
DRINK THIS.
WHAT IS IT?
IT'S GOOD FOR ANEMIA.
YOGURT 50
...
ANEMIA?
glub
LIKE IT?
IT'S LUKEWARM.
Bleh.
OH.
IT WAS LEFT OVER FROM LUNCH.
...
DON'T WORRY, IT'S STILL OKAY TO DRINK.
PROBABLY.
GOOD.
That is so like you...
I CAN TALK TO HIM LIKE BEFORE...
...
YOU KNOW...

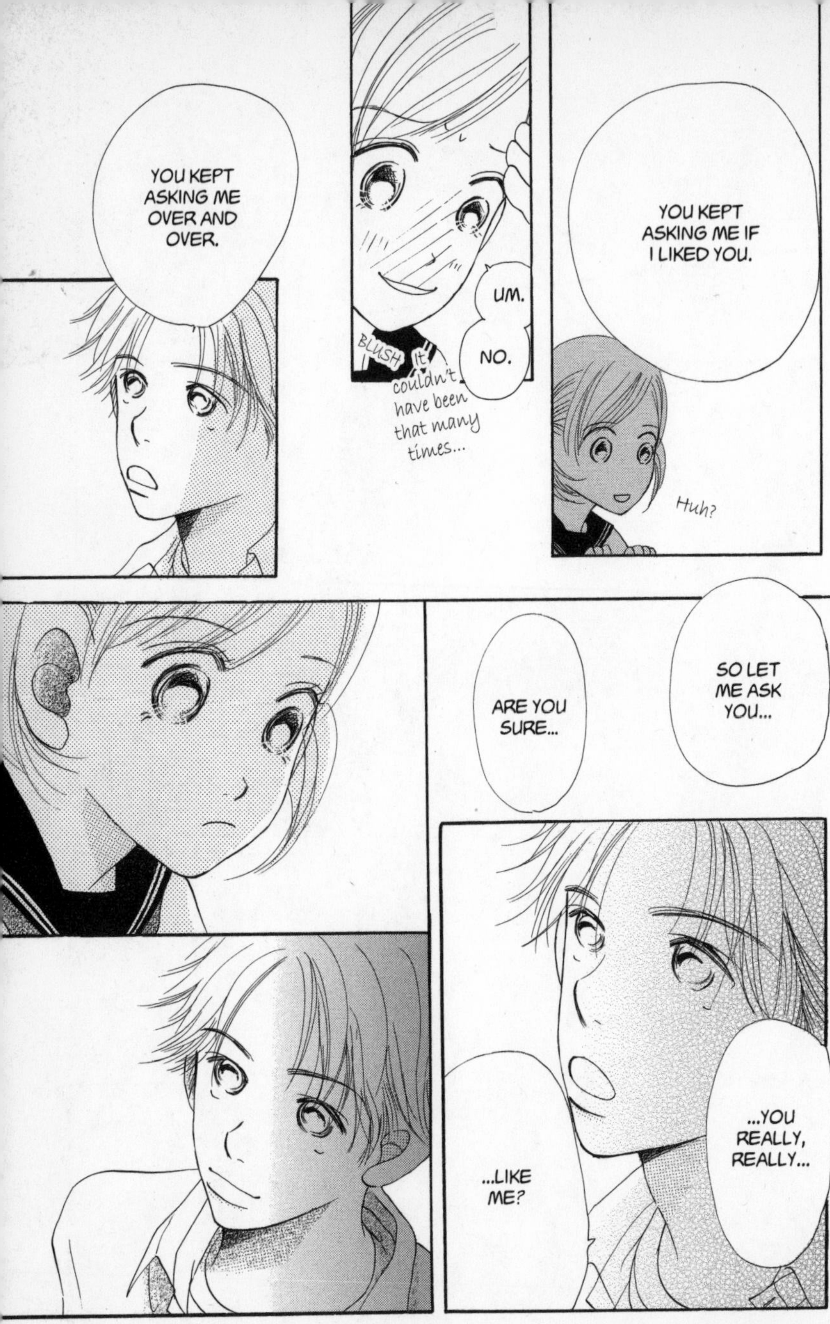
YOU KEPT ASKING ME IF I LIKED YOU.
Huh?
UM.
NO.
BLUSH
It couldn't have been that many times...
YOU KEPT ASKING ME OVER AND OVER.
SO LET ME ASK YOU...
ARE YOU SURE...
...YOU REALLY, REALLY...
...LIKE ME?

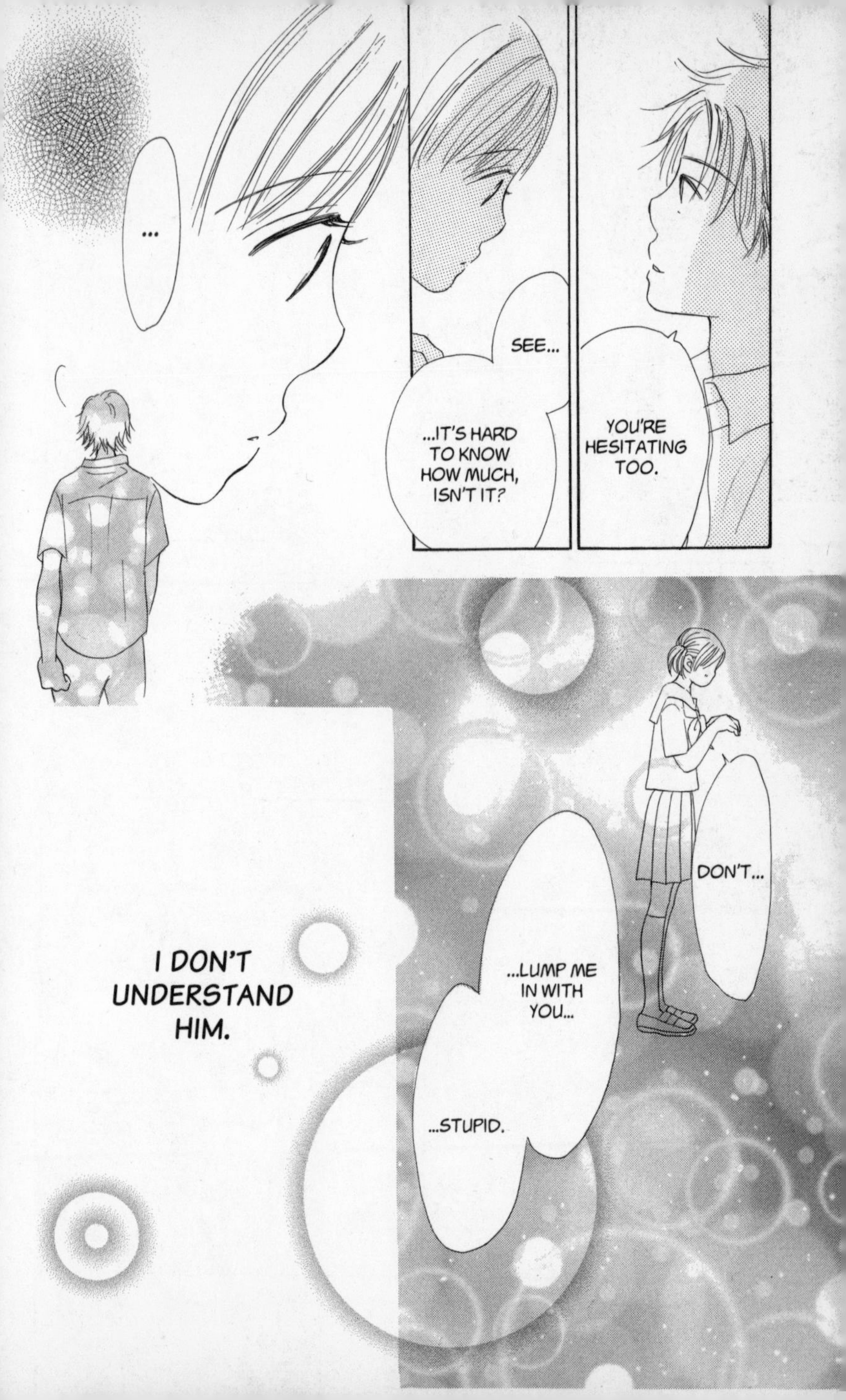
YOU'RE HESITATING TOO.
SEE...
...IT'S HARD TO KNOW HOW MUCH, ISN'T IT?
...
DON'T...
...LUMP ME IN WITH YOU...
...STUPID.
I DON'T UNDERSTAND HIM.

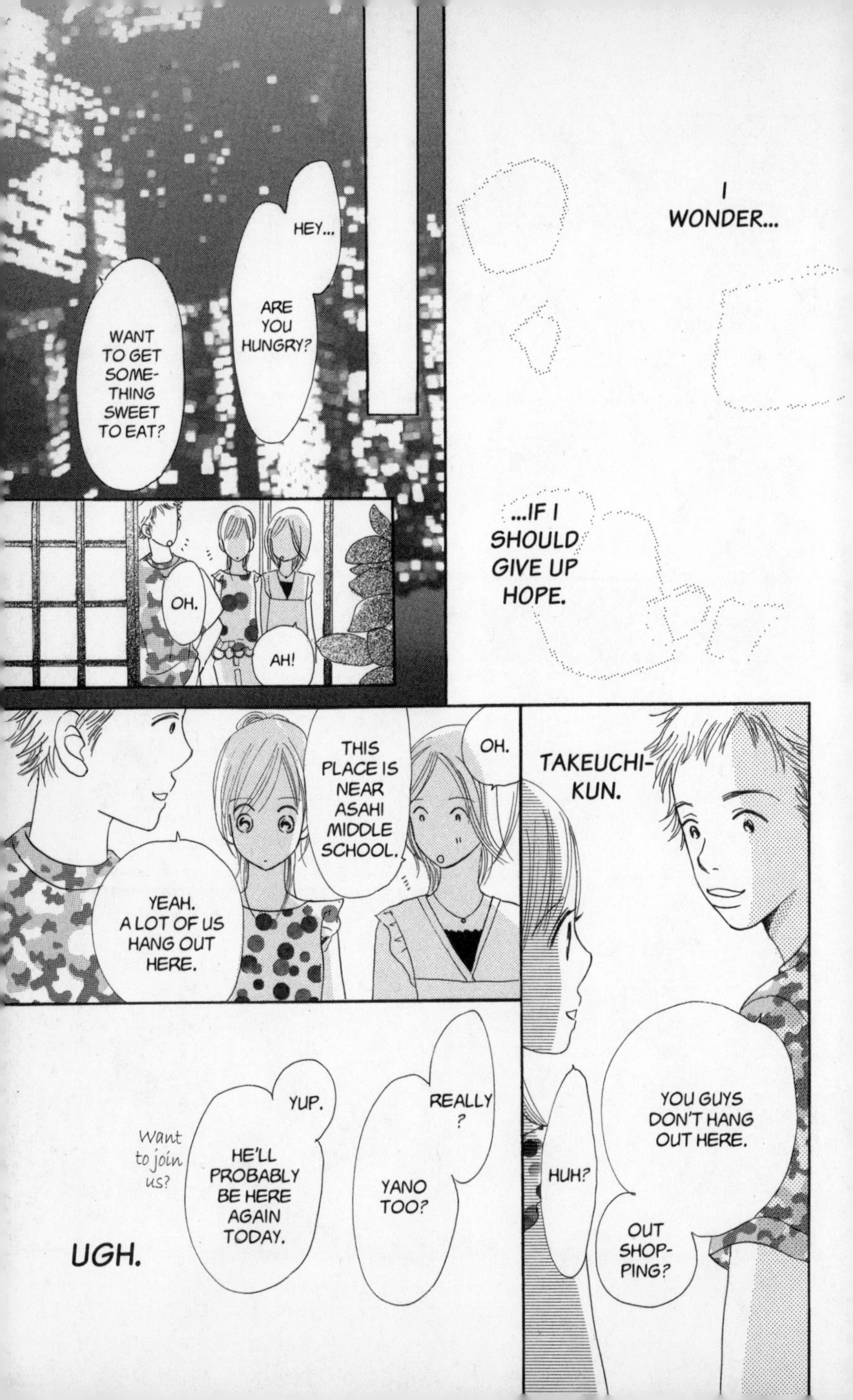
I WONDER...
...IF I SHOULD GIVE UP HOPE.
HEY...
ARE YOU HUNGRY?
WANT TO GET SOMETHING SWEET TO EAT?
OH.
AH!
TAKEUCHI-KUN.
YOU GUYS DON'T HANG OUT HERE.
OUT SHOPPING?
HUH?
OH.
THIS PLACE IS NEAR ASAHI MIDDLE SCHOOL.
YEAH. A LOT OF US HANG OUT HERE.
REALLY?
YANO TOO?
YUP.
HE'LL PROBABLY BE HERE AGAIN TODAY.
Want to join us?
UGH.

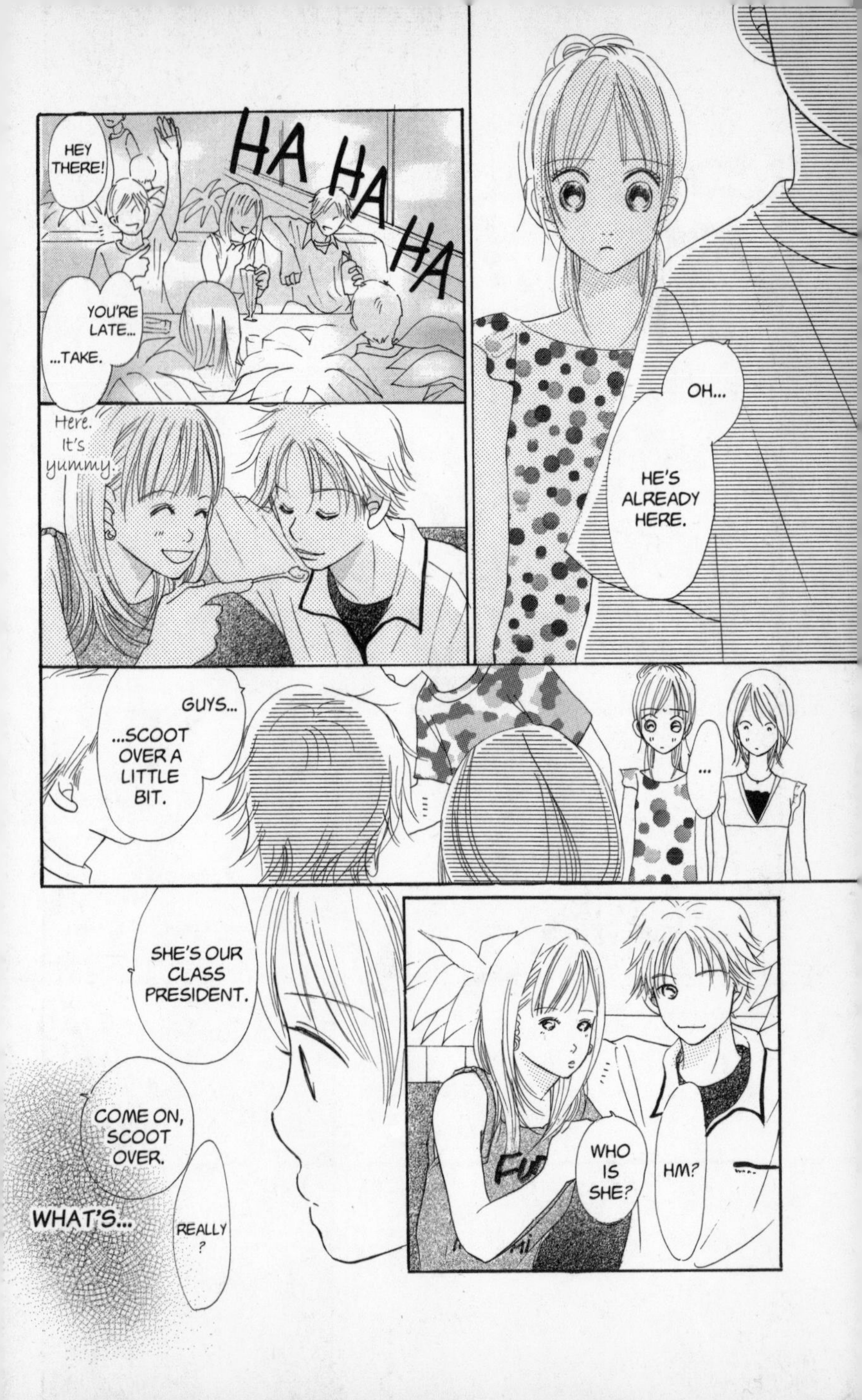
OH...
HE'S ALREADY HERE.
HEY THERE!
HA HA HA HA
YOU'RE LATE...
...TAKE.
Here. It's yummy.
...
GUYS...
...SCOOT OVER A LITTLE BIT.
HM?
WHO IS SHE?
SHE'S OUR CLASS PRESIDENT.
COME ON, SCOOT OVER.
REALLY?
WHAT'S...

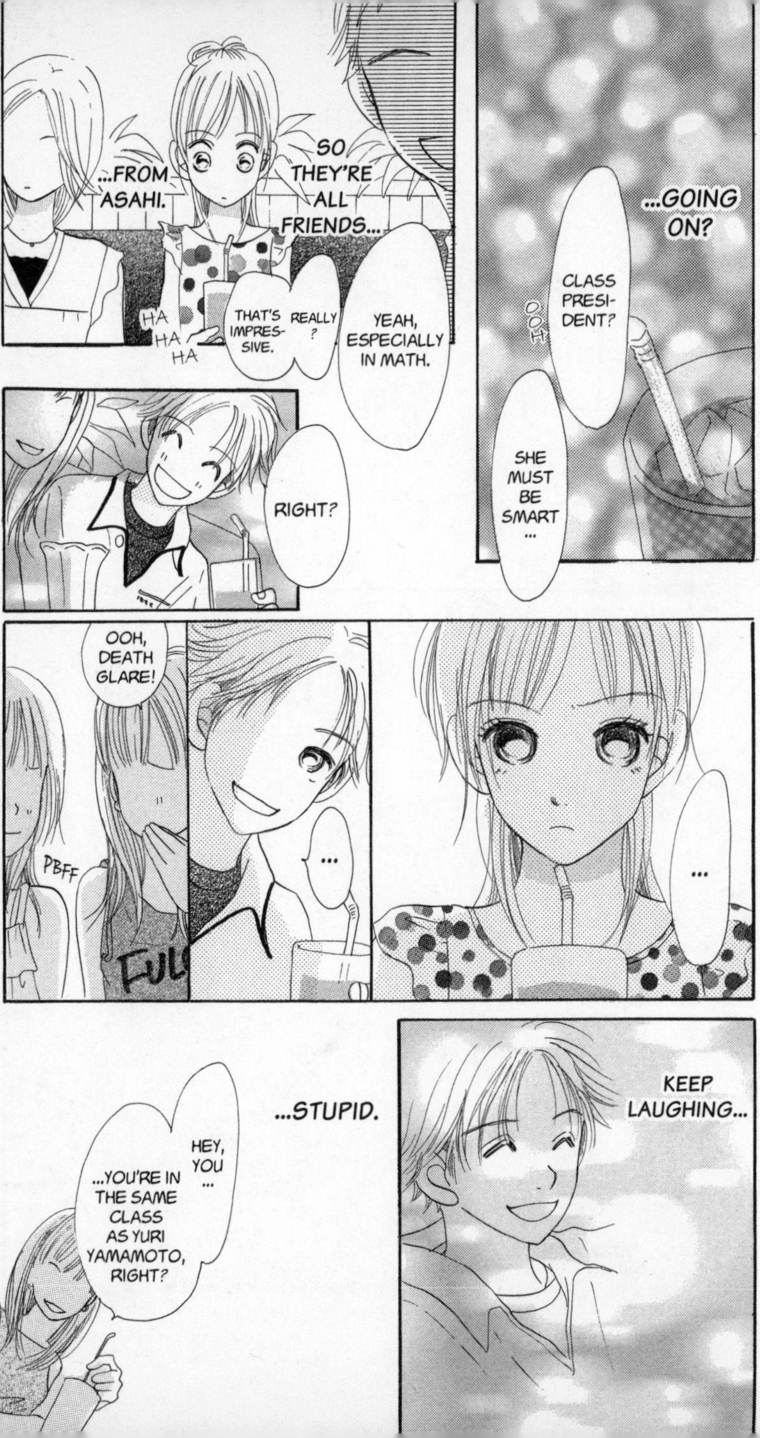
...GOING ON?
CLASS PRESIDENT?
OOH
SHE MUST BE SMART...
SO THEY'RE ALL FRIENDS...
...FROM ASAHI.
YEAH, ESPECIALLY IN MATH.
REALLY?
THAT'S IMPRESSIVE.
HA HA HA
RIGHT?
...
...
OOH, DEATH GLARE!
PBFF
FUL
KEEP LAUGHING...
...STUPID.
HEY, YOU...
...YOU'RE IN THE SAME CLASS AS YURI YAMAMOTO, RIGHT?

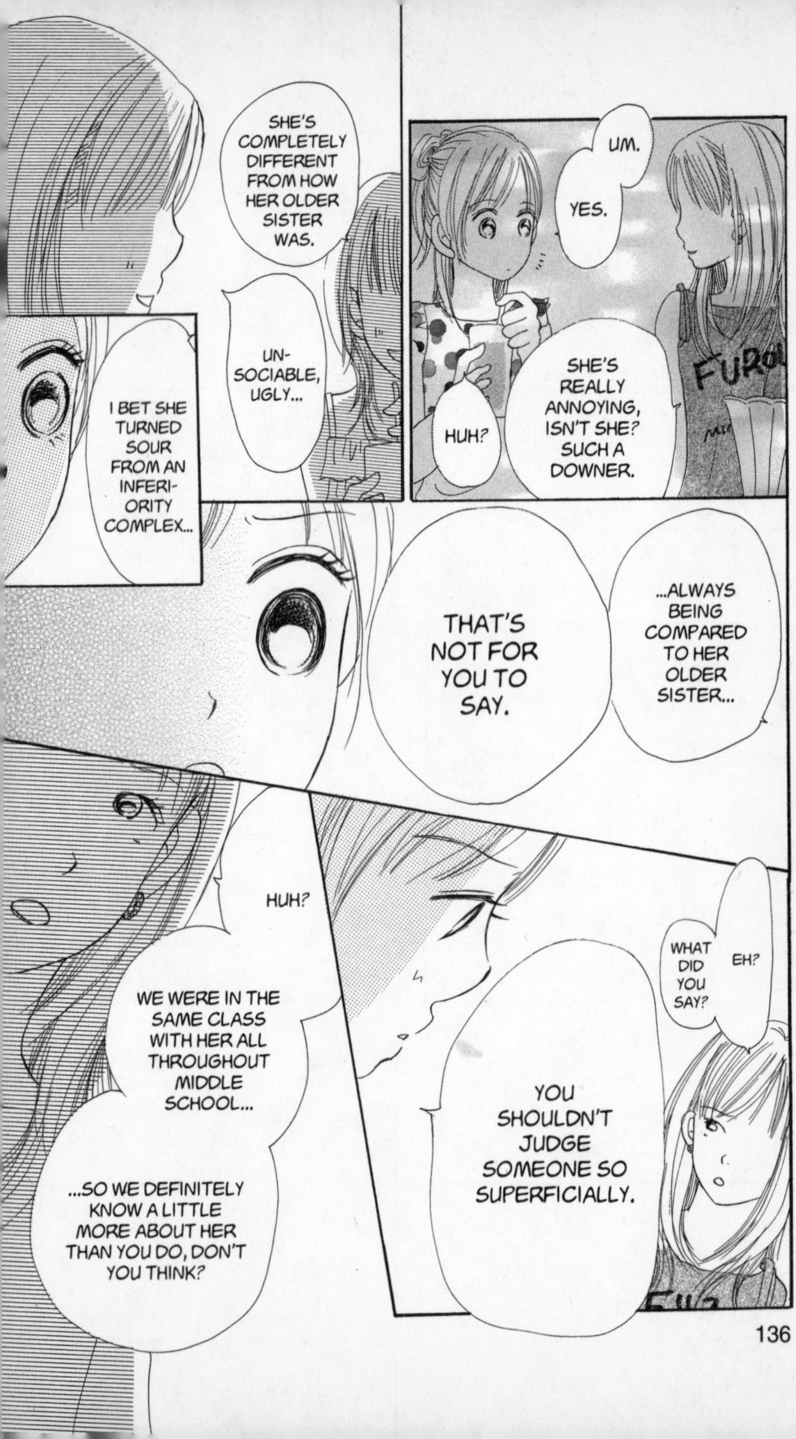
UM.
YES.
SHE'S REALLY ANNOYING, ISN'T SHE? SUCH A DOWNER.
HUH?
SHE'S COMPLETELY DIFFERENT FROM HOW HER OLDER SISTER WAS.
UN-SOCIABLE, UGLY...
I BET SHE TURNED SOUR FROM AN INFERI-ORITY COMPLEX...
...ALWAYS BEING COMPARED TO HER OLDER SISTER...
THAT'S NOT FOR YOU TO SAY.
EH?
WHAT DID YOU SAY?
YOU SHOULDN'T JUDGE SOMEONE SO SUPERFICIALLY.
HUH?
WE WERE IN THE SAME CLASS WITH HER ALL THROUGHOUT MIDDLE SCHOOL...
...SO WE DEFINITELY KNOW A LITTLE MORE ABOUT HER THAN YOU DO, DON'T YOU THINK?

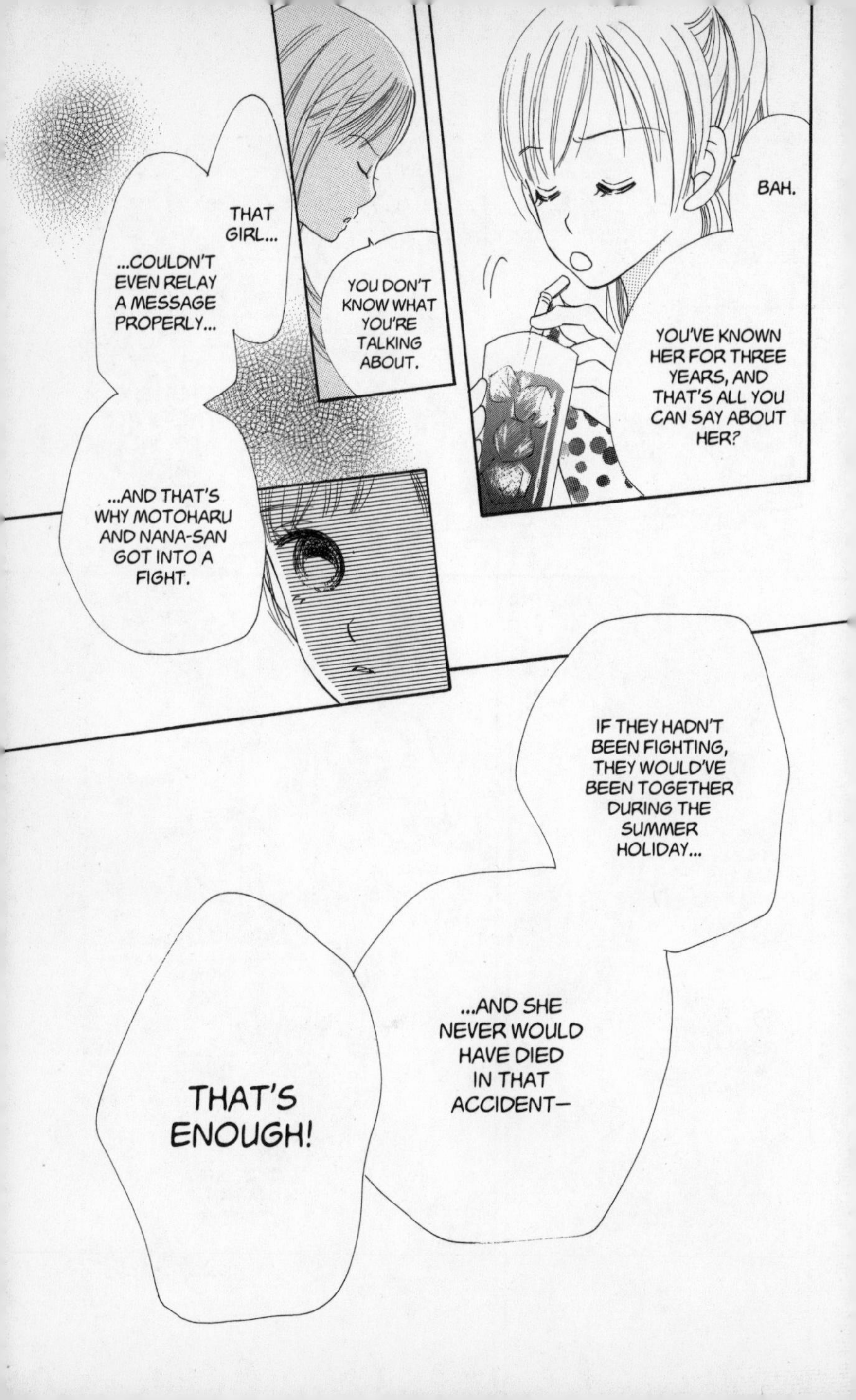
BAH.
YOU'VE KNOWN HER FOR THREE YEARS, AND THAT'S ALL YOU CAN SAY ABOUT HER?
YOU DON'T KNOW WHAT YOU'RE TALKING ABOUT.
THAT GIRL...
...COULDN'T EVEN RELAY A MESSAGE PROPERLY...
...AND THAT'S WHY MOTOHARU AND NANA-SAN GOT INTO A FIGHT.
IF THEY HADN'T BEEN FIGHTING, THEY WOULD'VE BEEN TOGETHER DURING THE SUMMER HOLIDAY...
...AND SHE NEVER WOULD HAVE DIED IN THAT ACCIDENT—
THAT'S ENOUGH!

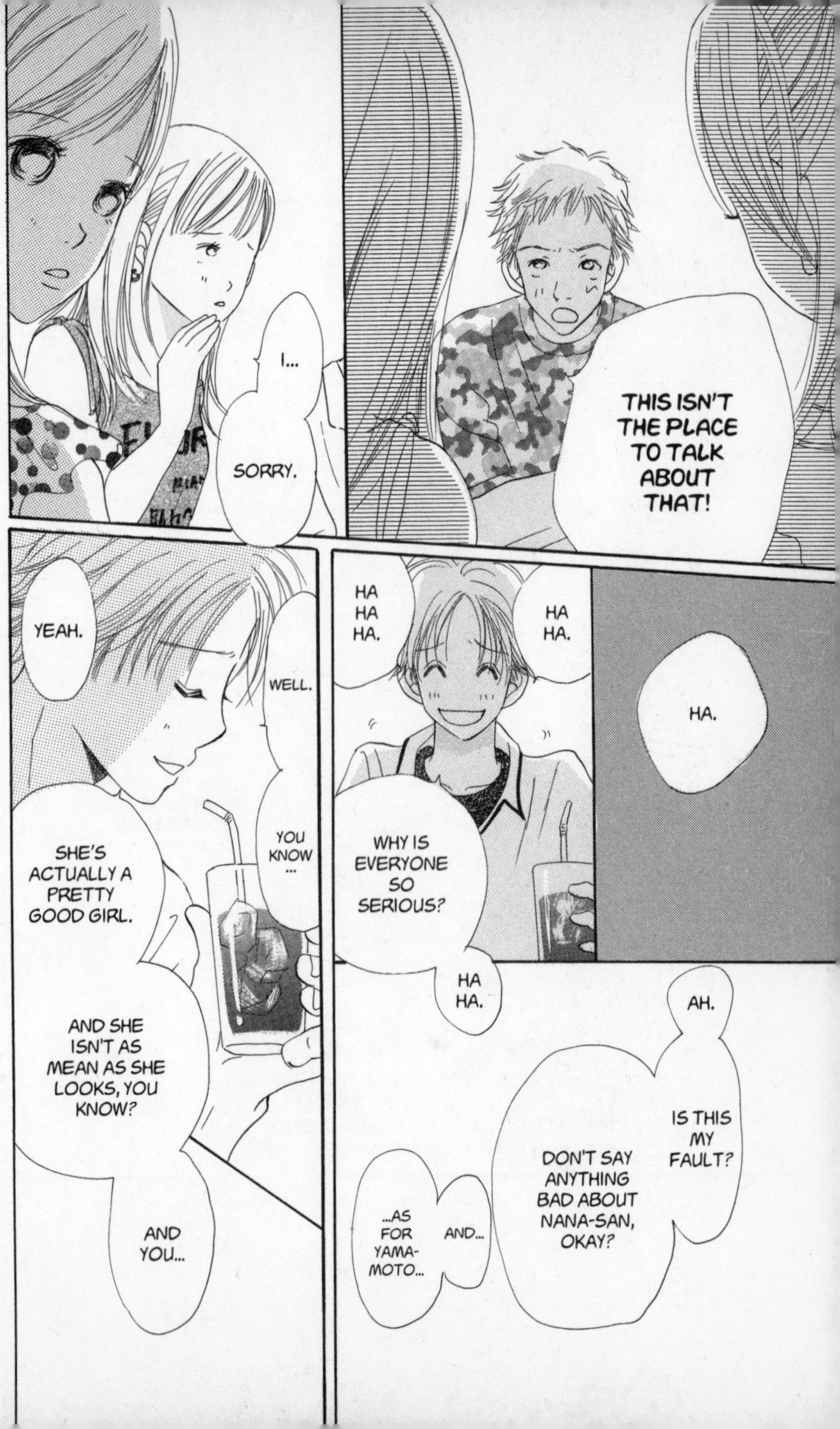
THIS ISN'T THE PLACE TO TALK ABOUT THAT!
I...
SORRY.
HA.
HA HA.
HA HA HA.
WHY IS EVERYONE SO SERIOUS?
HA HA.
AH.
IS THIS MY FAULT?
DON'T SAY ANYTHING BAD ABOUT NANA-SAN, OKAY?
AND...
...AS FOR YAMA-MOTO...
YEAH.
WELL.
YOU KNOW...
SHE'S ACTUALLY A PRETTY GOOD GIRL.
AND SHE ISN'T AS MEAN AS SHE LOOKS, YOU KNOW?
AND YOU...

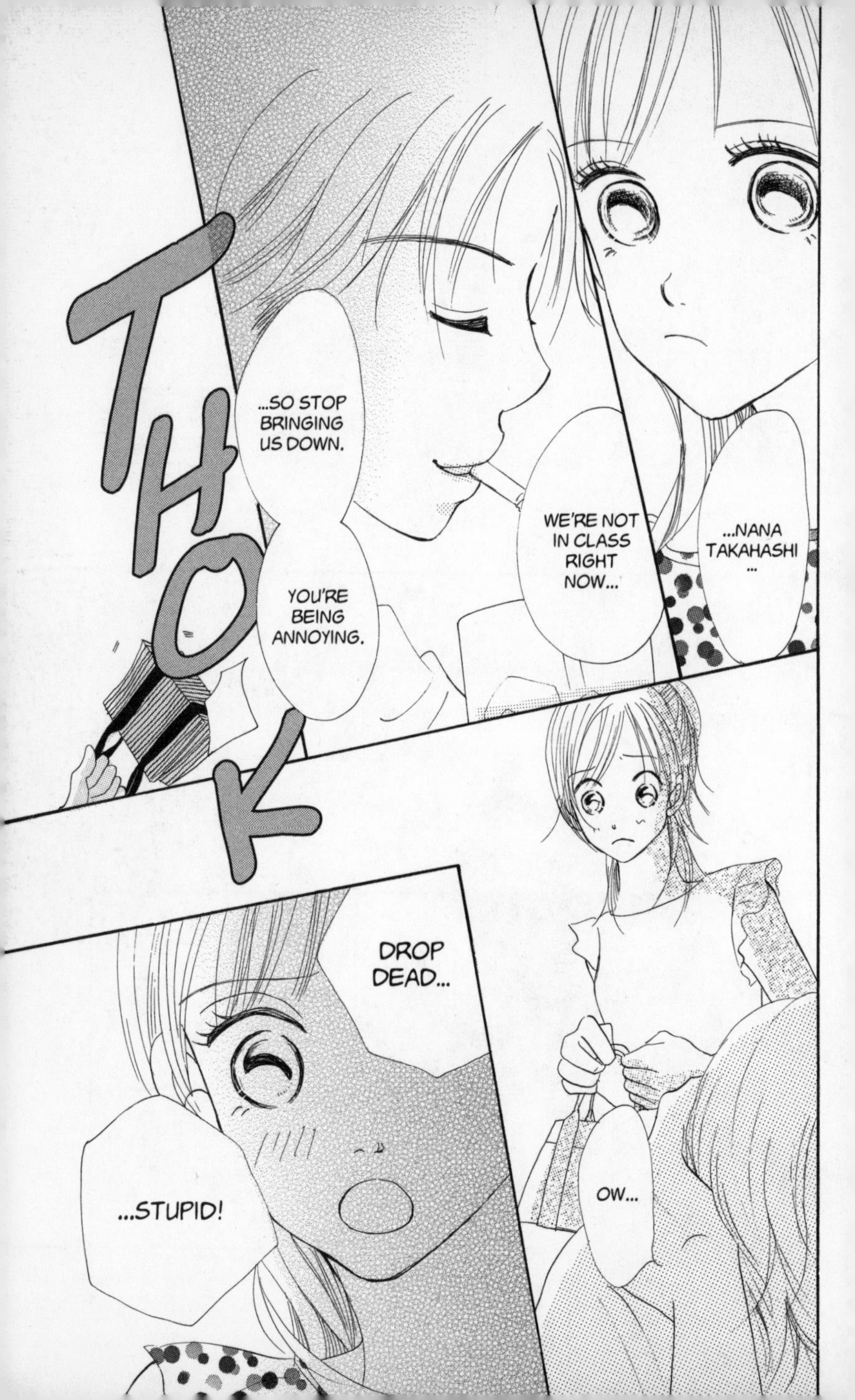
...NANA TAKAHASHI ...
WE'RE NOT IN CLASS RIGHT NOW...
...SO STOP BRINGING US DOWN.
YOU'RE BEING ANNOYING.
THOK
OW...
DROP DEAD...
...STUPID!

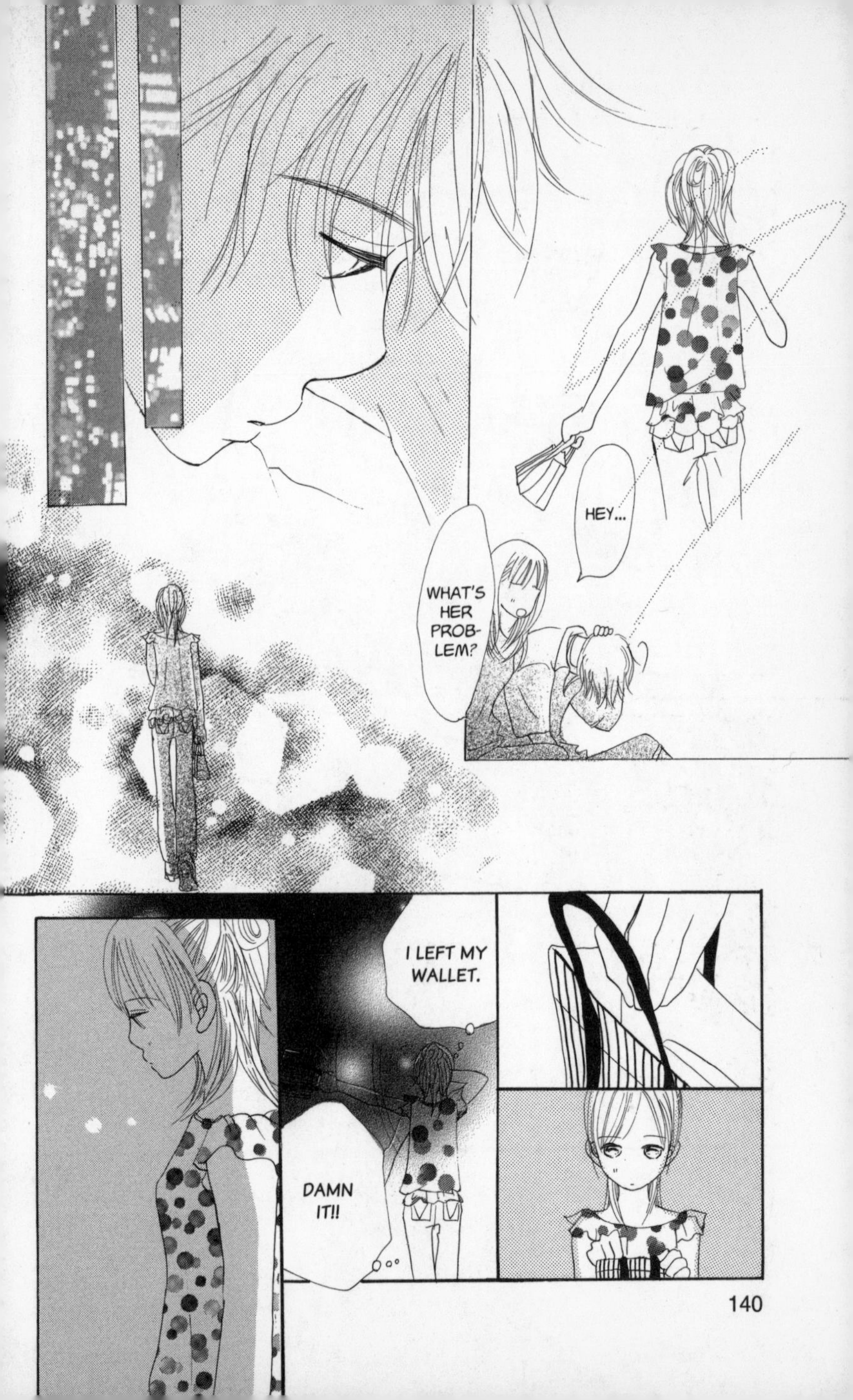
HEY...
WHAT'S HER PROB-LEM?
I LEFT MY WALLET.
DAMN IT!!

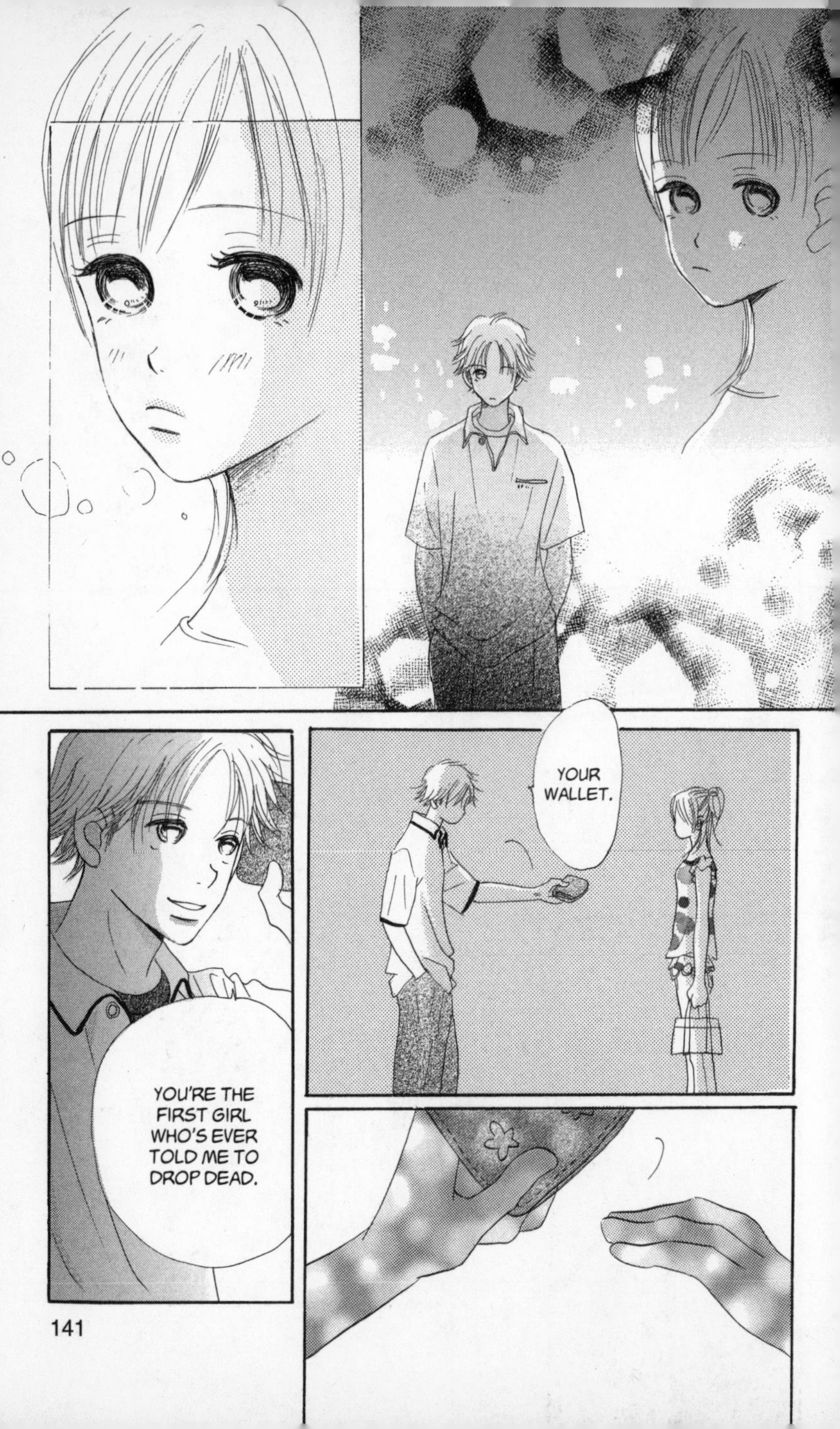
YOUR WALLET.
YOU'RE THE FIRST GIRL WHO'S EVER TOLD ME TO DROP DEAD.

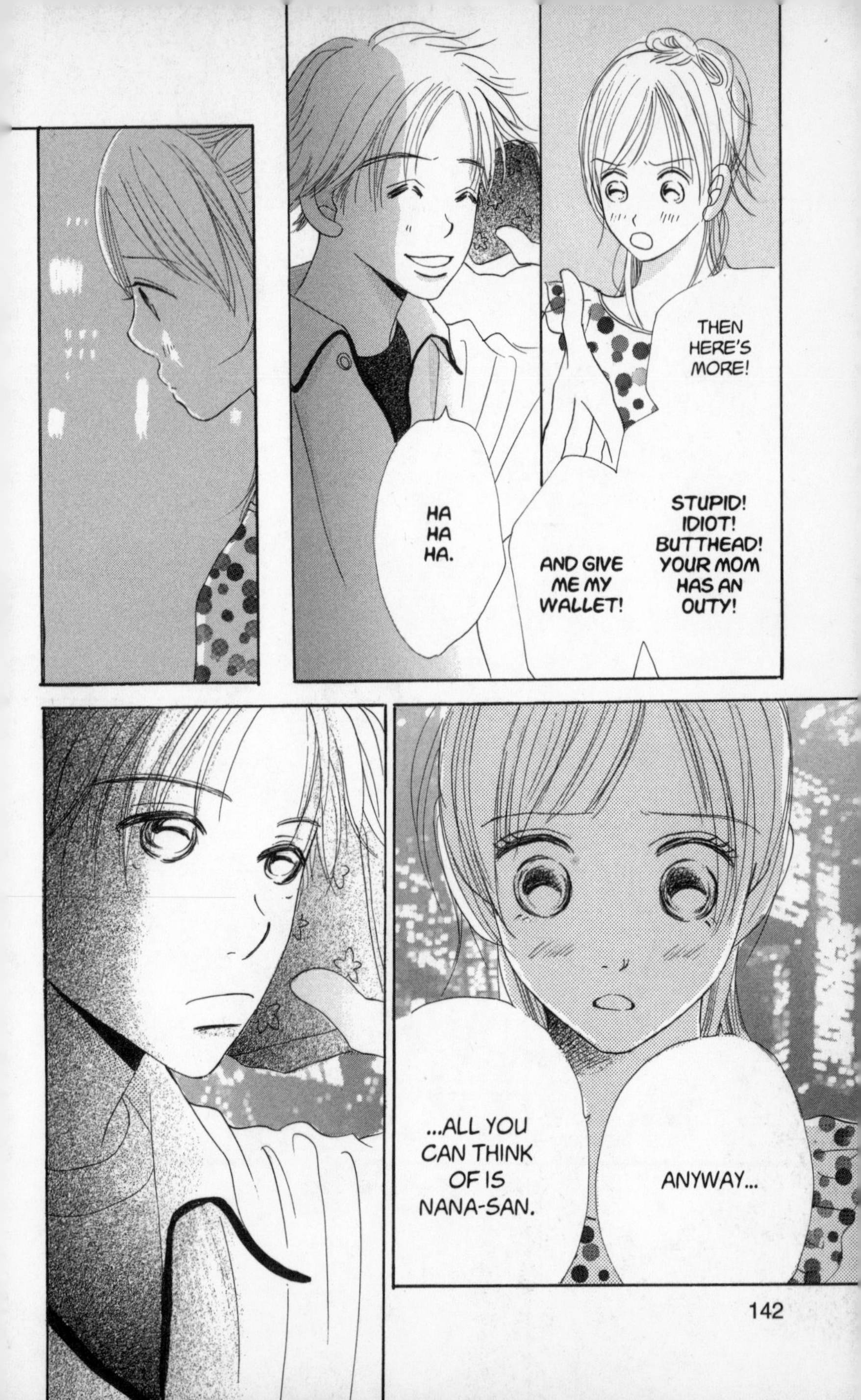
THEN HERE'S MORE!
STUPID! IDIOT! BUTTHEAD! YOUR MOM HAS AN OUTY!
AND GIVE ME MY WALLET!
HA HA HA.
ANYWAY...
...ALL YOU CAN THINK OF IS NANA-SAN.

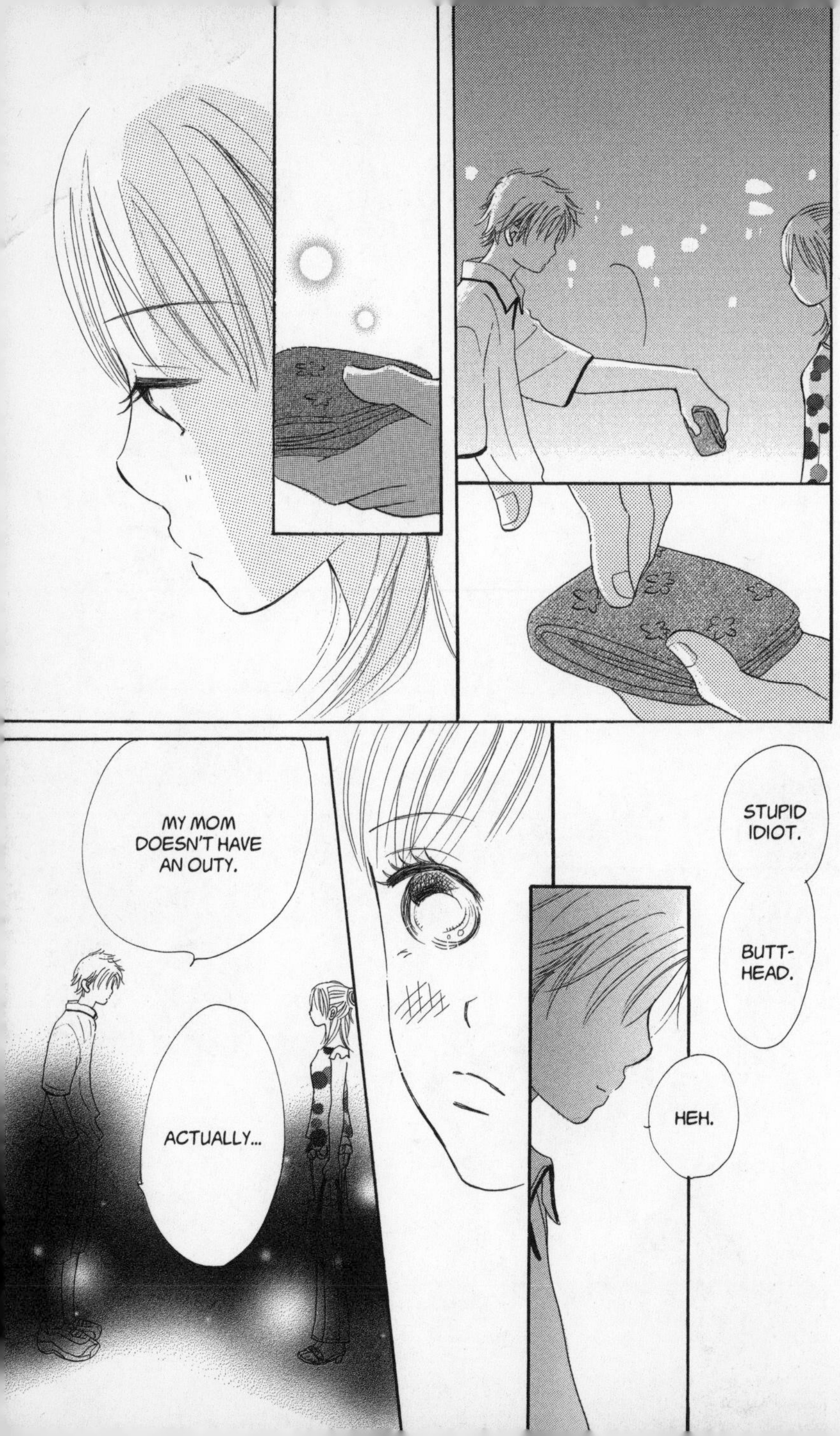
STUPID IDIOT.
BUTT-HEAD.
HEH.
MY MOM DOESN'T HAVE AN OUTY.
ACTUALLY...

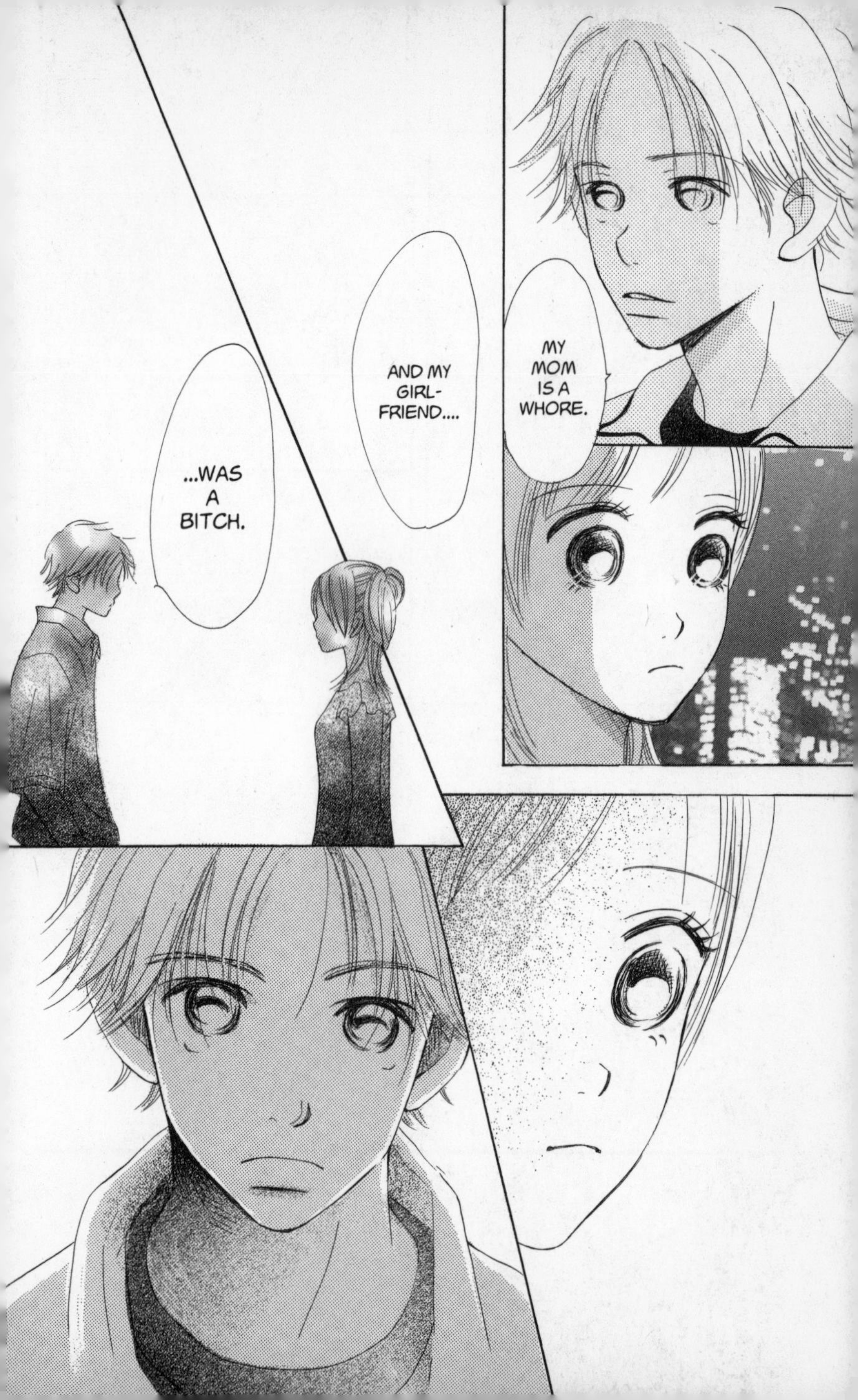
MY MOM IS A WHORE.
AND MY GIRL-FRIEND....
...WAS A BITCH.

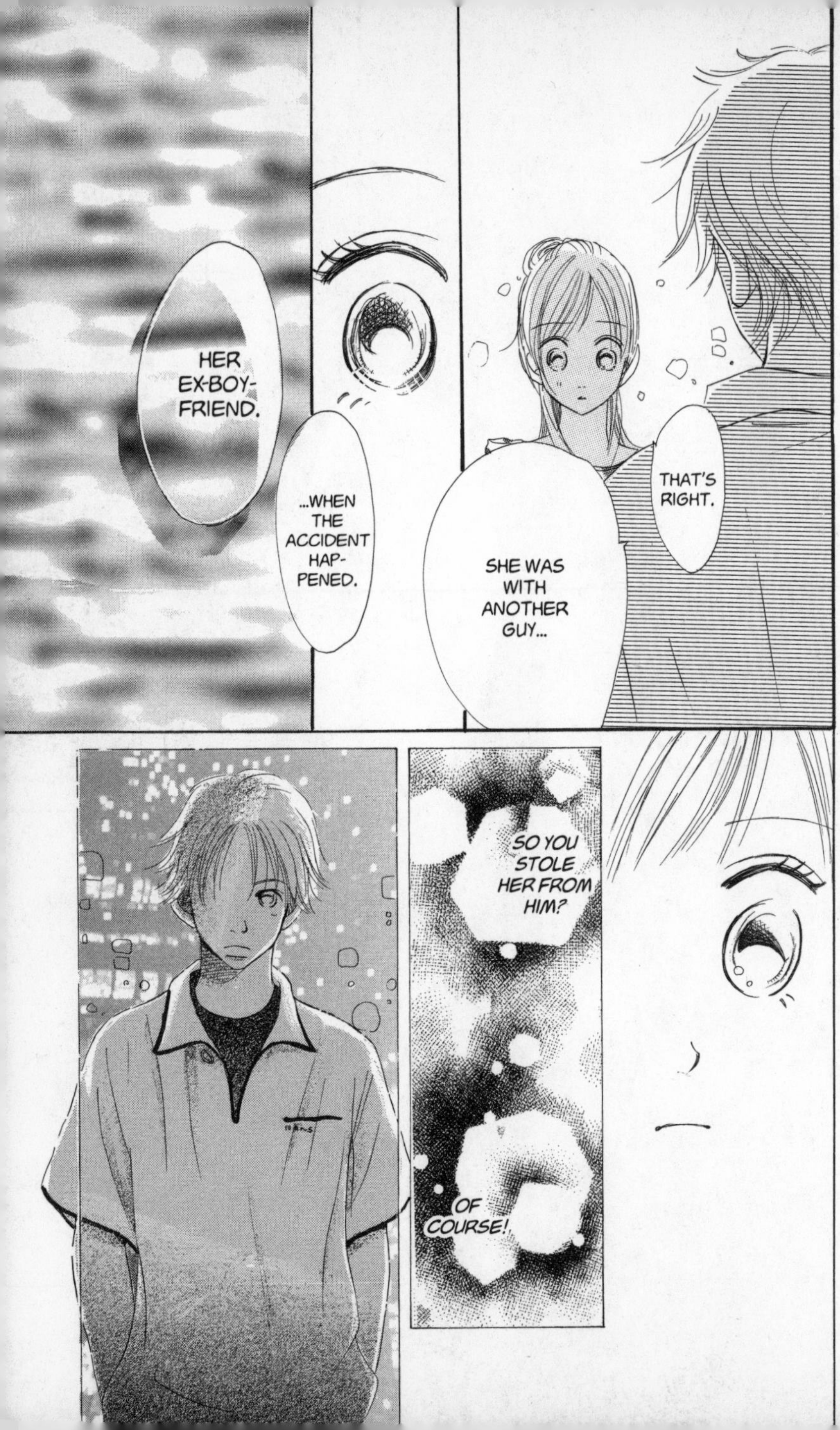
THAT'S RIGHT.
SHE WAS WITH ANOTHER GUY...
...WHEN THE ACCIDENT HAP-PENED.
HER EX-BOY-FRIEND.
SO YOU STOLE HER FROM HIM?
OF COURSE!

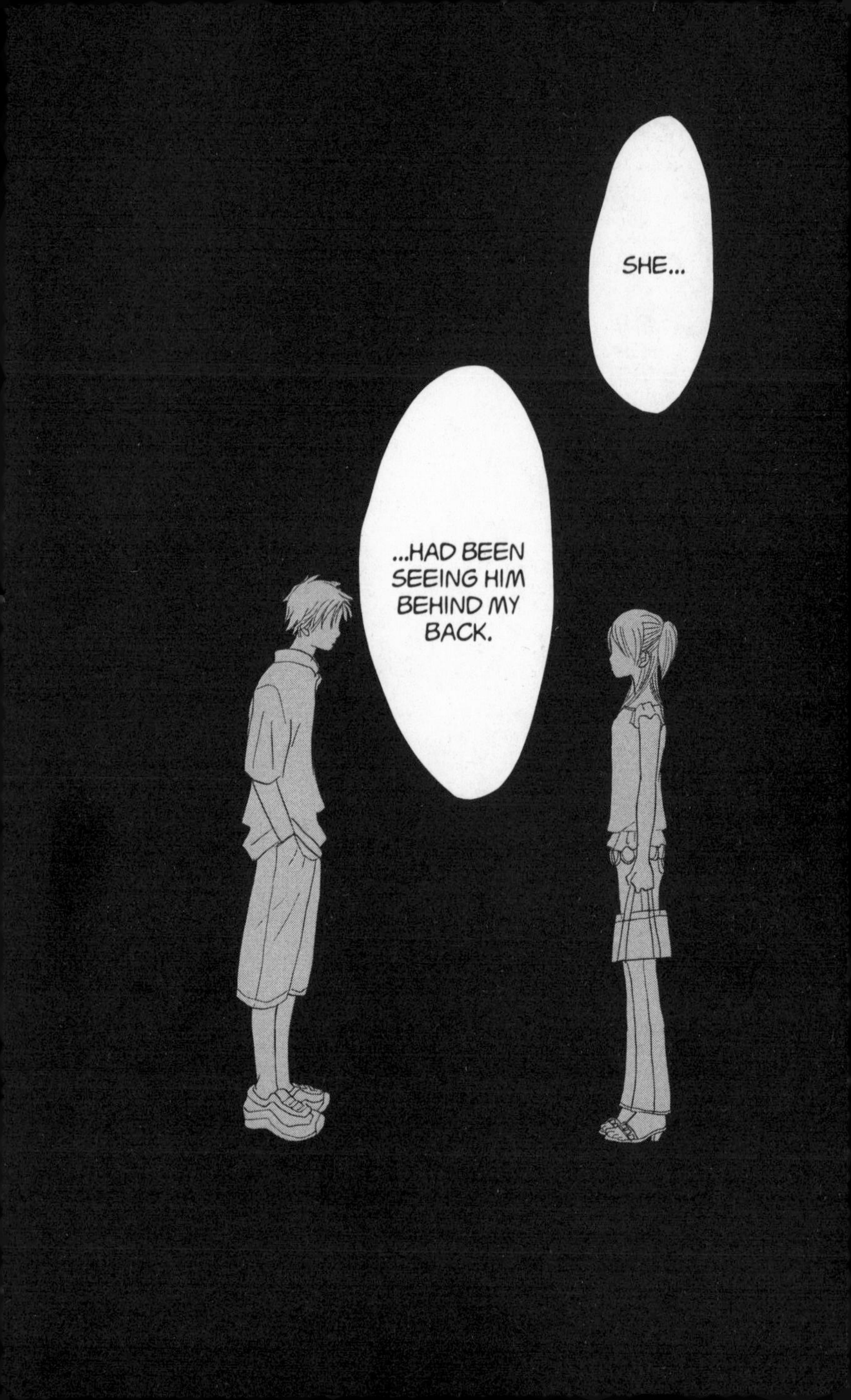
SHE...
...HAD BEEN SEEING HIM BEHIND MY BACK.

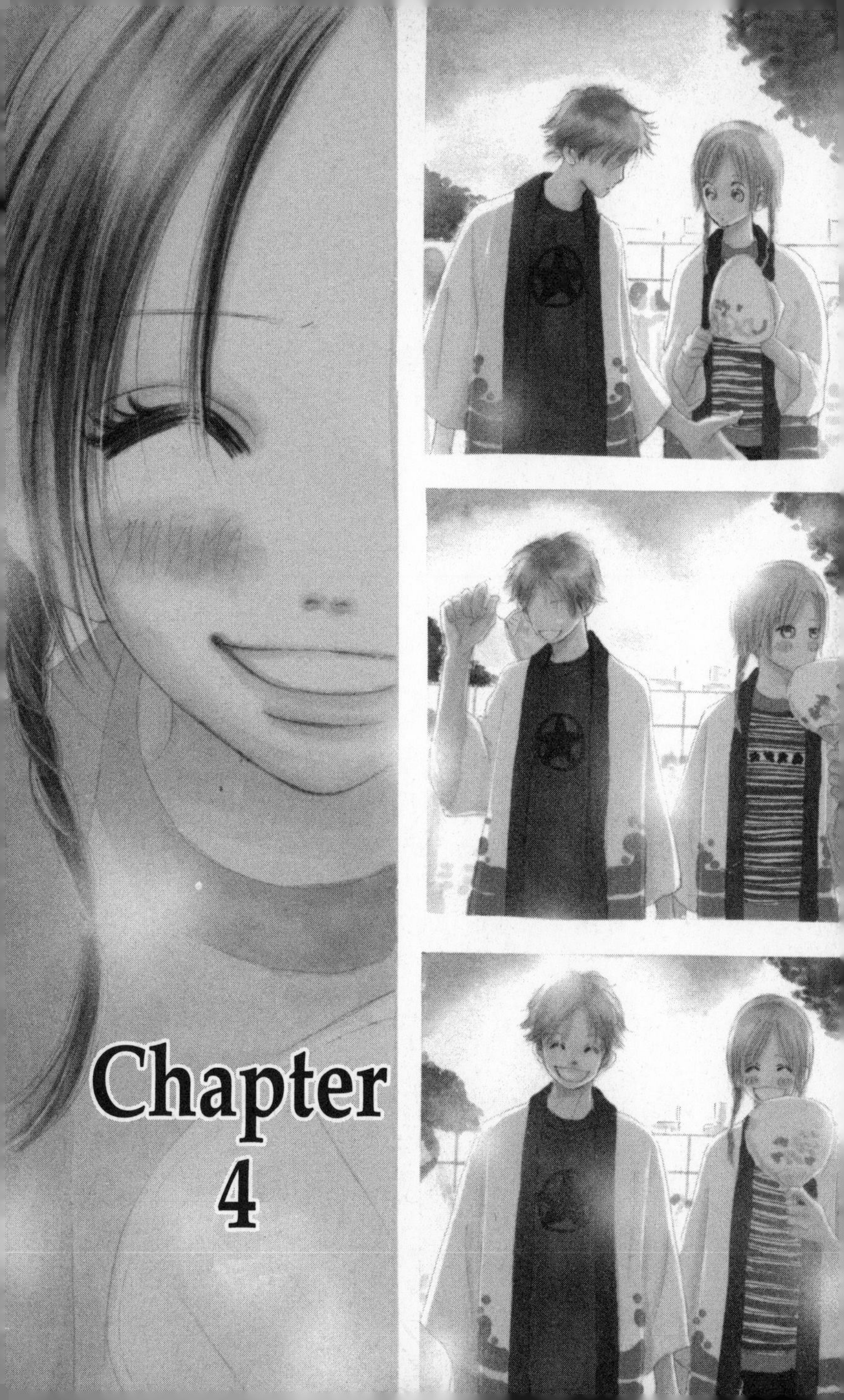
Chapter
4

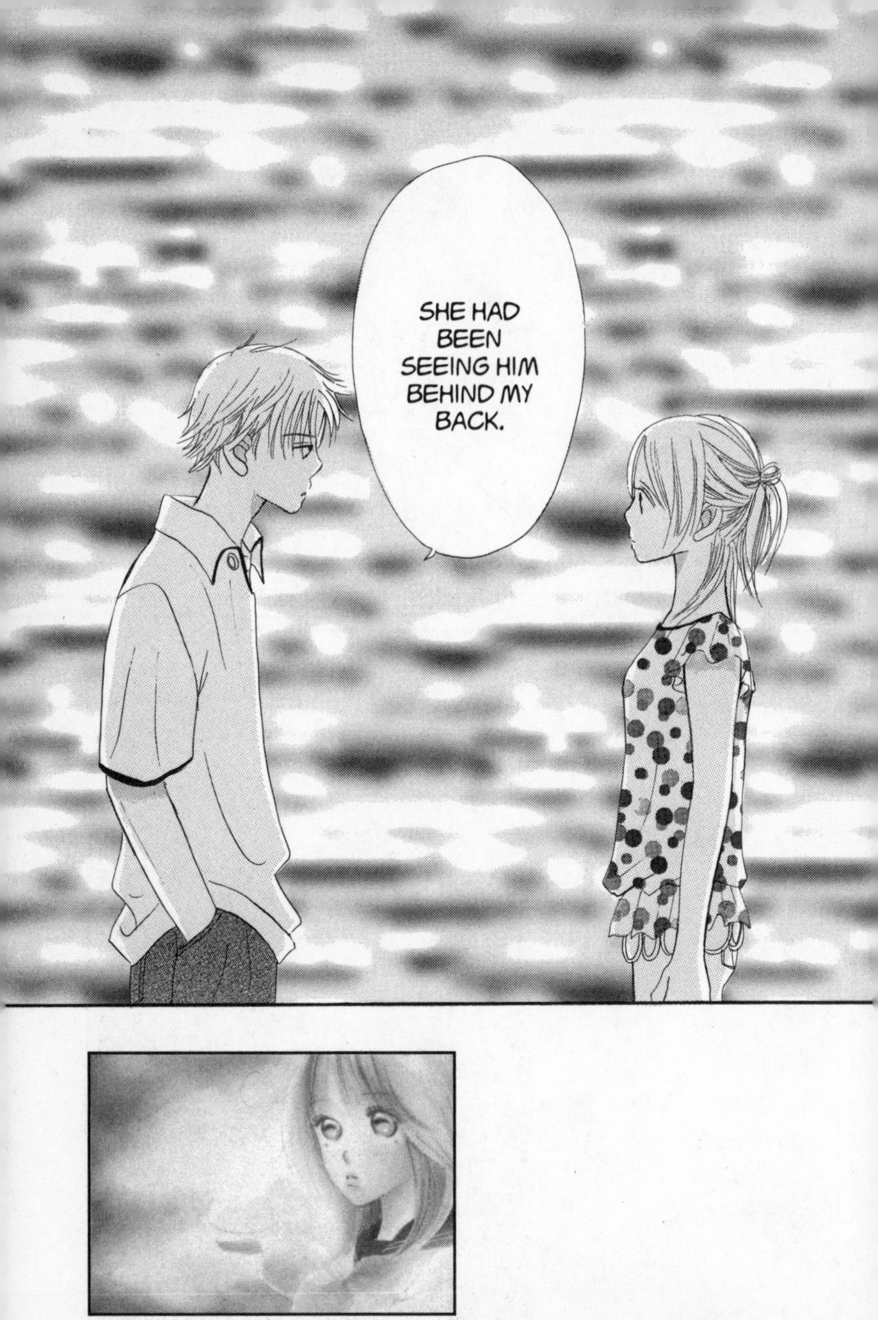
SHE HAD BEEN SEEING HIM BEHIND MY BACK.

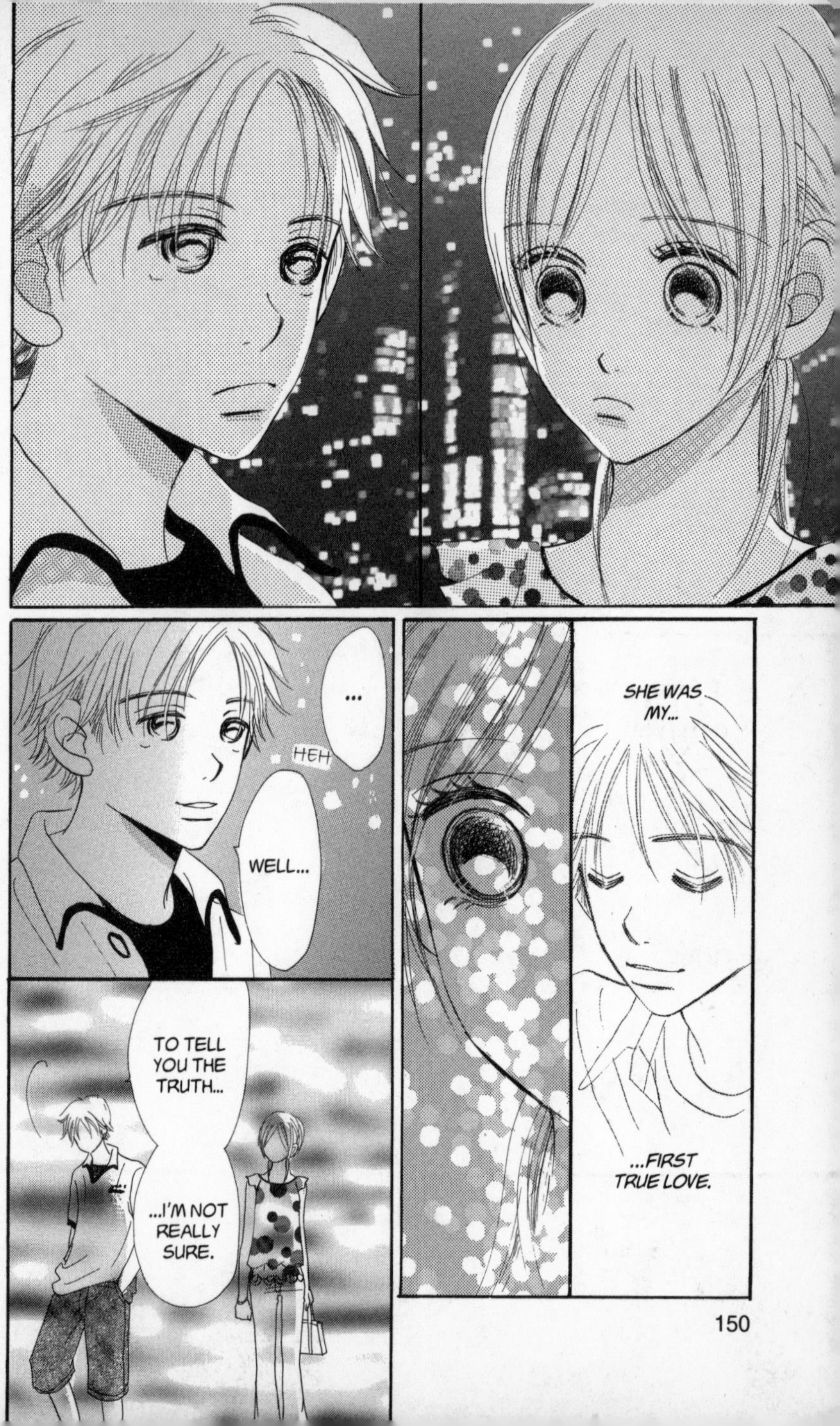
SHE WAS MY...
...FIRST TRUE LOVE.
...
HEH
WELL...
TO TELL YOU THE TRUTH...
...I'M NOT REALLY SURE.

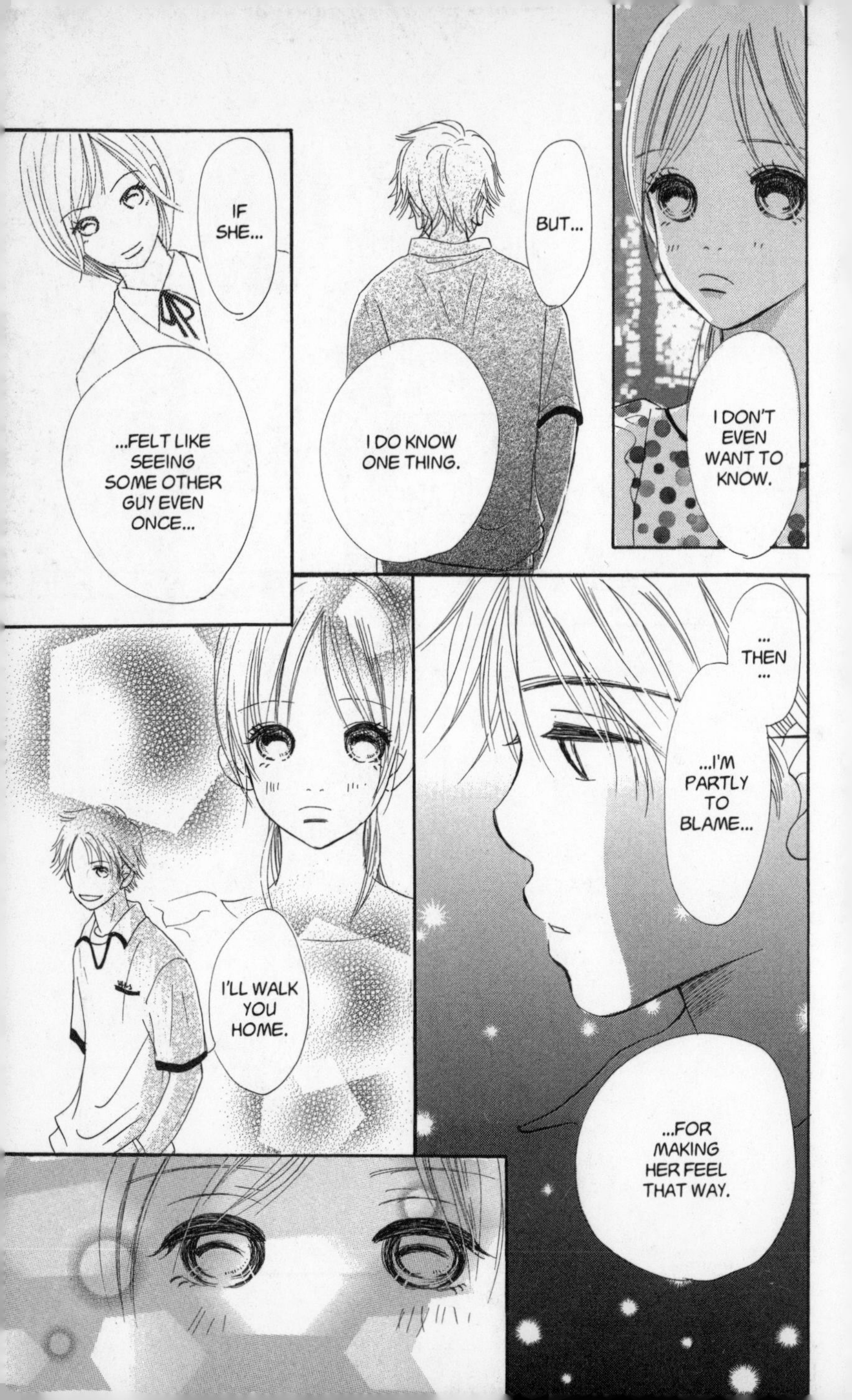
I DON'T EVEN WANT TO KNOW.
BUT...
I DO KNOW ONE THING.
IF SHE...
...FELT LIKE SEEING SOME OTHER GUY EVEN ONCE...
...THEN...
...I'M PARTLY TO BLAME...
...FOR MAKING HER FEEL THAT WAY.
I'LL WALK YOU HOME.

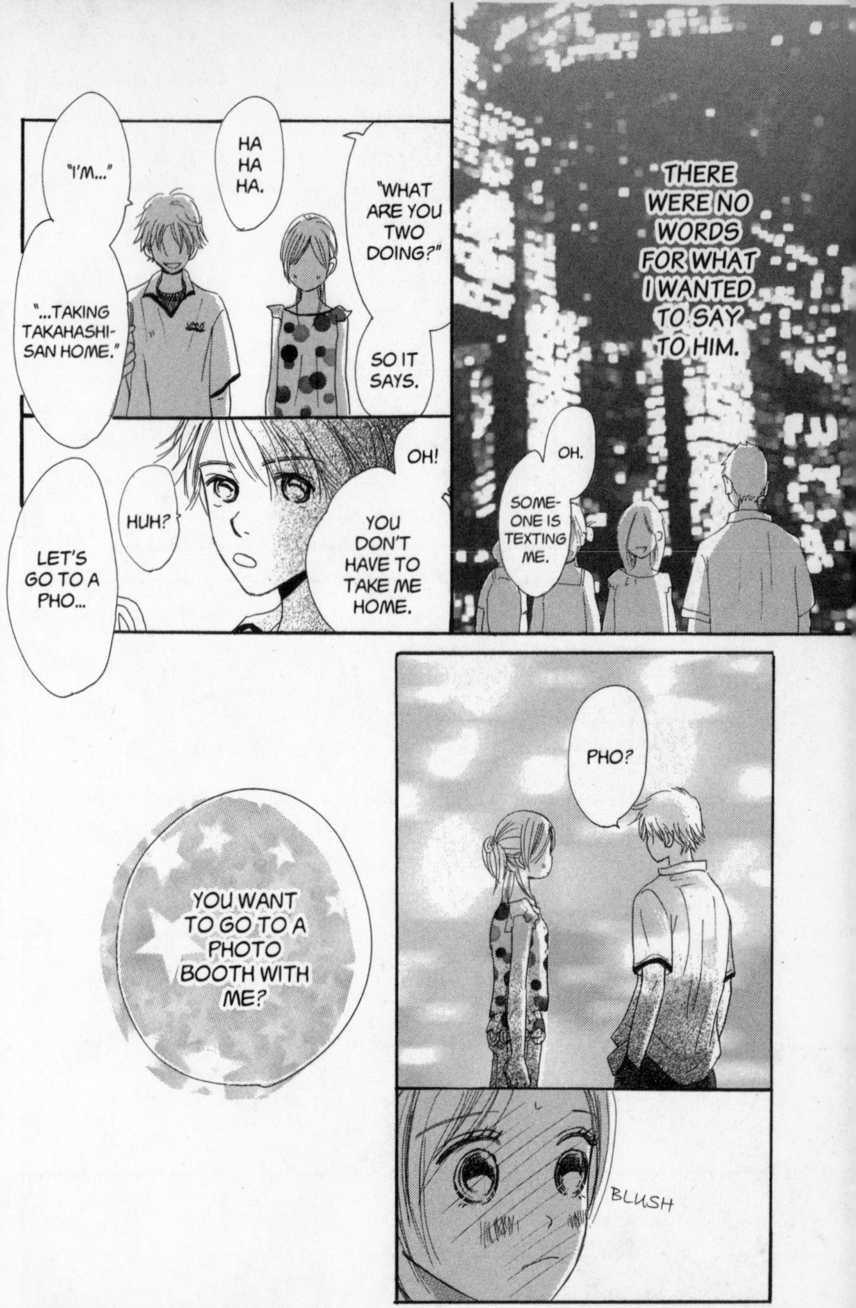
THERE WERE NO WORDS FOR WHAT I WANTED TO SAY TO HIM.
OH.
SOME-ONE IS TEXTING ME.
"WHAT ARE YOU TWO DOING?"
SO IT SAYS.
HA HA HA.
"I'M..."
"...TAKING TAKAHASHI-SAN HOME."
OH!
YOU DON'T HAVE TO TAKE ME HOME.
HUH?
LET'S GO TO A PHO...
PHO?
YOU WANT TO GO TO A PHOTO BOOTH WITH ME?
BLUSH

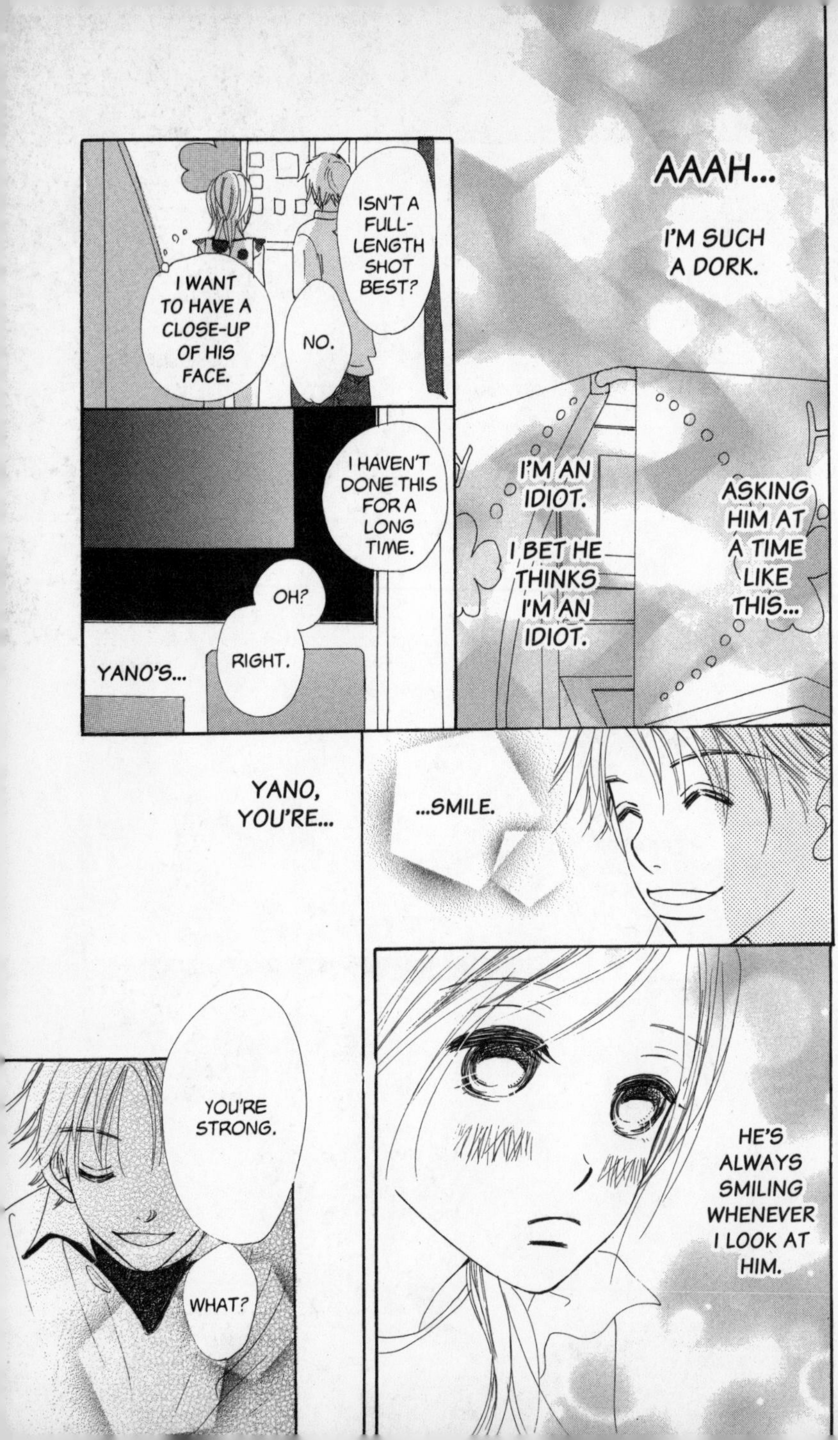
AAAH...
I'M SUCH A DORK.
ASKING HIM AT A TIME LIKE THIS...
I'M AN IDIOT.
I BET HE THINKS I'M AN IDIOT.
ISN'T A FULL-LENGTH SHOT BEST?
NO.
I WANT TO HAVE A CLOSE-UP OF HIS FACE.
I HAVEN'T DONE THIS FOR A LONG TIME.
OH?
RIGHT.
YANO'S...
...SMILE.
YANO, YOU'RE...
HE'S ALWAYS SMILING WHENEVER I LOOK AT HIM.
YOU'RE STRONG.
WHAT?

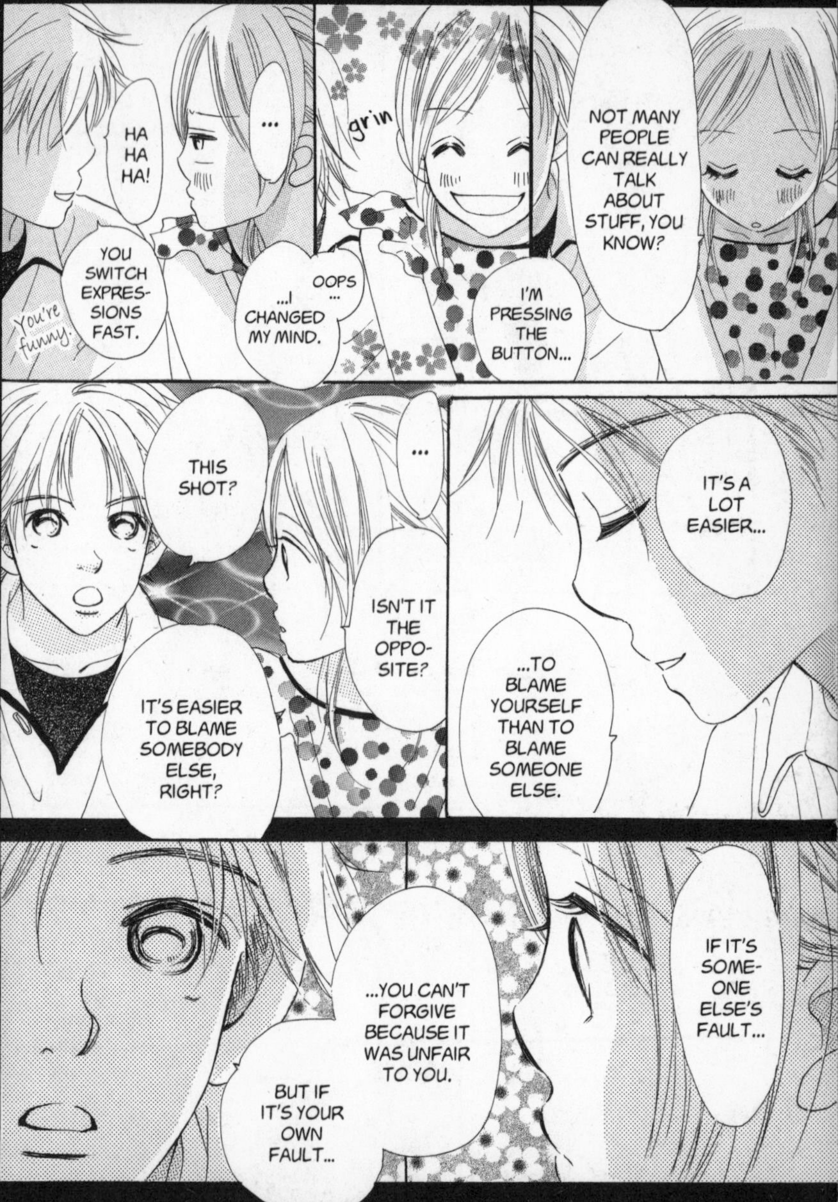
NOT MANY PEOPLE CAN REALLY TALK ABOUT STUFF, YOU KNOW?
grin
I'M PRESSING THE BUTTON...
OOPS ...
...I CHANGED MY MIND.
...
HA HA HA!
YOU SWITCH EXPRESSIONS FAST.
You're funny.
IT'S A LOT EASIER...
...TO BLAME YOURSELF THAN TO BLAME SOMEONE ELSE.
...
ISN'T IT THE OPPOSITE?
THIS SHOT?
IT'S EASIER TO BLAME SOMEBODY ELSE, RIGHT?
IF IT'S SOMEONE ELSE'S FAULT...
...YOU CAN'T FORGIVE BECAUSE IT WAS UNFAIR TO YOU.
BUT IF IT'S YOUR OWN FAULT...

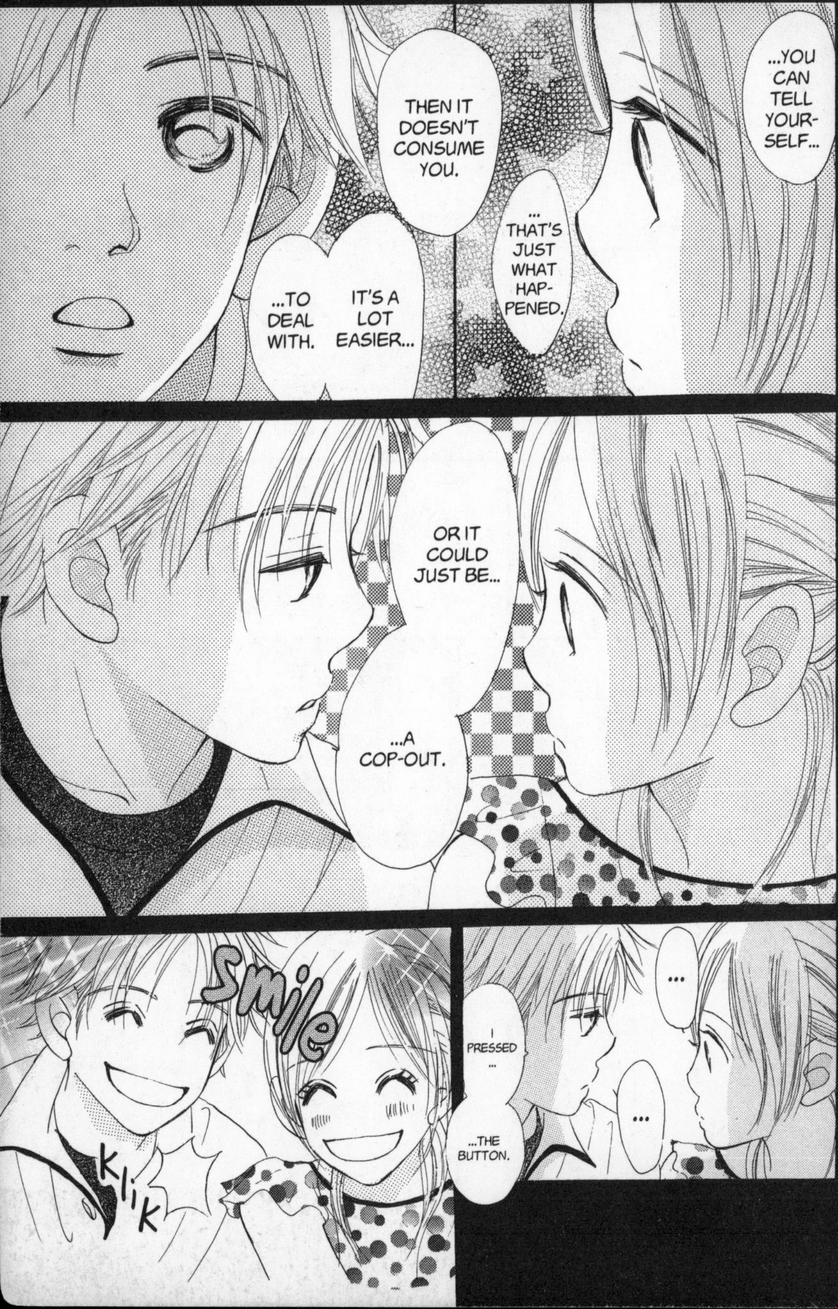
...YOU CAN TELL YOURSELF...
...THAT'S JUST WHAT HAPPENED.
THEN IT DOESN'T CONSUME YOU.
IT'S A LOT EASIER...
...TO DEAL WITH.
OR IT COULD JUST BE...
...A COP-OUT.
...
I PRESSED...
...
...THE BUTTON.
Smile
Klik

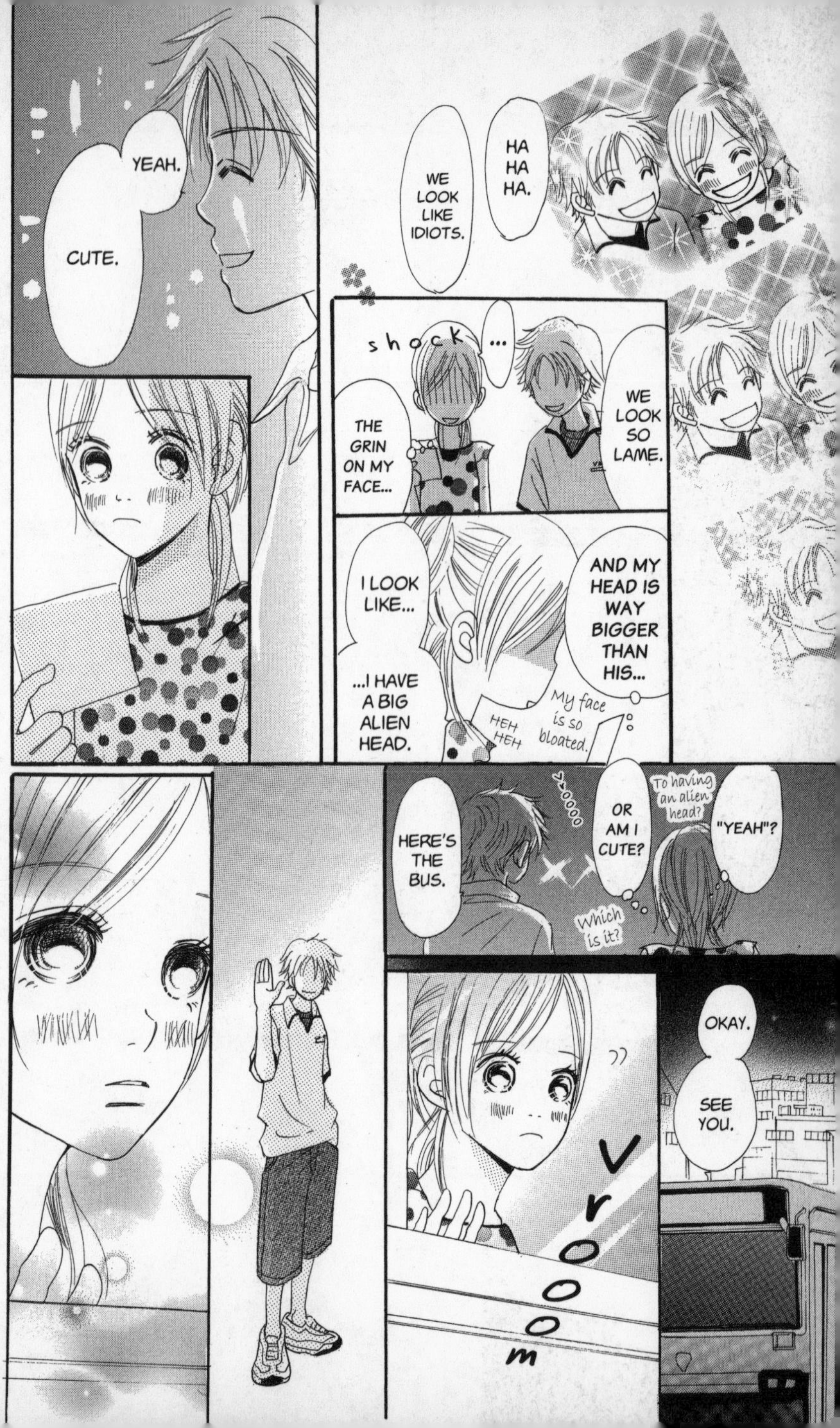
HA HA HA.
WE LOOK LIKE IDIOTS.
shock
...
WE LOOK SO LAME.
THE GRIN ON MY FACE...
AND MY HEAD IS WAY BIGGER THAN HIS...
My face is so bloated.
HEH HEH
I LOOK LIKE...
...I HAVE A BIG ALIEN HEAD.
YEAH.
CUTE.
"YEAH"?
To having an alien head?
OR AM I CUTE?
Which is it?
HERE'S THE BUS.
vvoooo
OKAY.
SEE YOU.
Vrooooom

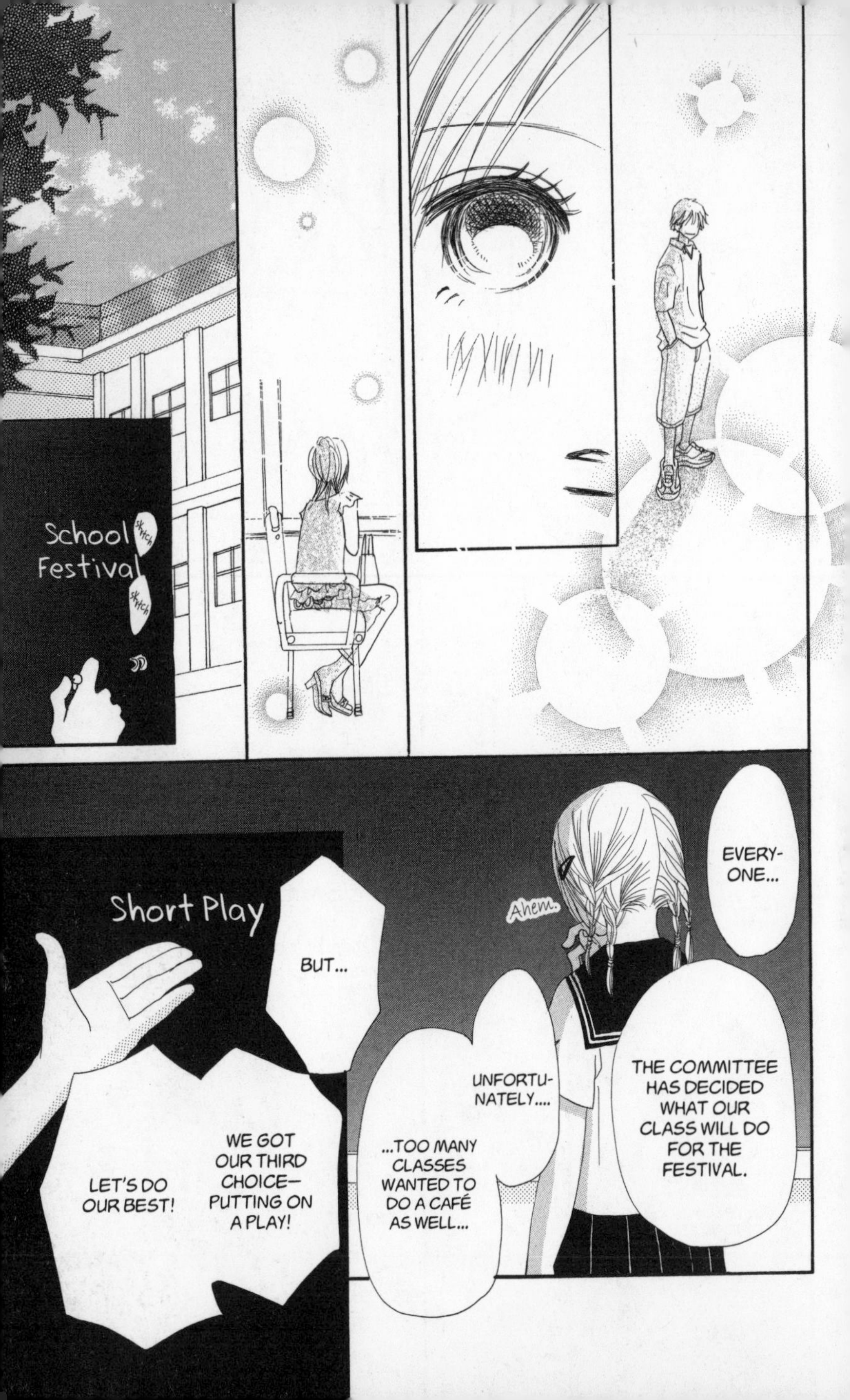
School
sktch
Festival
sktch
EVERY-ONE...
Ahem.
THE COMMITTEE HAS DECIDED WHAT OUR CLASS WILL DO FOR THE FESTIVAL.
UNFORTU-NATELY....
...TOO MANY CLASSES WANTED TO DO A CAFÉ AS WELL...
Short Play
BUT...
WE GOT OUR THIRD CHOICE— PUTTING ON A PLAY!
LET'S DO OUR BEST!

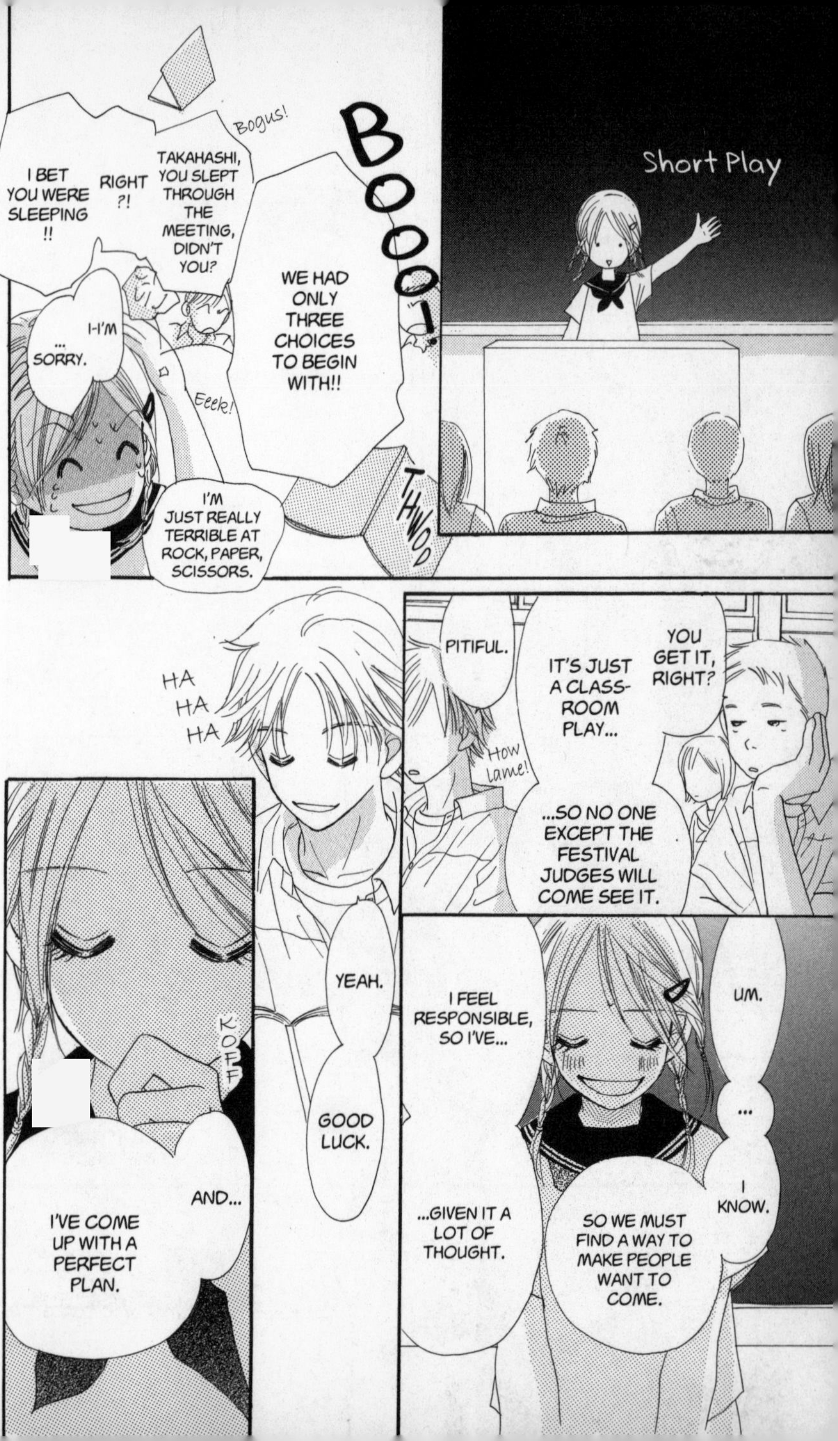
Short Play
BOOOO!
Bogus!
TAKAHASHI, YOU SLEPT THROUGH THE MEETING, DIDN'T YOU?
RIGHT ?!
I BET YOU WERE SLEEPING !!
WE HAD ONLY THREE CHOICES TO BEGIN WITH!!
Eeek!
I-I'M ... SORRY.
THWOD
I'M JUST REALLY TERRIBLE AT ROCK, PAPER, SCISSORS.
YOU GET IT, RIGHT?
IT'S JUST A CLASS-ROOM PLAY...
PITIFUL.
How lame!
...SO NO ONE EXCEPT THE FESTIVAL JUDGES WILL COME SEE IT.
UM.
...
I KNOW.
I FEEL RESPONSIBLE, SO I'VE...
...GIVEN IT A LOT OF THOUGHT.
SO WE MUST FIND A WAY TO MAKE PEOPLE WANT TO COME.
HA HA HA
YEAH.
GOOD LUCK.
KOFF
AND...
I'VE COME UP WITH A PERFECT PLAN.

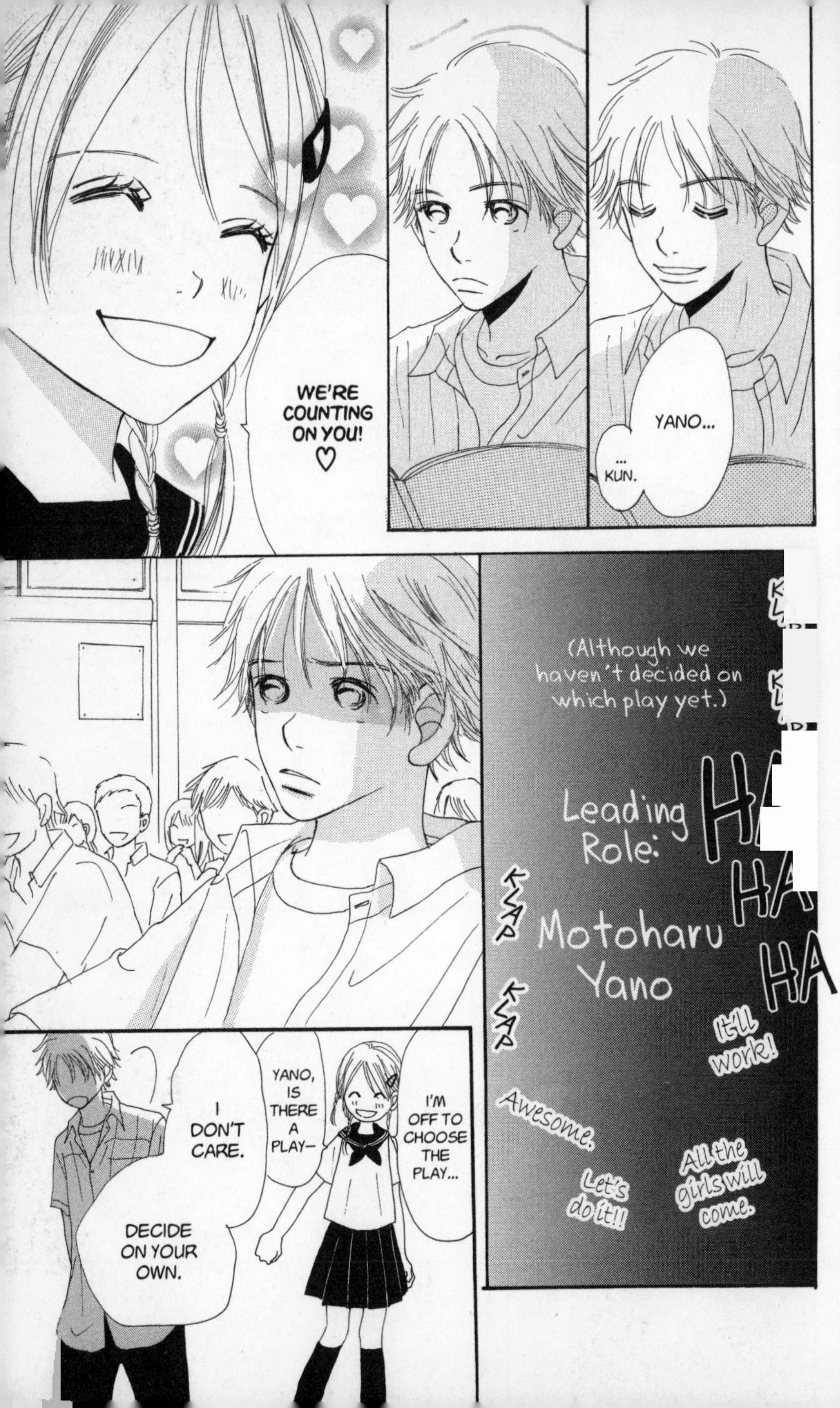

YANO...
...KUN.
WE'RE COUNTING ON YOU! ♡
(Although we haven't decided on which play yet.)
HA HA HA
Leading Role: Motoharu Yano
KLAP KLAP
It'll work!
Awesome.
All the girls will come.
Let's do it!!
I'M OFF TO CHOOSE THE PLAY...
YANO, IS THERE A PLAY—
I DON'T CARE.
DECIDE ON YOUR OWN.

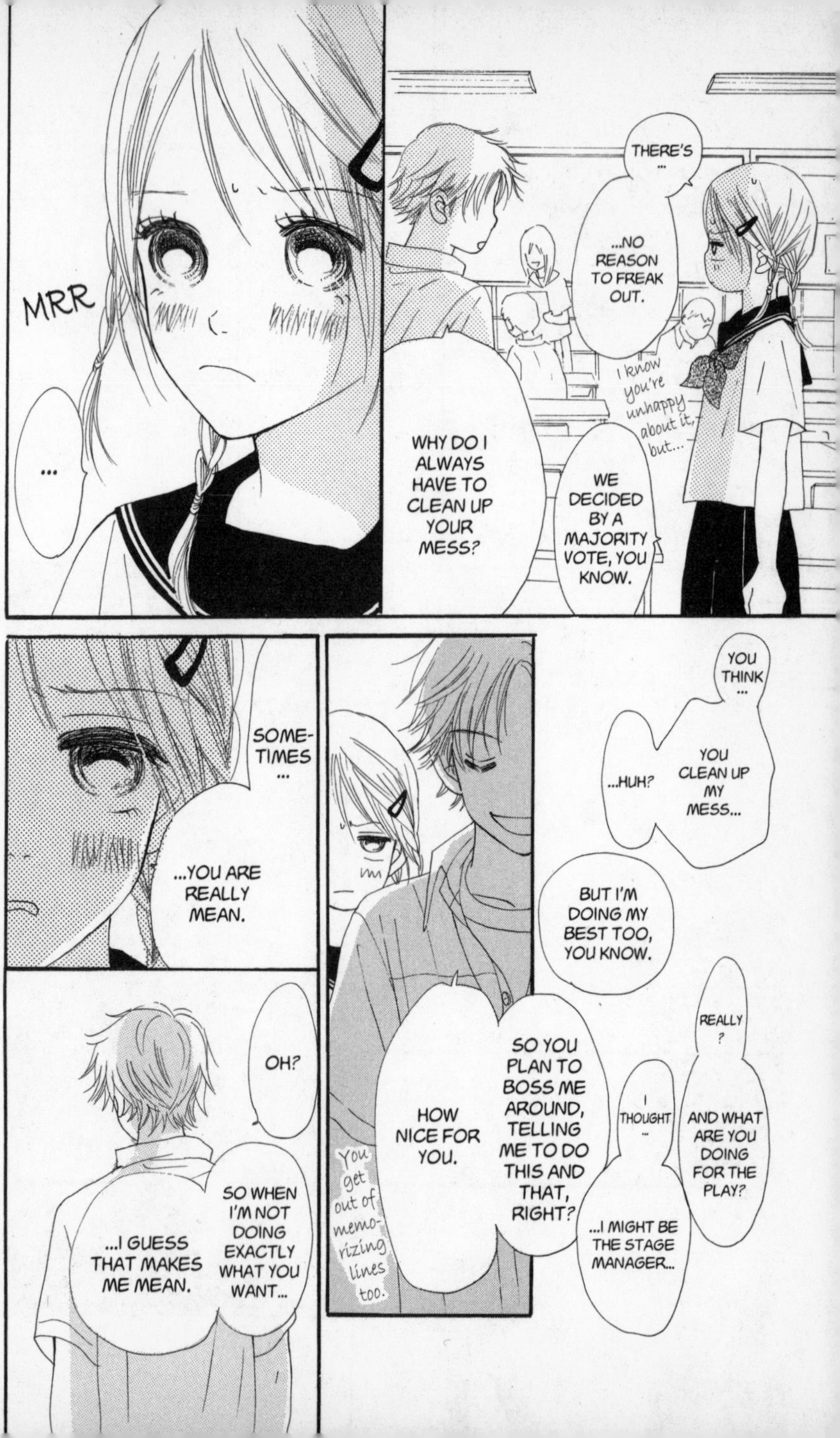
THERE'S...
...NO REASON TO FREAK OUT.
I know you're unhappy about it, but...
WE DECIDED BY A MAJORITY VOTE, YOU KNOW.
WHY DO I ALWAYS HAVE TO CLEAN UP YOUR MESS?
MRR
...
YOU THINK...
YOU CLEAN UP MY MESS...
...HUH?
BUT I'M DOING MY BEST TOO, YOU KNOW.
REALLY?
AND WHAT ARE YOU DOING FOR THE PLAY?
I THOUGHT...
...I MIGHT BE THE STAGE MANAGER...
SO YOU PLAN TO BOSS ME AROUND, TELLING ME TO DO THIS AND THAT, RIGHT?
HOW NICE FOR YOU.
You get out of memorizing lines too.
SOME-TIMES...
...YOU ARE REALLY MEAN.
OH?
SO WHEN I'M NOT DOING EXACTLY WHAT YOU WANT...
...I GUESS THAT MAKES ME MEAN.

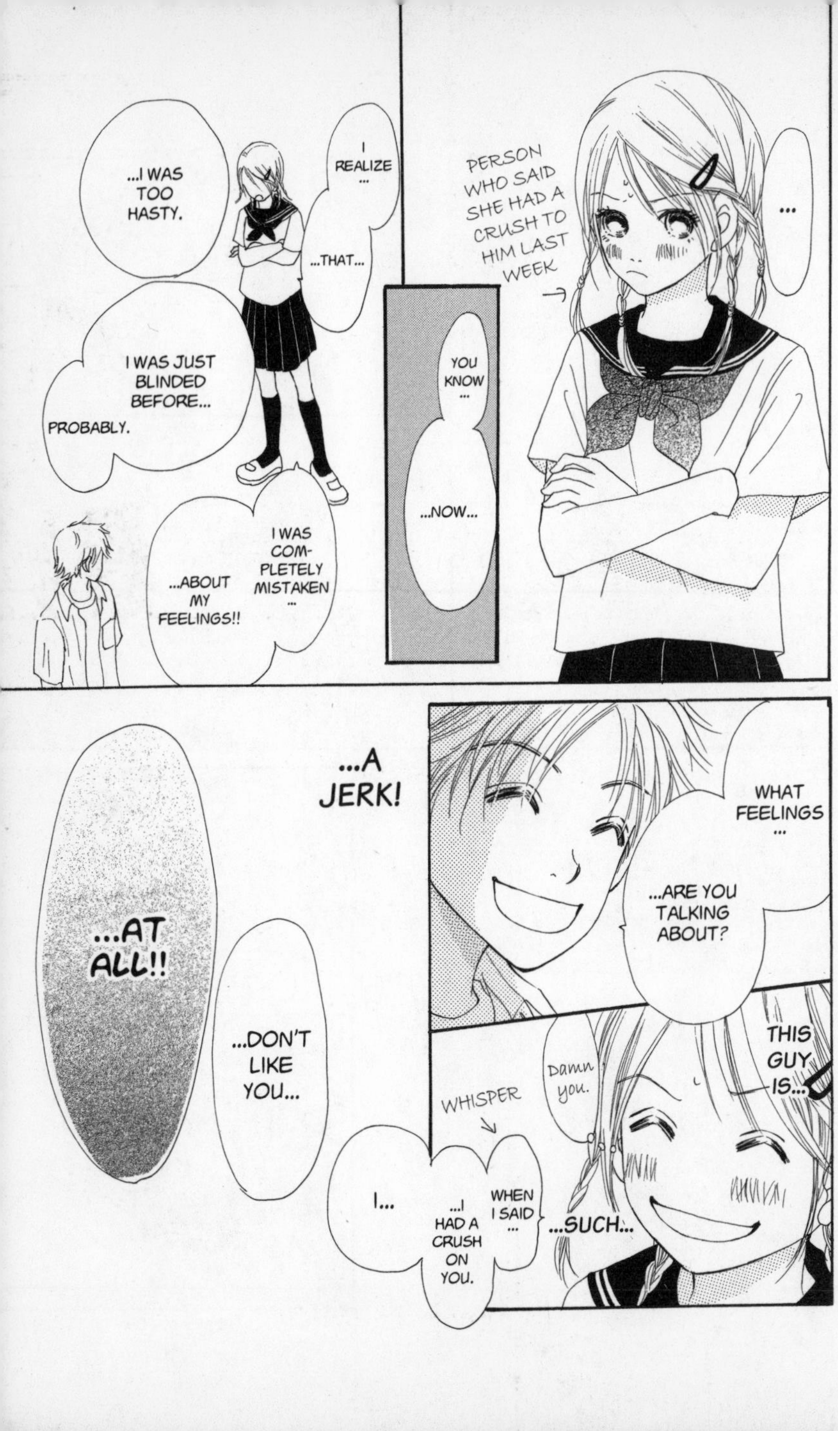
PERSON WHO SAID SHE HAD A CRUSH TO HIM LAST WEEK
...
YOU KNOW...
...NOW...
I REALIZE...
...THAT...
...I WAS TOO HASTY.
I WAS JUST BLINDED BEFORE...
PROBABLY.
I WAS COMPLETELY MISTAKEN...
...ABOUT MY FEELINGS!!
WHAT FEELINGS...
...ARE YOU TALKING ABOUT?
THIS GUY IS...
...SUCH...
...A JERK!
Damn you.
WHISPER
WHEN I SAID...
...I HAD A CRUSH ON YOU.
I...
...DON'T LIKE YOU...
...AT ALL!!

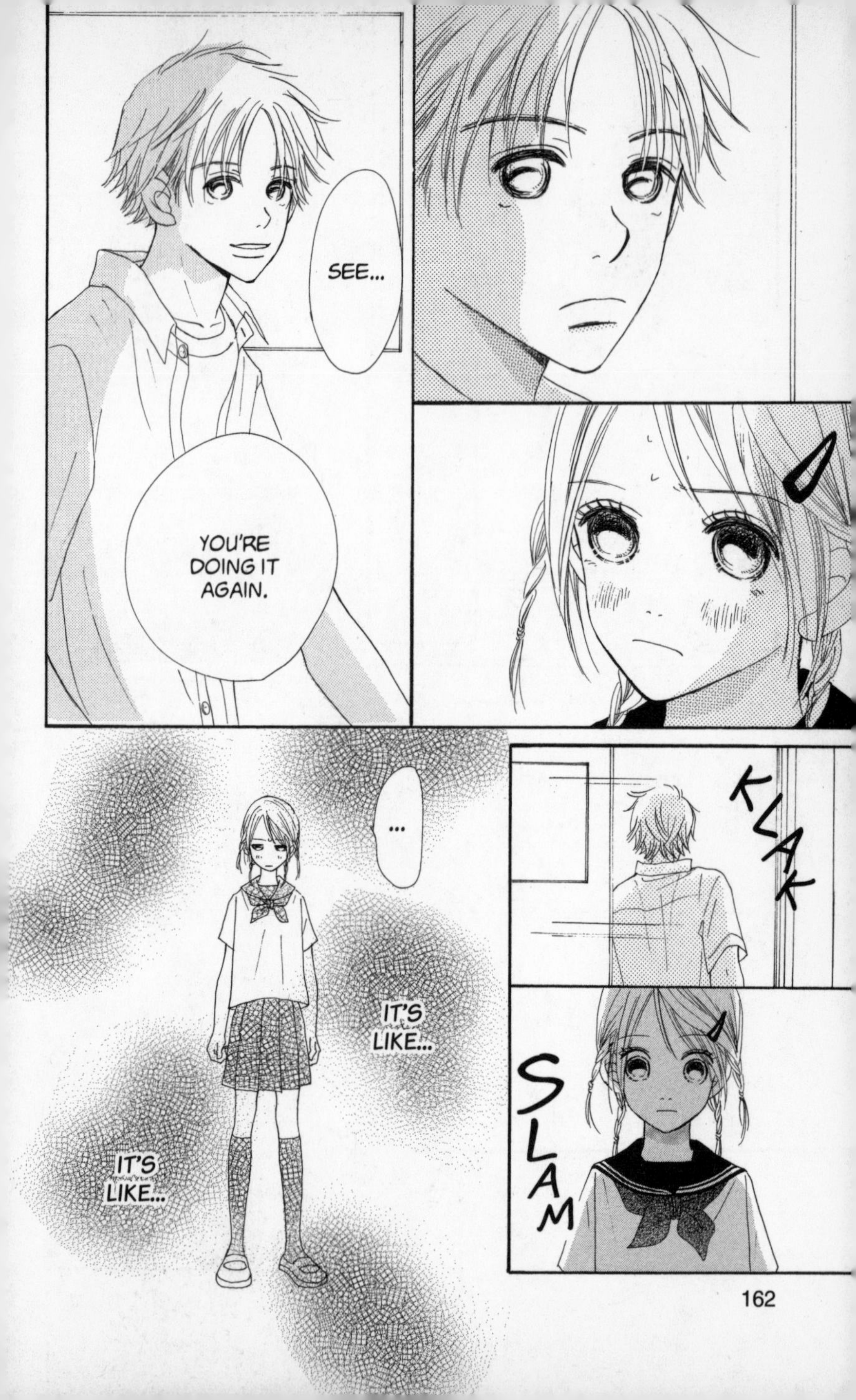
SEE...
YOU'RE DOING IT AGAIN.
KLAK
SLAM
...
IT'S LIKE...
IT'S LIKE...

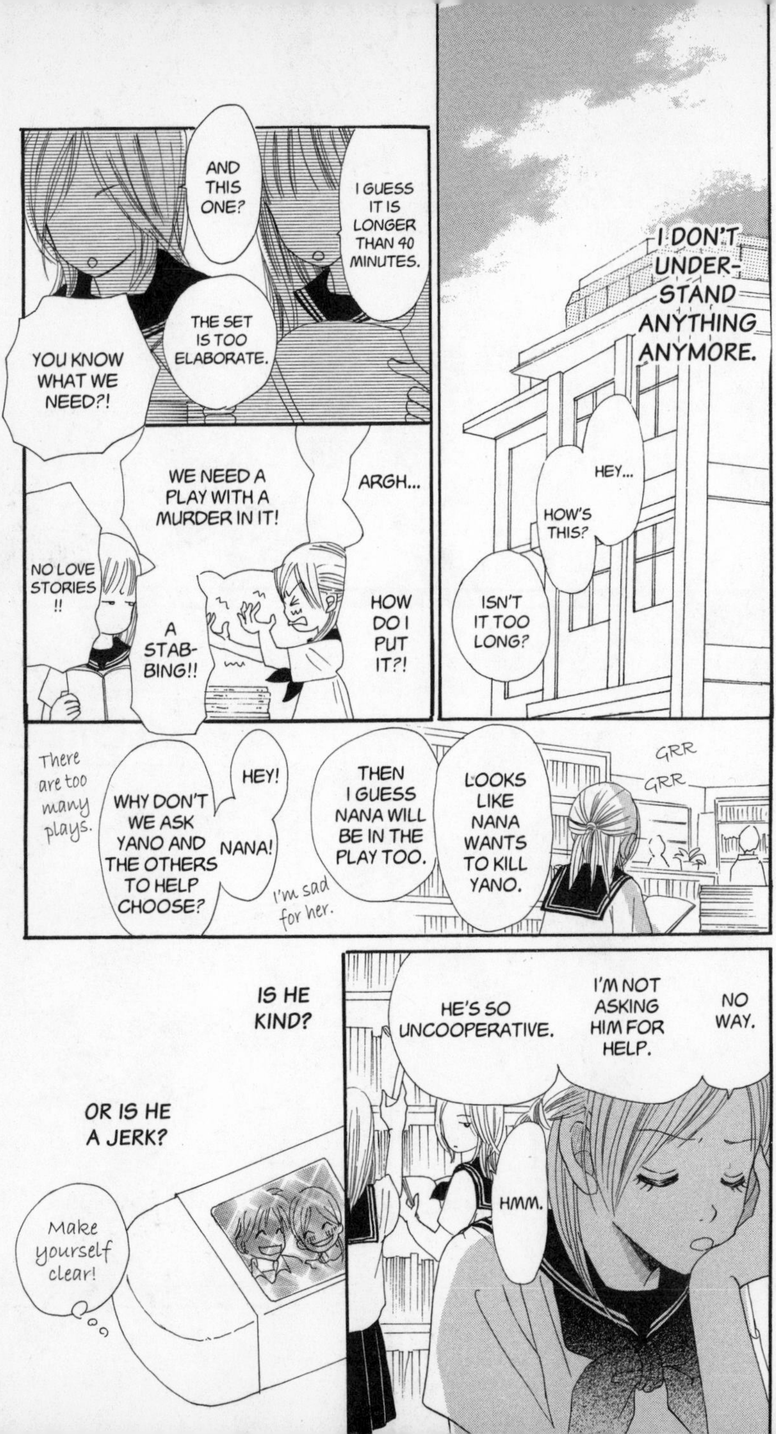
I DON'T UNDER-STAND ANYTHING ANYMORE.
HEY...
HOW'S THIS?
ISN'T IT TOO LONG?
I GUESS IT IS LONGER THAN 40 MINUTES.
AND THIS ONE?
THE SET IS TOO ELABORATE.
YOU KNOW WHAT WE NEED?!
ARGH...
WE NEED A PLAY WITH A MURDER IN IT!
HOW DO I PUT IT?!
A STAB-BING!!
NO LOVE STORIES !!
GRR
GRR
LOOKS LIKE NANA WANTS TO KILL YANO.
THEN I GUESS NANA WILL BE IN THE PLAY TOO.
I'm sad for her.
HEY! NANA!
WHY DON'T WE ASK YANO AND THE OTHERS TO HELP CHOOSE?
There are too many plays.
NO WAY.
I'M NOT ASKING HIM FOR HELP.
HE'S SO UNCOOPERATIVE.
HMM.
IS HE KIND?
OR IS HE A JERK?
Make yourself clear!

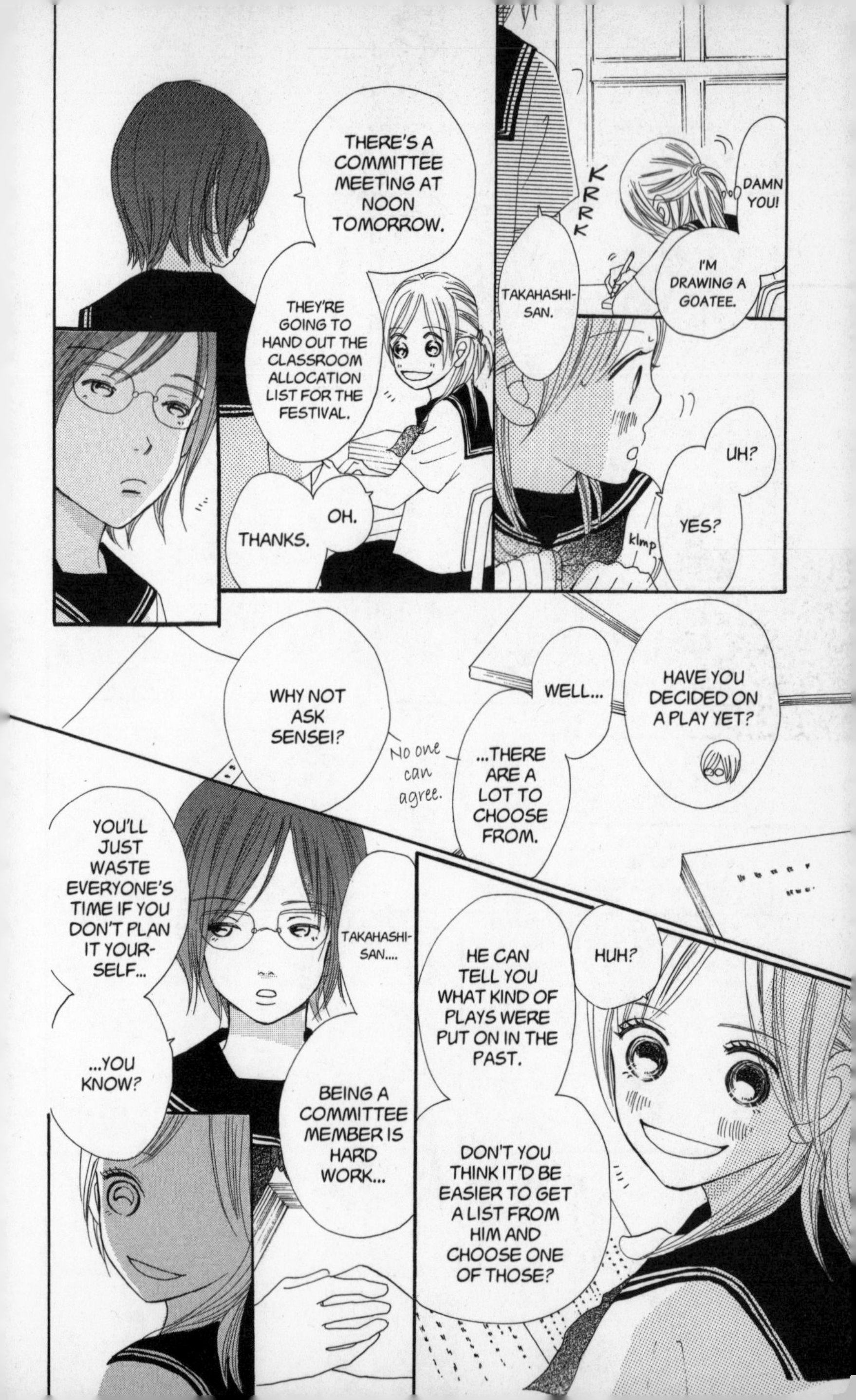

DAMN YOU!
I'M DRAWING A GOATEE.
KRRK
TAKAHASHI-SAN.
UH?
YES?
klmp
THERE'S A COMMITTEE MEETING AT NOON TOMORROW.
THEY'RE GOING TO HAND OUT THE CLASSROOM ALLOCATION LIST FOR THE FESTIVAL.
OH.
THANKS.
HAVE YOU DECIDED ON A PLAY YET?
WELL...
...THERE ARE A LOT TO CHOOSE FROM.
No one can agree.
WHY NOT ASK SENSEI?
HUH?
HE CAN TELL YOU WHAT KIND OF PLAYS WERE PUT ON IN THE PAST.
DON'T YOU THINK IT'D BE EASIER TO GET A LIST FROM HIM AND CHOOSE ONE OF THOSE?
TAKAHASHI-SAN....
BEING A COMMITTEE MEMBER IS HARD WORK...
YOU'LL JUST WASTE EVERYONE'S TIME IF YOU DON'T PLAN IT YOURSELF...
...YOU KNOW?

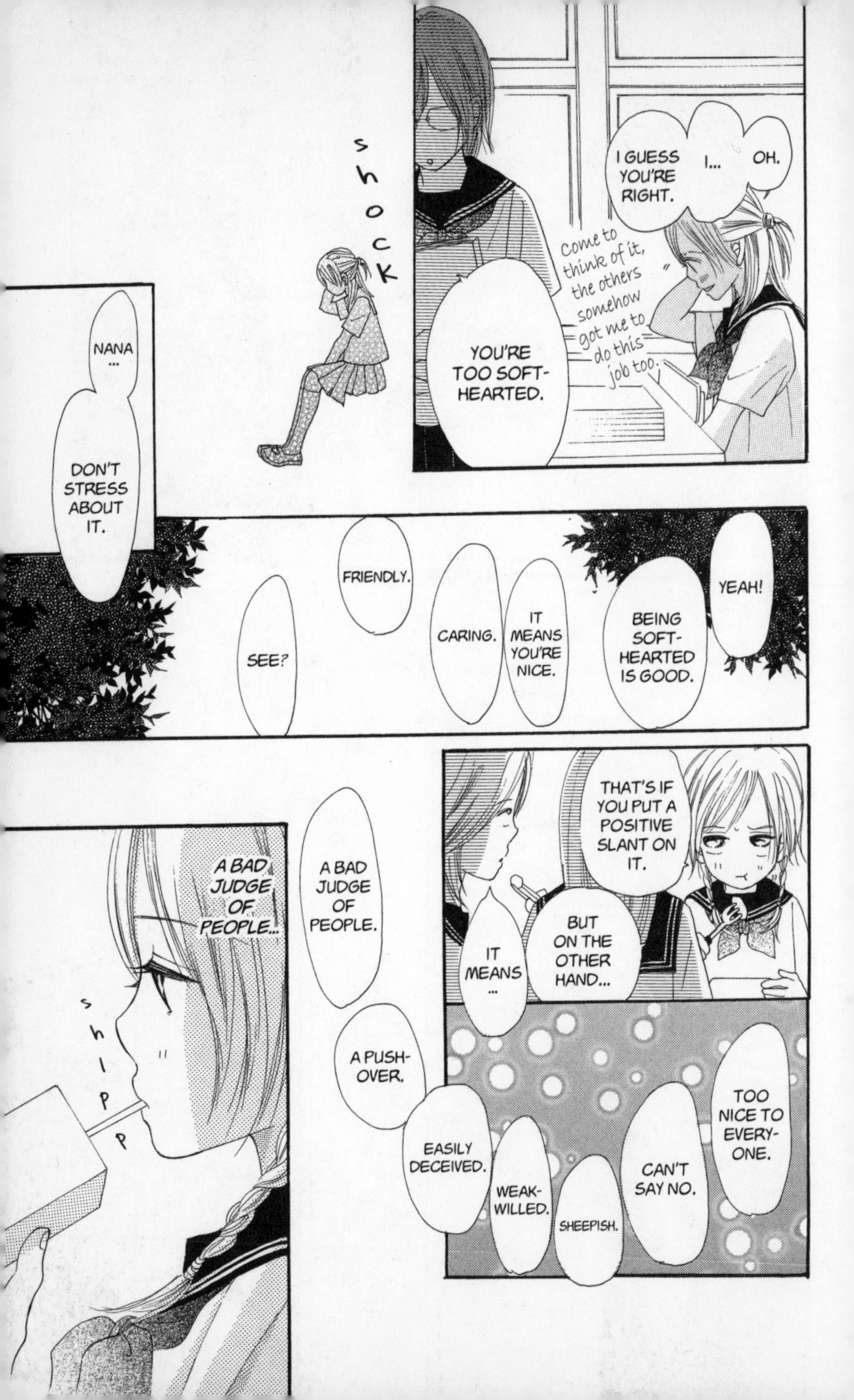
OH.
I...
I GUESS YOU'RE RIGHT.
Come to think of it, the others somehow got me to do this job too.
YOU'RE TOO SOFT-HEARTED.
shock
NANA...
DON'T STRESS ABOUT IT.
YEAH!
BEING SOFT-HEARTED IS GOOD.
IT MEANS YOU'RE NICE.
CARING.
FRIENDLY.
SEE?
THAT'S IF YOU PUT A POSITIVE SLANT ON IT.
BUT ON THE OTHER HAND...
IT MEANS...
TOO NICE TO EVERY-ONE.
CAN'T SAY NO.
SHEEPISH.
WEAK-WILLED.
EASILY DECEIVED.
A PUSH-OVER.
A BAD JUDGE OF PEOPLE.
A BAD JUDGE OF PEOPLE...
shipp

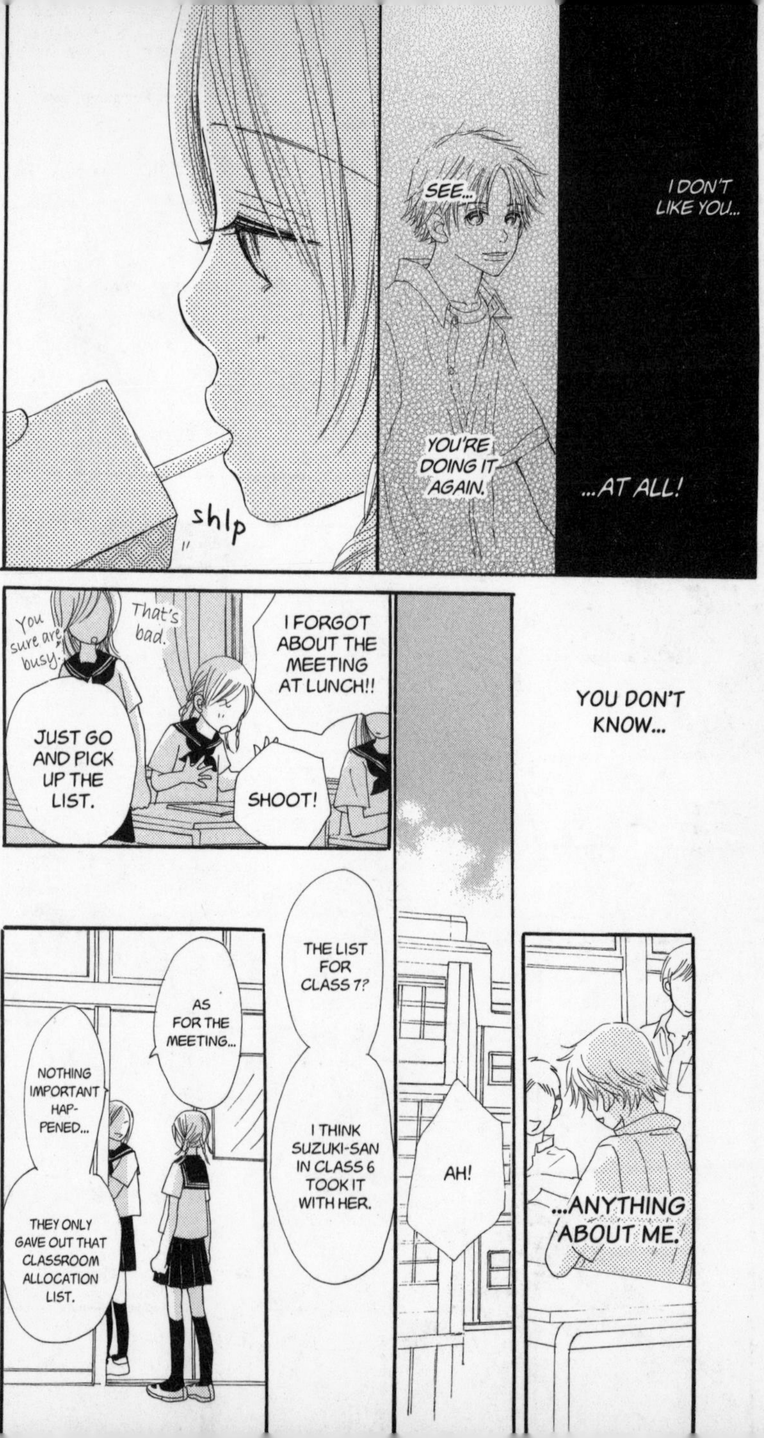
I DON'T LIKE YOU...
...AT ALL!
SEE...
YOU'RE DOING IT AGAIN.
shlp
YOU DON'T KNOW...
...ANYTHING ABOUT ME.
AH!
I FORGOT ABOUT THE MEETING AT LUNCH!!
SHOOT!
That's bad.
You sure are busy.
JUST GO AND PICK UP THE LIST.
THE LIST FOR CLASS 7?
I THINK SUZUKI-SAN IN CLASS 6 TOOK IT WITH HER.
AS FOR THE MEETING...
NOTHING IMPORTANT HAP-PENED...
THEY ONLY GAVE OUT THAT CLASSROOM ALLOCATION LIST.

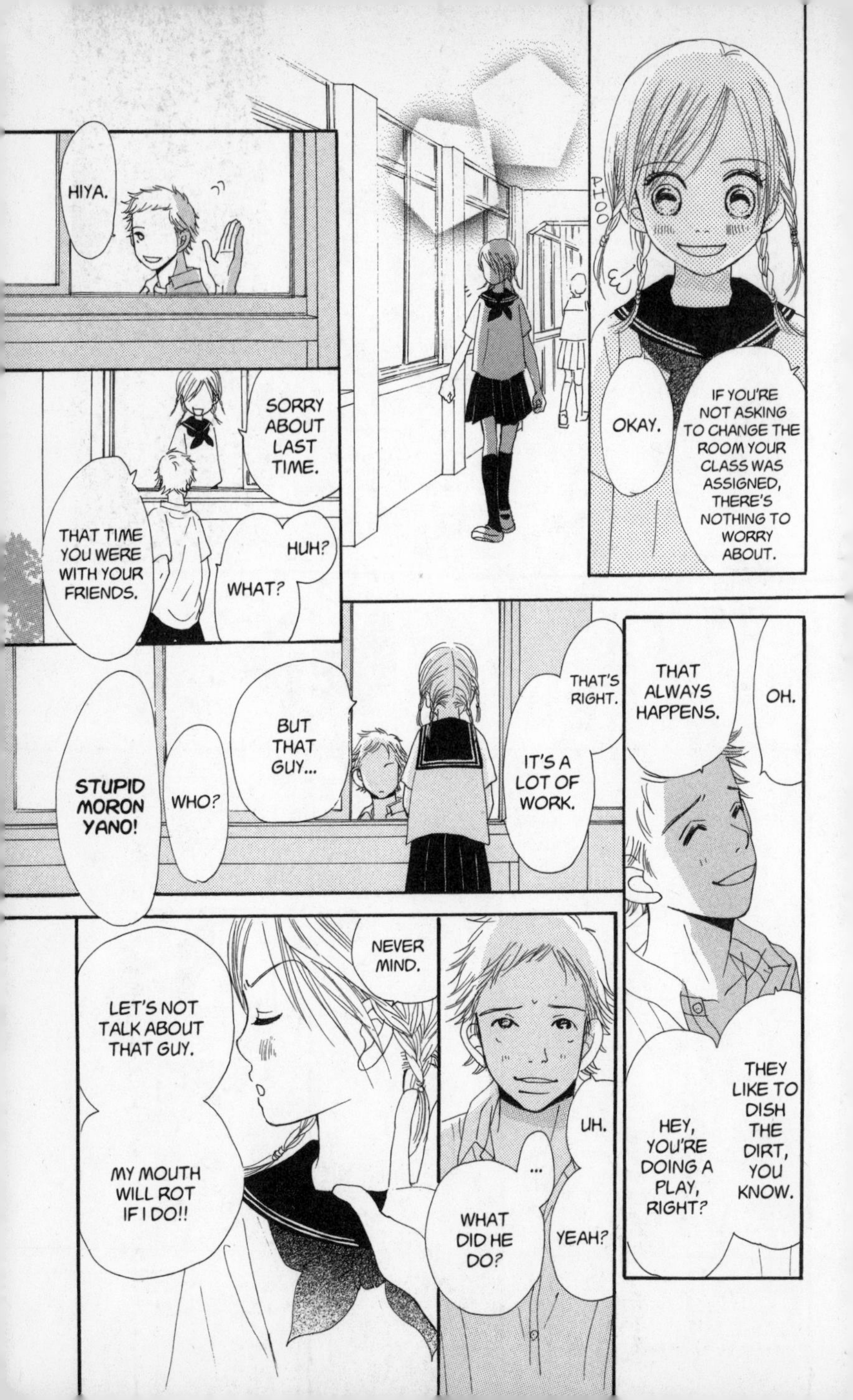
PHOO
IF YOU'RE NOT ASKING TO CHANGE THE ROOM YOUR CLASS WAS ASSIGNED, THERE'S NOTHING TO WORRY ABOUT.
OKAY.
HIYA.
SORRY ABOUT LAST TIME.
HUH?
WHAT?
THAT TIME YOU WERE WITH YOUR FRIENDS.
OH.
THAT ALWAYS HAPPENS.
THAT'S RIGHT.
IT'S A LOT OF WORK.
THEY LIKE TO DISH THE DIRT, YOU KNOW.
HEY, YOU'RE DOING A PLAY, RIGHT?
BUT THAT GUY...
WHO?
STUPID MORON YANO!
UH.
...
YEAH?
WHAT DID HE DO?
NEVER MIND.
LET'S NOT TALK ABOUT THAT GUY.
MY MOUTH WILL ROT IF I DO!!

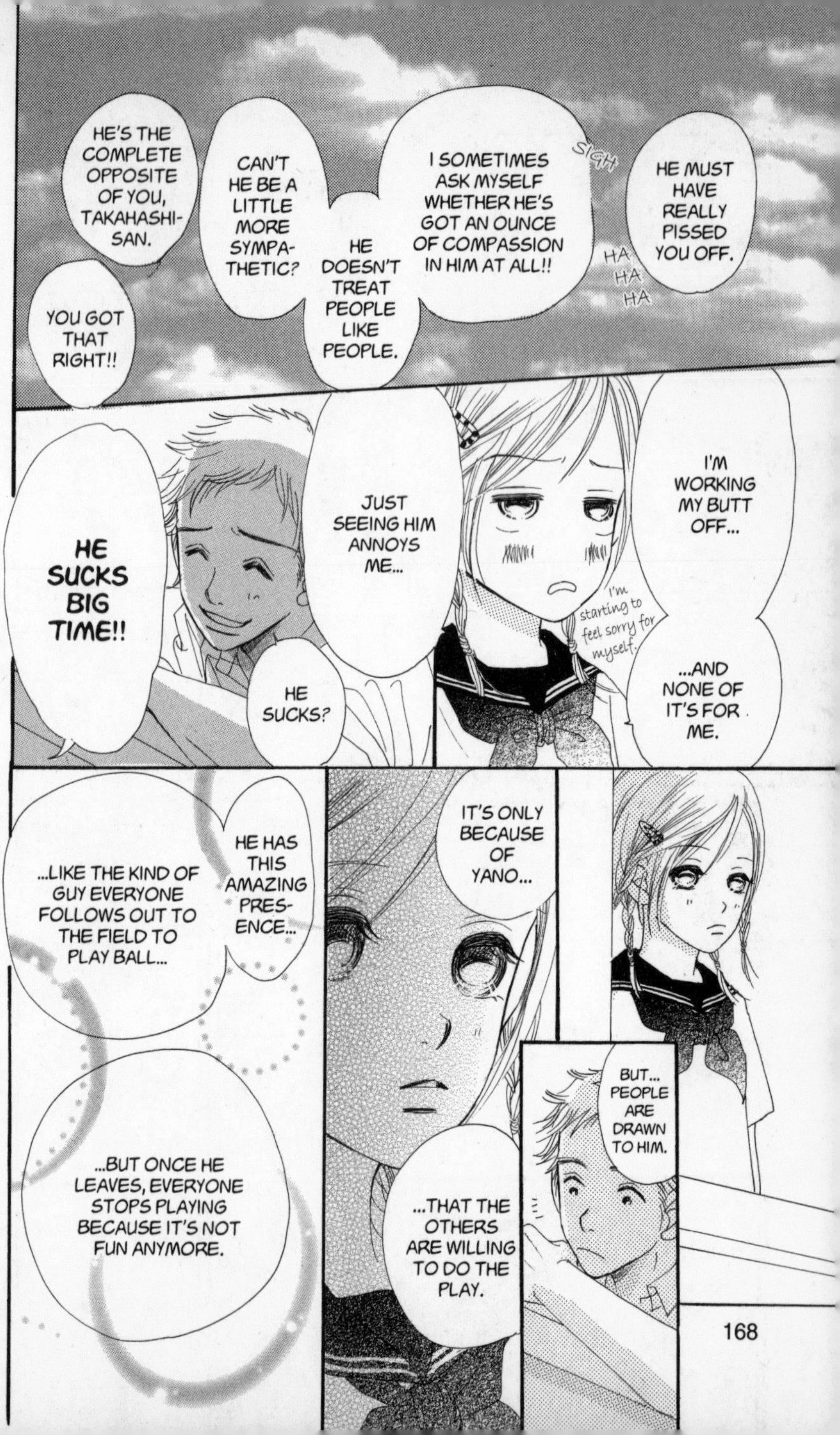
HE MUST HAVE REALLY PISSED YOU OFF.
HA HA HA
SIGH
I SOMETIMES ASK MYSELF WHETHER HE'S GOT AN OUNCE OF COMPASSION IN HIM AT ALL!!
HE DOESN'T TREAT PEOPLE LIKE PEOPLE.
CAN'T HE BE A LITTLE MORE SYMPA-THETIC?
HE'S THE COMPLETE OPPOSITE OF YOU, TAKAHASHI-SAN.
YOU GOT THAT RIGHT!!
I'M WORKING MY BUTT OFF...
...AND NONE OF IT'S FOR ME.
I'm starting to feel sorry for myself.
JUST SEEING HIM ANNOYS ME...
HE SUCKS BIG TIME!!
HE SUCKS?
IT'S ONLY BECAUSE OF YANO...
BUT... PEOPLE ARE DRAWN TO HIM.
...THAT THE OTHERS ARE WILLING TO DO THE PLAY.
HE HAS THIS AMAZING PRES-ENCE...
...LIKE THE KIND OF GUY EVERYONE FOLLOWS OUT TO THE FIELD TO PLAY BALL...
...BUT ONCE HE LEAVES, EVERYONE STOPS PLAYING BECAUSE IT'S NOT FUN ANYMORE.

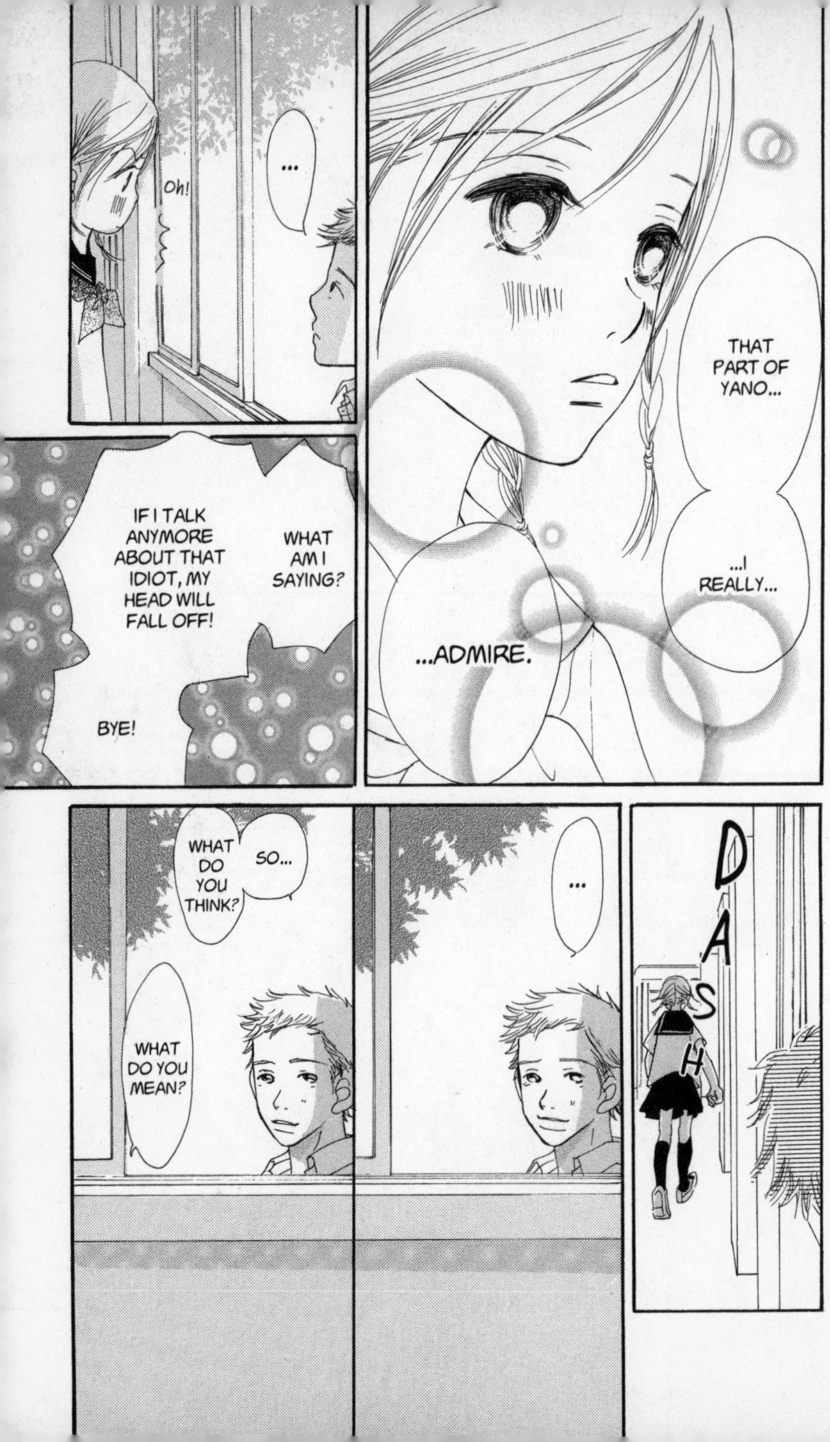
THAT PART OF YANO...
...I REALLY...
...ADMIRE.
...
Oh!
WHAT AM I SAYING?
IF I TALK ANYMORE ABOUT THAT IDIOT, MY HEAD WILL FALL OFF!
BYE!
DASH
...
SO...
WHAT DO YOU THINK?
WHAT DO YOU MEAN?

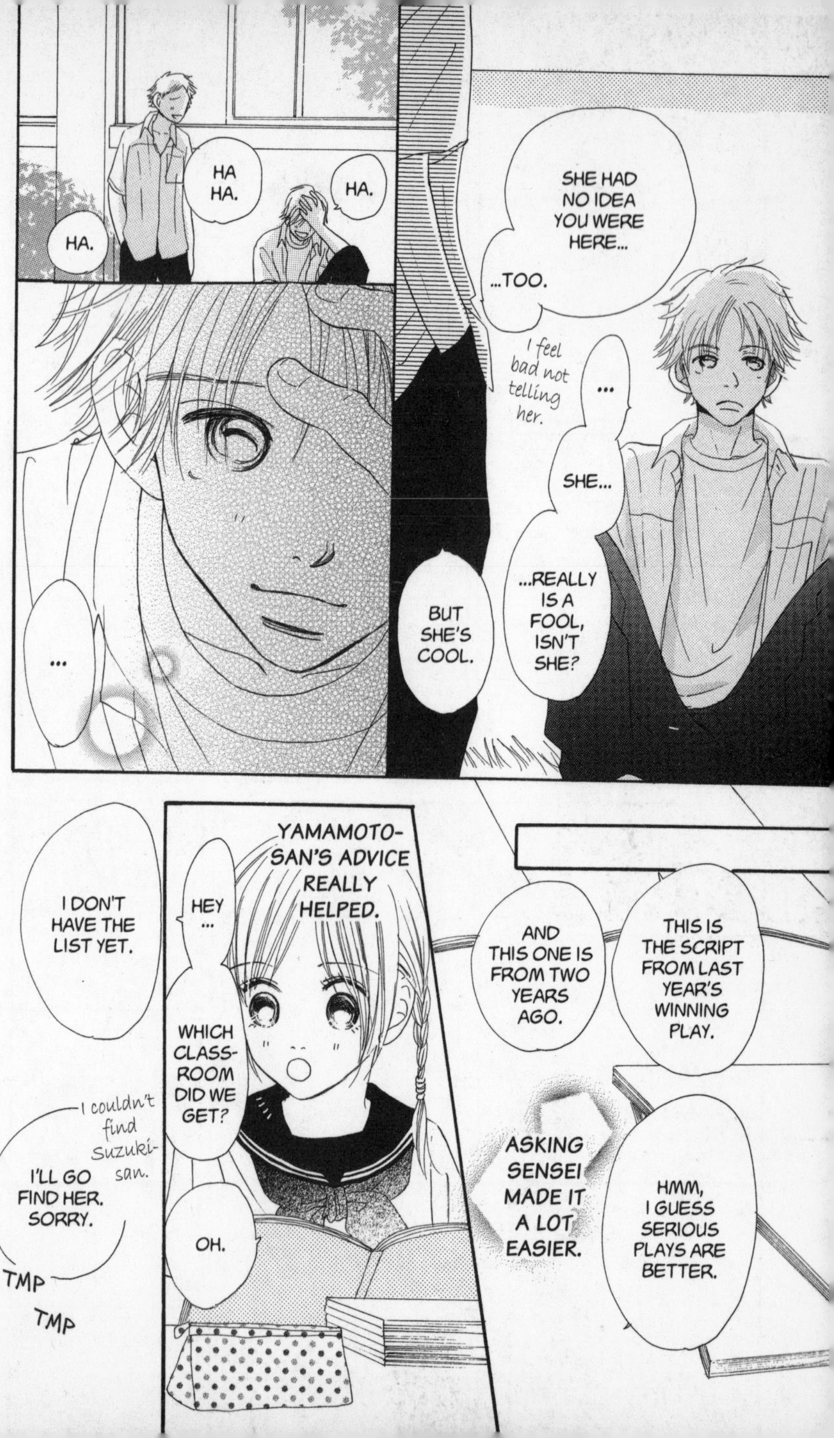
SHE HAD NO IDEA YOU WERE HERE...
...TOO.
I feel bad not telling her.
...
SHE...
...REALLY IS A FOOL, ISN'T SHE?
BUT SHE'S COOL.
HA.
HA HA.
HA.
...
THIS IS THE SCRIPT FROM LAST YEAR'S WINNING PLAY.
AND THIS ONE IS FROM TWO YEARS AGO.
HMM, I GUESS SERIOUS PLAYS ARE BETTER.
ASKING SENSEI MADE IT A LOT EASIER.
YAMAMOTO-SAN'S ADVICE REALLY HELPED.
HEY...
WHICH CLASSROOM DID WE GET?
OH.
I DON'T HAVE THE LIST YET.
I couldn't find Suzuki-san.
I'LL GO FIND HER. SORRY.
TMP
TMP

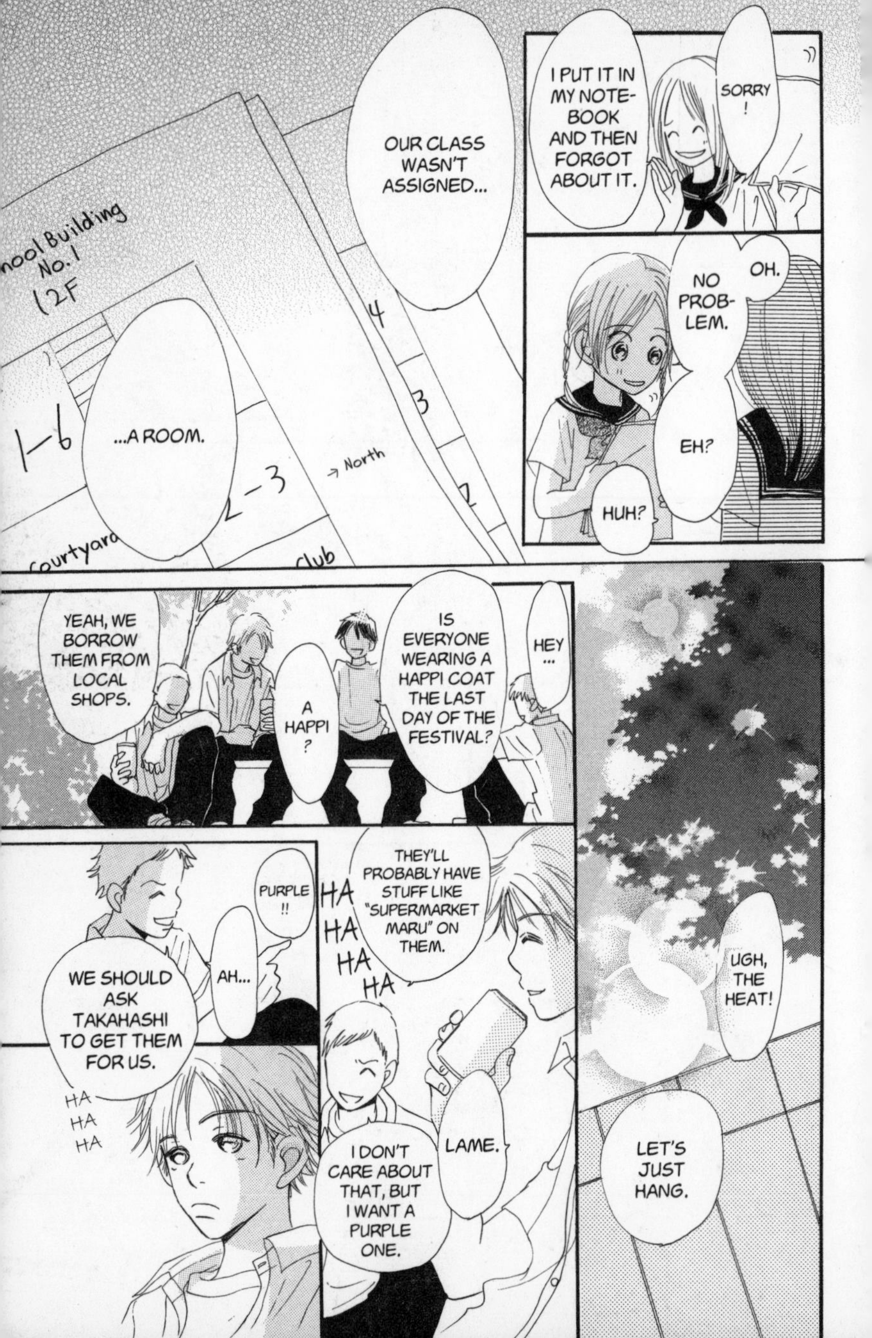

SORRY!
I PUT IT IN MY NOTE-BOOK AND THEN FORGOT ABOUT IT.
OH.
NO PROBLEM.
EH?
HUH?
OUR CLASS WASN'T ASSIGNED...
hool Building No.1 12F
4
3
2
1-6
2-3
→ North
Courtyard
Club
...A ROOM.
UGH, THE HEAT!
LET'S JUST HANG.
HEY...
IS EVERYONE WEARING A HAPPI COAT THE LAST DAY OF THE FESTIVAL?
A HAPPI?
YEAH, WE BORROW THEM FROM LOCAL SHOPS.
THEY'LL PROBABLY HAVE STUFF LIKE "SUPERMARKET MARU" ON THEM.
HA HA HA HA HA
PURPLE!!
AH...
WE SHOULD ASK TAKAHASHI TO GET THEM FOR US.
HA HA HA
LAME.
I DON'T CARE ABOUT THAT, BUT I WANT A PURPLE ONE.

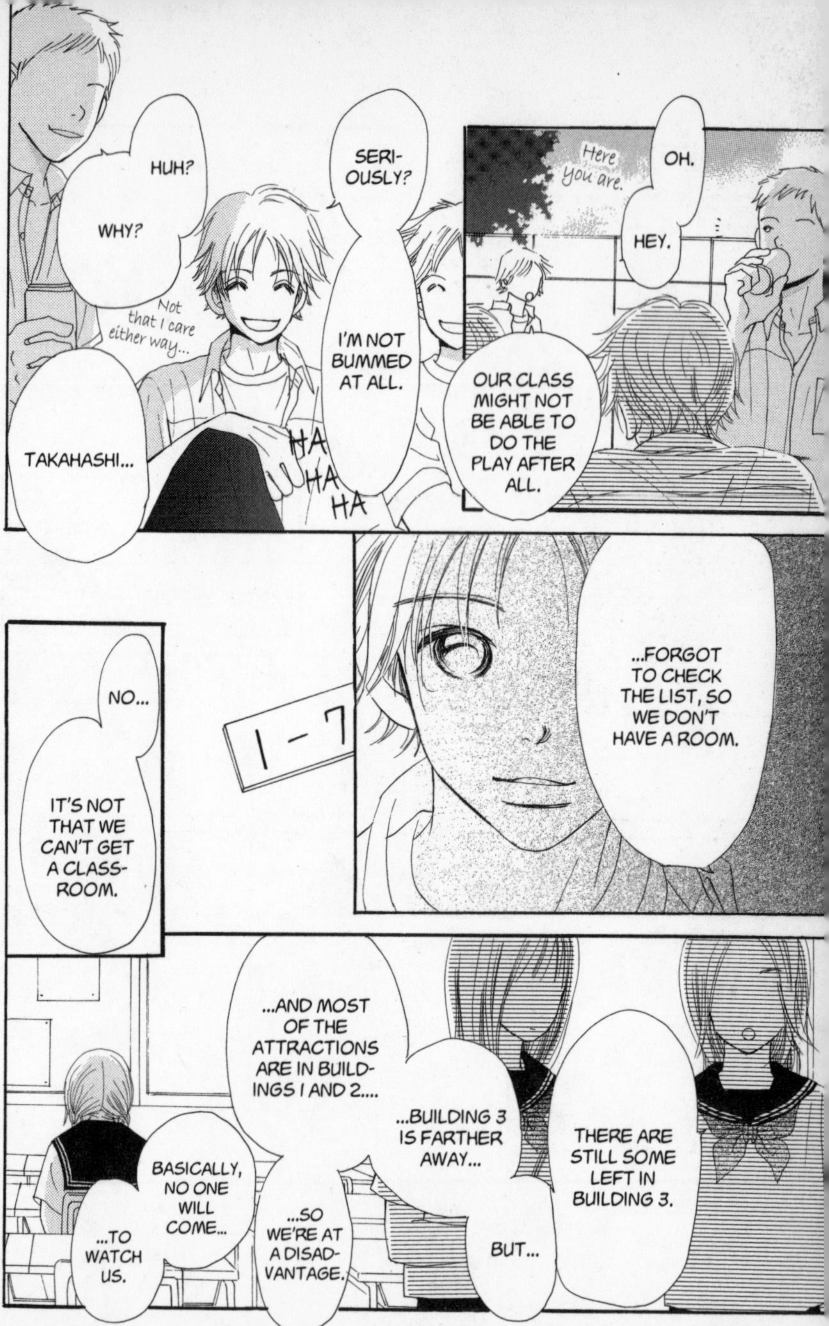

OH.
Here you are.
HEY.
OUR CLASS MIGHT NOT BE ABLE TO DO THE PLAY AFTER ALL.
SERI-OUSLY?
HUH?
WHY?
Not that I care either way...
I'M NOT BUMMED AT ALL.
HA HA HA
TAKAHASHI...
1-7
...FORGOT TO CHECK THE LIST, SO WE DON'T HAVE A ROOM.
NO...
IT'S NOT THAT WE CAN'T GET A CLASS-ROOM.
THERE ARE STILL SOME LEFT IN BUILDING 3.
BUT...
...BUILDING 3 IS FARTHER AWAY...
...AND MOST OF THE ATTRACTIONS ARE IN BUILD-INGS 1 AND 2....
...SO WE'RE AT A DISAD-VANTAGE.
BASICALLY, NO ONE WILL COME...
...TO WATCH US.

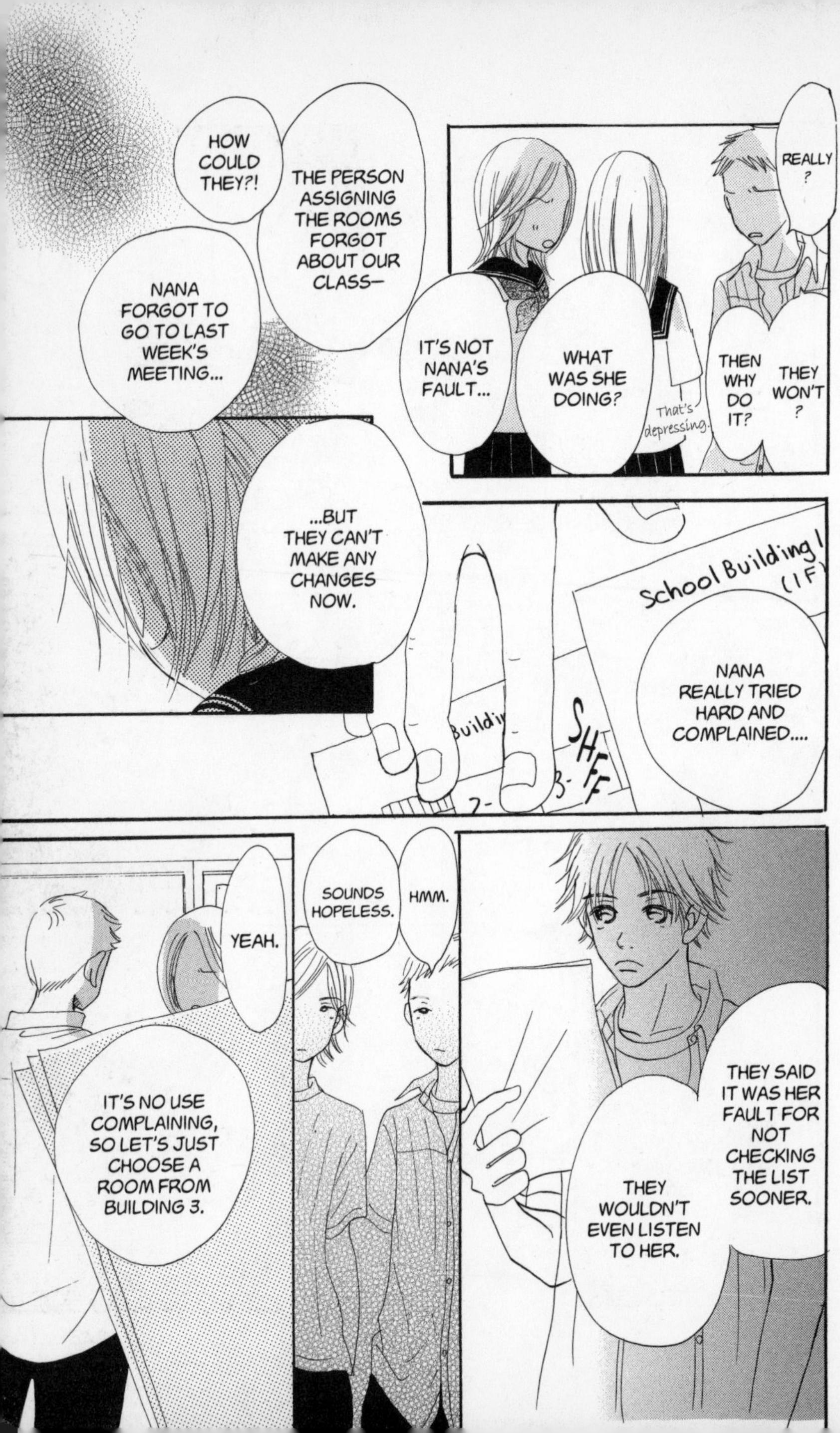
REALLY?
THEY WON'T?
THEN WHY DO IT?
That's depressing.
WHAT WAS SHE DOING?
IT'S NOT NANA'S FAULT...
THE PERSON ASSIGNING THE ROOMS FORGOT ABOUT OUR CLASS—
HOW COULD THEY?!
NANA FORGOT TO GO TO LAST WEEK'S MEETING...
School Building 1 (1F)
NANA REALLY TRIED HARD AND COMPLAINED....
SHFF
...BUT THEY CAN'T MAKE ANY CHANGES NOW.
THEY SAID IT WAS HER FAULT FOR NOT CHECKING THE LIST SOONER.
THEY WOULDN'T EVEN LISTEN TO HER.
HMM.
SOUNDS HOPELESS.
YEAH.
IT'S NO USE COMPLAINING, SO LET'S JUST CHOOSE A ROOM FROM BUILDING 3.

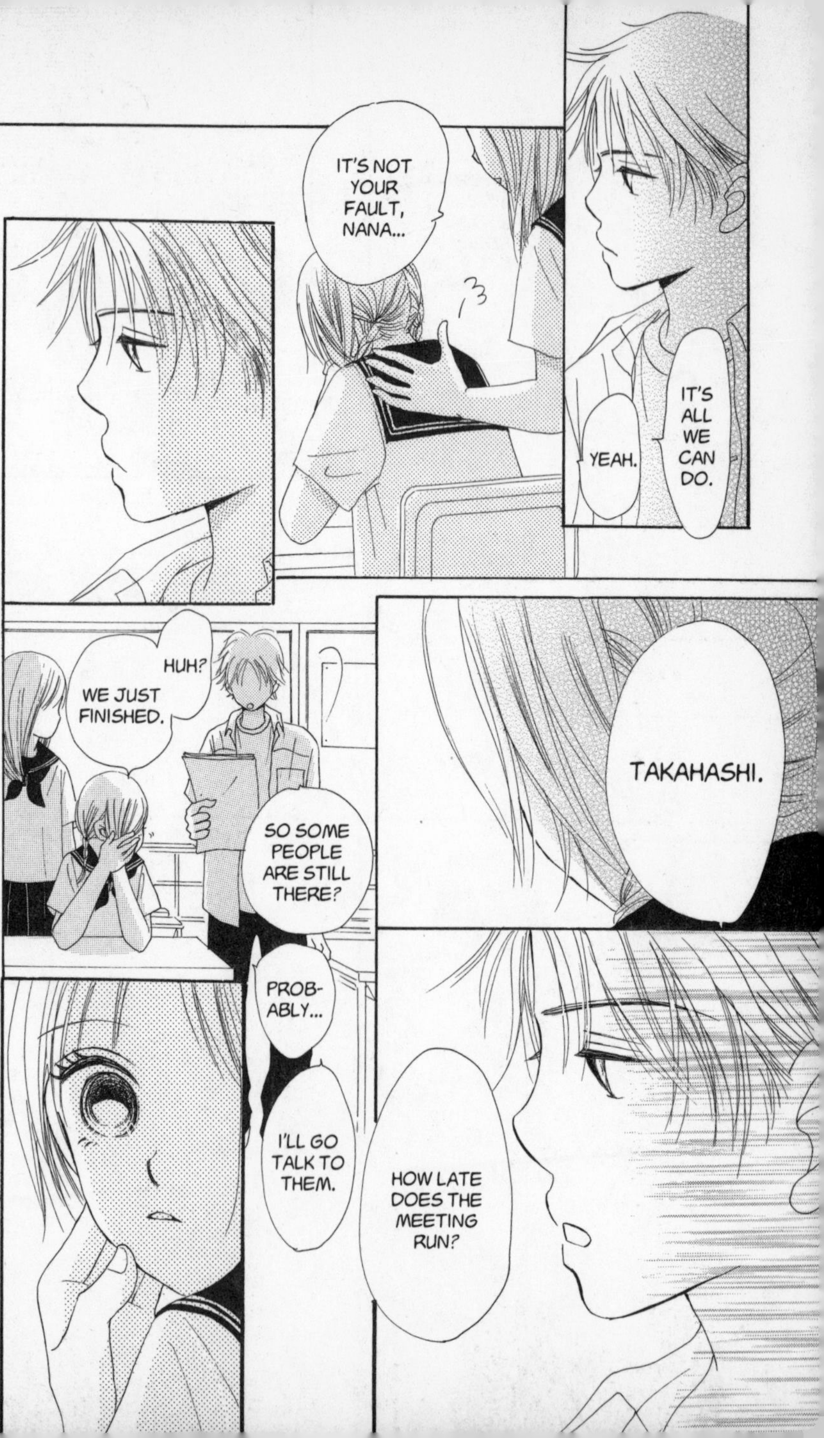
IT'S ALL WE CAN DO.
YEAH.
IT'S NOT YOUR FAULT, NANA...
TAKAHASHI.
HOW LATE DOES THE MEETING RUN?
HUH? WE JUST FINISHED.
SO SOME PEOPLE ARE STILL THERE?
PROBABLY...
I'LL GO TALK TO THEM.

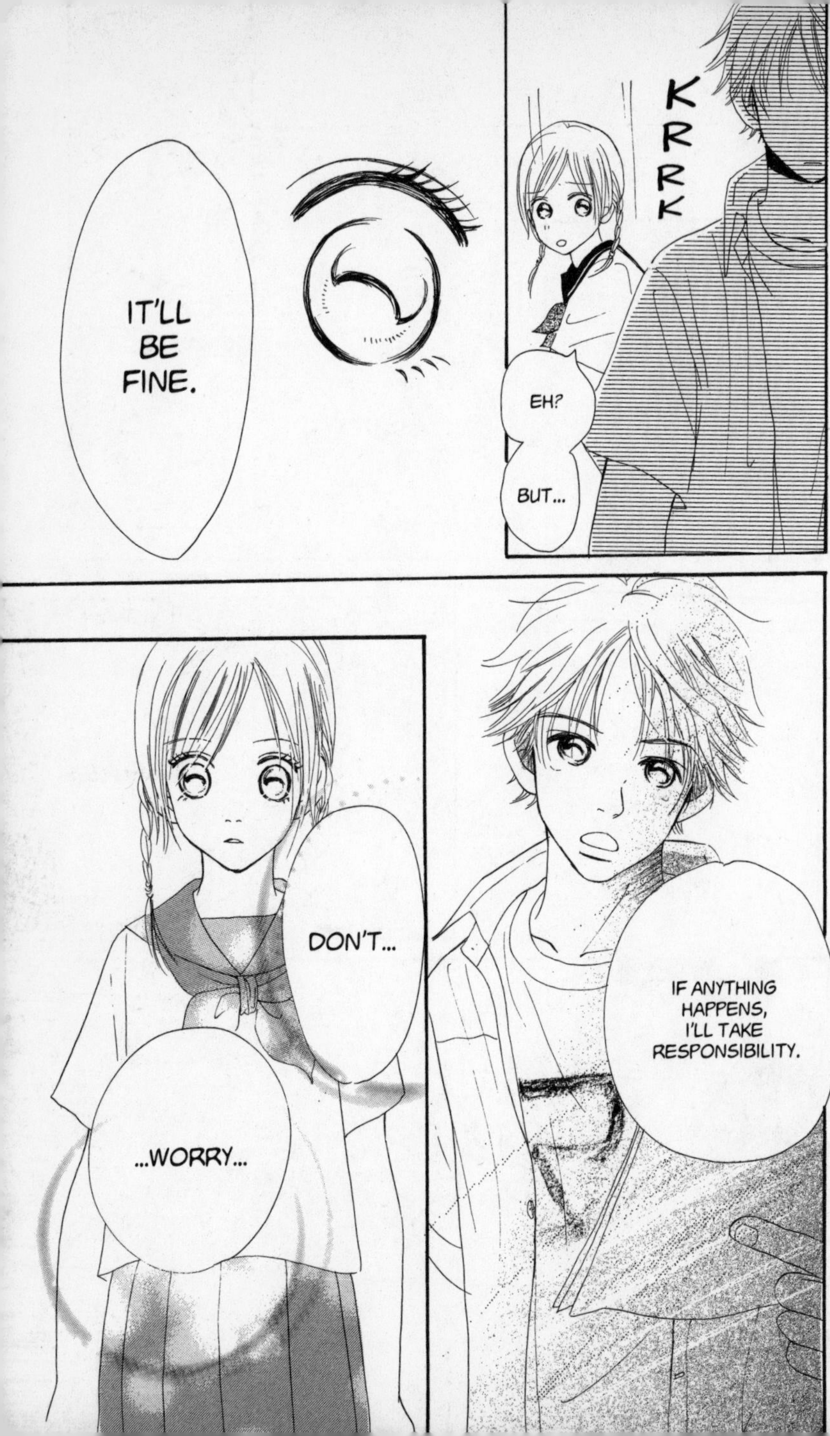
KRRK
EH?
BUT...
IT'LL BE FINE.
IF ANYTHING HAPPENS, I'LL TAKE RESPONSIBILITY.
DON'T...
...WORRY...

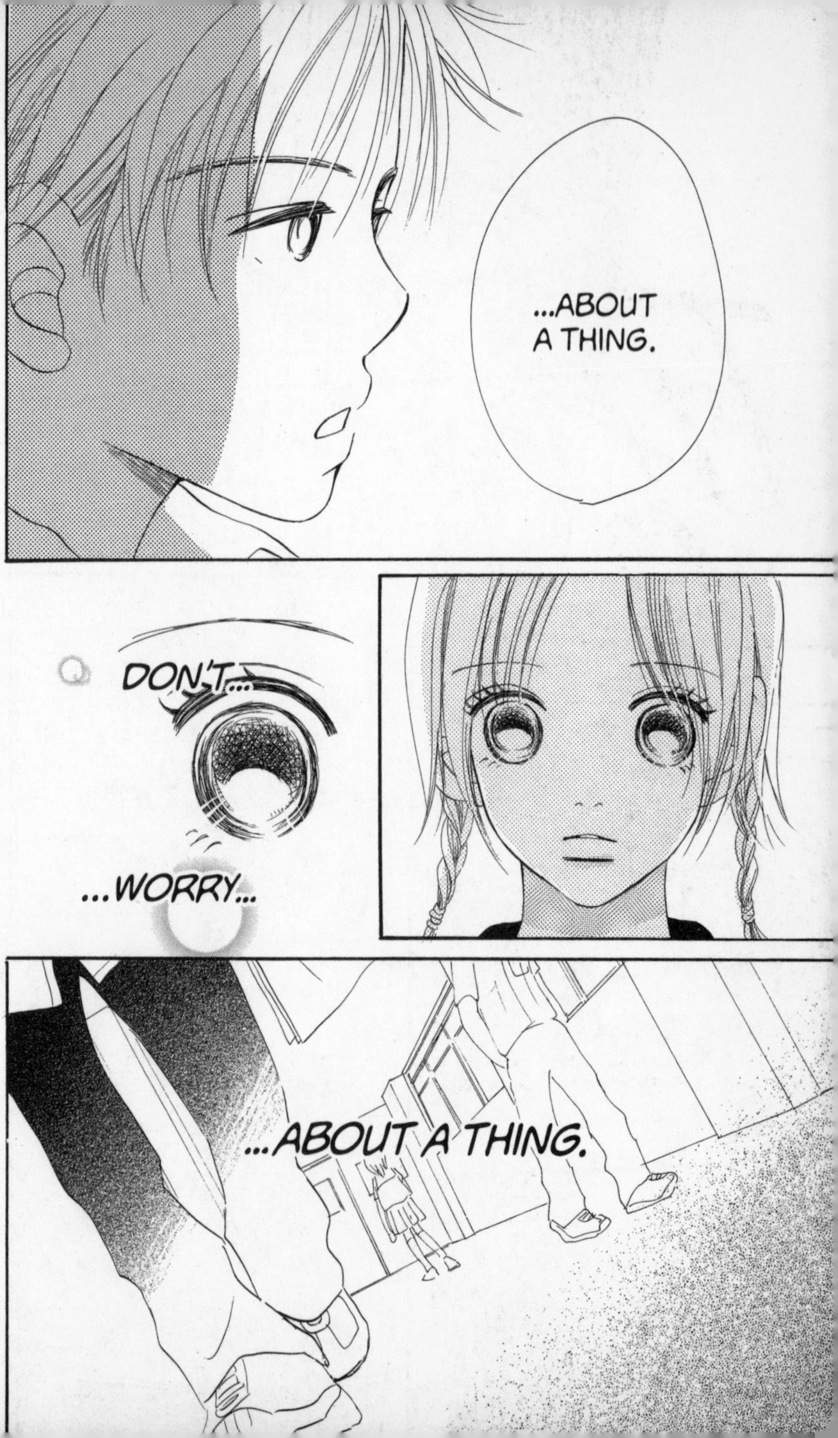
...ABOUT A THING.
DON'T...
...WORRY...
...ABOUT A THING.

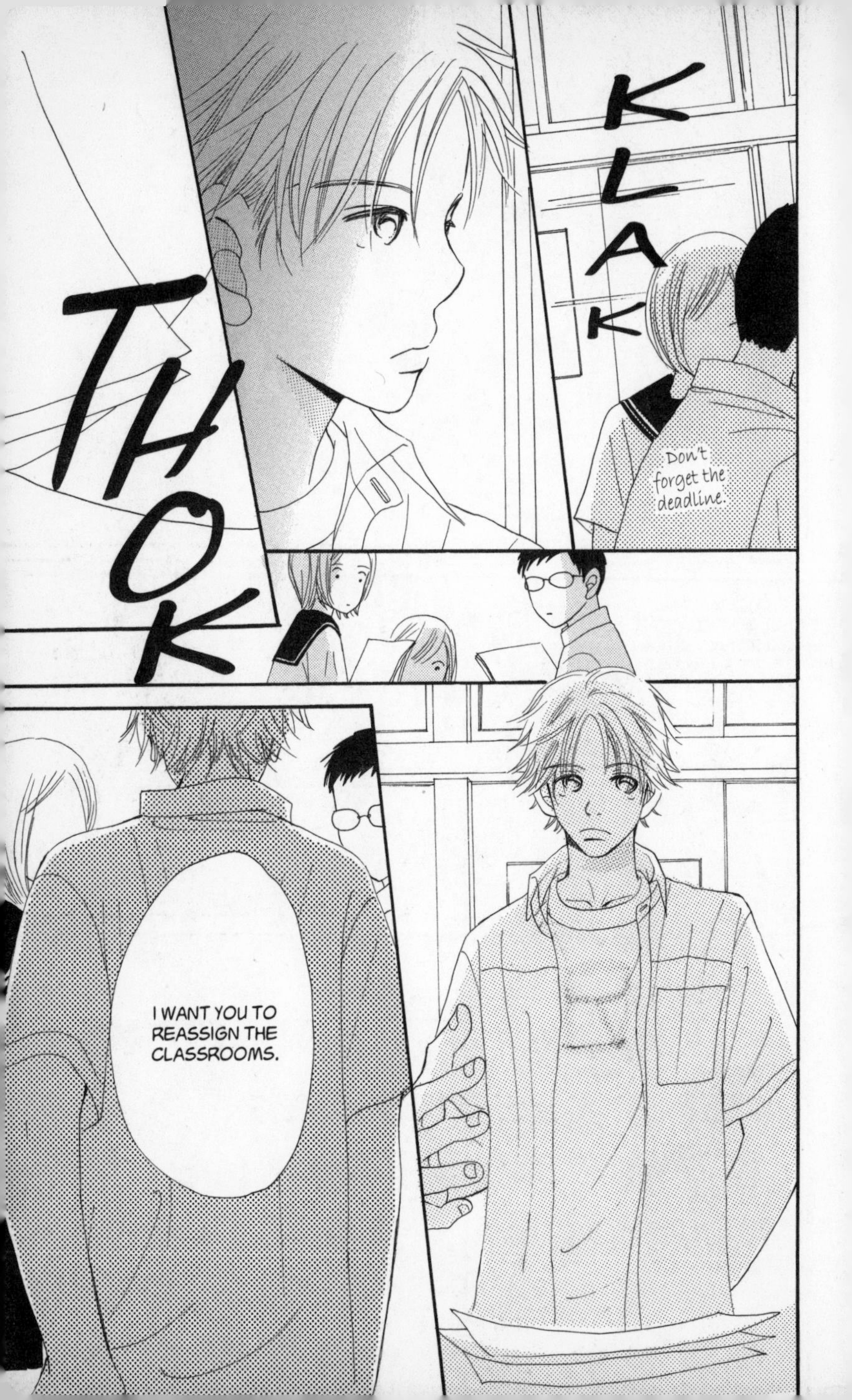
KLAK
Don't forget the deadline.
THOK
I WANT YOU TO REASSIGN THE CLASSROOMS.

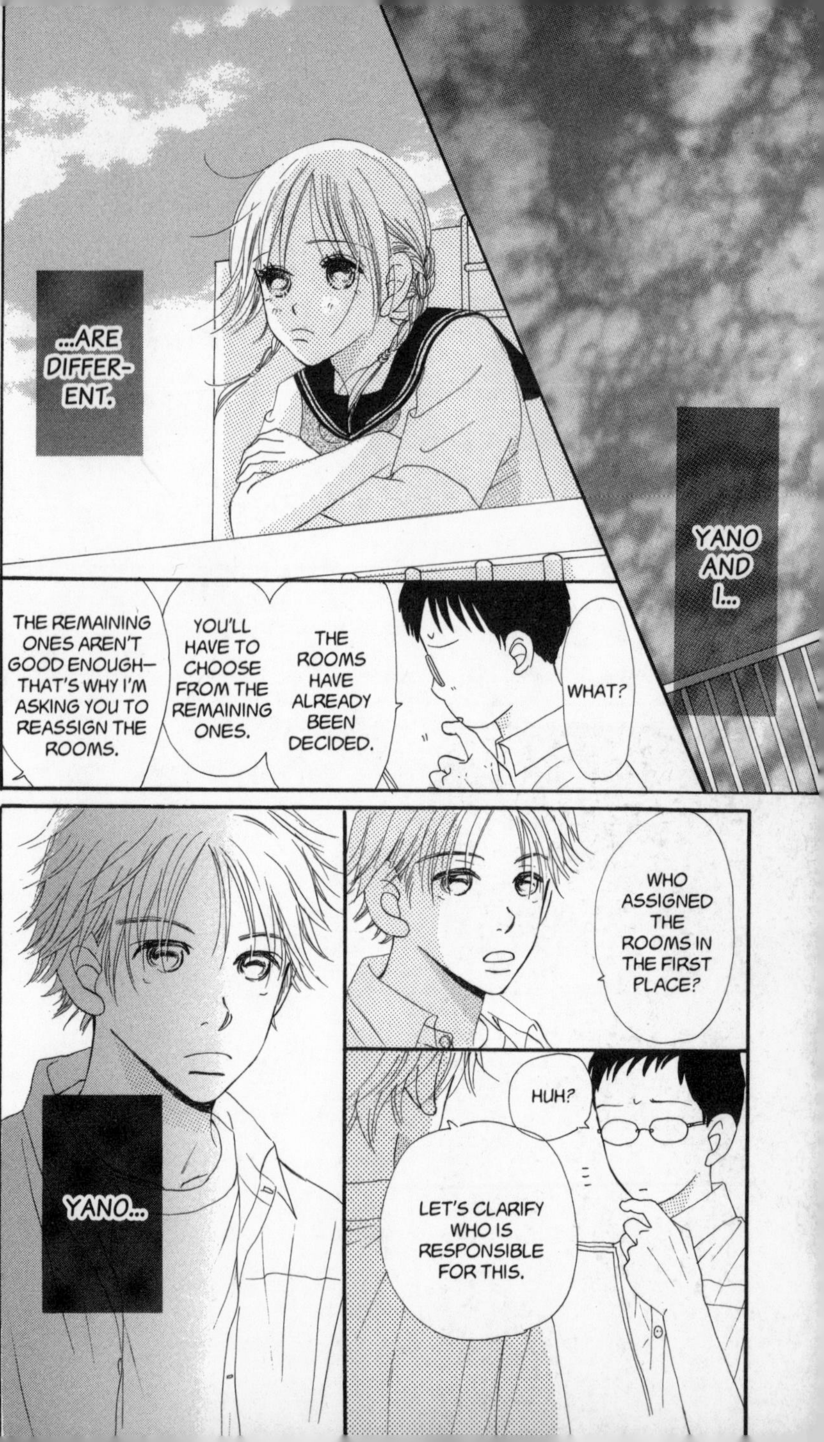
YANO AND I...
...ARE DIFFER-ENT.
WHAT?
THE ROOMS HAVE ALREADY BEEN DECIDED.
YOU'LL HAVE TO CHOOSE FROM THE REMAINING ONES.
THE REMAINING ONES AREN'T GOOD ENOUGH— THAT'S WHY I'M ASKING YOU TO REASSIGN THE ROOMS.
WHO ASSIGNED THE ROOMS IN THE FIRST PLACE?
HUH?
LET'S CLARIFY WHO IS RESPONSIBLE FOR THIS.
YANO...

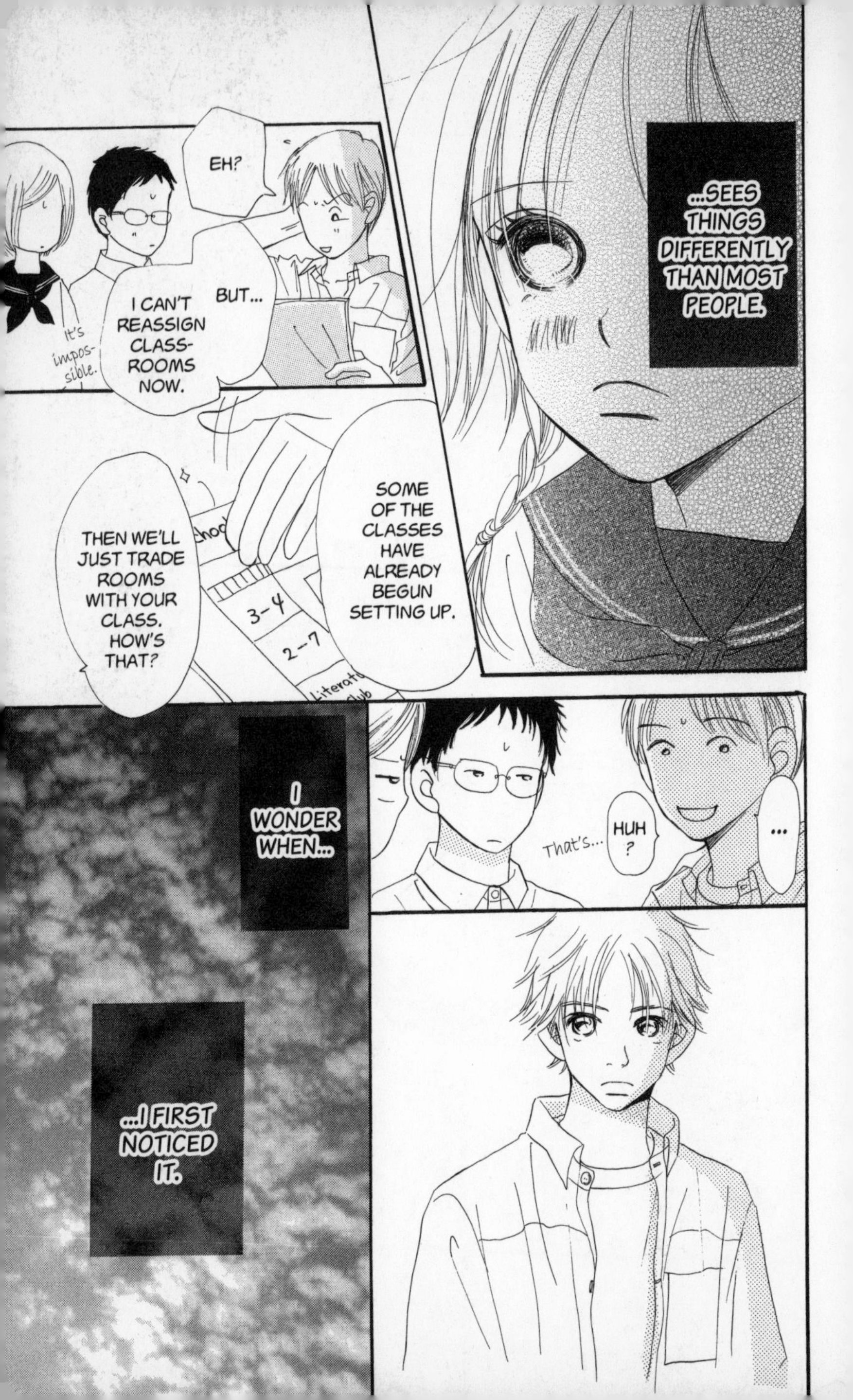
...SEES THINGS DIFFERENTLY THAN MOST PEOPLE.
EH?
BUT...
I CAN'T REASSIGN CLASS-ROOMS NOW.
It's impos-sible.
SOME OF THE CLASSES HAVE ALREADY BEGUN SETTING UP.
THEN WE'LL JUST TRADE ROOMS WITH YOUR CLASS. HOW'S THAT?
3-4
2-7
...
HUH?
That's...
I WONDER WHEN...
...I FIRST NOTICED IT.

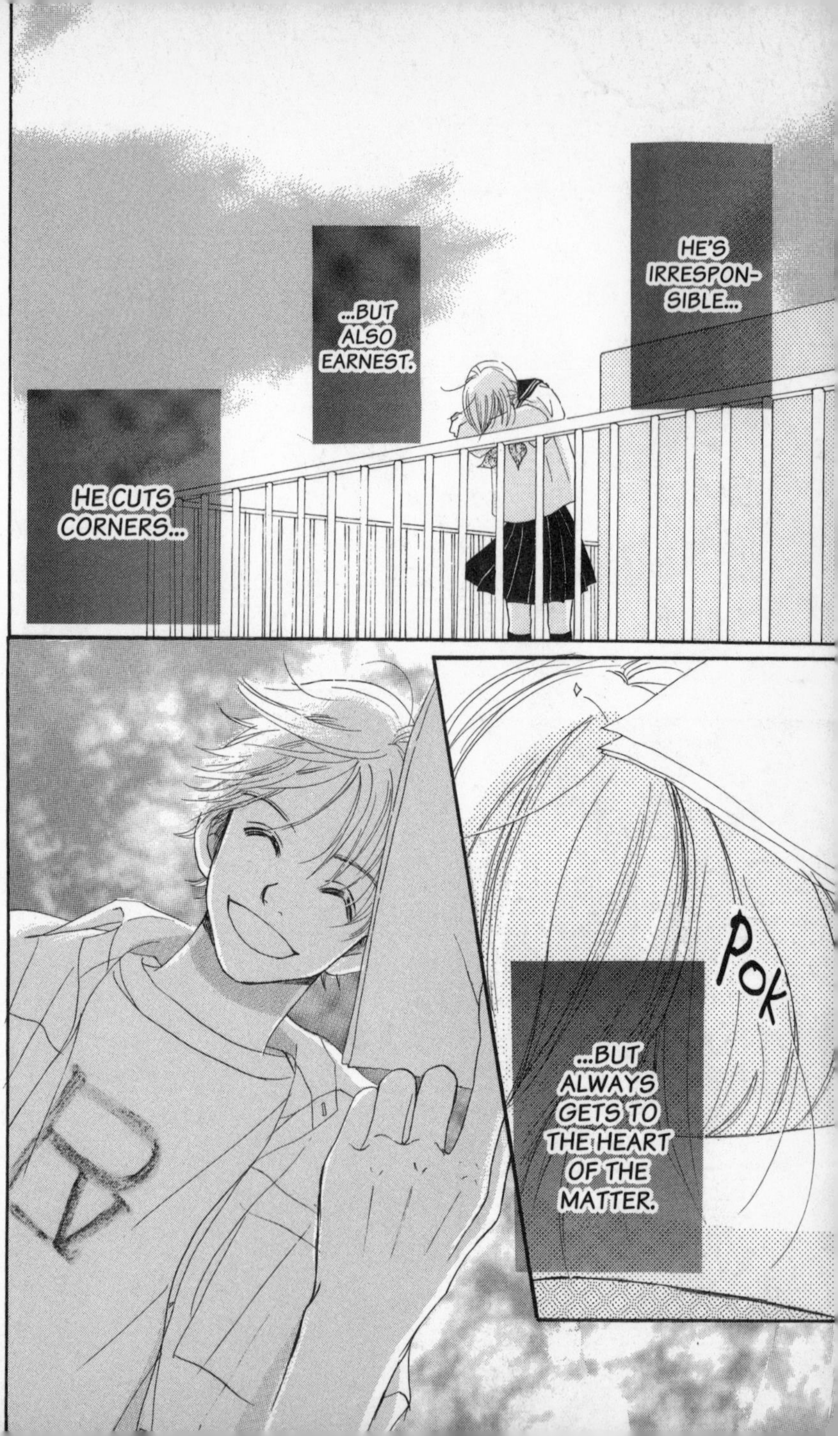
HE'S IRRESPON-SIBLE...
...BUT ALSO EARNEST.
HE CUTS CORNERS...
POK
...BUT ALWAYS GETS TO THE HEART OF THE MATTER.

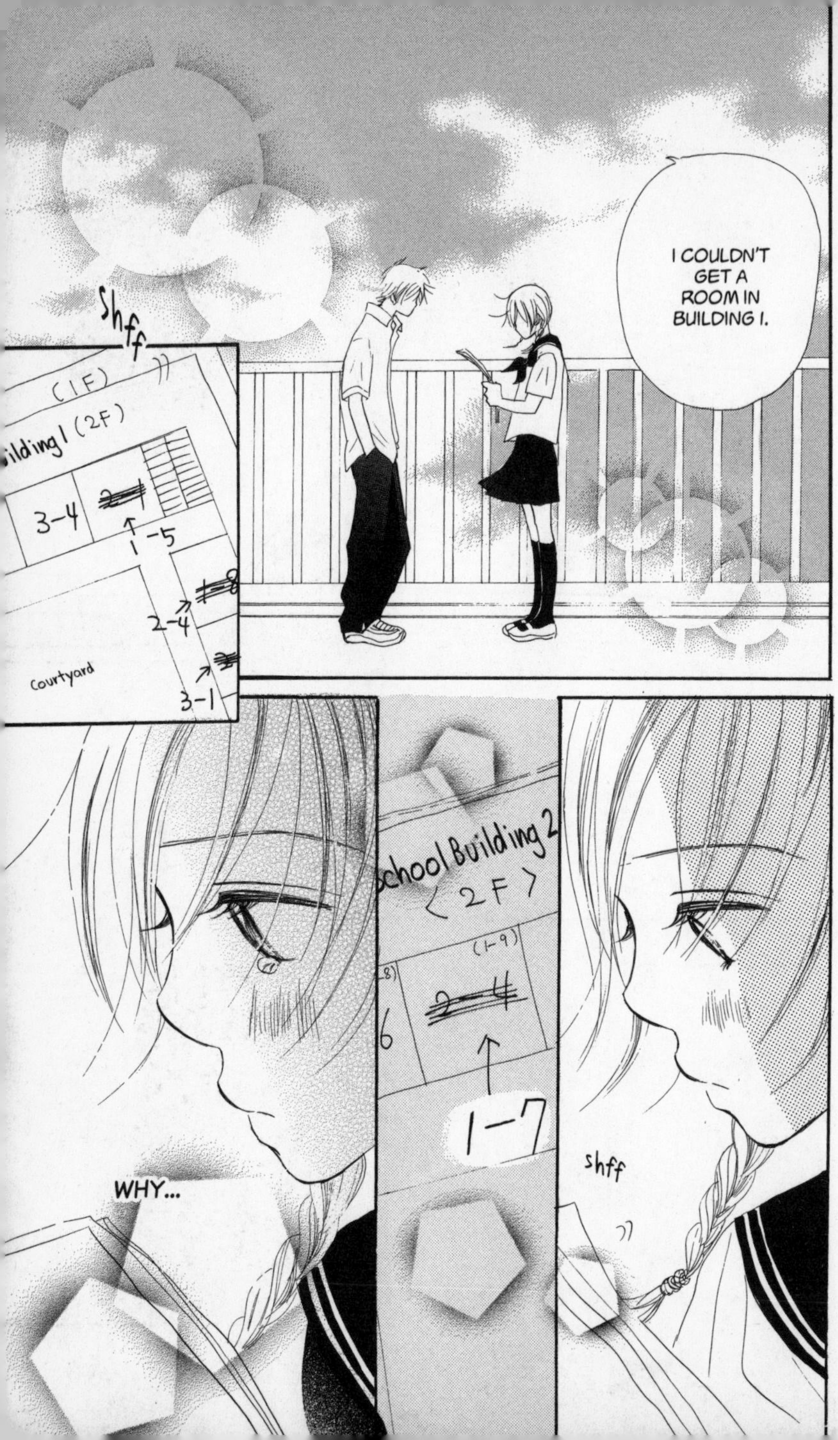
I COULDN'T GET A ROOM IN BUILDING 1.
shff
(1F)
ilding 1 (2F)
3-4
1-5
2-4
Courtyard
3-1
shff
School Building 2
〈 2F 〉
1-7
WHY...

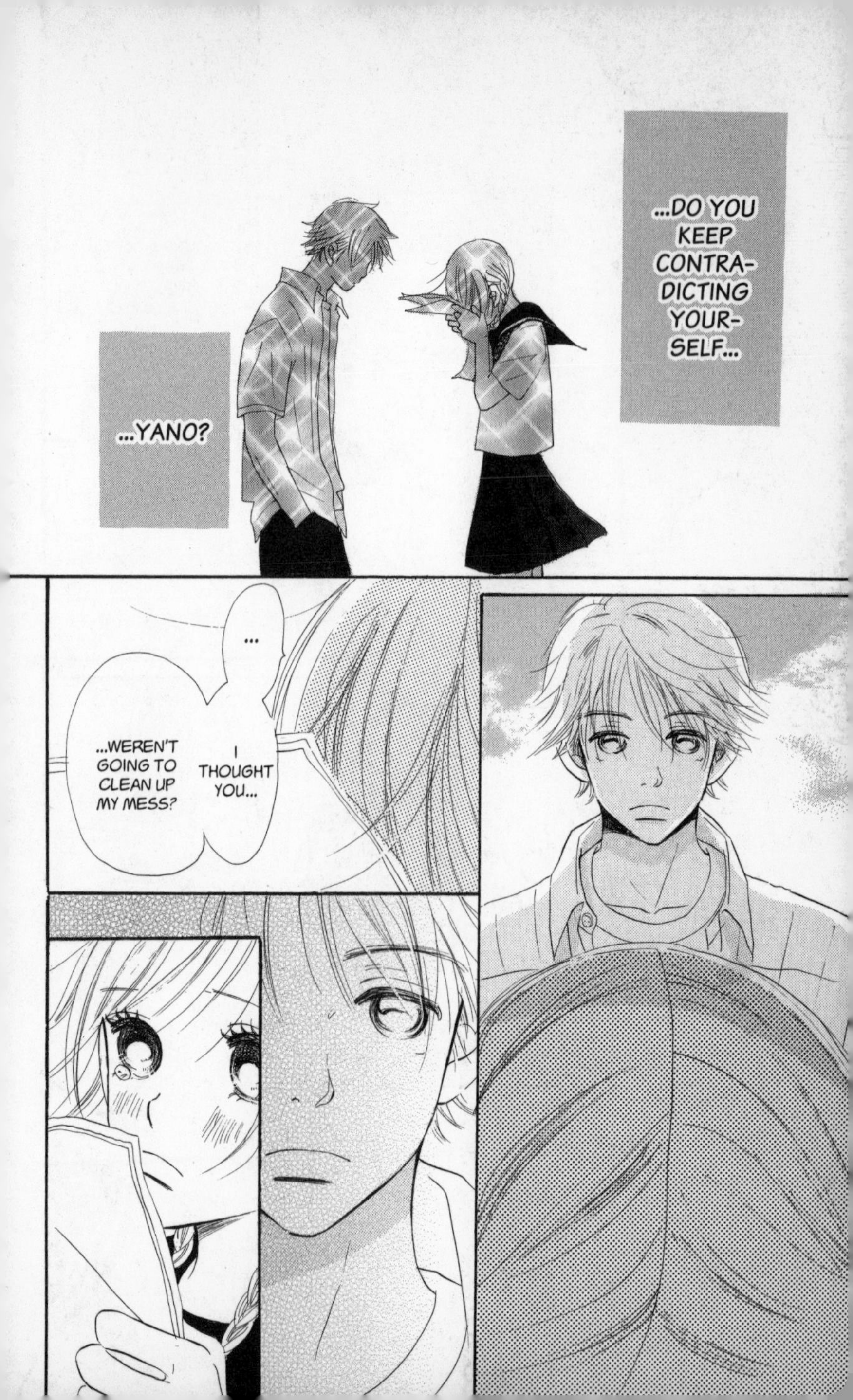
...DO YOU KEEP CONTRA-DICTING YOUR-SELF...
...YANO?
...
I THOUGHT YOU...
...WEREN'T GOING TO CLEAN UP MY MESS?

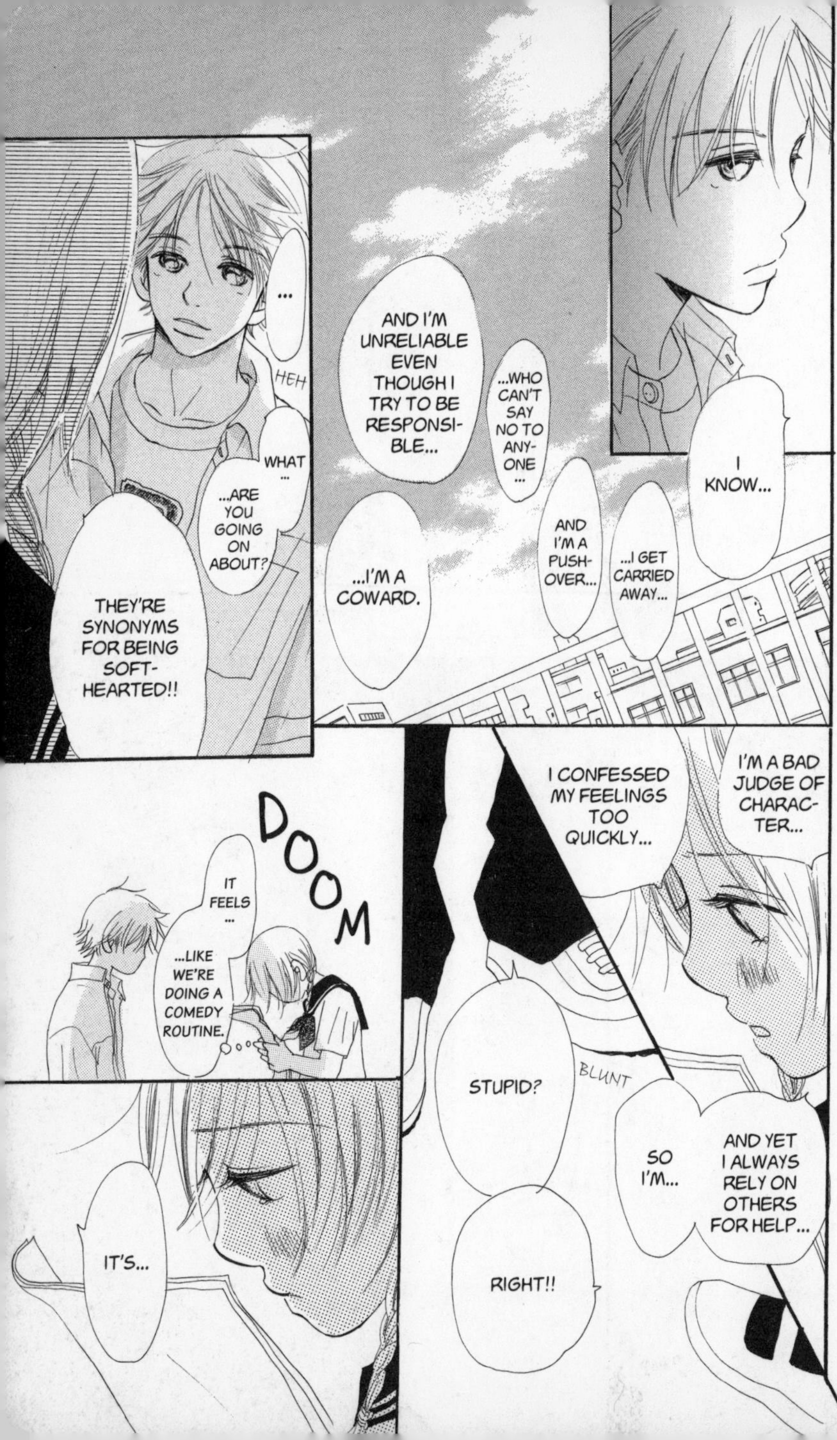
I KNOW...
...I GET CARRIED AWAY...
AND I'M A PUSHOVER...
...WHO CAN'T SAY NO TO ANYONE...
AND I'M UNRELIABLE EVEN THOUGH I TRY TO BE RESPONSIBLE...
...I'M A COWARD.
...
HEH
WHAT...
...ARE YOU GOING ON ABOUT?
THEY'RE SYNONYMS FOR BEING SOFT-HEARTED!!
I'M A BAD JUDGE OF CHARACTER...
I CONFESSED MY FEELINGS TOO QUICKLY...
AND YET I ALWAYS RELY ON OTHERS FOR HELP...
SO I'M...
BLUNT
STUPID?
RIGHT!!
DOOM
IT FEELS...
...LIKE WE'RE DOING A COMEDY ROUTINE.
IT'S...

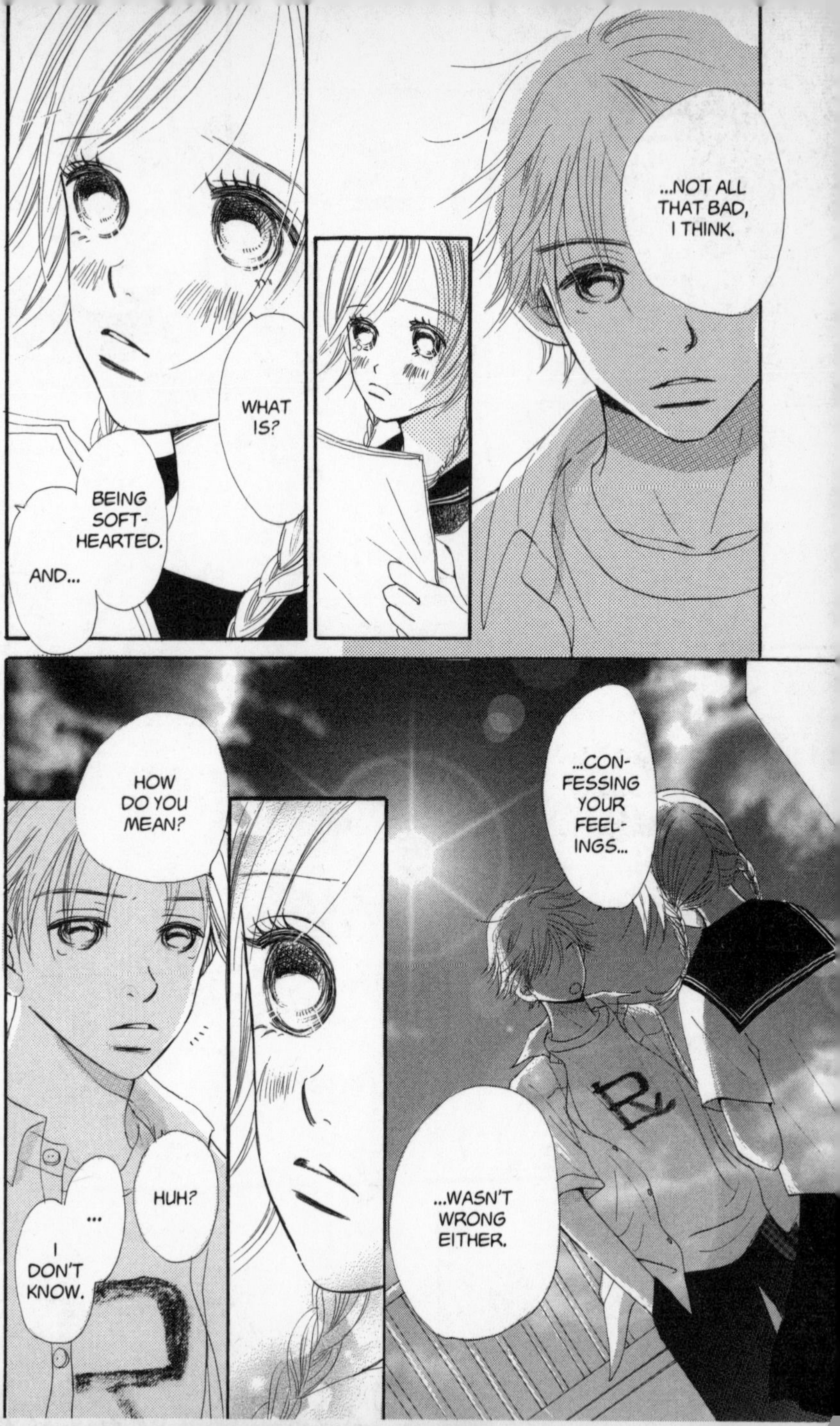
...NOT ALL THAT BAD, I THINK.
WHAT IS?
BEING SOFT-HEARTED.
AND...
...CON-FESSING YOUR FEEL-INGS...
...WASN'T WRONG EITHER.
HOW DO YOU MEAN?
HUH?
...
I DON'T KNOW.

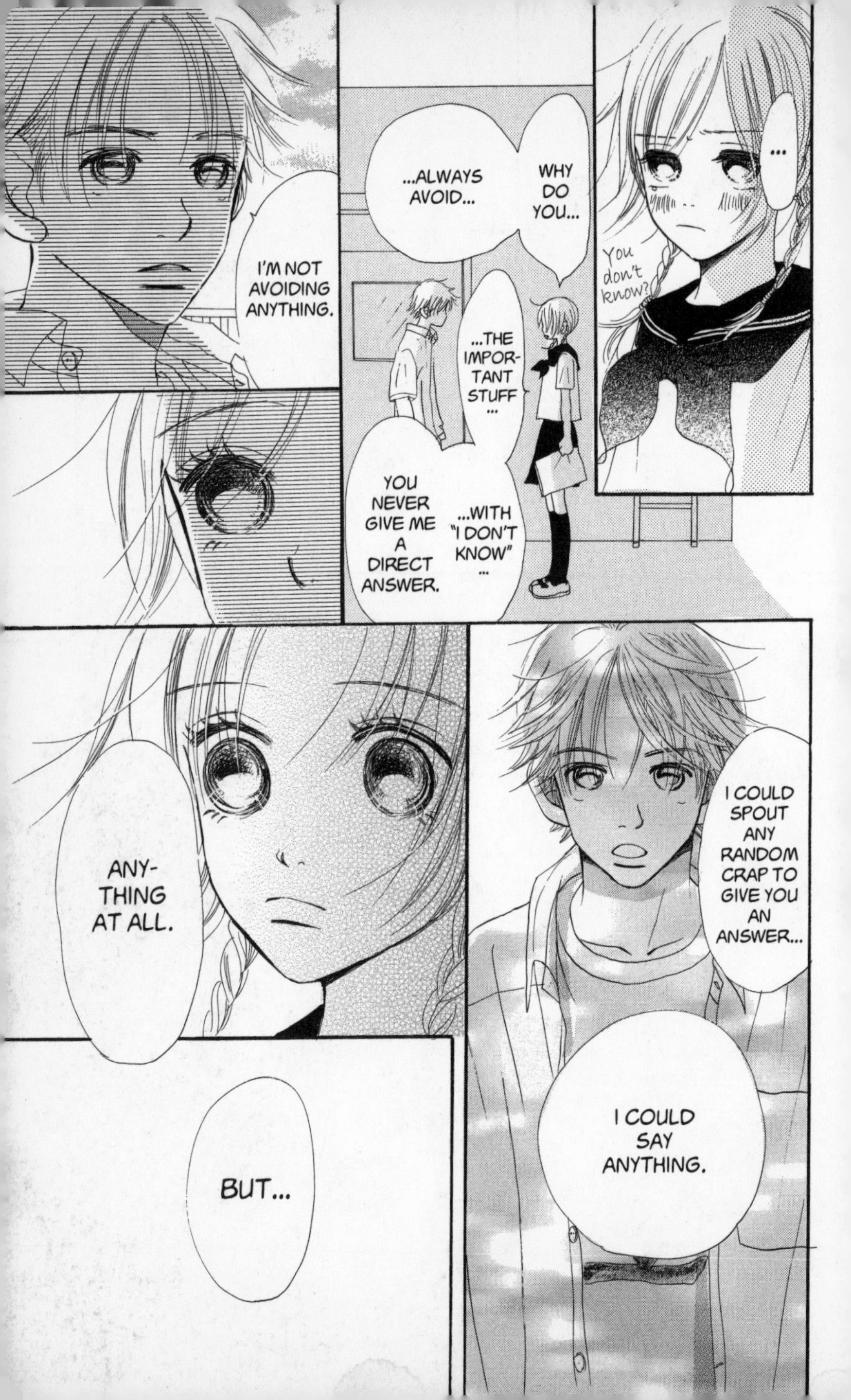
...
You don't know?
WHY DO YOU...
...ALWAYS AVOID...
...THE IMPORTANT STUFF...
...WITH "I DON'T KNOW"...
YOU NEVER GIVE ME A DIRECT ANSWER.
I'M NOT AVOIDING ANYTHING.
I COULD SPOUT ANY RANDOM CRAP TO GIVE YOU AN ANSWER...
I COULD SAY ANYTHING.
ANY-THING AT ALL.
BUT...

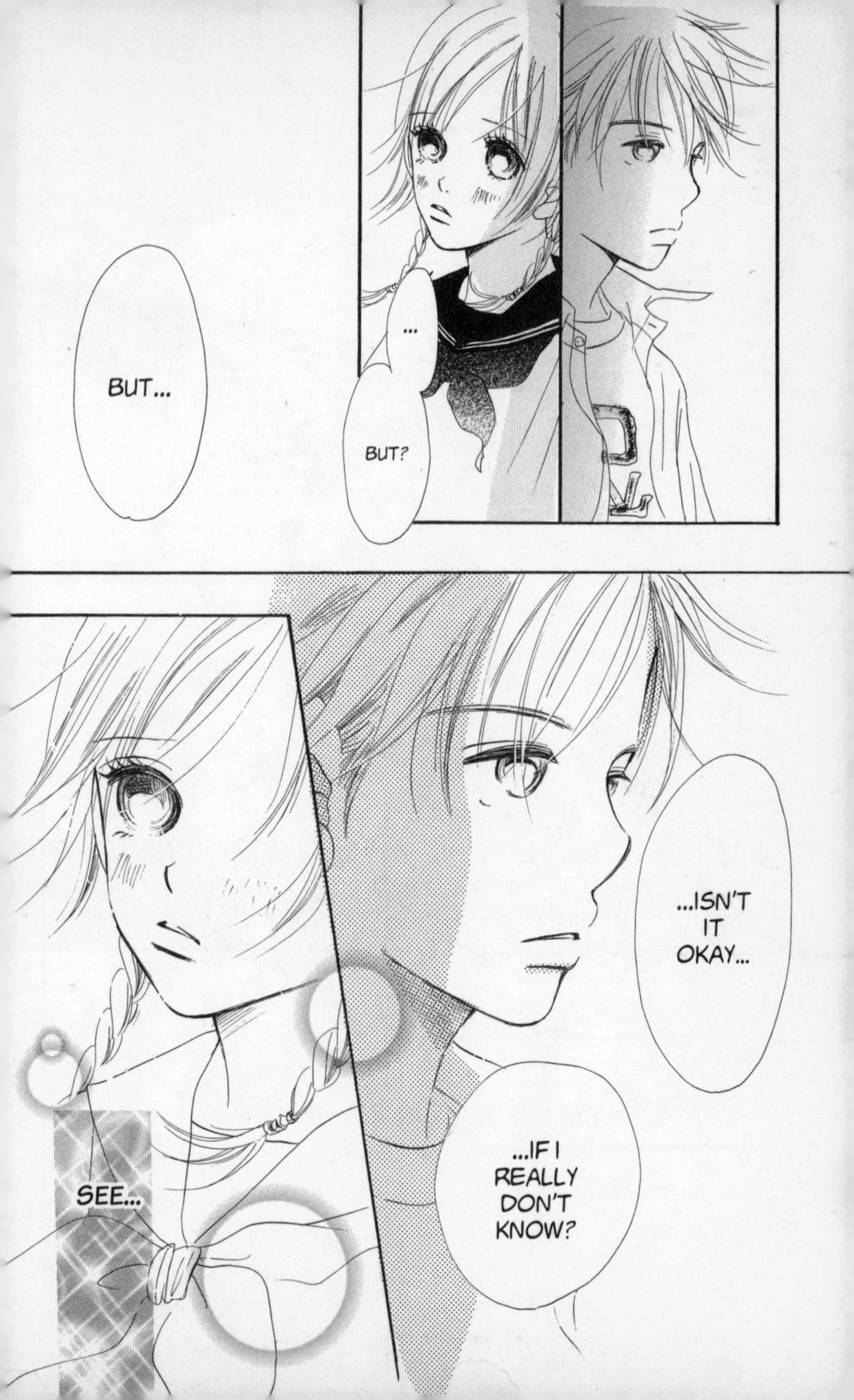
...
BUT?
BUT...
...ISN'T IT OKAY...
...IF I REALLY DON'T KNOW?
SEE...

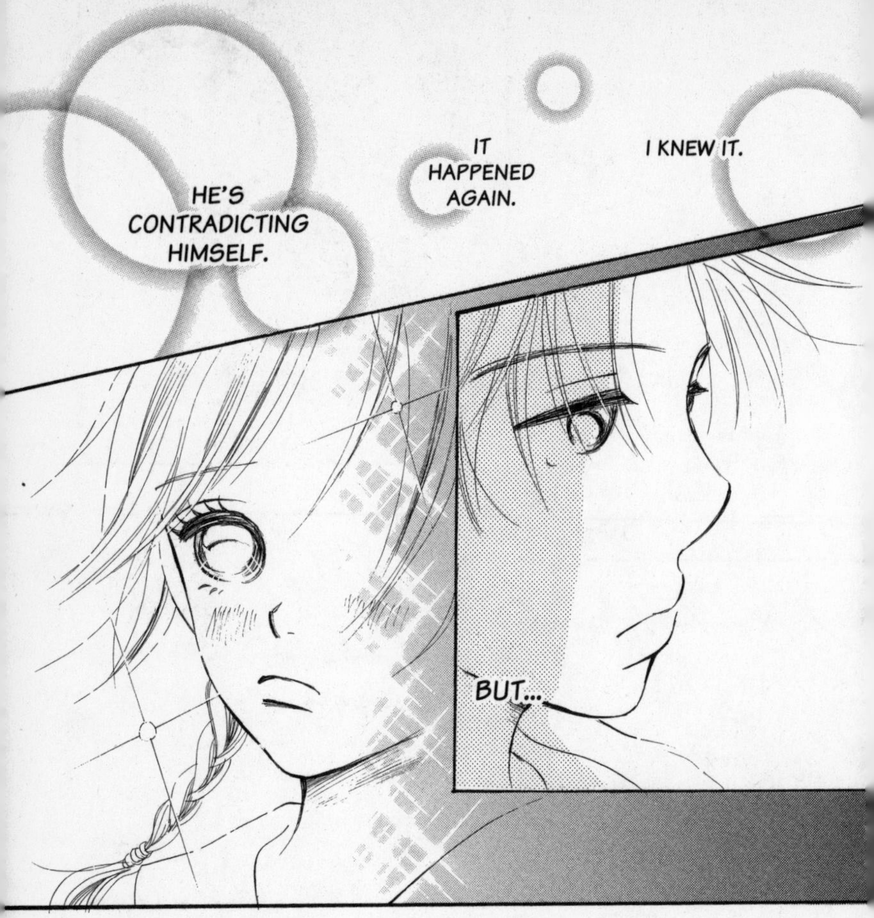
I KNEW IT.
IT HAPPENED AGAIN.
HE'S CONTRADICTING HIMSELF.
BUT...

I GUESS IT'S OKAY NOT TO KNOW.

WE WERE THERE VOL. 1/END

Notes

Honorifics

In Japan, people are usually addressed by their name followed by a suffix. The suffix shows familiarity or respect, depending on the relationship.

Male (familiar): first or last name + kun

Female (familiar): first or last name + chan

Adult (polite): last name + san

Upperclassman (polite): last name + senpai

Teacher or professional: last name + sensei

Close friends or lovers: first name only, no suffix

Nana-chan vs. Nana-san

Nanami's nickname is "Nana-chan." Yano's ex-girlfriend was a year older, so she was known as "Nana-san."

Terms

Day duty is for classroom chores.

Bunny apples are apples that have been cut into bunny shapes in *bento*, or Japanese lunch boxes.

Miyako konbu is a Japanese seaweed snack.

Horumon are pig innards.

Happi coats are traditional Japanese garb worn during festivals.

Yuki Obata's birthday is January 9. Her debut manga, *Raindrops*, won the Shogakukan Shinjin Comics Taisho Kasaku Award in 1998. Her current series, *We Were There* (*Bokura ga Ita*), won the 50th Shogakukan Manga Award and was adapted into an animated television series. She likes sweets, coffee, drinking with friends, and scary stories. Her hobby is browsing in bookshops.

We Were There
Vol. 1
The Shojo Beat Manga Edition

STORY & ART BY
YUKI OBATA

Adaptation/Nancy Thistlethwaite
Translation/Tetsuichiro Miyaki
Touch-up Art & Lettering/Inori Fukuda Trant
Design/Izumi Hirayama
Editor/Nancy Thistlethwaite

Editor in Chief, Books/Alvin Lu
Editor in Chief, Magazines/Marc Weidenbaum
VP, Publishing Licensing/Rika Inouye
VP, Sales & Product Marketing/Gonzalo Ferreyra
VP, Creative/Linda Espinosa
Publisher/Hyoe Narita

Printed in Canada

Published by VIZ Media, LLC
P.O. Box 77010
San Francisco, CA 94107

Shojo Beat Manga Edition
10 9 8 7 6 5 4 3 2 1
First printing, November 2008

www.viz.com

store.viz.com

Find the Beat online!
Check us out at

www.shojobeat.com!